Strategic
Public
Relations
Counseling

LONGMAN SERIES IN
PUBLIC COMMUNICATION
SERIES EDITOR: RAY ELDON HIEBERT

Strategic Public Relations Counseling

Models from the Counselors Academy

Norman R. Nager, Ph.D., APR
Richard H. Truitt, APR

Longman
New York & London

Executive Editor: Gordon T. R. Anderson
Production Editor: Halley Gatenby
Production Supervisor: Eduardo Castillo
Compositor: R/TSI

Strategic Public Relations Counseling

Copyright © 1987 by Longman Inc.

Longman Inc.
95 Church Street
White Plains, N.Y. 10601

Associated companies:
Longman Group Ltd., London
Longman Cheshire Pty., Melbourne
Longman Paul Pty., Auckland
Copp Clark Pitman, Toronto
Pitman Publishing Inc., New York

Library of Congress Cataloging-in-Publication Data

Nager, Norman R., 1936–
    Strategic public relations counseling.

    (Longman series in public communication)
    Includes index.
    1. Public relations consultants—United States.
2. Public relations—United States. I. Truitt,
Richard H. II. Public Relations Society of America.
Counselors Academy. III. Title. IV. Series.
HM263.N255 1987   659.2   86-21136
ISBN 0-582-28529-1

87 88 89 90   9 8 7 6 5 4 3 2

CONTENTS

PREFACE

This book is the product of a joint venture of two organizations, Longman Inc., a publishing corporation founded in 1724, and the Counselors Academy of the Public Relations Society of America, created in 1961.

While the Academy recently celebrated its 25th year, historians trace the heritage of counseling firms to early-20th-century pioneers such as Carl Byoir, William Wolf Smith, Hamilton Wright, Pendleton Dudley, John Hill, Ivy Lee and Edward Bernays.

But it really wasn't until after World War II that the industry took shape. Only in the past few decades has it gained the sophistication needed to guide the decision-makers of business and the institutions of society.

Some day, public relations counseling will be old enough to warrant the writing of history books. Certainly, the time may already have arrived that a textbook for newcomers to the field would be useful. But *Strategic Public Relations Counseling* was researched and written to serve a higher purpose and a different audience.

Public relations counselors, in the words of one leader in the field, have begun to "accelerate the momentum to future greatness." Not only industry leaders but also client executives recognize the growth and progress of counseling firms. This book has been published to help build that momentum and to fuel it with ideas and information.

We take issue with the 37 percent of survey respondents at the 1985 PRSA National Conference who "strongly agreed" that "we are in a 'golden age' of public relations." We argue that the "golden age" millennium will elude us until boards of directors, CEOs and other decision-makers are well-grounded in the potent strategies and resources of today's and tomorrow's counselors.

The need now is for a definitive book exploring the strategies that position the counseling industry to participate in and help guide the growth of its clients.

No one type of counseling firm, region of the country or area of specialization really can serve as the model for the strategic designs woven by counselors and their clients. We have drawn upon the experience, brainpower and vision of several hundred experts in the United States and Canada to do this.

Nearly three years of intensive field research were invested in examining the direction of public relations counseling, involving interviews with more than 200 counselors and client executives; review of some 300 cases submitted to the authors; and exploration of more than 150 speeches, articles and books.

Although the strategies presented here are strongly grounded in theory, this is no more a theoretical tome than it is a textbook. Instead, we present through our field research and literature sources the pragmatic counsel of a cross section of innovative public relations firms. The counselors we cite share the "what" and "how-to" of their strategies as well as the "why."

This book reviews trends that cut across the entire counseling industry. These chapters were based on the study of innovations along the vertically segmented areas of public relations counseling. First priority, however, was given to producing an in-depth book along the horizontal plane, dealing with such matters as creativity, objectivity, and professional and business growth.

The field and literature research on the vertical axis of contemporary strategic public relations counsel also provides the substance for another book, on such topics as marketing support, business and financial relations, employee and management communication systems, association relations, public affairs, government relations, international representation, crisis management, and public relations programs serving special fields such as non-profits, health care, culture, leisure, sports and special events.

Strategic Public Relations Counseling is designed primarily for the continuing professional development of officers of member firms of the Counselors Academy and for growth-conscious veterans of counseling service. It should be a significant resource for:

Senior counselors, for whom a work based on the wisdom of their peers will serve as a source of stimulation.

Mid-level counselors (independents as well as those in firms), who will discover ideas to stretch their capabilities and horizons.

Administrative, marketing, advertising and public relations executives in the corporate and institutional spheres, who will find the book useful for understanding what counseling firms offer clients.

Corporate and institutional public relations practitioners, who will benefit as counselors to management from exposure to strategies of counseling firms.

Journalists, for whom the book will illuminate the professionalism of modern counseling firms.

Academic researchers, educators and graduate students, for whom the book will provide an overview of the psychology and pragmatics of counseling.

PRSA, International Association of Business Communicators, Canadian Public Relations Society, International Public Relations Association and other societies, whose members will find the book useful for professional development programs.

We dedicate this work to those executives of client organizations who have made it possible for counselors to become adjunct members of their management teams and who have encouraged the development of innovative, results-oriented, research-based strategies.

The several hundred chapter notes and the text of the book testify to the major farsighted involvement of the officers and members of the Counselors Academy. We especially wish to thank the Academy's executive committees, who shared our vision, encouraged member cooperation with the research, and gave us strong and continuing support.

Finally, we wish to acknowledge the contributions of our editors and reviewers. We credit Petra Nager not only for her excellent copyediting but also for her valuable critiques. We cite Ray E. Hiebert, editor of the Longman Series in Public Communication, for building a collection of books to which we are proud to add this volume. We give heartfelt thanks to Longman Executive Editor Gordon T. R. Anderson for expert counsel, excellent ideas and spirited encouragement in making this book a reality.

Certain details of the editorial style used here deserve mention:

Sex: The strong presence of women in public relations firms and in the leadership of organizations such as PRSA (some former presidents are Barbara Hunter, Judith Bogart and Betsy Plank) suggests that phrases like "the public relations man" are anachronisms. Masculine pronouns, however, are retained in interview material, and gender-specific job titles (e.g., "chairman") are used for specific persons.

PR: The abuse of the abbreviation PR, particularly by some political figures and journalists, suggests that *public relations* be spelled out except when PR is part of a direct quote.

Firm vs. Agency: For reasons cited in Chapter 1, "Why 'Firm' Replaces 'Agency,'" this book uses *firm* or *consultancy* to refer to public relations companies except when *agency* is part of a direct quote.

Professional Titles: References to a person's professional society offices are made the first time that person is mentioned in the book. The professional title may be used again later if it is more germane than the firm title.

Firm Identification and First Names: Full names with corporate identification and titles are provided the first time individuals are cited in a chapter. The upward mobility of counselors and rapid changes in the industry are reflected in some titles and identifications of firms.

Citations: Full publication information and interview dates are in the "Notes" following the text.

Norman R. Nager, Ph.D., APR
Richard H. Truitt, APR

Strategic
Public
Relations
Counseling

I

STRATEGIC THRUST

Communication strategies, like technology, are constantly changing. Practitioners who commit to becoming and remaining state of the art will find themselves in great demand. They are already on the verge of being transformed from counselors into leaders.

Bruce S. Rubin, 1987 Counselors Academy Chairman[1]

Transformation of the role of public relations counselors from job shop publicists to enlightened guardians of client reputation and purpose was both a dream and a concern of leaders of the industry as the Counselors Academy observed its silver anniversary.

Senior counselors cited in this chapter presented separate visions with a unifying theme: As the practice changes and grows, efforts to assure that counselors keep pace with opportunity take on critical importance. Evidence of this transformation is examined.

Challenges will arise, to be sure. Competition from law firms, project orientation of some clients, the issues of costs, competition and even the economy—all these are examined as counselors look forward to their greatest growth period bolstered by their most telling resources, the capacities to share and to lead.

FACING THE FORCES OF CHANGE

The fortunes of most organizations depend significantly on gaining the favor and endorsement, if not participation, of many diverse groups. Customers, employees, suppliers, investors, analysts, labor leaders, government regulators and even dissidents—all these people, organized or not, can bear importantly on success of an enterprise.

Frequently the groups present differing points of view, causing concern. Sometimes they clash, causing crisis. Most often they just sit there, exercising influence and always portending the conflict (and the related opportunity) that a skilled counselor should be able to identify and capitalize upon before anyone else.

1

But counselors who put themselves in a position to deal with all these forces face an awesome task. For one thing, they are assuming a responsibility that has not always been theirs, by default. Clients, as a matter of fact, have traditionally assigned them a different role.

The public relations counselor, however, brings fundamental capability, invaluable experience and a new capacity for solving business problems to the situation. The capability is skill as a communicator—essential to public relations work. The experience is background with other clients—critical to counseling. The capacity is depth knowledge of business practice, initiated in professional school, given dimension in client campaigns and honed in universities and seminars now offering advanced education to counselors.

Counselors who are short of these strengths will have difficulty in serving their clients capably. But those armed with solid communications ability and able to synthesize and wisely apply concepts and solutions learned separately in professional development and from experience can expand the practice of public relations counseling to help build a new vision of its future.

From Traditional Services to Business-Wise Leadership

More than 1,100 members of the Counselors Academy of the Public Relations Society of America have embarked on a transformation from the traditional role of publicist to the more stirring and significant tasks of business leadership.

They and thousands of other public relations consultants already have made important progress in providing in-depth executive counseling and strategic planning.

The Counselors Academy is 1 of 15 special-interest sections of PRSA. It has embarked on its second quarter-century of service, only a few decades younger than the bulk of the public relations consulting industry it represents. Its roots, like those of counseling, lie deep in the entrepreneurial practice of providing independent public relations services to businesses, institutions and government.

In the early post–World War II days, only a relative few counselors strayed far from press agentry and publicity. But there were exceptions. Some looked beyond "doing" to counseling and based their counsel on research, rudimentary as it was.

Some began to consider themselves as problem-solvers, not just communication experts. Some began to act as adjunct executives to their clients, assuming responsibility for marketing support and public affairs objectives. Some began to strive for measurable objectives and started the struggle to transform a so-called art into a hybrid of business and social science.

Not all the motivation was—or is—altruistic. Much of the force for change has been dictated by economic realities as the costs of the talent and technology for counseling soared and as clients found they could handle some traditional public relations activities internally.

In response, leaders in the counseling business see a growing involvement in issues identification and much more sophistication in how they deliver messages to audiences. They're doing more fine targeting and moving into a very sophisticated business in which they'll be able to help clients mold opinions in very narrow interest groups. They are beginning to adapt from selling products to selling ideas. Monitoring of direct response is being used extensively now, and counselors expect to be doing much more direct response measurement in supporting or opposing legislation, in informing people why the products or services of clients are important to them.[2]

If counseling was to thrive, not just survive, new thrusts such as these were required. There would still be room for traditional services, but the future of the industry lay in opening new territory that internal apparatus could not handle and that a new aggressive generation of corporate and institutional executives could not resist.

Visionaries among the leadership have looked to involvement in research-based, results-oriented, change-sensitized, business-centered, socially responsive service to their clients. And domestic and international economics and the sociosphere have made conditions right for change in the 1980s and 1990s.

Conditions Right for Changing Role of Counselors

Innovative counselors already had begun to respond to the vacuum that persisted alongside attorneys, financial officers and industrial relations executives as existing and prospective clients struggled with a bewildering array of forces such as these:

International competition
Troublesome government intervention in business
Sharply changing demographics
Shifts in social values
Persistent special interest groups
Staggering trade imbalances
Changing patterns in government spending
Shifting tax burdens
Decay of the nation's infrastructure
Economic and natural disasters in the rural heartland

Breakneck growth of new technologies

Terrorism against civilians and sabotage of consumer products

Whirlwind mergers and acquisitions

Rapidly changing modes of communication in an era of satellite transmissions, video narrowcasting, vertical publications and heavy use of computers.

Building on Visions and Leadership

Public relations counseling, like the Counselors Academy, has built upon the leadership and vision of many individuals over many years. Elected leaders of the Academy have been influenced and guided in their work by the thousands of colleagues they have come to know through their conferences, literature and surveys.

The transformation of the craft and the vision of these leaders perhaps can best be crystallized by views of five recent chairmen of the Academy.

Counselors will be exploring and charting, and in the process they'll not merely be among the first to identify social and business trends— they'll often be at the leading edge.
    —Bruce S. Rubin, president, Bruce Rubin Associates, Miami[3]

I see decentralization of public relations counseling from a large-city base and more firms opening up in smaller cities and communities. New perspectives are coming into our profession and invigorating it. This produces much greater awareness in the marketplace of our expertness beyond our limited traditional roles.
    —Joe S. Epley, president, Epley Associates, Charlotte, N.C.[4]

It's a very competitive business, and when I first came into it you made a presentation to the client: "Here's what I would like to do, here's the budget, here's what I want to do now and here's what I'd like to do the following year." We did everything—news releases, brochures, special projects. Now, the client is saying, "I'll do these things in-house, here's what agencies will do." And the publics are becoming more sophisticated about how they're getting messages. They're open to credible public relations messages.
    —Paul H. Alvarez, chairman, Ketchum Public Relations, New York[5]

The real winners will be those counseling firms with specialized capabilities. We better either have that capability or be networked into the resources to get it. The real future is in high-level strategic consulting, fewer and fewer projects, more and more strategic counseling. We will never price ourselves out of the market for strategic thinking and management consulting. And the more we can demonstrate that what we're doing for clients is quantifiable and related to the bottom line, the more they're going to be happy with our counsel.

—Davis Young, president, Young-Liggett-Stashower
Public Relations, Cleveland[6]

For those of us who are independent consultants, the need is to understand and sell our expertise for its depth and total commitment to our prospects and clients, undiluted by fractionated, sometimes unrelated and frequently uncoordinated, peripheral communications services. The public relations consultancy must be on the cutting edge of the move from seat-of-the-pants subjective considerations to considering communications as an increasingly objective business discipline. Successful consultants will stand out just as corporate legal counsels or research and development chiefs, recognized for expertise and capabilities and positioned by performance.

—James B. Strenski, chairman,
Public Communications Inc., Chicago[7]

EVIDENCE OF TRANSFORMATION

Surveys Show Change from Traditional Public Relations Agency Roles

First has come the change from traditional implementation of communications programs to counseling. Evidence of the move to counseling and the beginning of the transformation to leadership may be found in several surveys:

Responsibilities: In-Depth Counseling, Strategic Planning
A survey at the 1985 PRSA National Conference in Detroit revealed that respondents selected client counseling and strategic planning as the two most important principal responsibilities of public relations firms.[8]

"In-depth counseling of senior executives" was ranked the single most important public relations firm responsibility by 37 percent and the second highest by 20 percent. "Strategic planning" also was supported for first-place choice by 37 percent. It was rated the second most important responsibility by 28 percent.

Although communication has long been considered central to the practice of public relations, "implementing communication programs" had only 16 percent of first-place votes. With 33 percent of respondents opting for the doing of communications as second most important responsibility, the total who ranked that in the top two was slightly less than half.

"Handling ad hoc assignments"—doing whatever came along—came in fourth among the five responsibilities tested, with 6 percent ranking it number one and another 13 percent ranking it number two, for a total of 19 percent.

The traditional duty of public relations firms up to recent years, the handling of "extensive publicity," received only 4 percent of poll support for number one responsibility and 6 percent for number two, a combined sum of 10 percent.

Of the respondents, 18 percent identified with the Counselors Academy as representing their field of primary interest. Four-fifths were associated with the 14 other PRSA sections.

Concern about Economic, Employee Relations, Marketplace Issues In the *PR Reporter* Annual Survey of the Profession, counselors mentioned the economy and employee relations as among the most important issues/ problems confronting the industry and their clients in 1985.[9]

The publication's survey identified "economy" as issues or problems related to deficit, tax reform and infrastructure, whereas employee relations was defined as concern with motivation and productivity.

Counselors joined with other practitioners in most mentions of marketplace issues, such as product quality and increase in domestic and foreign competition.

Planning, Counseling, Issue Management Account for Most Time An industrywide trend, involving counselors as well as their internal counterparts, is that public relations people are spending proportionately more time on activities that deal with planning, counseling and issue management than on more traditional publicity management and promotions.

Respondents to the *PR Reporter* 1985 survey rank-ordered the activities on which they spend at least 25 percent of their time. "Publicity" topped the list with 24.8 percent ranking it first. However, when the figures are summed for second place "public relations planning" (19.3 percent), fourth place "counseling" (16.3 percent), sixth place "strategic planning" (14.0 percent), and eighth place "issue management" (12.3 percent), "publicity" emphasis pales against the 61.9 percent who rated the new-thrust activities as most time-consuming.[10]

That 61.9 percent could be swelled, depending upon whether one considers the third place combination classification of "advertising and marketing" (18.6 percent) or the seventh place "community relations" (12.3 percent) as new-thrust or traditional activities. There also may be new-thrust elements in the fifth place "employee publications" (14.8 percent). The lowest ranking went to "promotions and special events" with 11.2 percent saying that these activities accounted for 25 percent or more of their time.

Academy Poll Reflects Supportive Trend by Client Top Management More evidence of the transformation was provided in Young's 1985 survey report

"The State of the Public Relations Consultancy in the United States." He found that the most important positive trend reported by members of the Counselors Academy was "growing acceptance of the importance and value of public relations by top management. . . . Nothing was even remotely close to the preponderance of mentions for increasing acceptance of the function as the single most important trend on the immediate horizon."[11]

In his poll of members on the most positive trends, he found that other trends mentioned with some frequency included:

"Corporate cost cutting with implications of more work to outside firms"

"Growth of public relations consulting services to professional service firms"

"Importance of counselors to the corporate planning process"

"Movement towards strategic and conceptual public relations"

"More first-time use of counselors as clients merge, expand or deregulate"

"Concern within the profession for higher standards, both ethically and professionally"

"Increased level of sophistication of what it is firms are asked to do"

Young concluded: "I would see the single most important positive trend being the fact that we are clearly able to do things with increasing precision. We have greater understanding of the concept of positioning as it relates to public relations, greater sophistication in the selection and use of fragmented media, and more reliance on results and less on intuition."

Growth of Counseling Industry—How and Why

PRSA Survey, O'Dwyer Reports, Show More Firms, Income Such changes have led to increased confidence and growth for the counseling industry.

For instance, the PRSA 1985 survey showed National Conference attendees bullish on growth of the public relations counseling industry. They were given the statement, "Public relations counseling has expanded significantly during the past few years" and then asked, "How much do you, personally, think counseling will change in the next two years?"[12] Their response:

46 percent: "Continue to grow substantially"

43 percent: "Continue to grow somewhat"

8 percent: "Little or no change"

3 percent: "May shrink somewhat"

Jack O'Dwyer's Newsletter chronicled the opening of 200 new public relations firms in 1985 alone.[13] "Quite a few were started by corporate people in their 50s who were laid off or who took advantage of early retirement plans," the newsletter reported. O'Dwyer said that many younger people opted to move into the counseling business in 1985 "feeling this would be a more secure career path."

In his year-end review of top stories for the same year, O'Dwyer found several trends related to counseling industry growth:[14]

"Profusion of new public relations firms to meet increasing demand for outside counsel by companies with caretaker public relations units"

"Unusually high loss of corporate public relations jobs due to mergers, takeovers and efforts by companies to slim down to meet lean foreign competition"

However, a subsequent report contradicted the connection between layoffs and increased retention of outside public relations counsel:[15]

One agency executive scoffed at the theory that companies are using more outside public relations because it's cheaper. Companies with sales of billions of dollars are not worried about saving a few hundred thousand on public relations. They are going outside because the advice is better. The agencies are not afraid to lay it on the line to the CEO and the agencies have the varied staff to carry out their recommendations.

Not only are the number of firms increasing, but so are the fees. The largest 50 firms experienced 20 percent growth for a 12-month total of approximately $520 million in net fees in 1985, the fourth consecutive year of gains for the counseling industry.

A year earlier, O'Dwyer reported that the 40 largest public relations firms had experienced a 423 percent increase in net fee income between 1974 and the end of 1984.[16]

Recession Fails to Dampen Growth   Yet this growth took place against the backdrop of one of the more serious recessions of the post–World War II era. That hurt business for some firms; many in certain economy-sensitive areas of specialization suffered loss of accounts. Some, such as the West Coast's ICPR, felt the impact of the recession as late as 1985, when the firm went out of business. But, for the most part, counselors did well.

In 1985, the *Los Angeles Times* reviewed the recession and reported, "Often the first to suffer in bad economic times because of its reputation as a business luxury, public relations has thrived recently as the economy has boomed and the industry has broadened its appeal beyond its traditional publicity role."[17]

In 1983, *PR Casebook* reported that the counseling industry was prospering in the midst of recession. At that time, the publication estimated that there were more than 6,000 firms in the United States alone offering public relations–related services and said that somewhat less than half were pure public relations operations. The majority represented publicity firms that averaged fewer than five employees.[18]

"Interestingly enough, the recession seems to have had little impact on the public relations trade." And then the article posed a rhetorical question: "With thousands of corporations going bankrupt, why has public relations done so well?"

David J. Speer, principal of Padilla, Speer, Burdick and Beardsley of Minneapolis, responded: "Our experience has shown that the downturn in the economy has, if anything, improved the climate for public relations counseling services. We attribute this primarily to the continuing increase in appreciation for public relations as a business discipline."[19]

Opportunities Increase as Management Turns to Counselors   An encouraging pattern that augurs well for firms seeking to build on this climate reveals that corporations are extending the public relations function beyond simple communications to include strategic planning and issue analysis.

Bill Cantor, head of the New York–based Cantor Concern, said changing patterns would open up greater opportunities. "Corporations that never felt the need to set up public relations departments or use outside counsel will be doing so in the near future. A surprising number today (some 10 percent of the *Fortune* 500 list) do not have a professional public relations staff or use outside counsel. This will be changing."[20]

As part of watching the bottom line, "top management is giving greater recognition to the role of public relations as its problems multiply in an ever-changing environment."[21]

Why "Firm" Replaces "Agency"

Symbolic of the thrust to counseling, many practitioners and client executives have abandoned the designation *agency* for public relations businesses in favor of the word *firm*.

For the most part, "agency" can be construed as a misnomer for public relations counselors, even including those whose firms function as part of advertising agencies. It may have been more appropriate in the heyday of press agents as a term for some companies. But the discipline has put a great distance between press agentry and the kinds of products clients increasingly expect from contemporary public relations firms.

There also is the matter of connotation. One connotation is that of an enterprise authorized to spend the money of another and, usually, draw a commission. Another is that of a franchise that acts as a vendor for another business.

Patrick Jackson, former president of PRSA, took the lead in campaigning for the new positioning of the industry in a mid-1980s article:[22] "Do we want to share the terminology of professionals, i.e., law firms, architectural firms, engineering firms, management consulting firms?"

The Exeter, N.H., senior counsel of Jackson, Jackson & Wagner said the term "agency" may be appropriate for advertising agencies, insurance agencies, employment agencies, talent agencies and food brokerage agencies. But its meaning in the public relations business tends to be that of getting "free space" to go along with the "paid space" of advertising.

His intent was primarily to differentiate public relations from advertising: "Ultimately, this subject boils down to realizing that public relations has the capability to become a true profession in our society. A profession must deal with something that is endemic and universal in human life like health, law, education, religion or public relationships."

Another counselor, the president of E. Bruce Harrison Co., Washington, D.C., endorsed the use of "firm": "Similar thinking led us to upgrade from PRSA 'section' to 'Academy' and to raise high the word 'counselor.'"[23]

Old habits die hard. On occasion, the word "agency" will continue to appear in print or in conversation. All name changes, when successful, count time as a most important ally.

CAMPAIGN VS. PROJECT

Overcoming Bias to Short-Term Gains

Contemporary management literature implies that a problem of U.S. industry in remaining competitive with companies abroad is a traditional North American bias in favor of pursuing short-term results at the cost of long-range investment.

Indeed, the value of patience and the expense involved in building for the long run have been intrinsic to the teaching of business administration in the United States and Canada. But somehow, the lessons seemed to have been forgotten in the haste to draw upon early profits.

Similarly, in public relations, the emphasis in many client organizations traditionally has been on short-term impact rather than on multiphased, carefully staged campaigns to influence opinions and behavior.

Toward the end of the 20th century, the trends toward short-term projects and long-range campaigns were clashing. Resolution was unclear but there was promising evidence of determination on the part of some counselors and client executives to opt for the long run. An example of a distinctively long-range campaign serves as the main case study in Chapter 2.

Many counseling firms are so young, they don't have a record of saying "no" to the large number of challenges presented to them. Some senior executives are beginning to recognize that asking a counseling firm to issue standard news releases is like asking the corporation's legal firm, "If I drove 38 m.p.h. in a 35 zone, would I get a ticket?" Client management, according to many counselors, is just starting to realize the potential of knowledge within public relations firms.[24]

Some Executives Willing to Be Persuaded More and more executives are willing to be persuaded. Increasingly, the public relations person's counsel is weighed together with that of other experts as the CEO listens and deliberates.

A CEO, or anyone in a decision-making position with the client, also listens to counsel from financial officers, lawyers, perhaps from marketing executives or people in charge of the technical aspects of the business, often from the director of personnel and equally as often from the industrial relations executive.

William H. Stryker, chairman of Honolulu-based Stryker Weiner Associates, said he viewed the responsibility of the public relations counselor as being "more concerned with the objectivity and pertinence of his opinions than with the course of action ultimately selected."[25]

One can credit CEO willingness to be persuaded, as well as counselor credibility and persuasiveness, for success in having recommendations accepted over objections of high-ranking operations officers who value short-range earnings at the expense of long-range corporate interests.

It may be, some counselors feel, that the field of "corporate communications" is a trap into which they might fall and one that might severely limit their growth potential over the long term.

James F. Fox, chairman of Fox Public Relations, New York, and former president of PRSA, said his vision of the long-range role of those who counsel is that they are futurists "mastering the calculus of long-range forecasting."[26] Such calculus takes into account economic indicators, technological assessment, social indicators, political trend analysis and early-warning signs of social change.

In being prepared to alert management to such signs and advise executives how to cope, the consultant could be reporting within a few years not to the CEO but to the board of directors. Fox said that counsel will help the board lead the company into new strategic directions, protect the corporation's social franchise, develop strategies for reconciling interests of stockholders, employees, customers, suppliers, the government and plant communities.

But most counselors know that those firms that insist public relations is corporate communications rather than advocacy and problem solving will find themselves suppliers to the executive strategist, perhaps a member of the board, "who will contract for their services as writers or communicators, just as one now contracts for photographers, graphic artists and printers."

Counselors Could Be Co-opted Some corporate executives apparently believe that as war is too important to leave to the generals, so public relations is too critical to leave to the practitioners. As far back as 1980, Fox foretold of the co-opting of public relations counseling.

> *We are not the only ones to whom management turns for advice on external affairs. Many others are in the public opinion/public affairs business, not the least of them lawyers, who see themselves as advocates to the public as well as in the courts.*
>
> *And what about economists, sociologists, academicians, retired politicians and bureaucrats, futurists, pollsters, trade association officials, management consultants, editors and even our own chief executive officers? We seem more and more to be in conflict when it comes to defining our area of responsibility. And more and more, because of the government regulatory problems, it is lawyers who are asked to assess and deal with the public environment.*

Luc Beauregard, 1985 president of the Canadian Public Relations Society, said he was concerned that without establishing professional criteria for public relations counseling, co-opting would be one of the consequences: "Other professionals, lawyers for instance, will go on invading this new area of management consulting—perhaps to the extent that at one point in time, they could pretend public relations is within their exclusive domain of jurisdiction,"[27] said the principal of Quebec's Beauregard, Hutchinson, McCoy, Capistran, Lamarre et Associes.

The confusion about domains is not unknown to counselors based in Washington, D.C., where the lines are thinly drawn between lawyers and public relations practitioners, especially where the field of "government relations" is involved. In addition, former members of Congress, former regulatory agency staffers and dozens of other kinds of Washington workers all lay claim to the title of "lobbyist" and to the promise that they can make things happen in the capital.

In 1985, Harold Burson, chairman of Burson-Marsteller, analyzed the situation this way:

> *There are a lot of lawyers around, but a lot of corporations rebel at the high costs of legal services. Lawyers are looking at "what else can we do?" Law firms are saying that we're stepping over into their area in the lobbying process.*

Management firms are saying that public relations is stepping over into employee benefit systems that they feel is their province.

We can't put a frame around counseling and reserve it for public relations people. But a really institutionalized public relations firm can be viewed as part of the business structure.[28]

Project Orientation Accompanied by Some Benefits   More strategic objectives and much more strategic planning are needed to position the public relations firm in an era becoming more oriented to projects than to long-range campaigns. Client executives used to ask themselves: "Do we do it ourselves or have it done externally?" According to Burson, "The day of the very large public relations department that does a complete job will be on the decline because of cost pressures. They have been trimmed down. They're looking to outside suppliers and resources to supplement their capabilities. That's why project orientation has become a trend."[29]

Burson reflected on the evolution of public relations over his career:

At first, the decision already was made by the executive, and he'd call the public relations person in and ask, "how do I say this?" That was largely a press function. In the era of the 1960s, the executive asked not only how, but also "what do I say?" That's gone on for a long time. In the 1980s, the public relations counselor is being asked more and more "what do I do?" That represents a tremendous escalation of the role of public relations.[30]

But although he has found that larger clients "tend to be more stable in their relationships with public relations firms," smaller, "marginal accounts are moving around."[31]

Burson said that one tends to have more success with larger client organizations in helping them "recognize that they have an investment in their counseling firm, and there is a two-way loyalty."

Move from Project Orientation Likely   As counselors become more sophisticated and strategy-oriented, the swing from project work to participation in the business management function is likely to accelerate. "The future of our business lies with strategic planners and thinkers, as compared with those whose hands are directly on a particular job," according to Young.[32]

That means clients will increasingly staff their own organizations for project execution purposes as hourly fees reach their upper limits. But those counselors who can command higher fees "will do so on the basis of counseling."

This may have an adverse impact on the hiring of journalism-trained persons by counseling firms. Newspapers and other media traditionally were the prime feeders of new talent into the counseling business. "If the demand shifts in the future to more consulting and less project execution, then there should be a dramatic shift away from hiring journalism graduates and towards the hiring of those with different backgrounds" oriented toward problem solving and management thinking, Young said.

It Helps if the Client Understands Complex Process Loet A. Velmans, chairman of Hill and Knowlton through the end of 1986, said he was encouraged "that a number of clients now are involving us earlier in the goal-setting process" although there are still some executives who "previously have identified their goals and want us to carry them out." Velmans also said that:

> I think we can be most effective for those clients who realize that public relations is a fairly complicated process.
>
> For example, if a client is trying to build market share and hasn't been successful, it might be due to a dealer relations problem. Or there could be public concern over product safety rather than the quality. Getting the client general placements in the press is not going to solve these problems. You can't simply use public relations techniques in a random fashion. You must concentrate them on the areas where the problems lie.[33]

NEW CHALLENGES FROM CLIENTS

Lower Barriers to Recognition of Accountability

The demands of clients for new roles for public relations counselors and the interests of a new generation of client executives in accountability have guided the growth of the counseling business. Concurrent with increased accountability is the abandonment of persistent myths shrouding the real functions and values of counseling and the sometimes rigid allegiance to following case precedent.

A Time to Get Rid of Mystique As the discipline developed, a mystique fed by some early practitioners and nourished by popular literature and a lack of client understanding grew around counselors and their role. One of the challenges to contemporary counselors is to strip away the mystique so that client executives—and counselors themselves—can focus on the substance of what public relations does in producing results.

According to Duncan T. Black Jr., president of the Montgomery-based firm of Cunningham, Black & Farley, theoretical constructs are valuable to counseling—much more so than mystique—because theory explains "why" something works and helps guide public relations firm services.[34] But theory can be taken to extremes. Black offered this note of caution: "Today's university graduates have lots of theory and think they can do the job. But in the rush to become professionals, some have focused too fully on philosophy rather than on the body of knowledge."

Neither the mystique of public relations nor theory isolated from the realities of doing counseling will suffice for long in the contemporary marketplace.

Case Histories—Fragile and Time-Bound, But Useful Cases in public relations counseling, as in medicine, law and physics, are time-bound and fragile. As examples, physicians long ago stopped using leeches, relying on the iron lung to combat polio and sending cancer patients off to die untreated. Over the years, medicine's knowledge of human systems, bodily processes, diagnostics and treatment has radically changed with new theory and research.

Attorneys may cite statutes and legal precedents of court cases up to the point that laws are changed and rulings of higher courts make their body of knowledge and cases obsolete. Physicists keep discovering new laws that supersede the previously "proven" explanations of the forces of energy and matter on this planet and in its solar system.

Similarly, casebooks about business success stories frequently become archaic as models. Even legendary industry giants topple under the weight of domestic or foreign competition, neglect by success-inured managers, government deregulation or unexpected, hostile takeovers. Case stories, however, can be stimulating for those who can learn from their lessons.

No two client situations are identical. Conditions subject to variation include such elements as time, place, marketplace conditions, competitor actions, prevailing attitudes of different publics, issues of temporal concern, behind-the-scenes forces and resources, including expertness and funds.

Placing Higher Financial Value on Counseling

Higher Fees Needed to Attract and Hold Talent The talent resources and know-how, in terms of business acumen and specialized areas of consulting, however, will be jeopardized unless public relations firms are able to command higher fees and allocate them to their staffs.

Services must be delivered in such a way as to justify higher fees to attract and hold good people as well as train better middle management, according to a California management consultant. Daniel H. Baer of Sherman Oaks said corporate public relations compensation packages often are more favorable than those in counseling firms.[35]

Baer recommended a conscious effort to attract competent recruits for "the myriad of gigantic new opportunities and challenges" in preparing for increased employment of research, planning, technology and business consultation strategies. His advice to recruit bright MBAs and lawyers as well as communications graduates would sharply increase the cost of talent.

Similarly, Michael Campbell, president of Toronto's Continental Public Relations, predicted that the costs of consulting time and services will increase significantly to allow salaries for senior staff to start to parallel those of many professional groups.[36]

Furthermore, compensation for entry-level creative talent in public relations counseling will have to rise to pay for the new skills and greater specialization counseling firms are increasingly demanding.

Business training heads the list of skills most firms are seeking. Other skills include postgraduate education and international communications experience. Although communication know-how will continue to be rated highly, it will become more exacting as technology dramatically alters the way in which we communicate.

Those higher costs, however, will tend to be offset partially by economies in time management and streamlined delivery of services. New efficiencies will enable many labor-intensive tasks to be completed in less time by less expensive junior practitioners. Such savings will be demanded by clients who develop even tighter cost control systems, Campbell said. "Public relations will be forced to become more accountable, streamlined, and cost-effective."

How to Reverse Undervalued-Underpaid Status Counselors can demonstrate their monetary worth to a campaign or project when they provide the tools to measure their contributions to the client bottom line and when they link what they do to such business compensation criteria as accountability, problem solving and know-how.

Alfred Geduldig, president of the New York management consulting firm of Chester Burger & Co., said "public relations is often undervalued and underpaid, largely because the evaluators do not appreciate and cannot measure its value." Geduldig also said he is aware that most compensation systems ignore or minimize "the value of intangibles."[37]

Prevailing criteria for the Hay System and similar "comparable worth" programs include the following points:

1. *Know-how*: This includes "specialized skills or technical knowledge, managerial savvy and human-relations skills."

2. *Problem solving*: This "takes into account the complexity of problems and the freedom one has to solve them."

3. *Accountability*: This "measures the reach of one's authority and the impact of the job on the bottom line, how much a particular public relations job contributes to profitability."

Geduldig raised questions important to demonstration of higher value:

"How can one quantify turning a potentially disastrous story into one that's only mildly damaging?"

"How can one set a point value on knowing when to speak to the media and when to duck?"

"How can one measure the worth of a community relations program that helps keep activist groups away from the company door?"

How can one quantify *"the effect on the price and stability of company stock because public relations people know how and when to communicate with financial analysts?"*

Increasing Value of Internal Staff Pays Dividends Another strategic approach to raising counseling firm fees starts with counselors helping internal public relations executives become more highly valued and paid by demonstrating their worth to top management in terms of accountability, problem solving and know-how.

Justifying a higher compensation for internal public relations services can serve the external counselor because:

The internal public relations executive frequently makes decisions or recommendations on when and how to utilize external counsel.

The internal public relations executive often serves as liaison person or point of contact for counselors. Even when that is not the case, the environment for counseling is enhanced when the client's staff is supportive and cooperative.

The internal public relations executive who includes external services in the budget might be encouraged, as well as given a basis, to place a higher value on services from counseling firms.

Fiscal officers who place a higher value on, and agree to better compensation for, the internal staff will not be surprised by the cost of retaining outside counsel.

Anticipating Needs of Client Executives

Business Acumen and Results Sought by the CEO CEOs are looking for people who know how their businesses work. Anything that can orient public relations people to management processes or help them understand business operations will make them better qualified to counsel their clients.

Counseling firms can become more efficient at anticipating client executive needs by:

Upgrading the creative process

Using research to a greater extent

Raising the level of professionalism by being oriented to results

Burson said that strong management development programs can help overcome the lingering problem of some corporate CEOs who have not viewed public relations executives as peers. The problem also can be addressed through initiative of individuals to learn everything they can about the client's business and industry.[38]

Clients and Counselors Need to Match Each Other's Know-How   The pressure to strengthen acumen for counseling power underlines the importance of professional development to build the broad business knowledge needed to match the communications skills of counselors.

By the same token, Young said that top corporate management must have a dialogue with America's special interest groups and learn to communicate with employees and a host of other constituencies.[39]

But this is difficult for those who have not had any formal training. Professional organizations, particularly the Foundation for Public Relations Research and Education, have planned initiatives to encourage business schools to provide such training. Until such a time comes, the responsibility will belong to public relations experts in communication.

Notable improvement in gaining business acumen has been achieved by public relations firms in recent years through financial management information processing systems.[40]

Treading on Management Consulting Firm Territory   Problem-solving consultation will bring public relations counselors into greater competition with management consulting firms. On the down-side, Fox predicted that "communications conglomerates, including their public relations wings, will themselves be swallowed, becoming part of the great management consulting firms, as such think tanks as Arthur D. Little, for example."[41]

On the up-side, public relations counselors can become more competitive by building and adapting such management consultant strengths in problem-solving as:

Technical competence in basic business functions

Understanding of strategic business planning and organization

Ability to be at home with computer-based information and control systems as well as comfortable in the world of ideas

Political sophistication

Knowledge of social forces and how to respond to changing public expectations

Ability to adapt to external affairs such proven techniques as risk management and auditing

Skill in government negotiations and communications

Willingness to deal with the underlying sources of dissatisfaction leading to the demand for action

Orientation helping management develop alternative means of dealing with problems

Capability to help executives develop alliances with other interest groups

Confidence of management to help them develop longer range measures to affect the business climate

Special strengths in interpersonal communication

Fox challenged North American counselors to "manage, measure, know more than others, have both insight and foresight and refuse to continue to recycle the old ideas" but, instead, be creative.

A TIME TO SHARE; A TIME FOR LEADERSHIP

Until the early 1980s, public relations counseling firms struggling for survival and attempting to build profitability in a very competitive industry tended to keep proprietary research data and innovative strategies to themselves.

Only one major book had been written that treated post–World War II counseling with any depth. It focused primarily on the perspective of a single firm, Hill and Knowlton, and the views of its senior author, H&K's late chairman Richard W. Darrow.[42] In 1982, another counseling firm, Burson-Marsteller, began to share proprietary data at PRSA national and regional conferences. A year later, Ketchum Public Relations followed suit.

The Counselors Academy, however, had shared monographs and special reports with its members since the 1960s. Yet those publications and the proceedings at the Academy's conferences have been unavailable to libraries, researchers, journals and even other members of PRSA.

When the authors approached the Counselors Academy in 1983 with a query about turning its literature into an edited anthology, permission was declined on the basis that this would violate the members' proprietary interests gained through membership. But it was a time to share. The Counselors Academy executive committee agreed to join forces with Longman Inc. and with Nager and Truitt in the development of an original book to be based on fresh research.

Of the more than 200 counselors from whom interviews were requested, only three declined. Others responded to requests for case and other materials, and entire confidential procedure manuals were made available for field research.

"Whatever we can do to upgrade the public relations counseling function will benefit us as an industry and as a company," one public relations firm chairman said in a comment that typified the responses of firm principals.[43]

"First you have to have data to share," he said, recalling the years it took for the industry to reach the point of having valuable materials to pool. "Second you have constraints about client confidentiality and client relations. You walk that fine line.

"In the research area, we were concerned about demonstrating what we could do through measurement from a public relations standpoint. We felt that if we could do that, it would contribute to the standing and good fortune of the field." And, perhaps, others would reciprocate.

The CEO of another firm reiterated a point often stated by his counterparts around the country when he told an interviewer: "Just let me know who you want to talk to or what you need, and I'll make sure you have access."[44]

Others suggested that corporate and institutional staff vice presidents for public relations should consider themselves internal counselors and that this book should take into consideration their professional interests and needs. "I trust your book will be broadly addressed to this larger audience, too," an executive advised.[45]

The leaders of the Academy during the research, writing and production phases furthermore supported the concept of a book that "would help CEOs, board members, advertising and marketing executives really understand what it is that counselors do so they can take fuller advantage of what our firms can deliver."[46]

In the November 1985 annual lecture sponsored by the Foundation for Public Relations Research and Education, University of Wisconsin–based author and researcher Lee Thayer challenged public relations people to "think leadership":

> The vital leadership role in the future, in human organizations of every sort, will be that provided by those who are equipped to sense what is going on in that organization's environment.
>
> This vital information-communication-intelligence-strategic leadership could and perhaps should be provided by today's public relations practitioner. You must lead the nation's decision-makers—in business and industry and labor and government and education, in social affairs and the arts and in science and technology—to make those decisions that will further our best and most human interests.[47]

For counselors, that leadership will mean a new dedication to the value of objectives-based public relations that is well-conceived, well-directed and well-sold. It also requires an interactive combination of strategic creativity, research and client relations. Perhaps the best starting point is creativity.

2

STRATEGIC CREATIVITY

In this chapter about the creative process as it works in public relations firms, critical elements of creativity are identified and illustrated as they have been applied in recent campaigns and projects.

Three essential parts of the creative process—keeping objectives in focus, restructuring existing information to fit a new situation and executing concepts and plans properly—are explained. Techniques for bringing out creativity and overcoming barriers are reviewed. The environment that supports a healthy creative process is examined in terms of counseling firm individuals, culture, incentives, training and use of expert consultants.

THE ELEMENTS OF CREATIVITY

The public relations counselor has been wrestling with creativity and its changing patterns for decades.

Needs of companies are changing, and clients are becoming more sophisticated about public relations. This change is demonstrated by the fact that so many of today's corporate executives grew up in marketing, finance and law. They continue to think in terms of those disciplines, and that has a significant effect on how they view the creative perspectives of their public relations counselors.

This makes it important to review certain new concepts, never yet fully defined, that govern the way public relations counselors strategize when they achieve creative excellence.

Creativity in the counseling business can happen in many ways, take many forms and be the product of many different forces. But three key elements almost always form the basis of a successful creative effort:

1. *It keeps targets in focus*: In public relations counseling, creativity that involves development of ideas to solve problems, meet needs or anticipate opportunities must mesh with hardened objectives of clients and research-tested interests of their publics.

2. *It builds upon the past*: Creativity, the intellectual finding of ideas or techniques that help solve problems or take advantage of opportunities, almost always involves the thoughtful restructuring of existing information.

3. *It requires diligence*: The success of a creative concept almost always depends on solid execution—the diligence and courage of the person in charge who is willing to make a good idea work and see it through to success.

Of these three, hitting the right target with the right message springs most frequently into the minds of objectives-oriented clients.

Keeping Objectives in Focus

Closing the Creativity Gap with Advertising Increasingly, client executives look for results beyond awards and media coverage, and that strongly affects their counselors' creative planning process.[1]

It used to be that creativity in public relations had the goal of capturing media attention. Sometimes, even today, practitioners pursue creativity for creativity's sake. But the business environment dictates that it have a broader, more carefully directed purpose.

A common denominator in most successful creative projects is the extra dimension that a strong sense of purpose can bring to clients. Creating new ideas, or building on ideas that went before, in such a way that they will make a contribution to the client's objectives is the most exciting part of the public relations business.

In their disciplined, research-based, objectives-oriented approach to creativity, advertising people frequently have been better at this. They study their audiences and messages endlessly. They test and retest nearly everything that counts. Only when they know what they're doing, do they start to think about starting production.

Thomas E. Eidson, president of Hill and Knowlton, USA, supported the argument that despite the traditional dominance of advertising in the sphere of creativity, public relations counseling firms now are growing dramatically in that area:

> *Creativity has been considered by clients to be largely the domain of advertising rather than public relations, but we're beginning to loosen the lock on creativity that advertising agencies have had. One of the challenges we have in public relations is to provide creative solutions that management now expects from us. In the past, they would expect mechanical aspects—SEC notification, media relations, basic information for consumer editors.*
>
> *Usually by the time we were called in, advertising and marketing already had decided on the name of a product and how the product was*

to be positioned in the marketplace. They had decided on packaging, distribution, market segments and targets and had already done strength and weakness analysis on a balance sheet. Public relations was told about this and then was asked to support the ad campaign.

But those days are gone and public relations is in a new era. We're going into the boardroom where we're embraced by more and more marketing directors. They're beginning to realize that in this mix of public relations, we have ability to segment the marketplace much more effectively than advertising and that we're more cost effective. For instance, advertising can talk to Hispanic females; public relations can segment the market of Hispanic females 10 different ways.[2]

Complex Audience Variables Require Research for Creativity Counselors remain under pressure, however, to assure that their creativity actually works. It has to carry the message they want it to carry, and they have to verify that this message really is effective for the client. It has to reach the people they're trying to reach, and they have to understand who they really are.

Do practitioners really *know* the people they're trying to reach? Consider this perspective of contemporary audiences:

They're exposed to more than 1,800 commercial messages every day. And they've got lots to think about in addition to that. Nearly 9 percent of the married people in this country seriously think their spouse is having an affair. Nearly 15 percent of our households contain someone who is chronically sick. At least one in five Americans feels he doesn't have enough money to buy food or clothing. Fully one-third are overweight, and they know it and worry about it. They have an average 4.6 cavities. A recent poll shows that one out of every five people has been threatened with a gun or shot at. No wonder "damn" is one of the 15 most frequently spoken words in our society.[3]

On the other hand, research-guided creativity itself becomes one of the best instruments for penetrating the consciousness of people who would just as soon be thinking of something else. Making that creativity work requires an understanding of the three critical elements noted at the beginning of this chapter and how they interact in the creative process.

Steak Will Prevail over Sizzle Increasingly, models of creativity in counseling build on the bedrock of substance concerning client products, services, and social responsibility. "Recognition will grow that the overriding objective of any public relations program will be trust," according to the president of Young-Liggett-Stashower Public Relations of Cleveland.

He counseled British colleagues that although "it has frequently been said in our country that it is the sizzle—not the steak—that sells, this axiom will be reversed in the years ahead. There still will be plenty of room for both sizzle and steak in what we do, but quite properly, it will be the steak that regains dominance. This is as it should be."[4]

Experience as Wellspring

Ways of Restructuring Experience for Creativity Creativity, almost without exception, springs from experience. There really is no such thing as a totally new idea, at least in the context of the counselor. Big ideas almost always come, in one way or another, from other big ideas, or small ones. That's why how-to books based on empirical experience sell so well.[5]

Counselors senior in experience and with broad exposure to cases, research methodology, events, societies and literature of their own and other disciplines start with an advantage.

That does not mean that creative thoughts flow merely from experiences. The creative process takes direct experience and melds it with what has been read or researched. Frequently, this process unites actual and vicarious experiences with reflections that come from synthesis, extension, intension, comparison, contrast, adaptation and other analytical methods explored in the C-R-E-A-T-E process of *Public Relations Management by Objectives.*[6]

Relative newcomers to counseling may bring more than their fresh perspective or healthy naiveté: up-to-date exercise of analytical and creative techniques, immersion in formal studies of theory and research and the experience of the "inexperienced."

In a recent creative session at a major firm, participants were trying to think of a name for a new commercial development being built for space commercialization. The working name for this venture was "Space Place," but the client wanted something better. The members of this creative team were young, bright, relatively inexperienced account executives and project managers who had an average of about one year with the firm and three years in the business.

Two things were important about the meeting. One is that they came up with a dozen superb ideas. The other is that each idea came from experience—obviously not from years of public relations work, but from experience in other areas such as their college studies, outside interests or extracurricular readings. The bright new public relations people leaned on the most useful crutch of all when asked to be creative—their own past. The most likely reason why they succeeded is that they intelligently used and adapted information already at their command.

The following case demonstrates how prior experience helped develop a creative solution that turned potential problems in public acceptance of a client merger into a favorable opportunity.

Whistle-Stop Case: Texas Bank Merger "The Interfirst/First United Special," a one-time whistle-stop train tour between Dallas and Fort Worth, celebrated the largest bank merger in Texas history.

A train of seven vintage cars transported 150 guests, media people and bank officials from Dallas to Fort Worth. There, the bank officials signed merger papers on the back of the "Houston," the rail car used by President Truman during the Texas swing of his 1948 whistle-stop campaign.

The merger of these two banks was a significant one and something of a problem at the same time. While the banks both were well-known, their joining came during a period of frequent mergers and acquisitions, and the officers feared it could be overlooked.

But most important, merger of leading banks in Dallas and Fort Worth, two highly competitive cities, touched on local sensitivities. It always had been hard to get these two communities to cooperate. The bank's public relations people and Tracy-Locke/BBDO attacked this problem head-on and used unification of the cities as a focal point.

"Experience worked wonders for us in the creative process," said Jean Farinelli, president. "We had to look outside and at what was happening between two cities, at commonalities and differences."[7]

Research showed transportation had been one of the most important growth factors in the area, and the two banks were founded about the time the railroad began to serve both cities.

"The idea of the train trip occurred in two ways. I noticed, coming from the East, that train trips were uncommon in Texas. I recalled the freight train whistle at home—and the ideas came up from the right hand side of the brain." Other experiences were explored—the Dallas-Fort Worth Airport opening a decade earlier, the Truman whistle-stop nearly a quarter century before.

The key to executing any event of magnitude is a solid plan of attack. "Why should the bank spend money, support the rationale and be willing to move to execution? We built the situation on analysis of the financial community and rivalry between cities, and then presented the train as part of the solution."

The public relations people got approval for the whistle-stop project, and their deadline was three weeks away. In that time, they successfully negotiated with Texas collectors who owned the vintage cars; cut massive red tape to lease tracks and engines; opened an old depot in Fort Worth that had been closed for years; cleaned and fixed it up; and arranged for beverage service, Dixieland band, barbecue caterer, buses, parking, security, credentials, decorations, photos, invitations, media kits and 300 oversized umbrellas in case it rained.

It worked. Politicians, media, bank officials, corporate friends and thousands of people were on hand as the train pulled into Fort Worth. Prime-time TV and front-page newspaper coverage played the unification theme heavily. One paper said in its three-column head over picture and story, "Banks Merge as Cities Bury Hatchet."

The 1984 Fort Worth-Dallas whistle-stop itself spun off an idea for the celebration of the state's sesquicentennial in 1986 with a train trip across Texas.[8] Moreover, the results of this creative adaptation of experience in turning a potentially negative situation into the beginning of a profitable venture prompted bank executives to move to a higher level of counseling relationship with Tracy-Locke.

EXECUTION: CRITICAL TO SUCCESS

The third key element that makes creativity work is execution. It is most certainly and most unfortunately true that some of the greatest ideas of our time probably were scoffed at and rejected while some of the least likely were made to work through force of diligence.

Client Courage and Vision Required, Too

It is not uncommon for a "great idea" to be dashed by impatience of a client who expected the idea to begin making money right away. Germs of ideas grow to excellence not only because counselors believe in them, but also because clients have the willingness to wait it out and let them work.

One major counseling firm executive said: "We can't deliver a big idea on paper because big ideas don't show up on paper. They show up after they have been conceived, budgeted, brought along, nurtured by very hard work and driven toward success. At that point the client, pleased, says something like 'let's see some more of that.' "[9]

Many companies, however, compare the early-stage proposals of their counseling firms with profitable ideas that already have come to full-term realization in their own or other client organizations. These clients benefit from exposure to continuing education about the creative process as much as their counselors do.

But human emotions also are involved, particularly fear and the insecurity of risk-taking. Judith Rich, Chicago-based executive vice president of Ketchum Public Relations, supported the point that fear and risk frequently are companions to creativity: "Fear has something to do with the client company itself. When you're in a competitive business like fast food, you've got to dare to be different. You can't afford to do what everybody else is doing." Fear and risk, however, are offset when "you get the chance to prove yourself, the chance to do a pilot campaign in a couple of cities, when you discover there are no limits except in imagination."[10]

Tel Aviv Hotel: Simple Idea Executed with Diligence
The important awards in public relations recognize excellent thinking and performance, but they

aren't necessarily won by geniuses. They're mostly captured by people who work smart and hard.

One example of this was a case submitted for a public relations award in the hotel industry. Hotels from around the world competed in the customer relations category. The winning project was conducted by a Tel Aviv hotel. What gripped the judges was that it was incredibly simple. It was called "Meet the General Manager" and consisted of only one idea, superbly executed.[11]

The idea was that the hotel's general manager would show up for coffee in the lobby every morning for about 45 minutes and make himself available to all who had complaints or questions. Guests were told about this at check-in time and reminded by cards in their rooms.

That's all there was to it—except that the judges thought it was the most creative of the many programs they studied because it simply worked so well. The cards were, indeed, placed in the rooms; the guests were, indeed, notified when they arrived; and the general manager did, indeed, show up for coffee.

Customer complaints that plague even the finest hotels were nipped in the bud before they reached the irritation point. Other problems never came to the complaint stage because guests found a responsive executive who listened.

Case Study of Exercise in Futility   Advertising agency executives, as their counterparts in public relations firms, have faced the forces that discourage creativity—not only pressures from clients, but barriers from within the agencies and from the individuals themselves.

An executive vice president of Dancer Fitzgerald Sample/Corporate Advertising Group reviewed several such sources of frustration that interfered with creative execution in his industry. Here is a condensation of concerns voiced by David S. Hill.

> *Some advertising people don't want to seem hard to get along with. They tell themselves it isn't worth it to struggle for creativity, that it's better to allow compromises to emasculate their creative ideas. They tell themselves it's useless to run the gauntlet of approvals and not worth the pain to undergo the poking and probing of the process. They worry that their caring for—and supporting—an idea will be interpreted as arguing and that caring too passionately will interfere with spontaneity.[12]*

Some public relations counselors have encountered similar concerns to those described by Hill. And, perhaps, more than their advertising colleagues, they have faced unrealistic expectations of clients. For instance, consider the frustrating experience of a well-known counselor who learned the hard way that creativity often is not appreciated until it is put into effect.[13]

The client company was large and privately held, with a strong reputation in the arts and in public service. In a sense, its success could be measured by effective execution of good ideas. It was a fine client for many years. But when things started to go sour, mainly because of disruption due to client management changes, the senior people began to wonder where all the innovations had gone.

The counselor who was supervising that client account was summoned by top management to explain. He said he was ordered and, "for some unbelievably stupid reason agreed, to present the company with three major new projects—big ideas—each quarter."[14]

None of those 12 ideas he submitted in the first year was recognized as such by the client. None was encouraged, backed with a budget or put into action.

The reason is that, as the television commercial for an investment company used to report, "good ideas don't just come up, bite you on the bottom and say 'we're here.'" Their quality depends not only on the thoughtfulness of the idea itself, but also on the willingness of the person in charge to see it through.

This takes courage, the third component of this book's definition of creativity—the self-assurance that makes an idea work.

Creative Excellence and Failure Tolerance   Client rejection of the germ of an idea, withholding of budget and other resources within a firm, or failure of a program that was approved and adopted have conditioned some counselors to fear fear itself and the risk of innovation.

Public relations firms, not only the *Fortune* 100 corporations researched by management consultants Thomas J. Peters and Robert H. Waterman Jr., know that "creative champions emerge because numerous supporters encourage them to, nurture them through trying times, celebrate their successes and nurse them through occasional failures."[15]

A tolerance for failure does not mean condoning; it does mean the creation of a positive environment in which policies and attitudes support reasonable risk taking, in which emphasis is placed on incentives for future creativity and in which individuals are freed from rigid structures ensnarled with procedural red tape. Nor does a tolerance of failure forbid open communication among creative personnel and their clients relative to execution.

Execute or Not? Some Pragmatic Concerns

Questions about Perspective on Creativity   It not only takes diligence and courage to execute ideas but also to subject creativity to analysis, field test before implementation, monitor during execution and make hard decisions that safeguard client and counselor alike while preserving the spark.

Pragmatic concerns have been raised by counselors such as James A. Little, president of Diversified Communications Inc., of Findlay, Ohio. The former PRSA president emphasized building discipline into the creative process and offered this perspective:

> *The physician and public relations counselor often deal with the same part of the human—the brain. But the brain surgeon goes to work with the knowledge that, at least mechanically, all human brains are the same. The public relations person finds no two are alike, and he often finds that hardening of the attitude occurs long before hardening of the arteries.*[16]

Improper use of creativity can jeopardize the well-being of a firm. As Little put it, "you can get hung up on creativity to the point that you don't deliver services in a cost-effective manner."

Some executives discover their account teams spending too much unproductive time on the creative process. For instance, "an engineering executive will buy only a certain amount of creativity, thus standing in contrast to a marketing person."

"A program may be supercreative and even win a Silver Anvil—but if it's not something with which the client will go along, why do it? Why not bring in creative ideas for a program the client will support?"

Dangers Loom for Backlash   Jack F. Agnew of Agnew, Carter, McCarthy Inc., a Boston counselor whose long-term clients include Ringling Bros., Barnum & Bailey, said hyperbole may have its place with a circus that has more than a century of tradition of "outrageous press releases." But even with that account, "if people remember the gimmick and not the message, you're doing a disservice to your client."[17]

This may require assuring that both client and counselors are sensitized to the potential for creative flair—taken too far—to distract key publics from the substance of an action or communication. Worse than distraction, however, are dangers of creative excesses turning into gimmickry. Possibilities of backlash loom when publics perceive they're being manipulated, tricked or treated without respect as intelligent consumers, employees or community supporters. Agnew said:

> *There's always a business reason behind any attempt at creativity; you're trying to accomplish something, trying to reach a goal. Creativity has to further the message, not be the message. Creativity is not worth anything unless you're counseling with certain professionalism that is perceived by your client's publics as commitment to excellence.*

One control is to make sure that creative personnel understand the guidelines within which they will operate.

Some counselors—or clients—may be tempted to impress peers or the media with creativity. Agnew, for instance, expressed concern that creativity for the sake of creativity could become "gimmickry for the sake of gimmickry and be viewed by the media or publics as hokum."

In a study analyzing dynamics and processes in the television-dominated media, one university researcher found that reporters and editors may buy the bizarre and hokum in competition for human interest angles that get coverage on the evening news. The research, however, found a backlash effect in which media may present such stories cynically or members of publics may have negative connotations of clients even if none are implied by journalists.[18]

Sometimes a client will order the staging of an event and its attendant publicity. "Maybe, under those circumstances, you ought to reconsider the event itself," Agnew said. "The client may feel that's not your concern. Does that leave the counselor blameless? If we serve the client and his highest purposes, we should point out potential risks. Even if we follow the client's lead, we're still associated with the event. If you sense the possibility it could be a disaster, don't do it."[19] Worst cases come to mind:

The military precision flying team doing a crowd-pleasing dangerous maneuver that killed the crews and resulted in congressional investigation of such promotion

An elegant Manhattan store staging a window display that an outraged public perceived as insensitive to the tragic existence of bag ladies

Jumbo crowds pressing into grandstands as intended evidence of sponsor success but resulting in structural collapse and mass casualties

A rock star's hair catching fire in a pyrotechnic accident during the filming of a commercial

Innocent rallies turning into riots

Satellite hookup for live transmission at a national convention blocked by interference from surrounding skyscrapers

Crippling of the U.S. space program following the explosion of a rocket booster carrying the first teacher—despite warnings of icing and design problems

On a lower level of backlash, some creative materials may be perceived by significant segments of publics as slick and wasteful.

Little offered as an example the corporate internal publication that may be designed and written in the vein of slick commercial publications "when what is needed is to keep it modest—not to save money particularly, but to have it appear as communication directly from management."[20] Agnew uses this rule of thumb: "If an item has little use, it probably will appear as extravagance. One person's wastefulness will be seen as depriving another person of the practical value of the expenditure."[21] In this respect, alert counselors are particularly sensitized to perceptions of:

Shareowners who may envision a slick annual report or lavish meeting as depriving them of increased dividends or stock value and whose confidence in management erodes

Employees who balance public relations services and products against the bottom line of their paychecks and see the costs as money taken from them

Members of Congress and taxpayers who seek retribution when government contractors bill excessively for a simple claw hammer or a toilet seat cover

Donors who have second thoughts about continued philanthropy to a nonprofit client that deflects money from the cause

Such damning perceptions may not be justified in a number of cases, and therein lies a challenge to counselors whose creative excellence in support of client and public interests may be seen differently.

Counselors such as Agnew accept the challenge this way: "Test it! Maybe you need to do field research, work with focus groups, do dry runs, consult experts, commission a survey. . . ."[22]

For smaller client companies, however, generally there is little or no budget to test concepts. Trusting one's own judgment, regardless of experience, can be deceptive. But at a minimum, account groups can invest a certain amount of time exploring down-side risks—the worst things that could happen, while anticipating client and public reactions.

The up-side opportunities, however, present an array of other challenges, including the strategies for maximizing creative potential within public relations firms. One area of strategy deals with enhancing the environment for creativity.

Following Orders or Leading the Way?   In the field research for this book, and in studies of the literature and of several hundred cases, the authors discerned a seeming paucity of originality that was claimed by public relations firms in program development and problem solving.

In interview after interview, in case after case, public relations firm executives simply said they did what the client asked them to do. Some— even when in-depth probing or collaborating research revealed otherwise— insisted on giving credit for creative programming to their clients. This was not normal professional modesty, they said.

Certainly, differences in the quantity and quality of applied creativity abound in the non-monolithic world of public relations counseling. Some counselors and firms do decidedly better in delivering creativity and strategic guidance. And some move so easily from crescendo to crescendo that the work no longer seems—to them—to be creative.

One school of psychology calls for deftly guiding clients to the discovery of options that best meet objectives with a touch of flair and leaving the clients with the credit and pride of authorship.

Could it be the same dynamic at work? Is it possible that counseling firms, in the main, are filling the role of public relations teachers, providing fundamental instruction in public relations methods and then putting those methods to work? Probably not, even though the firms themselves might suggest this is so. But the issue is clouded by the relationship between style versus substance in modern client/counselor campaigns.

Leading the Way

Several key principles of this chapter and the following chapters on objectivity and research are unified in a significant creative case that leads the way in several important respects.

Burson-Marsteller/IVECO Case: Multiphased, Eight-Year Campaign In the Burson-Marsteller/IVECO case, counseling firm and client built upon the substance of the European-based commercial vehicle conglomerate in a program aimed at important, measurable corporate objectives. A multiphased public relations thrust was constructed on a foundation of research.

Scope, application and a combination of other features make the IVECO case unique. But it also illustrates sharp restructuring of ideas that were not unique in isolation but that became so as an interactive combination. The duration of the project alone speaks for the creative courage and diligence of IVECO.

In 1985 and 1986, Burson-Marsteller and IVECO brought the culmination of an eight-year, three-phase program to bear on sales objectives for the wholly owned subsidiary of Fiat.

Client and counselor showed unusual creative courage in planning and executing the first six years of program action and communications to prepare IVECO for a third-phase strategy focusing exclusively on sales and product messages.

Postprogram research on the first two phases found the public relations investment positioned IVECO well. In the United States, 32 percent of *Business Week* readers told researchers that they recognized IVECO and knew the company makes trucks. That was a quantum leap for a firm that was known to only 3 percent of the American business public after the public relations firm initiated the program in 1978–1979.

In Europe, readers of *International Management Magazine* were sur-
veyed. The benchmark, or first, survey found that almost a third of the
European target publics had identified with IVECO within a few years of
its 1975 founding. A repeat survey after the first two phases of the program
found that recognition accelerated to 79 percent.

Throughout the program, and on both sides of the Atlantic, counseling
firm and client focused on people most likely to influence purchase of
trucks or other capital equipment for companies. According to Nicholas E.
Kilsby, Burson-Marsteller vice president and group manager:

> *We determined up front that most of the target audience had twin
> interests of sports and natural history/animal programs. The first phase
> (1978–1981) was purely to introduce the new company, which was es-
> tablished as an amalgamation of five European truck manufacturers
> under the Fiat banner. The second phase (1981–1984) was designed to
> build awareness of the name itself.*[23]

Kilsby said counselors faced a "somewhat unusual situation" in which
all five companies had been in business 80 to 110 years prior to their 1975
amalgamation. "It might be controversial strategy to give up or phase out
established brand names that had a lot of support in terms of dealers or
customers in exchange for a new name and organization," Kilsby said.
"You seldom get the opportunity to get involved in that kind of long-
range, multistage strategizing."[24]

That long-range, multistage strategizing, indeed, was a key factor in
distinguishing the creativity involved in the IVECO case. Those elements
rank high when successful client/counseling firm relationships are analyzed.

The kind of public relations results sought by clients such as IVECO
tend to require long-term adherence to basic strategy. Andy Cooper, the
counseling firm's senior vice president for creative services, said that "A
sustained effort in which you have a client that commits to the program
early on and sticks with it over a long period of time can generate very
significant results."[25]

Benefits of each of hundreds of activities fit into a strategic mosaic with
all that preceded and was to follow, just as Cooper noted that "generation
of awareness and support of sales work best when done in concert."

Burson-Marsteller's program had to be designed to reach IVECO's major
markets in America, Western Europe and Africa. Because of the culturally
and geographically diverse audience, Burson-Marsteller research indicated
sports and ecology as twin areas where language would not be a barrier.
Sports served as "an obvious medium where you don't have to speak any
one language." In this case, it was "done not for a consumer product but a
capital goods product, which is quite unusual."[26]

The program called for IVECO vehicles to be displayed or otherwise positioned in what the counseling firm designated as high-impact media, primarily television, with a measure of frequency.

Sports events included World Cup Soccer qualifying rounds in 120 countries and the 24-nation finals in Spain; Davis Cup Tennis qualifying rounds in 36 nations and finals in France and America; and the World Track and Field Championships inaugural featuring teams from 60 countries and a package of 12 world championship boxing matches.

To support cultural activities, client and counseling firm provided vehicles and logistics support for several expeditions, including Jacques Cousteau's, and created a project to translocate an endangered species of black rhinos from Africa to Texas.

Burson-Marsteller identified and coordinated specialized organizations involved in each of 57 events in 15 countries over the second phase. Reported attendance and media reach broke down to 264 million boxing fans, 500 million soccer fans, 200 million for tennis events, 350 million track and field enthusiasts, 100 million viewers of the Cousteau series in America alone and 50 million U.S. network television viewers who watched the rhinos arrive in Texas.

One challenge was to transform IVECO's approach from standard corporate advertising with public relations support to a multimedia, multicountry, total communications program transcending virtually every discipline of communications. Cooper said that direct participation was important: the relative role of advertising was small, and most of the job was done through sports marketing and event-oriented public relations.[27]

IVECO and Burson-Marsteller made the transition from primary dependence on advertising creativity and results to a long-range commitment to boldly creative public relations strategies. Intrinsic to such leadership is the environment for creativity.

ENVIRONMENT FOR CREATIVITY

Public relations counseling firms, as also is true of a growing number of *Fortune* 500 companies, have paid increasing attention to developing environments for economically healthy creativity in what has come to be known as their organizational cultures.

Model from a Large Counseling Firm

Hill and Knowlton Environment Made More Conducive to Creativity Loet A. Velmans, Hill and Knowlton's chairman through 1986, noted that increasing complexity in the counseling business now requires "people and modes of organization that can simultaneously meet client needs; provide thoughtful, objective counsel; and create a working environment that stimulates independent thought, creativity, quality of work and self-motivation."[28]

Thomas E. Eidson, president of Hill and Knowlton, USA, shared his visions on strengthening a counseling office's creative environment and illustrated his points with examples from the Los Angeles office:[29]

1. *Plan ongoing staff audit*: Eidson stressed the importance of initial—and ongoing—assessment of staff in person-by-person evaluation. Such an audit is neither easy nor speedily done. He estimated that it takes six months to a year, depending upon the size of staff and other considerations.

2. *Start with evaluation of managers*: He counseled first-phase examination of primary managerial personnel. "They're really the people who should set the pace and tone for client service." So: "Evaluate information received from clients and how the managers are handling situations."

3. *Set up mock client situations*: He recommended creating mock training sessions in given areas of counseling, such as financial, "setting up XYZ Co. with such and such a problem and forcing my people to come up with a solution and bring it back to me as if I were the client. I would examine people very carefully, forcing us into mock client situations until I saw their mind-sets and modes of functioning."

4. *Cultivate, recruit expertness beyond PR*: His views about education, however, were not limited strictly to public relations subjects.

We've been segmenting a great deal and, for example, have a division devoted to labor relations. They know PR and some have legal training. They have an intellectual approach that breaks problems down to what is manageable, palatable. Education doesn't mean only a degree from an accredited school; a lot of practitioners will be renaissance-type people coming out of different areas.

5. *Help staff see selves as problem-solvers*: Eidson said such individuals should view themselves as "problem-solvers, not just order takers. We continue to be business people with creative solutions and communications in one body. We're not just dealing with whether figures are right; we're forced to solve problems."

6. *Help staff look for creativity in mechanical aspects*: Eidson doesn't denigrate use of communication tools in his approach to strengthening the environment for creativity. But he said a counseling firm staff should be positioned to recognize that they have the opportunity to do their jobs from a creative, strategic point of view "every day in even the most mechanical aspects of this business."

7. *Differentiate those who are creative problem-solvers*: For example, he suggested differentiation of practitioners who, when called upon to do an annual report, will:

Provide that company with an interpretive, evaluative look at where they stand today in the financial community

Apply necessary energy to examine how the company is perceived in the marketplace by analysts

Verify from research what analysts, consumers and others think about annual reports

Think of the individuals the report will reach, what objectives should be achieved and what message is needed

8. *Let peer pressure enhance psychological environment*: Counselors need the personal desire and willingness to invest time and effort. Peer pressure can become an important part of the psychological environment for creativity. "We have tremendous peer pressure at Hill and Knowlton, constant evaluation of performance by peers, supervisors and clients. That constant process of evaluation tends to force people to think through solutions."

9. *Management must play its part*: In developing such a process in counseling firms, the question becomes: Does management share the feeling? Eidson said that the vast majority must in order to make the process work effectively throughout a counseling firm.

10. *Look outside the system*: One way to stimulate internal leadership was exemplified by Eidson during his second year in the Los Angeles office. He invited creative directors of advertising agencies to talk to the staff "philosophically and pragmatically so we could begin to expose people here to others who are creative and to learn how to apply creativity in a very intangible business."

Not all counseling practices approach Burson-Marsteller or Hill and Knowlton in size. Actually, most consist of one or several creative individuals with some support personnel.

Environment for the Single-Counselor Practice

Options beyond Involvement in Professional Organizations   The lone practitioner may exercise other options beyond the more obvious environmental change strategies such as continuing education and professional involvement in statewide or local associations, the Counselors Academy, PRSA, Canadian Public Relations Society, Canadian Counselors Institute, International Public Relations Association, International Association of Business Communicators and the like.

One option blends concepts involved in some of the examples of informal networking and formal counseling firm amalgamations reviewed in the chapter on strategic alliances. The lone practitioner might get together with two or three other heads of small firms and make a pact. ("Look over three of my programs, and I will look over yours.") Find other compatible managers to form an ad hoc committee to challenge each to rise to greater performance. Such a group also can provide stimuli for creativity through review of case histories.

Similarly, environmental change can come from participation in such peer review situations as national or regional award events that force the counselor to compete.

Building counseling creativity, however, is an internal process, not necessarily something acquired only by osmosis from other people. Keeping up with the state of the art through searching the literature, monitoring research and attending seminars and speeches goes to the foundation layer.

Public Relations: Strategies and Tactics, the 1986 book by Dennis L. Wilcox, Phillip H. Ault and Warren K. Agee, and the 1985 edition of *Effective Public Relations*, the classic by Scott M. Cutlip, Allen H. Center and Glen M. Broom, suggest modes of staying current. In *Public Relations Management by Objectives*, Nager and Allen review 12 steps for programming and incorporate them in a stylized objectives tree for professional growth.[30]

Models for Building Creativity through Leadership

There has to be clarity on what senior executives want from their people. These leaders also must contribute to the creativity environment by consciously serving as role models.

"Most people who run long-standing public relations firms are very intellectually solid people, original thinkers, who are able to grapple with problems," concurred Eidson. "You seldom find a person able to run an operation and survive without being a creative thinker who is able to bring original work to clients."[31]

Yet some executives may be unable or not positioned to provide the creative leadership envisioned by Eidson. "If I couldn't supply the leadership myself, I would look for a creative leader, an individual who can probe corporate problem solving and who can structure my organization to encourage account supervisors and professional staff to rally around that leader. Creativity is an intangible that only requires a spark of leadership to get it burning."

Principal Sets Firm's Style Daniel J. Edelman provides his own unique spark to the environment at the Chicago-based public relations firm bearing his name. In his *Public Relations Review* article "Managing the Public

Relations Firm in the 21st Century," the president of one of America's largest independent consultancies said, "the principal establishes the corporate culture; he sets the pattern for the operation. If he does things right, the chances are that the entire organization will follow."[32]

Addressing his ideas to other executives, Edelman noted the import of the principal's standards in a public relations firm:

If we work hard ourselves, if we are truly involved in serving the best interests of the client, if we enjoy what we're doing, if we make sure that we give the client more than the value received for his investment with us, then we're going to set an example for our people that will elevate their own self-image and encourage them to do likewise.

Whether public relations counseling is a profession, an emerging profession or a discipline will be explored later in this book. But it is worth noting Edelman's concepts for strengthening the corporate culture and environment for strategic creativity by developing professional pride among management members:

We're educated, with backgrounds in business, history, economics, political science, the arts. In my view, we're in a real profession. We're a solid part of corporate life and the social structure. We do make a tangible contribution, yet the old prejudices and misconceptions persist. As a manager, take it as one of your responsibilities to act in a way that builds respect.

Edelman also stressed management's role in making part of the organizational culture "a climate in our firms that makes internal advancement possible. We have to accord our people the same level of professional recognition given to young lawyers, accountants, management consultants, and business executives, and we must provide financial rewards that will help attract and hold the best prospects."

Use of Questions as Guidelines and Statement of Culture In its work for clients, Doremus Porter Novelli Public Relations of New York is guided by a set of standards that it provides each of its clients as well as its professional staff. Nina Palmer, general manager of the Corporate/Financial division in New York, said they tend to stand as a statement of the firm's culture as well as its approach to client service:[33]

"We believe that fundamental value is of great importance in public relations counseling. So we constantly measure the work of our professional staff against these questions, and it's surprising how frequently they come into play in guiding our work." They are:

1. *Is our material well researched, well written and on target?*
2. *Is the project creative, innovative and interesting?*

3. *Does work clearly address our client's interests and goals?*

4. *Is our counsel based on accurate and current information?*

5. *Are we totally conversant with the media we expect to reach?*

6. *Are we within budget and properly husbanding client funds?*

7. *Are we and our client communicating clearly and honestly?*

Bringing Associates into Group Value Statement   E. Bruce Harrison Co. in Washington, D.C., illustrates a common management tool used when its principal challenges the Harrison team to make a group value statement listing those characteristics that are most important to them as individuals.[34]

Typically in such group value processes, suggestions are elicited from members of the firm. In this case, an unprioritized list of ideas is prepared about organizational culture. Then staff members personally continue the dialogue with their managers.

Here is a sample "values" list condensed by the authors from two years of such exercises conducted by Harrison:

Working for a profitable firm

Turning out quality work

Teamwork

Positive client relations

Honesty, integrity in dealing with the client

Personal challenge on the job

Opportunity for professional growth

Personal growth, development of individual esteem

Creativity

Business responsibility

Unity of purpose in the work

Growing better as the company matures

Professional ethics

Employees Choose Criteria for Own Evaluation, Define Creativity   Another model is illustrated by Detroit's Anthony M. Franco Inc., where employees are encouraged to take an active part in choosing criteria by which they are evaluated and rewarded. This activity includes the definition in concrete terms of such nebulous concepts as "creative" and "initiative." Observable behavior provides the basis for performance review.

The process was designed to remove some of the ambiguity from public relations jobs and to create a performance appraisal system that leaves both the manager and the employee feeling there is "something tangible that can be done to make their jobs better," said Carol J. Gies, former senior vice president. The appraisal system includes the following points:[35]

1. *Managers specify observable actions*: The system incorporates an appraisal form constructed by asking a representative group of account executives and supervisors what observable, preferably measurable, actions constituted excellence in job performance. When words like "creativity" or "initiative" were suggested, the firm's officers asked: "What would you have to see the account executive doing to make you say, 'She's really creative' or 'She's not very creative'?"

2. *Subjective translated into tangible*: "Through this process, the subjective concept of creativity became translated into a series of tangible behaviors in the job of an account executive, such as: 'Offers new ways to approach a client problem. Does not rely on what was done before.'"

3. *Self-evaluations as well as managerial*: To involve the employee even more, the system was designed to have staffers do self-evaluation and managers do independent evaluation before meeting in formal appraisal sessions to discuss differences in ratings. Gies said that the next step calls for employee and manager "to identify the specific actions" implicated in a lower rating.

4. *Agree on objectives for improvement*: "Together, they can set a specific objective for the account executive to work toward—one that can be measured by noting the times that he was able to offer innovative, viable solutions." Part of the manager's job may include troubleshooting to identify and overcome perceived barriers to creativity—such as lack of time or trouble getting facts from clients.

5. *Reinforce and motivate excellence*: For professional staff already doing outstanding work, the system was designed to assure they are "told what behaviors make them valuable" and give them "something to shoot for in order to stay motivated." It has a provision for the employee to identify objectives for assuming new responsibilities and specifying what may be needed in training or other resources.

Dialogues Challenge Account Teams   In Dallas, Cynthia Pharr engages in strategic dialogues with C. Pharr & Co. staff to establish an environment in which they not only feel participative, but also know they may be challenged to rise to higher levels of creativity in servicing a given client.[36]

They argue, not in a combative sense, but in the way scholars and scientists use argument to open up thinking and strengthen the product through a healthy clash of ideas and raising of questions. Through that kind of dialogue, "you get terrific ideas," Pharr said. "I like to constantly challenge people so they will make their ideas sound good or prove me wrong if I feel they can improve upon them." Here are some of her approaches:

1. *Ask for three alternatives*: If an account team returns from a client assignment with a too obvious approach, Pharr said her response is to say something such as: " 'That's OK, now give me three alternatives. It's perfectly sound; there's nothing wrong with it, but you have not given it fresh thought.' When people come up with a predictable approach, that's not good enough; I tell them that's how everybody else does it, not how we would do it." At the same time, she reinforces strengths.

2. *Bring in outsiders as catalysts*: Her approach varies "from situation to situation when people seem to run dry or keep coming back to the same solution." She has suggested on occasion that an account team bring in a few colleagues and someone from the advertising agency with which her firm is affiliated. "And I tell the team to make a presentation to these people, and if they feel good about it, I'll go with the flow." This is done not only to bring in catalysts for fresh ideas, but also as a safeguard against her asking too much of a team. "Rather than be dictator and say absolutely not, I want to see if one of us is missing something."

3. *Set aside time for concentration*: As she has taught her staff: "When you have several issues to solve, set aside a half hour and do nothing for those 30 minutes but focus on one specific issue. If something else comes to mind, tell yourself it's not 1:30 yet. You practice intense concentration. It seems as if your mind is like a computer; thoughts begin to unload and spill out in a hurry."

External Environment Provides Stimuli   Life beyond the walls of a public relations firm and outside working hours shapes the counselor's environment for creativity and provides additional sources for stimuli.

Just as counselors like Edelman may encourage managers to participate in a diversity of outside activities and causes,[37] others, including Pharr, look for renaissance people with multiple interests.[38]

Employees at many firms work overtime and weekends to varying degrees. "But I expect my staff to get away so that they have sources of new ideas, different people as contacts. Public relations people who only talk to clients and other public relations people are not as valuable as those with broader exposure."

Pharr said she even advises counselors to put aside a problem, clear their minds and bring it back in a fresh light. She encourages them to "get away from the busy work atmosphere and go to a different place—the park, home—wherever they feel they can work better."

Freedom to engage in dialogues in which it's considered appropriate to either challenge or build a case for creative proposals and freedom to set aside a problem or get away from the work environment represent part of the shared values that have worked in the organizational culture of many firms.

Organizational Culture Institutionalized

The importance of shared values to counseling also was evidenced in the in-depth research done in 1985 by the *Public Relations Journal* on organizational culture in the discipline. Alyse Lynn Booth wrote, in concluding the two-part series:[39]

> *The inevitability of continuous change in public relations, as in business and society, will require that every organization have a shared sense of company values. That common set of beliefs—more than any business plan or financial system—will determine how successfully the company's structure, employee commitment and executional capabilities respond in the face of dramatic change.*

How Two Firms Institutionalize Values At Manning Selvage & Lee, the *Public Relations Journal* reported the institutionalization of a values system under Chairman Robert Schwartz and President Ed Stanton. The system consisted of a formal five-year plan of objectives and expansion from a base of consumer product publicity to high-tech public relations, with a thrust in financial and corporate relations. The firm was credited with building upon the legacy of corporate culture as it relates to client orientation.

"We are wrestling with our vision of the future. We are creating an ideology, searching for a united voice, a statement of who we are that distinguishes us from other agencies," Stanton said.[40]

Burson-Marsteller, with its global resources and network, not only institutionalized in a significant way the underlying planning and development that led to the 1985 "Vision and Values" program cited in the *Public Relations Journal* series, but also created the then-new SynerGenics company to help clients with their corporate cultures.[41]

Implementing Change Systems

Beyond the catch phrase of organizational culture and the substance of building environments for creativity lie sophisticated management strategies for changing systems within counseling firms.

One way to change a system is to bring in a catalyst from outside the system, much as corporations bring in public relations counselors. What works for clients also can work for counselors.

Counselors Counseled on Managing Excellence In late 1985, the Counselors Academy commissioned a former Harvard Business School professor to develop the first professional management school for senior executives and profit center managers in the public relations industry. In a discussion of the $3,000-per-person, five-day course, management consultant David Maister described an aura of excellence required by public relations people.[42]

What is essential is that members of a firm share one working definition of precisely the kind of excellence they strive to achieve. "The same piece of professional work can be either incredibly stimulating, inspiring the energy and attention necessary for creative, productive work, or appear meaningless, repetitive and dull." Helping public relations firm managers and staff find excitement in their work "is the key to quality and productivity." Maister's list of keys for "management of professionals" specified:

Provide clear goals

Involve them in decision-making

Seek their opinion often

Treat them like winners

Provide variety

Hold them accountable for results

Be tolerant of their impatience

Reward performance quickly

Always keep the next goal out front

Provide needed resources (i.e., don't get in their way)

Support risk taking[43]

Incentives for Creativity

Combining Self-Audits and Rewards Management for professional creativity can be approached profitably with a combination of strategies, much as Creamer Dickson Basford Inc. of New York has relied on creative audits, recognition and incentives. President Mitchell C. Kozikowski reviewed five components of that firm's system for change:[44]

1. *Periodic creative account reviews*: The firm adds to its creative departments people with specialties to enhance the whole problem-solving process. In larger offices, creative departments serve all account groups and arrange for creative account reviews as well as reviews of operational functioning of accounts. Such reviews include focus on Kozikowski's question: "How creative are the solutions we're devising for our accounts?"

Each account is scheduled for creative review twice a year or annually depending on size. The account is prepared for presentation to the creative director and a small management group. "Why don't we do it this way?"—type questions arise.

2. *Access reports for continuous account audits*: With ongoing accounts, the creative director receives copies of all reports "so somebody has the opportunity to run a continuous audit on how each client can benefit from new, fresh thinking," according to Kozikowski.

3. *Involve creative team in new business development*: Creamer Dickson Basford protocol, as that of some other firms, calls for a group led by the creative director to be brought into all new business development to share in research and serve as a resource.

4. *Problem-solving specialists on call*: A small group of former account people "who seem to have a bent in creative problem solving with particular areas of specialization" has become part of the creative director's team. They are freed from day-to-day account responsibilities to help create new programs and participate in periodic audits. Teams operating out of New York and Boston are made available to account people in other offices.

5. *Rewards for outstanding efforts*: As a spin-off of the creative audit, the creative director is joined by the board chair and president in a quarterly judging of better efforts by staff in all the firm's offices. They select the outstanding campaign, project and piece of writing. Brass sculptures and cash awards reward creative effort and "give us a good base of case history information of creative output to share with all of our offices," the president said.

One other purpose is achieved through the combination of audit, recognition and sharing of models, as indicated by Kozikowski when he observed that "those awards are eagerly sought after in our offices." The reason is to provide incentives to attain higher levels of results-oriented creativity.

Incentives in Compensation Systems   In many counseling firms, incentives for creativity and productivity are built into a diversity of compensation systems. The variety and complexity of such systems are beyond the purview of this book but are on the agenda of business seminars sought out by public relations firm executives.

An illustration of how one particular system is used to provide incentives for creativity was made available by Charles Lipton, chairman of Ruder Finn & Rotman New York and vice chairman of the national firm.[45]

Ruder Finn & Rotman began a three-component incentive system in 1985 for returning to staff a certain percentage of the profits they helped produce. The major part of that percentage is given to various groups that have contributed the most to the firm's profitability. Heads of these groups distribute the funds, subject to review of the policy committee. The second largest component is allocated at the discretion of top management "so we can reward a great program." In the third component, all employees in the entire company get something.

Altogether, the three components provide approximately a third of employee pre-tax profit, after all costs and benefits have been paid. "This should help motivate all our people to do the job with productive creativity, efficiency and appreciation for the bottom line," Lipton said.

Profit sharing incentives are complemented by other elements of the organizational culture, including orientation programs for interns chosen through Ruder Finn & Rotman national competitions and a thorough course of indoctrination for large groups of employees three times a year.

"You're getting people in our field more dedicated to public relations, not because they're frustrated journalists or frustrated novel writers. This makes our job of managing easier and better."

Equally important are strategies for making groups more homogeneous. Lipton said that to build commonality alongside individuality within groups, the firm tries to avoid situations in which junior staff become too specialized too early. "We move people around, particularly at the junior level so they can be more valuable to the client. By the time they're in the early to mid-30s, then it becomes better for them to specialize."

Public Relations Laboratory Offers Time, Budget Conditions and incentives for counseling creativity do not tend to follow set formulas but vary with the mix of clients, public relations firm executives' style and a number of other factors, including individuals who make up an account team. A growing number of counseling firms approach the 1990s with a proliferation of distinctive, provocative new strategies for stimulating creativity.

Ketchum Public Relations introduced a program in 1985 that, in essence, tells a counselor with "an outstanding idea for a new product that the firm can sell to clients, 'You have $5,000 of company time and $1,000 to $1,500 of out-of-pocket budget to develop your idea.'"[46] Paul Alvarez, chairman and CEO of Ketchum, explained that the $5,000 of time is awarded with corporate recognition and "encouragement to turn the idea into a full-blown proposal, complete with economics, in six months' time."

Of three ideas submitted in the New York headquarters the first year, one was funded. Alvarez said that the program, institutionalized as the "Ketchum Public Relations Laboratory," was designed to have no more than two new product proposals under development simultaneously.

Although specifics were confidential on the first such product developed, he said that its value to the firm would be considerable: "If we could get one new product out of the system like this every two years, we would consider the program well worth the investment."

Beyond giving Ketchum employees motivation to develop new products for the business, the chairman said the program offered this spin-off benefit: "Anything that encourages people to think about the business and that encourages employees to think about new ideas does the firm a lot of good."

Development of Individuals

At many innovative firms researched, creativity incentives are woven into the fabric of a larger organizational culture suprasystem, of which a key component is internal development of staff members.

Programming Creativity Early   Development of individuals for counseling creativity seems to produce more favorable results when initiated early in their career. Regardless of whether a consultancy offers programs for interns or concentrates on recruiting junior or senior staff, consensus seems to be that the orientation process remains important for new hires or for transfers.

Some firms, ranging from the youthful company founded by Sue Bohle in Los Angeles in 1979 and later merged into Ketchum Public Relations to the long-established firm founded by David Finn and William Ruder in 1948, invest intensely in programming for creativity at the student-intern stage.

Bohle, executive vice president of Ketchum/Bohle, and Finn said that although a large proportion of their trainees are recruited by other counseling firms, those who remain contribute to creativity from their first enthusiastic "why" and "why not" questions through their development into senior counselors.[47]

Some firms, such as D-A-Y/Ogilvy & Mather, emphasize the training of junior staff. Dudley-Anderson-Yutzy, even before its merger with Ogilvy & Mather, encouraged new creative staff with less than five years with the firm to set their own agenda in the "Under Fives" ad hoc group. Barbara Hunter and Jean Way Schoonover were cited by *Inc.* magazine for turning D-A-Y around by apprenticing people in their mid-20s and building an environment that maximized the potential of the "Under Fives" by encouraging them to learn about objectives, philosophy, new business, budgeting and client relations.[48]

As suggested by E. W. Brody, president of the Resource Group of Memphis, the orientation process constitutes an opportunity to introduce the newcomer to the mores, folkways, values, standards, traditions and concepts of service. It also expedites adaptation to new environments.[49]

At Padilla, Speer, Burdick and Beardsley in Minneapolis, the initial orientation generally runs 10 weeks and goes into such specifics as procedures for dealing with clients. President Lou Brum Burdick said that the initial orientation provides the base for more extensive orientation and training to follow.[50]

Burdick's senior management team follows through with a year of weekly training sessions. This is mandatory for new employees at every level, but it is also open to veterans for refresher training.

Three components are covered during the 52 weeks:

1. Skills, such as publicity, marketing, corporate activity and writing annual reports
2. Business and management, typified by studies in time management, how to hold meetings and building client relations
3. New business development, such as writing proposals, making presentations, and generating leads.

In addition to the year-long program, the firm also has had weekly staff meetings to share case studies and occasionally bring in a member of the media or client to discuss a public relations problem.

Younger members of the firm are asked to give presentations to the staff, either on case studies or seminars they attended, to develop skills needed in client relationship building.

But studies extend beyond the "how" of one-on-one communications to the "why." Burdick said it's important to provide younger counselors with a greater understanding of human dynamics and communication theory, particularly interpersonal.

The program endorses a combination of internal training as well as self-study, professional development courses, work toward advanced degrees in evening programs and ongoing education through professional organizations.

Experts and Other Support for Creativity Training Whether internal or external, such programs may be enhanced by involving expert talent as planners, faculty and facilitators. Frequently, such experts are brought in for creativity training. A growing number of firms also provide varying degrees of support for outside seminars and courses.

For instance, counselors from other firms and university faculty serve on the advisory committee and faculty in the Doremus Public Relations program. Employees enrolled in the company's "Curriculum 207" study creativity as part of the seven-week-long course that also includes classes on media, strategy and the business of public relations firms.

At Ketchum's New York, San Francisco, Chicago and Pittsburgh offices, employees enroll in a four- to six-week course on creativity taught by professors from local universities. The company matches the after-hours or before-hours time employees give to formal sessions. Homework assignments are extra-time donations by employees in the voluntary program.

Coursework is spread out so students have the opportunity to apply what they learn over a period of time. Outside courses and continuing education for creativity are reviewed periodically by executives.

Ketchum's policies tend to give the benefit of the doubt to the individual whose pragmatic, creative strengths may be somewhat latent; it also helps the individual with manifest, demonstrated abilities learn how to maximize them.

Alvarez drew a fine, but critical, distinction in what can be taught: "I believe you can teach people to recognize creativity. I don't believe you can teach creativity per se. The point is to stimulate people to think about things creatively. Any thoughtful approach will do."[51]

Ketchum-encouraged creativity analysis and training helps individuals and their executives determine if they're creative. "The worst that can happen is that some people who think they're creative will find out that they're not; but they'll still learn how to identify creativity when they see it."[52]

Creativity in public relations counseling, however, may evidence itself along a spectrum of degrees rather than as an either/or dichotomy. An individual's creative potential may not be apparent to that person or others because of lack of confidence or assertiveness. In addition, creativity, as with other human characteristics, may be subject to cycles, dependent upon everything from an individual's physical well-being to emotional and mental conditions.

How Creativity Is Lost and Gained

Probing the Mysteries of the Creative Processes   The brain may indeed be described in the terminology of the aerospace era as "a black box" whose processes not even experts in psychiatry and neurology can really observe. But it may be seen that the more individuals probe the mystery of the processes, the more they can prime the creative wellsprings of themselves and their colleagues.

John Softness, president of New York's Softness Group, pointed out that "creativity isn't something you can demand by executive fiat," but it's also "a very personal and strange thing that appears mysteriously from some inner wellspring of ideas."[53]

Aging, On-the-Job Systems Suppress Creativity   But study of creative processes and behavior has led to some conclusions that can help guide creativity development in public relations firms.

Advertising agencies traditionally have sought to apply the latest knowledge and theories about creativity, and their findings and models tend to provide counselors with insights. Norman Brown, CEO of Foote, Cone & Belding Communications Inc., described his corporation's top priority as restructuring authority, organization, processes and standards—"all to enhance the fundamental creativity of our operation."[54]

Yet "these steps, and similar actions by our competitors . . . are only primitive beginnings toward a better use of our whole creative potential," Brown added.

Brown said that "most on-the-job systems suppress much of the creativity of an inherently curious, expansive and intuitive mind." Furthermore, to compel individuals to specialize "narrows vision, even as we expand our knowledge."

Warning that one educational study indicates that a person's creative ability drops 90 percent between the ages of five and seven and that by the time adults reach age 40, they retain only about 2 percent of the creativity they had at age five, Brown called for strategies to minimize what was termed as a "tyranny of the left brain."

The left hemisphere of the brain rules over such activities as verbal, analytical, abstract, rational, temporal, digital and propositional functions. It works in a careful, sequential, logical, step-by-step manner. It stays on the track, but "usually on a familiar or conventional track," Brown observed.

The right brain hemisphere, with its territory covering such lines as preverbal, synthetic, concrete, emotional, spatial and analogic, looks at everything all at once, seeing whole pictures, skipping around as necessary to fill in gaps. It works intuitively. "It loves speed and complexity and, frankly, disorder."

To reduce the tyranny of the left brain, Brown outlined a strategy that balances intuitive views and analytical positions; strong feelings and hard facts; and unstructured, spontaneous developments and highly organized and carefully planned situations.

"We'll shift back and forth in solving problems, breaking them down into parts, approaching them sequentially, using logic on one hand and looking at the whole, approaching it through patterns, even hunches, on the other."

Ninety-four Percent Benefit from Creativity Courses Regardless of the mysteries, complexities and schools of thought on how best to cultivate creativity, one thing stands out: Most firms and their clients tend to profit from a combination of encouraging staff attendance of specialized courses and following through to ensure that they apply what they have learned.

Those who take courses in creativity show a 94 percent improvement in their ability to think up good, usable ideas, according to Thomas E. Kuby, principal of his Chagrin Falls, Ohio, public relations firm and author of a monograph on creativity.[55]

In his monograph, Kuby recommended a number of principles for gaining creativity, including:

Become more of a generalist: Acquire a deep and broad knowledge about many subjects.

Become more flexible: See the alternatives to various situations.

Recognize "the need for curiosity: a mature childlikeness; the ability to keep asking, 'Why?' "

Recognize "the need for originality: ability to come up with something new that will become acceptable."

Recognize "the need for independence: ability to withstand pressure."

Manipulate ideas with such methods as a check list. Ask yourself such questions as: "In what ways might I put this or that idea to other uses?" "How might I adapt this to the public relations problem I face?" "How might I modify it to better suit my needs and purposes?" "What can I substitute, rearrange, eliminate, combine?"

Strive for quantity of ideas. "Research proves that from quantity you'll get quality."

Use "brainwriting in which each participant writes ideas on sheets of paper or cards in response to a problem. Pass the sheet into the pool after writing four ideas. Then read the ideas of others and write more on their papers."

Build a library on creativity methods.

Take advantage of altered states of consciousness through relaxation and biofeedback.

Pharr has observed that creativity may arise in the twilight period when falling asleep, on waking, while driving or walking, and in periods of singular concentration.[56]

How to Overcome Creativity Blocks   One gains creativity by understanding and overcoming a number of psychological blocks.

1. *Cultural blocks*: This block is characterized by the logical fallacy of "I've always done it this way; I must continue doing it this way." It may be overcome through the block-shattering questioning technique of Stanford University's Paul Watzlawick, a psychologist who has challenged individuals to ask "Why not?" when confronted with the block that a new approach has not worked in the past and to ask "Why?" when faced with the knowledge that a certain way always has worked.[57]

2. *Fear-of-making-mistakes blocks*: "What is the worst possible thing in the world that can happen to you if you make a mistake?" Farinelli asked.[58] Other questions could include: How much would the benefits of exploring a new and better solution outweigh the chances of making a mistake? What safeguards can I build into the testing of an idea to minimize the risk of making mistakes?

3. *Perceptual blocks*: A perceptual block may be compared to the math or mechanical block some individuals learn to overcome, even the temporary "writer's block." Such blocks relate to an individual's perception of self-capabilities. Farinelli said: "You probably can do a lot more than you think you can do when you're put to the test, but perceptual self-image gets in the way. To get out of that trap people have to change their self-images to get in touch with inner strengths. We tend to adhere to the stereotypes with which we grew up—women can't fix cars, men can't cook, only somebody who has worked for a newspaper can write a good story."[59]

Some public relations counselors interviewed told of overcoming such blocks at seminars or in independent study of psychology; others reported breakthroughs in sessions with psychiatrists.[60]

4. *Only-expert-problem-solvers-can-be-creative blocks*: Similar to the experience of learning to use a computer in middle age, this block tends to be overcome by not demanding too much of oneself at the start, by taking—and mastering—small steps at a time, by seeking counsel and by studying the literature.

5. *Getting started blocks*: Sometimes it takes the commonplace, such as laughter, to break the tension or structure to warm up to the creativity process.

Different approaches to breaking this block were illustrated by several counselors:[61]

Start with common problems.

Introduce humor.

Use a form. From George Hammond, retired chairman of Carl Byoir & Associates, came the idea to place in the right-hand column of a grid all possible topic areas of activity. He listed industries across the top of the grid; then he tried to force a relationship process. For instance, in looking at the grid intersection of issues and advertising, he asked himself what they have in common.

Use a system. From Dr. Edward DeBono's research came the Plus-Minus-Interesting approach to lateral thinking. The counselor, for example, asks what's plus—positive—about an idea. It can start with a minus, such as a challenge to the status quo, for instance, "Let's say annual reports should be done away with." The interesting idea: There may be a new, better way of doing an annual report.

Understanding Risk Taking One area on which experts on creativity in public relations, advertising and the social and physical sciences seem to agree is risk taking. Although risk taking and creativity tend to go together in public relations counseling, it is not always obvious to an individual that an idea is creative, let alone worth any risk.

James Arnold, a partner in Chester Burger & Co. of New York, put it this way:

More often than not, a lot of great ideas are not recognized as great ideas when they come along. It often takes the perseverance of a knowledgeable professional, who filters ideas through a trained mind and understands what's possible, who is willing to take a risk, but a risk that is qualified by experience and good judgment. The way to focus on creativity as a problem-solving dimension of the public relations business is to emphasize the role of the individual as a part of the team.[62]

An executive creative director of an advertising agency in Los Angeles underscored the import to creative development of the risk-taking spirit with a sports analogy.[63]

When Ken Stabler was a quarterback for the Raiders football team before its move to Los Angeles, a reporter interviewed him after visiting the Jack London Museum. Inspired by London, the journalist said, "Ken, I want to read you something Jack London wrote:

" 'I would rather be ashes than dust. I would rather that my spark should burn out in a brilliant blaze than it should be stifled by dry rot. I would rather be a superb meteor, every atom of me a magnificent glow, than a sleepy crumbling planet. For the proper function of man is to live, not exist. I shall not waste my days in trying to prolong them. I shall use my time.' "

And the reporter then asked Stabler: "What does that mean to you, Kenny?" Without hesitating, Stabler said: "Throw deep!"

Passing the ball far downfield—throwing deep—"That's taking a risk" and illustrative of an integral principle to creativity, FCB's Michael Wagman concluded.[64]

But the risk may be too costly when a passer throws deep and no receiver is in the clear. It takes teamwork as well as risk taking in sports as well as in public relations. A problem may demand more than a strong creative person can work out alone; it may call for strategies by an account team with input from other resources in the firm and from clients.

Brainstorming and Alternative Creative Sessions

Differing Perspectives Lead to Variety of Techniques Brainstorming sessions appear to be an effective means within public relations firms of developing strategic ideas and programs for clients. Under the rubric of "brainstorming," counseling firms have built a rich repertory of techniques. New techniques seem to be constantly evolving, although some old ones have a widespread acceptance and longevity.

Models from other spheres of management consulting, including organizational communication, have their followers, as well as their opponents.

In a sense, one finds that adoption of a paradigm—a widely accepted model—encourages some individualists to seek to disprove it or come up with a better one. This process of developing, challenging and refining basically follows the pattern described by Thomas S. Kuhn in his seminal work *The Structure of Scientific Revolutions.*[65]

Even within the same public relations firm, the perspectives on, and approaches to, improving upon the group process may be widely disparate.

A case in point was found at Ketchum Public Relations: Chairman Alvarez said he is "death on brainstorming," whereas Executive Vice President Rich has a reputation as a disciple of, and innovator in, brainstorming. (This example of the counseling industry equivalent of academic freedom illustrates defiance of the discipline to adhere to monolithic stereotypes of lockstep uniformity.)

Because the Alvarez perspective represented a bold move toward a new paradigm, albeit one that was still a minority viewpoint expressed by counselors, this section starts with the proposed alternative rather than the traditional practice.

In his advocacy of differentially structured small group sessions over brainstorming, Alvarez offered these reasons for his "death on brainstorming" outlook:[66]

1. *Large groups are costly, ineffective*: "Some people don't work well in a large group and can be intimidated in such sessions." In arranging a creative session, Alvarez advocated passing over people without a proven record in creativity and limiting the number of participants to four.

> *If you have 10 people in the room with an average billing rate of $60 or more per hour and you spend an hour or two hoping somebody will come up with something, that's not too practical. The popular theory is that everybody is creative. Mostly you'll find uncreative people. That doesn't mean that almost everybody doesn't have a good idea one time or another.*

2. *Freedom from censure is impractical*: He also challenged the brainstorming concept of participants being "free to say things that might be silly or impractical."

Alvarez, however, has observed traditional brainstorming sessions in which "people go off track. Impossible! You can focus people's thinking by saying why something doesn't work. I think you should be able to say 'that's a dumb idea; let's move on.' They can say that to me. Time is too precious to massage people. Nobody's going to be hurt. Sitting there being polite in a creative session wastes time."

In an organization in which the chairman can have his ideas censured along with any other participant and in which the group understands the priority placed on productive time, the creative session may have a special balance of advantages and disadvantages.

Here are some of the components of the Alvarez approach to small group sessions as an alternative to brainstorming:

1. *Use briefing papers; have more detail ready*: He follows an accepted practice of executives in his preference "to have a briefing paper before a creative session, but not in colossal detail." But if questions arise: "I like to have somebody in the meeting who understands colossal detail and who has assembled most of the information we might need." That's part of his protocol for preparation for what he calls "idea day." Telling people who will participate several days in advance, if feasible, starts the creative germination.

2. *Start with "best, top-of-the-line thing" challenge*: In structuring the sessions, Alvarez said he prefers to open with "what's absolutely the best, top-of-the-line thing we can do for the client." An example might be to get on the cover of *Time*. "Maybe we can or can't. Maybe we can lead up to it. What are the creative ways, the strategies for doing this?"

3. *Encourage the very big idea, but within limits*: Although he eschews ideas that might be "silly or impractical," he said that "frequently I like somebody to give us a very big idea: 'How about if we linked hands coast to coast' might not work, but we could do it across the city limits of Des Moines or Pittsburgh or some states."

(In 1986, a year after Alvarez offered this analogy, a fundraising organization found that its vision of an unbroken human chain in Hands Across America foundered in some regions. A thin line, however, might be seen between what is silly and what is stimulating and what is impossible or adaptable. One is reminded of a really big idea that excelled in execution—the 1984 AT&T and Burson-Marsteller Olympics torch running relay through America.)

4. *Let idea stand test of time*: He recommended that "once you get an idea, you must let it sit, preferably 48 hours. If it's a good idea, it will come back at you. Another test is that you can tell it so simply that everybody understands it."

5. *Know when to change mix of people*: He said he would give a session up to four hours to see if it's really productive. "If not, change the mix of people. It works. People should understand the change is not because anybody is 'bad'; you're just trying to change the chemistry of the mix of people contributing to ideas."

Getting the Most out of Brainstorming   Brainstorming sessions vary even within the same public relations firm depending upon the people, client's needs, leader's style, other activities within the company and experiences of previous sessions. Whether they are termed *brainstorming, brainwriting,* or *small-group creative meetings,* they share the central purpose of giving the client the fullest benefit of the creative thinking the firm can bring to bear through the stimulation of idea sharing by internal—and occasionally—external resource people. Here is a score of ideas to get the most out of brainstorming:

1. *Look for a creative mix*: In her two decades with Edelman, where she was executive vice president and national creative director before moving to Ketchum, Rich refined and innovated procedures for brainstorming: "In creative sessions, you try to bring in a mix—your own account team creative personnel, people from outside, secretaries."[67]

2. *Draw in junior people*: Boston's Agnew said that beyond solving client problems, the value of drawing in junior people is that it enables them to contribute more than they customarily would when just servicing accounts. "In brainstorming, everyone is equal. In client service, you have strata of responsibilities. Contributions of young persons to ideas can be just as valid as those of the owner of the company."[68] Moreover, the process builds junior personnel confidence in working with senior members of the firm and its clients.

3. *Keep it positive*: Rich said she advocates the "free thinking" kind of session in which "nothing negative is said about ideas brought up in brainstorming; you listen to the lowest person in the room."[69] Agnew explained why and how:

> The account executive or supervisor will present the goal or objective of the client, and then you have a period of time for unrestrained discussion, in which concepts are thrown out and recorded. No negative words. Sometimes, younger people with their freshness of approach will have really creative ideas, but if they're told right then they wouldn't work because of cost or feasibility, they wouldn't put out another idea. People can throw off shackles and be emboldened to throw out ideas. The function of the leader is to occasionally call on or stimulate younger people. Just being in an environment where they hear others' ideas has a stimulating effect.[70]

4. *Bring in outside views*: Other considerations determine who participates in a session. It helps to get a crossover effect from one account group to another so ideas flow not just from the narrow sphere of one account team or the specific account assigned to it. It can prove invaluable to get outside views from people not living with the account day-to-day.

5. *Build team feeling within the firm*: Agnew cited an additional benefit for firms small enough to periodically bring in much of the staff— "enhancing the feeling of the firm as a team."[71]

6. *End on a high note*: Like Alvarez, Agnew is concerned with time invested in a creative session. He said his firm limits brainstorming to a half hour. "If we're on a real roll, we don't always have to cut it off." He recommended that whatever time a meeting is allowed to run, "try to end it on a high note rather than let it peter out, become repetitive, or reach too hard."

7. *Consider the pros and cons of CEO or client presence*: Top executives of counseling firms and officers of clients may help or hinder the process. Such a presence may have the unexpected effect of causing others to withhold ideas that they fear might be perceived as far out or impudent in the wake of a suggestion from the client.

8. *Consider expert resources*: It's essential sometimes to invite an outside consultant as catalyst as well as expert resource, particularly if the focus is on a technical field. It also may be advantageous to involve persons who represent consumer thinking when certain clients are present.

9. *But take advantage of lay curiosity*: At times, however, the best ideas spring from lay curiosity. "Ignorance—in the nicer sense of the word— during the early brainstorming stage on barriers, negatives or even knowledge of high technology, may yield wonderful ideas," Rich said. "Obviously, expertness must be taken into consideration in later stages of the creative process."[72]

Creativity, as indicated by research, may require different brain hemisphere traits other than planning. Rich did not underrate the involvement of experts with a solid base of research who are also eloquent when discussing client and product needs. At the same time, however, she said that "people who think in the most simplistic forms sometimes are the best; those who try to think in the most philosophic vein, sometimes are not the best—their verbiage gets in the way."

10. *Plan for comfortable interaction*: The psychological environment of a creative session is important. Part of it depends upon the way individuals interact. According to Rich, people need to feel comfortable with each other. "When they get to care about each other, they become more comfortable." That doesn't mean forcing certain individuals together in the hope that they will learn to care. "You get to know people in your firm, and after a while you don't bring certain individuals together at the same session if someone tends to be sarcastic or demanding, or puts another person down."

11. *Schedule strategically*: Timing influences the creative energy and excitement brought to brainstorming. Sessions should be scheduled in non-stress time, when participants can think with minimal distraction.

Rich recommended structuring a session as "a positive break in the day rather than as an extra burden." This calls for early notice, not only to pique the participants' curiosity and allow time for ideas to germinate but also to let them clear their schedules and look forward to the creative interaction. Although it seems logical to avoid Friday afternoons in the belief that most employees are preoccupied with the weekend, it depends on the subject and on how the invitation is expressed and the session planned. "People can get their wildest ideas on Friday afternoon and their worst on Monday mornings."[73]

12. *Use retreats*: Retreats may be scheduled if the client can afford the costs. Some public relations firms may schedule joint creative retreats away from the office. Retreats can be structured to go beyond the scope of normal sessions, exploring intermediate and long-range objectives and even the dreams of the client.

Retreats require lead time so people can plan on being away from their offices, and specific times can be scheduled for phone check-ins. Create an environment for relaxation, not only in terms of clothes and environment, but also in regard to agenda and range of topics. Participants, however, need enough of an advance agenda to assure that they know the priorities, including the time required to cover certain topics. Make the sessions casual enough that "as much as possible, the lines are erased on who's client and who's agency," Rich said.

13. *Build pleasure expectations*: The idea is to make the session more appealing than conventional activities and prime the individuals for creativity. Many firms put out snack food and light refreshments; some stage special attractions, such as prizes, invitations that pique curiosity and passing around product samples.

Rich recalled a session she scheduled for Orville Redenbacher popcorn marketing when she was with Edelman. It was 4 o'clock on a wintry Chicago afternoon, and the aroma of fresh popcorn wafted down the corridor just before employees got ready for the session.

14. *Create emotional involvement*: "The more crazy you get—to a degree—something may come out of it. That's if you put everybody in a relaxed mood, have something for them, get people competing positively, get them emotionally involved in the problem and move them to put themselves in the position of consumer."

15. *Change their orientation*: Farinelli advised: "You change the orientation to the unaccustomed to force people to stop being habitual. We tend to be creatures of habit" and that can impair creativity. Examples used range from changing seating patterns to inflated planes dangling from the ceiling to symbolic photo projections and upbeat theme music.[74]

16. *Keep focus on client problem*: Anything, however, can be taken to extremes, and Rich, Farinelli and other counselors cautioned that if sessions are too much fun, the problem at hand may not receive serious attention.

17. *Bring out what's new and special*: The greatest challenge comes when a product or client seems like all the others. Such situations punctuate the importance of well-prepared written materials and oral briefings, of selecting a skillful session leader who can bring out the subtleties of what is new or special. Rich said: "It's easy to trip over little facts that can be all important. You have to make sure whoever runs the session listens to all nuances."[75]

18. *Recognize the import of individual experience*: If participants can go into a session and touch and use a product, the experience may stimulate their creativity. "You don't want to interpret the product or service to others—the idea is to have people translate to themselves," she said.

19. *Take the lead in stimulating excitement*: Whatever the concept, the session leader should be excited and positive about it in order to get a positive feedback. Rich observed that some leaders are tempted to start a session by saying: "Here's such and such, and there's not much we can do about it." In her studies of, and experiences with, creative sessions, she concluded that "the one common denominator for results-producing brainstorming is curiosity. The best happens when you bring together people with passionate curiosity. Then you can build drama. If you feel excited, you'll get other people excited. It's believability, credibility itself."

20. *But consider allowing negatives to be vented*: Negatives can be helpful at the beginning of a session if doubts about a project's value or a client's commitment threaten to stifle creativity. Kay Berger, executive vice president of Manning, Selvage & Lee, recommended that leaders "get those negatives out on the table." But "make no attempt at judgment or solution. Say: 'Fine, now we have the negatives out; we can put them aside and deal with them later, but now we don't have to worry about them.' "[76]

21. *Build creative lift beyond sessions*: Successful creative sessions often have effects beyond the ideas and discussion yielded, beyond the strengthening of teamwork within the firm. Rich said: "People leave brainstorming sessions and go back to their desks or homes and feel better about themselves and their jobs."[77]

And the creative lift may last long after the session is over and even build upon itself.

Creativity with Expert Consultants

Clients of public relations firms often get their creative lift from their involvement with expert consultants—from taste psychologists to nuclear physicists, from former government regulatory agency executives to cardiologists, from retired congressional leaders to specialists in futures or network research.

At larger counseling firms, many of the experts assigned to special client situations are on payroll or working under contract as senior consultants. Some firms have panels of experts on call; yet others subcontract their services as problems or opportunities arise. Of course, the client's own experts also are consulted or made ad hoc members of account teams.

In the multiple stages of a campaign—from preliminary diagnostics through postmortem and from the preparation for brainstorming sessions through idea execution—the working relationships of outside public relations counselors with expert consultants provide an edge to clients in developing innovative strategies. This is particularly so when dealing with highly technical or complex client needs, although the payoff potential also may be discerned when dealing with relatively common products.

The involvement of a taste psychologist in Fleishman-Hillard's Diet Pepsi cola war battles of the mid-1980s serves as a case in point.

Case of Taste Psychologist and the Cola Wars Before Coca-Cola decided to reformulate its century-old formula to fight the Pepsi challenge with the "New Coke" and reintroduce its original formula as "Coca-Cola Classic," St. Louis–based Fleishman-Hillard Inc. gave Pepsi the initiative in the seesaw cola wars by harnessing the expertness of the head of Duke University's weight-loss unit.

Robert E. Keating of New York, F-H executive vice president and senior partner, reviewed some implications and highlights of this case. "Use of expert consultants is one of the strengths we and other firms offer clients. This was done haphazardly in the early days of counseling without the fine degree of planning we have today."[78] Some experts not only work as consultants but also are publicly identified with certain clients and their products. A case in point is the Fleishman-Hillard mid-1980s media tours for Diet Pepsi. Keating said that "the image of the expert is related to the product and the target audience, and that person is prepared to talk intelligently about the subject and around the subject with great confidence. We're seeing more credentialed people on media tours today."

One such person was Dr. Susan Schiffman, who not only had credentials as Duke's weight-loss unit chief, but also as a psychologist, scientist, taste researcher and advisor to the FDA and makers of NutraSweet. She consulted on the Diet Pepsi account and came into the public spotlight in her media tour activities.

Initially, Diet Coke used a combination of saccharin and NutraSweet and, according to Keating, "had the jump on Pepsi coming to market" with such a sugar substitute blend. Pepsi decided to step up the competition with Coca-Cola by introducing its own NutraSweet blend. Later Pepsi regained the lead in being the first to adopt 100 percent NutraSweet in its diet line.

The public relations firm that also helped develop the strong association between Pepsi and Michael Jackson during his mid-1980s concerts first had to handle the "difficult assignment of how to get a commercial product—sweetener-blend Diet Pepsi—on television news and interview shows." This was complicated by Diet Coke's new sweet taste beating Diet Pepsi to market.

Schiffman, billed by the account team as a "taste psychologist," had her Broadway-show-like tryout in the "sophisticated, tough-minded Boston market," Keating said. The Diet Pepsi–sponsored expert appealed to the media with her demonstration of the five senses, distinctive style and credentials. The "overwhelming positive response from Boston media" continued as the tour was put on the road in 20 major markets around the country. Everywhere, the firm was able to arrange for the taste psychologist to appear on two or three television shows and do well with leading newspapers and radio programs. "Most wanted to have her back," the executive said.

Although she always got around to Diet Pepsi, her appearances featured a number of exciting demonstrations involving the senses. In one, people were blindfolded and fed carrot baby food. Some identified the baby food as ice cream, others as yoghurt, none as carrots. In another, involving the sense of smell, she had people sniff Chanel perfume that had been poured into such containers as peanut butter jars. Some said it was turpentine or paint remover. Many were confused by appearance and said they would prefer perfume of a different color.

In the soft drink test, she asked people what they heard and had them tune into the fizz. They then examined the color of the drink and were asked whether they would drink it if it looked different. Much as in a wine tasting, she would have people pick up the beverage and check whether it smelled right. And, then, they would be asked to taste it and describe the sensation on the palate. "To the consternation of Coke she would mention Diet Pepsi by name," Keating said. "In many cases, she got the TV host to sample the Diet Pepsi and comment on its good taste and flavor."

One of her discussion themes was that people who were trying to reduce should focus on low-calorie foods that provide a satisfying flavor. Diet Pepsi—first in its NutraSweet-blend flavor, then as reformulated with 100 percent NutraSweet—was cited as such a food and shown on the air as an example. "It was one of the most effective media tours in history," Keating said. And sales increased in every market.

In the public relations counseling industry, the significance of creativity depends on what the strategies actually accomplish for the client, not how a counseling firm uses expert consultants, runs creative sessions, develops creativity within individuals, establishes an environment for creativity or follows through on ideas.

As significant as it may be, creativity is only one of the fundamental bases of contemporary counseling. Another is objectivity, which is defined in the following chapter.

3

OBJECTIVITY

Objectivity, certainly one of the most substantial values offered by public relations counselors, can contribute significantly to building client confidence. Most important, however, it is the foundation upon which most major client programs are built. As such, the term *objectivity* deserves to be put in fresh perspective as it applies to contemporary counseling practice.

The public relations audit, often a cornerstone of objectivity in counselor-client relations, is presented in this chapter as a management resource useful to both counselor and client. The optimal role for practitioners as problem-solving strategists, not program executors or communicators, is studied.

OBJECTIVITY IN PERSPECTIVE

From Cliché to Commodity

Sophisticated counselors and client executives reject the timeworn claims about "objectivity" in the trite, "either/or" sense of the word—"public relations firms are objective; internal departments are subjective."

"Objectivity"—like "total objectivity" in outmoded journalism books and lectures—has become a cliché at the top of most lists that weigh the advantages and disadvantages of using a counseling firm. As with many clichés, "objectivity" has been clothed in vague, abstract and oversimplified language that clouds its meaning.

One 1986 book places objectivity at the head of a list of seven primary advantages of external counsel. *Public Relations: Strategies and Tactics* defines it as the capability of a firm to "analyze a client's need or problem from a new perspective and offer fresh insights."[1] And *The Practice of Public Relations* said:

The biggest difference between an external agency and an internal department is perspective. The former is outside looking in; the latter is inside looking out—often, quite literally, for itself. . . . Sometimes the use of an agency is necessary to escape the tunnel vision syndrome that affects some firms, where a detached viewpoint is desperately needed. An agency unfettered by internal corporate politics might be better trusted to present management with an objective reading of the concerns of its publics . . . but outside agencies are often unfamiliar with details affecting the situation.[2]

Effective Public Relations said counselors rank "their objectivity, as relatively free agents untrammeled by the politics within an organization" second only to a "variety of talents and skills compared with internal staffing."[3]

Chester Burger, founder of the New York management consultancy bearing his name, however, was quoted in the same book as ranking "independent judgment of an outsider" as last in a list of six reasons why organizations with internal public relations departments retain counseling firms.[4]

Twelve Elements of Research-Based Objectivity   Strong support was voiced by a number of counselors and client executives for a formal definition of "objective" as that observation of reality that is based on facts, free from personal feelings, unbiased and existing independent of subjective thought.

A dozen elements may be identified in research-based counseling objectivity:

1. Relative—matter of degree—state of counseling that is
2. Dependent not only upon freedom of thought, but also
3. Grounded in applied research and
4. Strategically engineered through exposure to and
5. Evaluation of a number of different clients' experiences.
6. Rigorous analysis of factual and observational materials
7. Developed from a relatively independent perspective and
8. Subjected to tests of predictable behavior or
9. Tested in the crucible of opinion of experts within and outside the counseling firm and incorporating
10. Options developed and advocated from a
11. Relatively independent perspective that seeks to
12. Identify and balance biased influences.

There seems to be no automatic "righteousness" attached to either external or internal public relations operations by virtue of their "outside" or "inside" relationship to the organization.

Some internal departments operate with independent judgment and up to several of the dozen or more elements of objectivity exemplified by the counsel of a number of public relations firms. Some external counselors are able to develop in a short time a better understanding of a client's situation, details involved and the motives and needs of client executives than some internal staff practitioners develop in the span of a career.

As a case in point, David Ferguson, who made the transition in the mid-1980s from senior public relations staff executive for United States Steel (now USX) to senior consultant with Hill and Knowlton, has observed that a willingness to engage in opinion research and audits, for example, may vary with how internal staff persons perceive conditions. The 1985 PRSA president also said that "corporate public relations can be more objective in good times and more subjective in bad times; in good times, you tend to be more positive and willing to look around at the world about you."[5]

THE AUDIT

Cornerstone of Research and Client Relations

Human fallibilities that predispose varying degrees of subjectivity make it all the more important that a painstakingly designed, solid structure for objectivity be built and maintained. That structure is research; its cornerstone is the audit.

The audit serves as cornerstone for the research structure by providing the basis for decision-making on which additional research may be needed. It also provides the research base on which counseling and public relations programming are built.

At the same time, the audit often serves as the first critical-path planning step in developing a counselor-client relationship by yielding even more than research-based intelligence.

Key corporate executives new to their positions often commission their own audits of management effectiveness for reassessing—or developing anew—goals, objectives, priorities, management structure and managerial strategies.

The public relations audit can serve as a natural extension of this technique, but it also has its own set of unique purposes. The precedents are well established. So is the use of external firms with specialized know-how, resources and objectivity to give internal public relations staff confidence in the reliability, expertness and objectivity of the process.

David A. Meeker, Akron, Ohio, counseling firm principal, agreed that "the audit helps get you in the door. It's an instant means of getting into an organization, a good way to get to know the client. Client executives are accustomed to financial, if not legal, audits."[6]

Experience with Audits Builds Marketplace Support

Fortune 1000 Executives Favor External Audits   Over the relatively short history of public relations counseling, the audit occasionally has seemed difficult to sell because of its cost and because of some cynicism in the marketplace.

Executive confidence nurtured by experience with audits and increasing sophistication of audit research systems appears to have enhanced the market in recent years. This is borne out not only by the sanguine posture of the counseling industry but also by surveys of corporate customers.

Two-thirds of *Fortune* 1000 public relations directors who used research told interviewers that they conducted financial relations and employee relations audits. Moreover, virtually all of them spoke up for the useful-ness of these audits. "The most popular type of public relations research is the audit," concluded Research & Forecasts chairman Peter Finn.[7] Analy-ses of corporate perspectives are given in the PRSA Professional Library audiotape "The Public Relations Audit: A Management Tool."[8]

Nine out of 10 *Fortune* 1000 public relations executives who responded to the 1980s survey said they believed research can provide a realistic overview of how their corporations are perceived. Eight out of 10 said they believed that research can measure how well a specific program is meeting objectives, according to John C. Pollack, research director of the Ruder Finn & Rotman subsidiary.[9]

Of *Fortune* 1000 executives who used outside research consultants, more than 9 out of 10 cited as their reason for going external the need for specialized capabilities not possessed internally. More than 8 out of 10 said they needed research "by an objective third party—that is, they needed a perspective that was not poisoned by the internal problems of the com-pany itself." And better than 5 out of 10 said they needed credibility to as-sure that the results would be accepted as scientific by an outside audience.

The potential audits market for counseling and research firms could be larger than even some opinion leaders in the field anticipate. For instance, the Research & Forecasts survey found that 82 percent of the *Fortune* 1000 executives believed primary areas of growth would be in public relations audits of external audiences and internal publics. By those who had not used research, financial and employee audits were considered most likely future trends. The survey also found much popularity for program impact and media relations audits in the future.[10]

Barriers to Overcome   First, however, some barriers would have to be over-come for non-users. These barriers are chiefly budgetary, but they appear to be rooted in a lack of awareness or understanding on the part of execu-tives of new research capabilities, applications and cost effectiveness.

Pollack said that consultants have not adequately helped corporate executives understand the methods and uses of research and "the wide array of research possibilities open to us." In their decisions not to use research earlier, 65 percent said that the greatest barrier was budgetary.[11]

Finn attributed this to a tendency of many clients to believe that money is better spent on other programs or on staff. "Many others realize, however, that $25,000 can really save $100,000 if used for research that directs a professional to effective programs—and away from costly, misguided ones. . . . The critical point is that they can operate better—more effectively, efficiently and economically—with research."[12] Pollack noted that 50 percent of non-users felt that their executives have insufficient understanding of how research works and what it can achieve.[13]

One-Shot Device or Part of a Program?

Financial Audits Provide a Model for CEOs to Schedule Public Relations Audits This seems to present an opportunity for counseling firms to work with internal public relations staffs in helping them ground management in the use of audits. The reasons given by those who contract for research and counsel can strengthen the case for making public relations audits the equivalent of financial audits. Chief among these reasons are expertness, third-party objectivity and credibility.

Client executives have found exceptional value delivered in many cases, particularly when counselors bring depth and breadth of scope with the resources, experience and style of a scientifically based objectivity.

Financial audits provide a model of scheduling. Although financial audits may be most appropriate when an organization changes leadership or direction, executives recognize the value of a continuing audit process in the day-to-day management of organizations. Ongoing audits allow management to recognize problems before they reach crisis proportions, monitor fiscal effectiveness of programs and take advantage of changes that portend profitable trends.

In public relations, there seems to be a dichotomy among clients who subscribe to one-shot audits and those who believe in making auditing an ongoing, systematic program.

At one end of the spectrum, audits may take from a few hours to a day and may include intensive focused interviews, perhaps together with data analysis from computer banks, files and existing opinion research.

At the other end of the spectrum lie full-scale operations in which counseling firms mount extensive—and intensive—programs incorporating a powerful combination of such methods as observation, survey, Delphi futures research and laboratory and field experiments.

Counselors and their clients may find the conventional audit a one-shot device despite the duration and resources committed and the expertness and programmatic and persuasive skills applied to assuring a follow-through on the findings. In this case, it falls short of the potential of a "rolling" audit that never stops.

Audits can help clients thrive financially while raising the level of counsel and capabilities in problem intervention and prevention and in opportunity projection and capitalization. The first priority challenge for the counselor, therefore, lies in persuading client management to invest in the appropriate level of public relations audit.

How to Persuade Client Management to Invest in Audits

Counselor Must First Convince Self of Value, Then Client Public Relations Executive Counselors often have to learn themselves about the value of sophisticated research methodology before they can persuade client executives to invest in audits. Similarly, counselors may have to help internal public relations management persuade themselves of the value of an audit before gaining their support. What convinces the external counselor also may convince the internal staff.

"There's no substitute for an enthusiastic presentation by a professional who believes deeply in the product he or she is selling," according to Daniel H. Baer, consultant on public relations management, Sherman Oaks, Calif. But therein lies a principal problem in selling audits. In his *Public Relations Quarterly* article on "Selling Management on Public Relations Research," Baer wrote:

> It often is exceedingly hard to argue in favor of research when it is quite possible that you perceive that the time and dollar allocations you seek might be spent more cost effectively on program implementation. This conflict is exacerbated when dollars diverted from your program would go to another profit center or outside supplier.[14]

Even those who embrace research as an integral part of the planning-programming-evaluation process "all too often raise an amazingly large number of objections as to why research is not appropriate for this particular activity at this particular time," according to Walter K. Lindenmann, vice president of Opinion Research Corp. in New York.[15]

Counselors may find some client public relations executives hesitant because the executives may feel they know all the answers to research questions before they are asked. For example, when Lindenmann was president of Hill and Knowlton's research subsidiary, he had a client who commissioned an audit of federal government opinion leaders to double-check the organization's own convictions. The client's public relations director told him: "We already know the views of Washington government opinion leaders toward us and our industry."

"Boy, were they ever in for a shock," Lindenmann said. It turned out that government officers were telling corporate leaders one message in public, but conveying a completely different message in private when promised confidentiality.[16]

Counselors also may anticipate the client's instinctive desire to rush to action rather than get bogged down in research that may not be fully understood by an executive or that may be perceived as too time-consuming. Furthermore, counselors may anticipate client—if not self—reluctance based on a concern that program and first-class research cannot be done adequately at this time due to budget constraints, thereby causing research to be scaled back.

Client education must begin with a careful analysis of the relative cost/value ratio of the different available options—from no audit whatsoever to first class, extensive audit procedures—because the opportunity may exist for low cost/high value research. Opportunities also may exist for planning an audit in several phases, each phase to be submitted and approved for budget as the previous results are analyzed and presented.

It may be helpful to remind internal public relations executives of the special dividends audits pay as objective, third-party support for inside departments' objectives, priorities, programs, strategies and budget. Top management may unfairly, but subconsciously, perceive even the most objective of internal public relations staff as asking for research with the intent to promote their own causes.

What Works for Internal Public Relations Executive Can Work for External Counselor The third-party selling of public relations services such as audits may work as effectively for the external public relations counselor as for the internal executive.

Although the image of third-party objectivity may be well-earned by a counselor who offers audits together with other public relations services, client management may unfairly ascribe profit motives—rather than a concern for the organization's interests—to counselor recommendations for a thorough preliminary audit.

In such cases, it may prove helpful to recommend independent auditors, who do not have available the comprehensive operations of full-service counseling firms but who do concentrate on preliminary audits and who can recommend guidelines for client use when commissioning services from others.

Twenty-two Techniques for Clients New to Public Relations Audits Counselors may use a number of techniques with clients who have little or no experience with public relations audits. The following 22 are derived from, and inspired by, several sources:[17]

1. Probe to understand exactly what—and why—reluctance or negative perceptions may exist about the breadth and depth of the range of inquiry that should follow in the audit.
2. Make clear, with a well-reasoned, solidly documented discussion, what the client is likely to get for the investment.
3. But spare the client from technical details that may distract from the results to be achieved.
4. Specify how long the audit will take. This is particularly important if the client has experienced, or heard of, an operation that seemed to wander.
5. Help the client understand that the amount of research determines what he needs to spend.
6. Set close parameters so that you and the client will know what the entire audit and its components will cost.
7. Involve in the presentation the expert researchers who will participate in the proposed project.
8. Cite successful case histories that are relevant to the client's situation.
9. But be sensitive to situational variables that may be perceived as making some case histories not applicable to the client.
10. Cite examples of profitable audits in allied fields such as management consulting and explain how these applications can be adapted to meet current public relations needs.
11. Provide reprints or concise summaries of relevant articles from business or trade publications that are respected by the client.
12. Identify professional development seminars on audits to which the client may wish to send internal public relations staff.
13. For the first audit proposal, consider selecting those areas of greatest importance to the CEO and board. One possibility might be an audit focusing on public attitudes toward a possible price increase to guide the client in marketing strategies; another might be in issues identification to aid in programming for public affairs.
14. Elicit the support of those members of management who are research-oriented to help you open the door, precondition key decision-makers and, perhaps, even make the sale.
15. Consider acclimating the client to audits first by selling a project to middle management. This builds a base of successful experience internally for selling the next level of audits to top management. Moreover, it offers the potential of arming middle management to do the persuading. Examples: Propose an employee attitude study to the personnel director or an analyst survey to the investor relations officer.
16. Consider proposing varied levels of audits while supplying the additional benefits and costs of each increment.

17. Prepare a fallback proposal for the client who wants the benefits of an audit but who won't invest enough initially to go first class. But make sure the executive understands the degree to which reliability or comprehensiveness is sacrificed as well as the relative value of a short-cut audit.
18. As an alternative to the fallback proposal, develop a several-phase proposal with time-certain review dates and built-in criteria to guide decision-makers in adding stages and refining earlier phases.
19. Investigate the potential of a joint project with the client's management consulting firm or advertising agency. This could add powerful allies to the presentation and appeal to the client's sense of economy.
20. Learn from the experiences of counselors with similar client situations. It is useful when preparing proposal and presentation and when collecting and analyzing data from the actual audit.
21. Determine what studies and information can be gleaned from existing resources without the cost of fresh research. Be sure to brief the executive on the resultant economies.
22. Plan to build upon intelligence already developed through the client's departments and advertising agencies, management consultancies and accounting and legal firms.

An example of the value of this last point is found in Baer's experience in an audit for the Southern California McDonald's owner-operators.[18] At the onset, most members of the group indicated that they did not want to sacrifice advertising dollars for public relations counsel or services.

Baer interviewed public relations professionals at national headquarters and in counseling firms across the country, starting with Chicago's Golin/Harris Communications Inc., which was under national contract to McDonald's. He also interviewed in public relations firms and advertising agencies under contract with other regional McDonald's owner-operator groups.

In cities where both public relations and advertising companies were under contract, he explored how they worked together. He also interviewed people from the local advertising agency. The insights gained were useful to him in planning, conducting and analyzing owner-operator interviews as part of the audit. Equally important, Baer was positioned to understand the keys to persuading owner-operators to invest in public relations services.

A public relations firm was retained as part of the follow-up to the audit. At the end of its first year of service, McDonald's operators, who had earlier opposed such budgeting, called for more public relations budget dollars.

What to Do if Client Is Unhappy with Past Audit An infinite number of factors may prejudice a client against public relations audits, including experiences in which executives felt funds and time were spent with little tangible return. Here are several points to consider:

1. Keep in mind that although some client decision-makers may be favorably disposed by their experience with financial and other audits, others may attach an onus to the word "audit" because it may connote to them an investigation or a challenge to their authority. Those that bridle at the term may find synonyms such as "strategic review" less threatening.

2. Anticipate that some clients may have encountered public relations auditors who they perceived did not have the necessary grounding to conduct an audit. Because of such experiences, they may be scared of somebody with little expertness in their business "meddling" in delicate areas. This requires building confidence in the process as well as building the auditing skills of counselors.

3. Anticipate that other clients may have been audited by consultants without public relations research expertise or strength in communication. Antipathy to auditing may flow from disappointments resulting from such auditors, inability to ask the right questions of the right people, let alone know how to interpret or apply effectively the data.

4. Be sensitized to real-time constraints. Client CEOs frequently look for instant results after commissioning audits not realizing that the necessary careful and patient cultivation of such sensitive publics as government officials, security analysts, corporate executives and journalists takes time. They may not know what is needed to secure the cooperation of or to schedule appointments with such important contributors of audit data.

5. Part of the challenge may be to brief such a client on what the proposed new auditing is expected to produce, when the process will begin to yield payoff, exactly how much it will cost and how the improved process will be used in support of corporate objectives.

6. Resolve the question: Do you sell your work as a communications audit or do it as a communications audit and sell it as a management intelligence tool?

7. Consider another option: Should a public relations audit be restricted to communications or should you do—and sell—a management intelligence audit that includes, but is not limited to, traditional communications questions?

8. More than the audit's objectives may have to be made clear; this may be the kind of client and situation that requires explaining how the audit investment, itself, will be evaluated.

9. That point suggests proposing of a benchmark audit as part of a process in which later research will measure progress at predetermined intervals.

Follow Through to Interest Client in More Sophisticated Services An effectively conducted audit can be used as a catalyst in the chemistry between
client and public relations counsel. Armed with the public relations equivalent of financial and legal audit data, counselors can position themselves
to contribute to long-range planning, policy counseling and the change-
agent role of professionals.

Similar to the follow-through employed by a golfer who plans the trajec-
tory of the ball and then keeps the club in the same arc of motion after
hitting it, sales-minded counselors incorporate long-range client conditioning, beginning at the point of initial proposal through and beyond
presentation of recommendations based upon audit results.

Positioning strategy requires carefully planned presentation as part of
the follow-through by a public relations firm:

1. Because an audit is generally the first thing done for a client, how
well a counselor proposes it and follows through tends to prejudice the
client toward a long-term relationship.

2. Expert auditors build on their successes by assuring that profitable
results of well-done audits are communicated effectively to various levels
of management, including the board.

3. Involvement of important individuals and publics in intelligence
gathering can be put to advantage not only with client top management,
but also with such important publics as securities analysts, financial media, prime contractors and dealers. Their audit interviews signal management interest in strengthening the corporation and respect for the
opinions of stakeholders. With adroit handling, this leads to greater confidence in management and creates an interest in investing in, contracting
with or otherwise supporting the organization.

4. The astute counselor also may build upon the intrigue generated
among these external publics in the audit process by helping them understand how they, too, can take advantage of this kind of research.

5. Although, ideally, presentation of results and recommendations may
best be done after auditing and analysis are completed, client needs and
exigencies may demand relatively quick feedback. This may do more than
serve the client's interests; it also may help convince the client that there
are short-term—not just long-term—dividends to be realized.

6. Just as the design of interview sessions with key board members and
executives may strengthen support of the auditing process so, too, may the
design of the presentation sessions.

7. Many counselors present voluminous reports and documentation to
clients. Indeed, some executives appreciate the opportunity to scrutinize
the data personally. In addition, some users of the reports may find a
scanning useful in interpreting material that may have special meaning to
them because of their intimate knowledge of the situation. However, just

as proposing an audit requires conciseness rather than overly long detail-
ing of process, so, too, does the presentation of results require special
organization. This includes:

Brief overview of what is learned

Organization with an easy-to-use table of contents and index

Organization of report sections to fit salient interests of executives in
topical areas

Preparation of oral presentations and written text to make material
conform to brevity, tight organization and directness sought by many
client executives

Coordination of citations and appendixes for easy perusal by executives
who wish to check documentation

Coordination of timing and planning of presentations with internal executives who are understanding and supportive of auditing process and
who have stakes in making audit reports more than an agenda filler at a
meeting

Presentation of a series of attainable objectives

Presentation of a series of actionable recommendations

Presentation of a manageable session, or series of sessions, in which
interaction of auditors, counselors and client executives is programmed

Planning of follow-through questions to decision-makers allowing them
to participate in certain critically important interpretations and inviting
their participation in choosing among options for action

Execution

Long before this stage, of course, comes the need to develop a systematic
approach to auditing operations, a need dictated not only by economics
but also by the necessity that incremental lessons learned in the execution
of audits are applied in future operations.

Even firms that have such auditing systems in place consider the benefits of cross-fertilization of ideas by looking to models from other organizations.

Models from Burson-Marsteller for Marketing Audits Two Burson-
Marsteller documents are combined here for the convenience of readers:
"The Marketing Audit" internal training procedure, and "Marketing Audit
Form" for guiding questions.[19]

MARKETING AUDIT

I. Purpose

To understand the prospect's/client's total marketing situation.

- *Externally*
- *Internally*

II. *Procedures*

First, collect and interpret marketing-related materials to focus subsequent personal interviews on areas not covered by these materials, or to clarify issues covered by them.

Conduct personal interviews with relevant marketing executives:

- *Marketing*
- *Sales*
- *Advertising/Promotion*
- *Research (Market)*

Concentrate audit questions on areas of executive's expertise

III. *The Interview*

In-person

Open-ended, tape-record if possible, otherwise, take copious notes

Have a second person as part of the interviewing team

Cover issues missed

Record responses

IV. *The Content Areas*

1. *Before You Start—Get Copies of:*

   Ads

   Literature

   Articles, publicity reprints

   Sales tools

   Marketing plans

   Marketing research reports

   Organization charts

   - *Check the information areas covered by the above and focus the audit on those areas* not *covered by them*

2. *Marketing Situation*

   a. *Sales analysis*

   What have sales been the past two years? Market share?

   What is your sales forecast for the next two years? Market share?

   What accounts for the increase? Decrease?

   What is being done about that?

   How many of your customers are key accounts, both in

*numbers and by percentage? How much of your business
do they represent?*

*If you do have key accounts, how are monies and efforts
being allocated to them?*

What about geographic trends?

- *Is business concentrated in a limited number of
  markets?*
- *Are your efforts taking this into account?*

*Are there market trends? i.e., should we begin to "plant
seeds" in growing markets?*

*What about seasonal/lag time between order and
delivery?*

- *Is your product seasonal?*
- *Does that create problems?*
- *How are you solving those problems?*
- *Can you help flatten the demand curve?*

b. *Increasing Sales*

Increased sales will come from:

- *Expanding markets*
- *New markets*
- *Broader line, new products*
- *Greater use of product*

What is being done to secure these increased sales?

What are you doing to support that effort?

c. *Your Competition*

Who are your primary competitors?
*What is your competition's unique selling proposition
(USP)?*

*Compare your own strengths, weaknesses across the board
to those of your competitors.*

How are you communicating those strengths?

d. *Your Reputation*

What is the reputation of your product(s)?

What is your reputation in terms of service?

What is your corporate reputation?

Do your reputations need refining? Building?

How do you communicate the reputation you want?

Do you know the effectiveness of such communications?

Have you identified your own unique selling proposition(s)?

e. *Promotional Mix*

Items in the mix and how each is determined:

- *Personal selling*
- *Advertising*
- *Public relations*
- *Trade shows*

3. *Market Analysis*

a. *Market Structure:*

What are the markets? Size, etc.

- *Primary*
- *Secondary*
- *Tertiary*

b. *Audience Segments*

Who are the decision-making influences in each audience category?

How is each being addressed?

How are you reaching the key decision-makers?

c. *Audience Needs*

What are the needs of each audience?

What do they look to you for?

How do you know their needs?

What are their current problems, if any, in terms of product, service, etc.?

What are each audience's primary motivating factors in terms of accepting your product? Your service?

How does each of your audience's needs match up with your own marketing objectives?

d. *Purchasing Factors*

How does the purchase develop?

Is the purchase for new products the same as for existing ones?

How do your communications take this into account?

Are you addressing the influence of an intermediary (e.g., dealer, distributor, etc.)?

e. *Brand Loyalty*

Why is your brand purchased vs. others?

Why are competitors' brands purchased vs. others?

Which competitor or market segment is vulnerable? Why?

4. *Distribution Analysis*

   a. *Channel Analysis*

What is the role of your intermediaries?

What is their relationship to your company?

What percentage of your business is through intermediaries as opposed to direct sales?

Are proper time and attention devoted to this audience?

   b. *Problems*

Is your distribution system satisfactory? Why/why not?

Are you offering solid sales support? Training?

What is this audience's primary complaint (if there is one)? How are you dealing with that?

   c. *Communications*

How do you routinely communicate with intermediaries?

Are they satisfied? If not, why?

5. *Sales Force Analysis*

   a. *Communications*

How is it done?

Does it take into account other demands placed on the sales force?

How do you measure its effectiveness?

What is the sales force's biggest problem with communications from headquarters?

Are you addressing that concern? How?

   b. *Support*

How do you help the sales force communicate to their audiences?

How effective is what you provide them?

How do you know?

6. *Internal Management Analysis*

   a. *Does Management Know What You're Doing?*

Does it know the results?

How does it know?

Is the measurement valid? How do you know?

      b. What Are Your Problems/Challenges with Marketing?

        Do they understand your needs?

        Do you understand theirs?

        If they need to be better informed about your efforts (and the value of those efforts), how do you propose to do that? When?

V. The Write-Up

1. *Briefly summarize main points for each content area. If they have a marketing plan, use it as basic source document.*

2. *Identify areas of little or no information. These serve as investigative opportunities.*

3. *Concentrate on integration of marketing elements: product, promotion, and distribution. Any inconsistencies, gaps?*

4. *Assess where Burson-Marsteller research can be of major help: in obtaining additional information or in communications strategy/tactics?*

Combining Benefits of Qualitative and Quantitative Data Counseling firms often employ collection methods that combine qualitative and quantitative data. Public relations audits usually start with a collection of secondary data (materials from the literature, much of it now accessed by computer); these may include historical perspectives, analytical information about the publics and industry, survey data, reports filed with government agencies and articles from trade, financial and other media.

To this base, auditors add interview data, which may include a profile of client executive attitudes as they pursue issues in a relatively unstructured fashion. Then the audit fans outward to important, segmented publics, and it may return to management as the loop is closed.

Lloyd Kirban, Burson-Marsteller's research director, said that

perceptions, attitudes, and observations of people auditing an area may be as important as if we had collected highly structured scientific responses. This makes us better able to understand actions taken by the client company.

It's interesting to contrast attitudes, opinions and perceptions of executives in the client company against what they believe to be attitudes of target audiences. There may be chasms between the two. It's important to recognize the differences between what executives believe to be out there in the real world and what is really out there. The counseling firm's role is to convert the executive to a better understanding of target audience perceptions rather than convert the target publics.[20]

North Carolina Firm's Model of Client Presentation For a model from a smaller firm concerning audit structure and client presentations, the authors condensed and synthesized an actual client proposal and a staff training document of Epley Associates of Charlotte, N.C.[21]

PROPOSAL FOR A COMMUNICATIONS AUDIT

Phase I: Define Parameters of Audit and Plan Course of Action

The purposes of the audit are to determine assets and weaknesses of the organization; put into perspective communications, marketing and public relations activities as they relate overall to the client's goals and objectives; identify needs by priorities; and plan cost-effective programs with greater assurance.

The audit provides a measuring point for future evaluations and assessments.

Phase II: Study History and Organization

1. Overview of corporate organization, communications policies, history, services, method of operation, emergency plans and philosophy concerning employees; marketing; and relations with media, community, government, shareholder and internal publics.
2. Review organization of communications functions, including duties of public relations department and personnel.

Phase III: Internal Media

The internal media phase begins with a general overview prior to management interviews and employee surveys. The material is reviewed again after interviews and feedback from employees. Then assessments and recommendations are made.

1. Review communications for content, flow to recipient, consistency, appearance and way originated. Examine messages from top management. Attend staff meetings to observe group communication organization and effectiveness, including reactions. Analyze feedback from employees and one-on-one communications. Look at bulletin boards and signs. Review company handbooks, benefit programs and policies. Study rumor control.
2. Interview midmanagement. Get their opinions not only concerning what exists but also concerning their desires and ideas for improvements.

Phase IV: Top Management Interviews

Beginning with the chief executive, conduct interviews to:

1. Ascertain concurrence on goals and objectives of client.
2. Learn attitudes and philosophy toward communications.
3. Determine key publics.
4. Determine the CEO's assessments of strengths and weaknesses with all publics.

5. *Assess views on marketing and on relationships with the news media, local and state governments and community.*
6. *Assess views on effectiveness of internal communication such as formal, written, chain of command, lateral, bottom-to-top and rumor control.*
7. *Identify key public issues affecting the client. Other interviews to be conducted include those with the executive vice presidents of major divisions, senior vice presidents of marketing and public relations and the senior regional officers.*

Phase V: Mid-Management and Employee Attitude Assessment

1. *Survey client's city executives, branch managers and other senior officers for their understanding of corporate goals and objectives, communications effectiveness, community and government relations, media relations, marketing objectives and techniques and perceptions of client loyalty by managers and employees.*

This survey design is based upon the data gained in previous studies and is to be distributed to individuals to complete at their office and then mail to an outside independent research firm for evaluation. An alternate approach would be to conduct a focus group session in each region.

2. *Survey rank-and-file employees for attitudes toward company, goals and objectives, superiors, colleagues, effectiveness of major communications systems, customer relations, their role in overall marketing efforts and effectiveness of training programs.*

Survey forms are distributed to each branch and coded to identify specific locations but not individuals. An alternate, but less effective, approach is to conduct three to five focus group sessions across the state.

Phase VI: External Communications

Media

1. *Review all news releases disseminated over the past two years to mass, trade and special interest media. Examine editorial treatment of the organization and its products and management.*
2. *Analyze content of releases and style of writing. Are all important elements present? How does the company respond to queries? How does it maintain contact and rapport when nothing is going on? Does management understand media requirements?*
3. *How are emergencies handled?*
4. *Review clips from major newspapers in the state to see how the company is compared editorially with other members of its industry.*
5. *Identify key media and key people in each medium. Speak to a*

representative sample and determine if they feel adequately informed; receive cooperation; respect the client and give it credibility; assure news releases are well-written, timely and complete; know client position on key issues; and support or oppose the company.

6. Talk with key business editors of major print and electronic media to determine their knowledge of client's perceptions of its target publics in relationship with other members of industry, how they get information and their likes and dislikes.

7. Review emergency information plan.

8. Review policy and procedures for officials in handling news media on a day-to-day basis.

External Communication

1. Public Affairs: Are key issues understood by midmanagement, employees? What is corporate orientation to local, state and federal government? Are people encouraged to vote? Can they identify allies and opponents in government? Do they know regulations that affect them, how to influence change? Do they understand industry efforts?

2. Community Relations: Do employees support community relations goals? What does the company do? How effective is it? What do community leaders think of the company? Do they know its leaders? Does management know community leaders? What impact does the organization have on community? How are employees recognized for community involvement? Can involvement activities be capitalized on?

Phase VII: Community Relations

1. Review by city markets the community relations activities in which client has involvement this year and plans for next year. Designate each activity, type of involvement, specific amounts of contributions, loaned personnel, active promotions, etc. Evaluate involvement: What material benefits did client receive, if any? What was the objective of participation? Was the objective achieved? Why do you recommend continuing or dropping participation? Review by city markets government and civic boards or commissions on which client officers or managers serve. Review community relations policy.

2. Shareholders: Review annual report and quarterly reports. Analyze relations with financial community.

3. Customers: Review rapport, credibility and communication programs and materials for existing and potential customers. Review advertising of past two years and the proposed program for next year.

4. Marketing: Determine attitudes toward client product line by small and mid-size business interests. In major cities, interview in person 30 to 40 representative CEOs of firms in the $3 to $100 million sales

category that do NOT do business with client. Ask what they look for in client's industry, how they assess the major firms in that industry—including the client, what these firms are not doing for them that they should, their knowledge of the client and its services, why they would change to another firm and their opinions about marketing techniques by members of the industry. Repeat the procedure with CEOs of firms that do business with the client.

Phase VIII: Report

Client is furnished statement on mode of report; projected costs reflecting a mini-maxi range, depending on client choices among parameter options for the audit; and a time line, such as six months.

1. *Analyze and compare concepts and perceptions to actual conditions. Identify discrepancies and strong and weak points.*
2. *Organize and write findings, comments and recommendations.*
3. *Assure that report will be concise and easily understood.*
4. *Use design to make reader more receptive to content.*
5. *Use declarative statements.*
6. *Give rationale for recommendations.*
7. *Say what exists—don't pull punches.*
8. *Express your interpretation of situations by how they are helpful or counterproductive to the organization's goals or objectives. Label comments as such. Keep them to the point. Make any criticism constructive. Provide warnings where needed.*
9. *State recommended action in a clearly labeled paragraph. If several recommendations are made, indicate at the start of each that it is a separate counsel. Explain rationale for recommendations.*
10. *Organize plan of work for counseling firm follow-up.*
11. *Review recommendations periodically and follow through.*

Key to Audit Payoff: Client Management Follow-Through

No matter how effectively the audit is executed, no matter how sound the recommendations, no matter how well organized the counseling firm plans its follow-up, audits still may do very little for the client except satisfy curiosity. The key to the bottom-line effectiveness of audits has to be the commitment of client management to follow through.

From a client perspective, it is not enough to get a commitment from management to programs based on audit results nor enough to have ongoing measurements in place. In separate reports to the PRSA Investor Relations Sections and the Society for Marketing Professional Services, Winthrop C. Neilson III and James B. Strenski reinforced the concept that management has a price to pay to realize the investment potential of audits.

Neilson, 1987 PRSA Investor Relations chair and managing director of Krone Communications, put it this way:

All too often, valuable audits become historical period pieces because of the lack of vital follow-through. It is critical that the audit becomes a jumping-off point whereby you have in place a reporting program through which management can follow the progress of your efforts. The purpose of the audit is not to judge how you have done in the past as much as what you can do for the future.[22]

Strenski, chairman of Public Communications Inc., counseled marketers that an audit not only becomes a research strategy document on which a great deal of marketing communications can be designed and a benchmark measurement tool against which to determine program effectiveness, "but also becomes an exploratory tool in discovery of potential new markets not seriously considered in the past."[23]

The cost includes client patience as well as management commitment to participation. The average marketing communications audit takes three to four months, depending on scope and complexity. Even more important than patience is willingness of management to listen. Several conditions for that willingness were suggested by Strenski: "Management must be willing to listen with an open mind, to learn and respond to new information, sometimes at variance with self perceptions. If listening is practiced, learning can be achieved. With a commitment to do something about what is learned, business can definitely be improved."[24]

It may be concluded that public relations objectivity provides only half of the equation in the formula for audits. The other half of the equation requires client objectivity in accepting and using the intelligence gained from audits.

It would be of value to succinctly incorporate in proposals and end-of-audit reports a section summarizing the general *and* specific individualized benefits the client should derive.

For example, Kate Connelly of Chicago's Hill and Knowlton office summarized eight general purposes of audits:

1. *Improve communications cost-and-time effectiveness.*
2. *Forge stronger management-communications staff links.*
3. *Move management closer to consensus on important issues.*
4. *Upgrade communications function throughout the organization.*
5. *Incorporate a long-range plan for communicating by objectives.*
6. *Strengthen CEO's grasp of communications function.*
7. *Articulate more effectively positions on important issues.*
8. *Communicate more effectively in crisis situations.*[25]

PROBLEM SOLVING

It is in problem solving that objectivity and mechanisms such as the audit attain their highest value to clients. *Problem solving* as used here extends beyond the common interpretation that defines problems in terms of "trouble." The meaning also fits within the framework of reference of the physical or social scientist who thinks of problems in terms of opportunities, needs or challenges that pose questions worthy of an answer.

Objectivity Fuses Creativity and Research for Problem Solving

Interdependence Recognized by Counselors Creativity, objectivity and research are interdependent components of problem solving in the public relations counseling function. The question of which of the three comes first is academic. These components of the problem-solving process are fused by effective counselors.

You need objectivity to determine the purposes and parameters of creativity, even to understand the creative processes themselves.

You need creativity to raise the questions for research to answer, to adapt or develop the research methodology, and to interpret the implications that expert researchers furnish counselors.

You need objectivity and research to test the creative strategies and to project the expected/desired results.

You need creativity to challenge research methods that may produce statistical significance for social scientists but sidestep the realities of complex causal and correlational relationships.

You need objectivity and research to find out what executives or publics really think they want or need. You need creativity to develop ways to tell the difference.

You need objectivity and research to provide measurements of effectiveness and creativity to determine what effectiveness should mean to be acceptable.

You need creativity and objectivity and research to develop and justify a program.

You need objectivity and research and creativity to determine how best to apply limited resources and choose among options.

Public relations counselors need creativity to bridge the gaps in the discipline's body of knowledge and research methodology.

The inexorable linkage of public relations planning and evaluation was explained by researcher David M. Dozier in the Summer 1985 *Public Relations Review*:

> *In public relations, the underlying foundation, the base of the professional pyramid, the body of public relations theory developed through*

research is shaky and unstable in comparison to medicine's and law's underlying structure of scientific theory that guides professional practice. Part of this is because of the relative immaturity of communication theory. The social scientific study of something as complex as human communication cannot expect to mature as rapidly as complex areas of inquiry, such as physics, chemistry and the biological sciences.

But public relations begins to collect a body of practical theory about what works and what doesn't work, in terms of program impact, when public relations programs are implemented. Over time, over repeated evaluations of many programs under different conditions, "the state of the public relations art" is systematically improved.[26]

Contemporary practitioners, including internal staff, have built upon the problem-solving fusion of creativity, objectivity and research developed over the years by earlier generations of counselors. Today's generation continues the systematic improvement of the counseling function through the fusion of these components of problem solving.

Uniqueness of Variables Guides Problem-Solving Counsel   The unification of problem solving, creativity, objectivity and research into a dynamic whole process, however, does not supply a panacea for discriminating counselors and clients.

There is a temptation, to be sure, for some executives to demand and for some consultants to supply relatively cheap, handy, off-the-shelf approaches to problem solving that do not take into consideration the uniqueness of any client and the variables involved in each of its problem situations.

David Finn, chairman of Ruder, Finn & Rotman, said that the major challenge in planning a public relations program is to look with a fresh eye on a client's interests and to develop creative ideas on how to achieve relevant benefits:

An almost sure sign that a program is not well thought out is the presentation of a standard list of objectives that would serve equally well for any organization. Serious planning can, for the most part, only take place when time and money have been set aside at the outset, and throughout the program, for adequate research.

The most convincing evidence that a program is on the right track is its unique appropriateness to the organization for which it is designed. It should be a program that seems right for this organization at this particular time in light of current and emerging conditions.[27]

A Look at the Roles Played by Counselors

Problem-Solving Process Facilitator Role Model Such sensitivity to client and situational variables in creative problem solving fits within the public relations role models reviewed in *Effective Public Relations*.[28]

One of the four major types of public relations role models seems to come closest to the thrust of counseling firms at the end of the 20th century. Cutlip, Center and Broom summarized it under the heading of "problem-solving process facilitator":

> When practitioners assume this role they collaborate with other managers in the organization to define and solve problems. Collaboration and consultation begin with the first question and continue as a joint effort to diagnose, plan, implement and evaluate. Practitioners in this role guide other managers and the organization through a rational public relations problem-solving process. . . . Without such participation, operating managers are likely to be uninformed about program goals and objectives, unenthusiastic about public relations program efforts and uncommitted to its function in the organization.

The involvement by counselors in client management, however, may have to yield to a second, more traditional role in public relations firms— in situations that seem to allow no time to go through the process of collaboration and joint problem solving because "action is imperative." The "expert prescriber role" finds "senior officers or clients content to leave public relations in the hands of the 'expert' and assume a relatively passive role" in problem definition, program development and responsibility for implementation.[29]

Communication Skills Vital but Secondary in Problem Solving Although communication and program execution skills continue to play an essential role in public relations problem solving, they tend to be secondary to other qualifications demanded of counselors, such as accountability.

One advocate of this thesis, James H. Dowling, president of Burson-Marsteller, observed: "In a world that needs more and more problem-solving strategists, we have continued too long to be executors. We are in danger of finding that communications is too important to be left in the hands of communicators."[30]

Corporate and institutional executives want an increasing amount of accountability from the function of communications. To be accountable, "you need also be responsible for the resolution of the issue the communications is supposed to address. To be ultimately accountable, one must have the ultimate strategic responsibility for the problem or opportunity at hand."

Dowling said that some practitioners have erected "artificial restraints on our ability to act and think strategically" by conforming to labels that categorize different communications tools and functions. He cautioned against letting "ourselves get compartmentalized by artificial barriers among these communications processes."

For instance, he said "one of the great myths is that public relations and advertising are somehow two disciplines at odds with one another, and should be kept apart as church and state." As two "communications techniques they need to work in a common strategy towards a common goal."

Strategic, results-oriented public relations not only means a joining of disciplines in a common cause, but also increasing the knowledge base and minimizing the risks of intuition. In the wake of the first Tylenol poisoning incident, for example, Burson-Marsteller and client had the equivalent of a national opinion poll conducted every night for six weeks.

Dowling ranked creative execution as the third essential component of the communications structure together with knowledge and strategy, but said that "creative execution not targeted against the real problem is merely an unguided missile that can do more harm than good."

In the perspective of a number of counseling firm executives, research is the fourth essential component of the communications process, along with knowledge, strategy and execution. And Dowling supported a basic premise of other opinion leaders of the industry: "It takes a combination of upfront research and post-activity measurement to meet the ultimate challenge of accountability."

Accountability Meshes with Counseling Firms' Own Business Interests Accountability to clients and related aspects of problem solving, however, do not take place in a vacuum; they tend to mesh with the business interests of counseling firms in more effective problem-solving campaigns.

William F. Noonan, vice chairman of Burson-Marsteller International, advised officers of other public relations firms that catering to client needs and accountability to client executives work best when melded with "substantive business plans for our own companies—plans that set specific goals, strategies, and actions to grow and strengthen our own company's business."[31] Effective planning strategies go beyond "raw numbers" to incorporate "the flesh and blood required to deliver those numbers." He said it is very important to close the loop on planning.

Public relations firms are becoming more systems-oriented than technique-oriented in their response to changing client needs. For example, Noonan projected that the sending of multiple messages in multiple environments would increase and, with that trend, counselors will need to understand not only their individual impact, but their cumulative impact as well.

This is symptomatic of a holistic approach to communications that is needed for counselors to solve clients' problems and, at the same time, thrive in their own industry. This also requires working from "the reality of the marketplace back, and not the other way" and of challenging whether "our communications techniques are the right ones, the effective ones, the only ones."

In their own systems/holistic approaches to client problem solving, Burson-Marsteller provides one of a number of increasingly sophisticated models.

Interdisciplinary Problem-Solving Model

Another example may be found at N W Ayer Inc., where public relations counselors work closely with the advertising agency in an interdisciplinary team plan for creative problem solving. Joan Parker, New York–based senior vice president, said the Ayer plan provides a vehicle to combine the creative strengths of both disciplines.[32] "Together, we identify the key fact—what you want public relations and advertising people to do for the client."

Problem solving starts with an analysis of client product or service objectives. These observations are used to guide research and further refine the team's analysis of client problems and opportunities. Ayer teams approach the creative process in problem solving with zero-based budget thinking. Parker said this initial no-budget-in-mind perspective provides a sense of freedom in exploring a wide range of ideas. Later, the program can be adapted to budgetary considerations. This fits with the concept of considering—or proposing—variable levels of problem-solving activities as options for the client. But she observed that "sometimes we in public relations think smaller than advertising people" because of the disciplines' different orientations to expense.

This implies that some of the more expensive proposals for public relations from advertising members of the team turn out to be sound cost/value propositions for clients. But the advertising components of client campaigns also benefit from the input of public relations members of the team who contribute their special knowledge on trends.

Model Integrates MBO with Client Relations Philosophy

Another firm, Epley Associates, has created a problem-solving model with core structure of management by objectives adapted to public relations counseling.[33]

This model takes a systems perspective and examines problem-solving aspects and results as they interact. For example, Epley said that "if you want to impact on one public, you have to be able to look at opportunities for impacting on another at the same time. The second audience would interact with the first and reinforce what you're doing with that public."[34]

Research for this book indicated that the trend in most organizations retaining outside counsel is toward short-term projects and limited-sphere assignments. This trend represents the essence of one of the greatest challenges to counseling firms engaged in creative problem solving. Long-term goals and budgets are established as part of counseling initiative. Even firms hired for specific short-term projects still need to know what the long-term goals are, to make sure that their efforts contribute as much as possible.

> *We may discover hidden agendas upon which we can capitalize with the same theme. For example, a cigarette manufacturing plant announced building plans. The government was talking stringent controls. What we did with the building story was to send out a secondary message that the cigarette manufacturer still had confidence in the tobacco industry and wanted to invest more than $150 million in new facilities. We can create secondary objectives for such events.*
>
> *But we do try to guide clients, when appropriate, into a primary long-term goal approach. When a client moves into a new town, for instance, you need to look beyond the move into the follow-through needed. Of course, you can't get close to some clients on long-term objectives. With others, you're right up there with the CEO.*

Even a number of client organizations that have an MBO policy may not use it to advantage throughout the organization or understand its potentials and procedures. That poses a challenge—and opportunity—to help develop the necessary goals and objectives and then focus on the priorities and the strategies to accomplish them.

A widely acknowledged "rule" of MBO-like systems within an organization is that solutions should be arrived at by joint agreement between employees and executives. In situations involving external counsel, the concepts of mutually agreed upon objectives and carefully coordinated client-counselor strategies and operations require special attention.

Ease of Application and Rigor vs. Rigidity in Systems   The models cited fit some of the criteria for what was termed "the process management of public relationships" in *PR Reporter*. Such a process involves standardized methods in a holistic model that takes elements of organizational life into account and allows stability through stresses of constant change.[35] Integral to this kind of problem-solving process is a combination of rigorous rules and a framework for ease of application and explanation.

The case for flexibility was supported by Dan Thomas, president of Thomas & Co. of Palo Alto, Calif. "A rigid planning process not only creates barriers that impact the implementation of the plan, but also stops strategy formulation from being the dynamic process it must be in adapting to changes in turbulent external and internal environments."[36]

The ease of application criterion, however, limits to a degree the rigidity built into creative problem-solving processes. There is an important difference between *rigidity* and *rigor*. Rigidity is illustrated by a refusal to acknowledge change. Rigor is illustrated by the clarity of the operational definitions used by scientists to assure that others can duplicate their experiments.

It is such rigor that helps make research reliable. It is reliable research that arms counselor and client with the power of knowledge.

To paraphrase Dale Zand, author of *Information, Organization and Power*, in a knowledge society, the counselor's effective power is the product of his formal persuasive power multiplied by his knowledge competence. Zand has said that "organizations today can be viewed as cauldrons of knowledge—rich with ideas about new products, new processes, new approaches to markets and new ways to improve management's effectiveness."[37]

It takes sophisticated, rigorous modes of research to systematically collect and accurately interpret the ideas and the knowledge to equip counselor and client with objective, useful, reliable data. But although the data base of knowledge from research provides the counselor with power, it is a data base that must constantly be tested, updated and strengthened with current, improved methodologies.

According to Phillip J. Tichenor, an authority on social and behavioral science, "there is no final or ultimate knowledge from science, only the best knowledge and the best interpretation that can be provided at a given time."[38]

That proclivity to obsolescence and vulnerability to fresh tests of evidence underlines the importance of rooting the counselor's objectivity in the most solid research mechanisms possible. The reason is simple and intrinsic to the concept of objectivity. As stated by Michael Rowan, president of Hill and Knowlton's research subsidiary, research should define problems "so that communications professionals can deliver advice on strategy and programs and do so with confidence, persuasion and intelligence."[39]

4

RESEARCH

Few modern counselors would approach their role as advisors to corporate management without first seeking support from some of the research systems described here. Research is a major tool of the practitioner, but research reports themselves are not the purpose of the work. That purpose is the strategy, the policy, the major campaign that derives from the knowledge research provides.

Properly put to use, research can breathe life into public relations programs—finding direction for the campaign itself, providing substance for the materials, steering counselors toward proper audiences, media and messages and, finally, evaluating the program's success.

Several systems for guiding and determining the results of campaigns are reviewed in this chapter, along with illustrations of how research can provide the substance for powerful, long-term programs.[1]

EXPERIMENTAL DESIGNS

Counseling Firms Open Up Proprietary Methodology

Medical Science Model: Pave Way for Progress by Pooling Knowledge The sharing of research methodology and findings at seminars, in journals and in books—even revelations of blind alleys and failure to support researchers' theories—has long contributed to the advancement of medical science. That sharing has been one of the hallmarks distinguishing medicine as a profession.

Similarly, researchers in the physical and social sciences have contributed to their pool of knowledge, even if this meant giving competitors an opportunity to take advantage of this sharing. Those who open up their research risk stimulating debate, even criticism. But the same dialogue that brings out the spirit of criticism also stimulates others to go public. It gives some counselors incentive to try new approaches to research or to the delivery of counseling services.

90

In the relatively young discipline of public relations, communication about privately developed research advances—particularly specifics needed to replicate someone else's methodology or to build those findings into a body of knowledge against which others can compare theirs—was restricted until the early 1980s to university-based research reports presented at academic seminars and to such publications as *Public Relations Review*.

Lloyd Kirban, international director of research at Burson-Marsteller, broke ground in the sharing of proprietary information when he held a series of workshops in 1982 and 1983 at national and regional professional development meetings.[2] He went beyond discussing general parameters of the experimental research to cite specific clients, media and situations and even furnish statistical data. Moreover, he revealed findings that contradicted some traditionally accepted counseling and media relations practices in the industry, those of his own firm included.

Monitoring Influences on Consumer Behavior

In 1985, Kirban disclosed that Burson-Marsteller and client Searle Pharmaceuticals applied to public relations a first-of-its-kind combination of sophisticated technologies derived from cable television and checkout-stand computerized optical scanning of purchases. This experimental research was used to monitor consumer behavior in test markets for the Nutra-Sweet Equal brand sugar substitute.[3]

This approach was significant in closing the sophistication gap between public relations firms and the advertising industry. The implications of this may be best understood after one has reviewed the state of the art in years preceding the introduction of Equal.

Backdrop: Pretest/Posttest; Experimental Group/Control Group Advances
At the beginning of the decade, leading counseling firms were starting to move into the well-charted depths of behavioral science by using pretest/posttest and experimental group/control group research methodology to measure effectiveness of client actions, communications and campaigns. Here's how and why this kind of testing works:

1. *Researchers select two identical groups*: Two identical groups of persons are scientifically selected as representative of important publics for a given campaign.

2. *Pretests administered*: Both groups are given two sets of identical tests before they are exposed to communication or action that is being investigated. This allows researchers to determine their "baseline" or "benchmark" level knowledge or feelings about a product before anyone sees or hears the public relations message.

3. *Experimental group exposed to message*: Then one group—designated as "experimental" because the experiment is aimed at changing their level of awareness, attitudes or behavior—is subjected to what researchers call "the treatment," which is exposure to part or all of a public relations campaign.

4. *Control group is isolated from message*: The other group—designated as "control" because controls are exercised to assure that it is isolated from the experimental treatment—is not exposed but just observed in comparison to the experimental group.

5. *Posttest given to both groups*: At the end of the treatment for the experimental group and lapse of the same time for the control group, both are given another evaluation, called the posttest.

6. *Comparison of results tests public relations effect*: The pretest and posttest results for both groups yield data to help counselors determine if there is a statistically significant difference between the experimental group and the unexposed control group.

7. *Control group used to exclude extraneous variables*: The comparison of pretest and posttest results within the control group enables researchers to rule out changes within a public due to what social scientists call "extraneous variables." (A public's attitude may change with time or as a result of social trends. Even the act of asking questions in the test procedures can shape opinion.) Researchers would have to rule out the public relations treatment as the cause if similar changes were to occur in the answers of experimental and control groups between pretest and posttest.

8. *Allows check before committing resources*: This allows a campaign to be scrutinized through a relatively low-cost, low-threat research mode before resources are committed to a full-scale program.

9. *Helps alert counselors to need for changes*: It also gives counselors a chance to modify or replace elements of a campaign that are shown to have relatively little impact or low cost-efficiency.

10. *Similar to test marketing*: Similar to test marketing of a new product before national roll-out, much of counselors' use of such research takes place in the natural environment of the field rather than in the artificial constraints of a laboratory. But rigorous rules for observation and controls assure reliability and validity of data that guides go/no go decisions or modifications in a campaign.

Burson-Marsteller researchers in the early 1980s had refined such research in more than two dozen studies, including the following three cases in which they measured impact of:

Placement of a four-page pictorial article in *Ladies' Home Journal* for increasing brand awareness of Celanese's Arnel and Fortrel fabrics used in fashions for businesswomen.

Preparing a mechanic as a television spokesperson for dealing with specific message points to position Fram Corp. as a company whose products help lower driving costs and lengthen automotive life.

Introducing Knox Gelatin as a nutritious plant food in the Canadian provinces, with treatments ranging from no promotion in some provinces, through print publicity in others and a media tour of a home-gardening expert in two provinces, to a full campaign of direct mail, print and broadcast publicity and a media tour in one province.[4]

In the Celanese and Fram cases, telephone surveys were done for pretest measurements just before the *Ladies' Home Journal* article appeared. Pretesting also was done before the first talk show interview in the Seattle-Tacoma test market. Surveys were repeated a week after publication and within 36 hours after the talk show.

In the case of Knox Gelatin, no pretest was performed, but comparative posttest data were collected to compare the various treatments against the no-promotion control group provinces.

By measuring impact, it is possible to diagnose reasons behind a program's effectiveness; in this manner, one can increase an understanding of what works, what does not and why and, moreover, produce better cost effectiveness comparisons among programs and program elements. Preliminary research findings led to the following three conclusions:

Success of a program cannot be measured in all or nothing terms: Some messages register on target audiences; others do not. Only some things companies want to say may be of audience interest.

A national campaign has to compete with a lot of related and unrelated communications that bombard the target audience. Other communications, or general noise in the system, may mask impact.

"Recognition is growing that location-by-location evaluation, rather than broad scale, may be more legitimate."

Although in 1984 it was enough for communications-based criteria to be used to measure impact on target audiences in terms of awareness, knowledge, attitude and propensity to take action, Kirban warned that in the future, mere change may not be enough because client executives "will eventually want to know *how much* change they can expect as a result of a public relations program."

Beyond Conventional Pretest/Posttest to Point-of-Sale Measurement   A year later, Kirban was able to talk about the arrival of a future in which he and his group could do an almost instantaneous measurement of consumer response to communications in terms of such specific behavior as buying the product.[5]

In its research to introduce Equal, Burson-Marsteller moved into more sophisticated modes than the traditional pretest/posttest measurement.

For the first time, a counseling firm used (and shared with competitors information on) point-of-sale behavior scanning to assess its program:

1. *Optical scanner technology used at checkstand*: Researchers adapted capabilities of optical scanners of the kind that supermarket, drugstore and other sales checkers use at checkout stands to translate UPC symbols on packages into data to record sales, check inventory, order goods and give customers itemized printouts of their purchases.

2. *Split cable TV signals used to send different messages*: At the same time, they took advantage of a technology that allows two different messages to be transmitted to identical groups of television viewers in the same area via split cable. To introduce Equal, counselors wanted to test the effectiveness of televised public relations messages before the national roll-out.

3. *Two test markets each got two sets of messages*: Marion, Ind., and Pittsfield, Mass., were selected as test markets for behavior scanning. Pittsfield and Marion provided cable television capabilities that enabled researchers to split each market in half and broadcast one set of messages to half the households and another set of announcements to the other half.

4. *Controlled exposure to track influence on sales*: "You put something on TV and see what it does in the market and then take it off and put something else on," Kirban said. "This permits you to control exposure to message and relate it in terms of sales."

5. *Followed impact of TV messages as sales rung up*: Both towns had stores with optical-scanning equipment that enabled researchers to follow product movement off supermarket shelves after exposure of consumers to the split-market messages.

6. *Immediacy reduced risks of interference*: Computerized optical scanning at checkout stands is accurate and almost immediate. That immediacy is important not so much in the speeding of data to research analysts as in monitoring changes in behavior with minimal risk of interference by other variables.

7. *Controlled for "maturation effect"*: Researchers have found that the time lag between experimental communication exposure and measurement of attitudes or behavior allows results to be distorted as test publics are exposed to uncontrolled communication or other unintended influences. ·

They can control for this "maturation effect" in laboratory settings, but real-world conditions as found in a natural, field environment may produce quite different results. Researchers can build in immediacy in behavior measurement in stores after exposure to messages at home. This enables counselors to harvest the combined advantages of laboratory and field research approaches without sacrifices that either, by itself, normally entails.

8. *Allows communication tools to be checked for interactive effects*: Traditional studies tended to prohibit measurement of benefits of using one communication activity in interaction with others. But checkstand optical scanning to measure behavior enables counselors to manipulate variables and determine the best mix of communication tools. Research can now tie in-store promotions to other communication activities, such as public relations or advertising, to look for synergistic effects.

9. *Added dividend—can study impact of pricing, packaging*: Similarly, optical scanning now enables researchers to study consumer behavioral responses to different pricing strategies and packaging approaches where they actually shop rather than in the artificial environment of the laboratory. Optical scanning, however, is not limited to monitoring behavior at the checkstand.

10. *Zip code tracking could guide strategies*: Kirban said it is feasible to develop research designs that use optical scans of postal zip codes of persons who write companies for information or who otherwise respond to a public relations event, article or direct mail. Tracking of such queries or responses by zip code could provide controlled tests to measure different strategies in postal zones.

He predicted that client companies will require systems to track inquiries and requests as well as sales—triggered by target publics' responses to particular strategies.[6]

Beyond Kirban's projections, counselors may see a number of potentially rich applications of new technological and research advances, such as the gathering of data on program effectiveness, that could broaden the study of what people actually do, not what they think they would do.

From "Gentle Survey" to "Highly Pragmatic Problem Solving"   In 1985, as another sign of the counseling industry trend to applied studies of behavior of publics, Hill and Knowlton disclosed that its research subsidiary would change the emphasis of its research from "gentle survey" to "highly pragmatic problem solving."[7] Part of that change consisted of renaming Hill and Knowlton's Group Attitudes Corp. to Strategic Information Research Corp. Also significant was the appointment of Michael Rowan, whose background in "highly behavioral political research" fit the new direction, as president of the subsidiary. "The name says what we're out to do—affect decision-making and problem solving at the highest levels for our clients. We want to deal with strategic research questions," Rowan said.[8]

As does Burson-Marsteller's Kirban, Hill and Knowlton's Rowan looks to research design and follow-through to provide objective data and reliable interpretations in support of counselors and clients and the bottom line. To Rowan, this means research that "helps clients make decisions—

strategic decisions, policy decisions, new product decisions—and not merely confirm opinions."[9]

The difference between gentle survey research and highly pragmatic problem solving is typified by the contrast between polls to find out who remembers a commercial and surveys to determine the best arguments to use in thwarting a corporate takeover.

Case in Point: The Power of a Single Word A single word, let alone a words-and-arguments combination, may affect behavior in profound ways, as Carl Byoir & Associates found several years earlier. Research done for the Road Information Program concerned the client's generic identification and resulted in a change from its "highway construction industry" designation to "the roadbuilding industry" in its own promotional materials.[10]

The research started with field surveys to determine the effects of word choice in news releases. A massive difference was found between what newspaper editors and others thought about the "road" business and the "highway" business. One source said that:

> In the minds of many, a "highway" is a hot, gleaming mass of pavement that pushes its way through a neighborhood or farm, upsetting life styles, spoiling the environment in many ways, causing lawsuits by the dozen and generally turning everything, including backyards and parks, from green to black. On the other hand, a 'road' is as noble as the day is long. It winds through the countryside, past churches and old willow trees, leading the way to the beach, the store, perhaps to grandmother's house.

Beyond the power of words or arguments lie intricate, complex interactions of varying degrees of reason and emotion related to the amount of involvement individuals feel in making a decision to buy a product, invest in a corporation or retain a public relations firm.

Advertising Agency Research and Planning Tool Adapted Byoir used a combination research and planning tool developed by its advertising parent to plot the location of client products and services on a matrix. The Byoir/ Foote, Cone and Belding instrument, the Vaughn Grid, positioned products on a grid against two dimensions, the degree of involvement a potential consumer has with a particular item or service and the relative rational or emotional nature of that involvement. Components of such a grid help the counselor position issues based on how much information segmented publics have about the issue and whether—and to what degree—they feel it affects them personally.

Client executives were told that the grid is based on substantial research about how decisions are made by potential consumers. "If few people know about an issue, the primary mission of counselors and client is to move that position through dissemination of information. If many know about the issue, but don't care much one way or the other, we will mainly increase their sense of personal involvement."[11]

The Vaughn Grid has been used to plot more than 300 products and services, such as those illustrated in the following figure:[12]

VAUGHN GRID

	RATIONAL (THINK)	EMOTIONAL (FEEL)
HIGH INVOLVEMENT	★ Money Market Fund	Tourism Attraction ★
LOW INVOLVEMENT	Disposable Pen ★	★ American Beer

In this example, the Vaughn Grid helped counselors determine that:

1. Purchase of a money market fund is a rational investment by highly involved buyers.
2. Decision to buy American beer positions the typical consumer somewhat on the emotional side of the spectrum, with a moderately low sense of involvement.
3. Clients who wish to attract tourists need a campaign oriented to a highly emotional decision by individuals with a high degree of involvement.
4. Campaign communication for disposable pens is best targeted to pub-

lics who approach such decisions with very low involvement and rational thinking.

But the grid was designed to do more when guiding decisions about how members of segmented publics evaluate products, investments or whatever element concerns a client. The grid calls for research, analysis and a positioning of subpublics based on their involvement and rational/emotional behavior; this can then be related to the company itself as well as to the specific product or service under study.[13]

The grid may prove useful in guiding such decisions as choice of media and targeting of publics, but it is not a magic tool for counseling research any more than any other single technique. As a matter of fact, before Byoir was acquired in 1986 by Hill and Knowlton, an internally distributed document reviewed 24 other areas of research in the firm's checklist for its own counselors and researchers.[14]

Interaction of Programs, Information, Attitudes, Behavior (PIAB) The research tools may be diverse, but the key concept at Manning, Selvage & Lee, as at many other firms, centers on the observable, measurable behavior: "We're hired to be applied behavioral scientists, not to get people to love our client organizations," according to Lloyd N. Newman, executive vice president.[15]

He stressed it is necessary to design and begin the evaluation process before a public relations program is implemented. In the P-I-A-B schemata for developing persuasive programs for results, the *B*—as in behavior—comes last; but it also comes first.

"We start at the behavior end of the spectrum." Behavior is influenced by attitudes (the *A* in P-I-A-B). Newman said that information (the *I* in P-I-A-B) influences attitudes, but he noted that information flows from three sources—"us, competitors and the environment." Programs—"ours and the competitors' "—(the *P* in P-I-A-B) influence the information. Although programs would seem to drive the process, the study of measurable behavior precedes program development, as does the measurement of attitudes. Monitoring the observable behavior helps counselor and client determine what targeted individuals "will do, not do and let us do."

Following factual research (such as investigating records), and as part of a system of studies, Newman said the firm engages in what he termed "moccasin research." This was defined as "walking around" to check the facts. It includes double-checking everything the opposition says as well as what may be accepted as "facts" by others.

As an example of moccasin research, he recalled the incongruous situation in which a company was charged by neighbors with spewing out nocturnal air pollutants—even though the client claimed to close down operations at night. "We had people positioned in cars in the neighborhood at night. They did smell a stink and tracked it as coming from plants—not the client's—downwind from them."

But facts backed up by moccasin research and mated with findings of attitudinal studies, concept and message testing, and believability may not win the day. "People can take all the rational reasons and play them back, even knowing the information better than we do," and yet be motivated by emotions. So together with the research and analysis of rational behavior go studies of emotional appeals. And, yet, "if you motivate with emotional appeals, people will begin to feel manipulated." In a sense, individuals say: "You must give me a rational reason for doing what you have made me emotionally want to do."

Rational and emotional grounds for behavior tend to be reinforced, if not stimulated, by persons most counselors would term opinion leaders. Newman prefers the term "mavens," defined by dictionaries as persons who are trusted by certain other individuals as experts in everyday matters or in special areas. The challenge is to find out who they are for a targeted public on a particular subject.

One way to identify mavens—or opinion leaders—is through a study of networking. But the time-honored and relatively primitive modes of charting networks, and the limited utility of network analysis in the recent past, are yielding to a revolution in research flowing from academe and think tanks and about to spill over into counseling.

NETWORK ANALYSIS

Sophisticated Tool Ready for Counseling Firms

Researchers Give New Meaning, Value to Study of Networks The state of the art in experimental network analysis methodology in 1986 had reached the point that it would soon be adopted for counseling on improving organizational structure and strengthening external and internal communication systems.

To many counselors, the term *network analysis* has meant informal evaluation of social and professional relationships to learn of job opportunities or to exchange information. To some university-based researchers, however, network analysis has become an exact science that measures and interprets the group patterns of communication relationships within and among organizations.[16]

The ability to identify and verify group membership by tracing communication behavior among individuals has powerful implications in targeting external or internal publics. This goes beyond diagnostic benefits accrued from merely grouping people according to values shared, norms, mores and attitudes. It extends to an examination of the frequency, topics, amount and kinds of contacts made in communication among group members.

Applications of network analysis to corporations and government agencies has found significant differences between what top management *thought* existed—and had institutionalized in organization charts—and what the *actual* relationships are among departments, executives, supervisorial personnel and other employees. Network analysis may employ such means as auditlike interviewing, systematic observation, appointment books, conversations log-keeping, telephone billing records, monitoring electronic mail and tracking computer modem traffic for on-line "conversations."

How Network Analysis Works

Kinds of Business Networks   A *network* is best understood as the pattern of communication linkages found—and verified to exist—within an organization. Researchers have found that within the same company or even division, a number of different networks of communication relationships exist, such as:

1. *Production networks*: communication related to doing work.
2. *Innovation networks*: relationships that can be traced and charted for communications among managerial and other personnel in developing new products and services or in coming up with better ideas.
3. *Crisis networks*: linkages within and among departments and individuals in responding to crises and emergent situations.
4. *Maintenance networks*: typified by social, non-work-related conversations, but "maintenance" in the sense that even a simple exchange of greetings may help keep the channels of communication open for production, innovation or crisis communication.

Although these are examples of networks found within businesses, studies could look at larger networks extending beyond an organization to involve vendors, prime contractors, sub-contractors, competitors, government agencies, media and stakeholder publics.

Conditions That Define a Network   Researchers have identified four conditions as particularly important in defining and interpreting network relationships:

1. *Frequency of communication among individuals*: It's up to the organization's executives and researchers to determine whether certain relationships are defined by contacts at least quarterly, monthly, weekly, daily or more frequently.

2. *Specifications of what constitutes communication*: Depending upon the type of network investigated or the client's particular needs, somebody must write clear, unequivocal definitions of what should be counted as certain kinds of communication.

3. *Resolving question of what is a group*: Researchers Richard Farace, Peter R. Monge and Hamish M. Russell said that network units are defined by their communication. All members of a group must have some minimum portion of their total communication with the others, such as more than half. Those with less, but still some substantial contact, may be considered multiple-group members.[17]

4. *Rigorous procedures*: The modes of tracing patterns and analyzing the message content or kind of communication to be studied require systematic procedures that are rigorously followed.

5. *Verification*: In the use of interview data, researchers check for reciprocity—what one individual said about frequency or content of communication is verified by data collected from other individuals involved. Social scientists have formulas for taking into consideration the ability of people to remember contacts.

Isolates Revealed in Network Analysis Charting patterns often reveals individuals, sometimes as high as the CEO, who cut themselves off—or are cut off by others—from much of the communications involved in production, innovation, crisis or other types of networks. Such individuals are called "isolates," even if isolation is not an absolute but a matter of degree. Sometimes communication flows between two or more individuals who, for all intents and purposes, are isolated from vital parts of a network.

Public relations counselors, even those serving *Fortune* 500 companies and the White House, have discovered isolates—frequently after a great deal of damage has been done—among key managerial personnel or others down to the level of supervisors in positions central to problem solving.

Similarly, teams, groups and whole divisions within an organization have been found to be isolated from processes involving problem identification, development of objectives, priorities and problem-solving activities.

Isolates can be counseled, given necessary training and brought more into the picture through reorganization or specially designed communication efforts. Evaluation can be programmed of communication strategies and campaigns can be monitored for early alerts to isolate-related breakdowns. Another value of network analysis to the counselor lies in its potential in public relations audits, where it may be incorporated in the interviewing, surveying and data analysis processes.

Bridges and Liaisons Provide Potent Links Bridges and liaisons provide potent linkages for public relations counselors and client executives to capitalize upon. The distinction between bridges and liaisons is an important one. Although at first glance the terms may appear as the jargon of researchers, the meanings become clear quickly when one commissions a network analysis. Because research reports use such language as "bridge" and "liaison," it is useful to know the difference.

A *bridge* has been defined as a member of a communications group who also has one or more links with members in other groups in the network. A *liaison* has links with two or more communications groups but is an individual who is *not* a member of any of them. (A typical criterion for "membership" is that each person within a "group" have at least 50 percent of communication with other members.)

There is greater likelihood that distortion in the communication flow throughout an organization will occur when linkages for a set of groups are provided largely by bridges rather than liaisons. In a bridge-linked network, a message introduced into the network must pass through each group and travel on to the next one. In a liaison-linked network, the message originates from the same source—the liaison—and there is less chance that details will be dropped out, added or modified.[18]

In the complex spheres of public relations client organizations, bridges and liaisons may be at work simultaneously. Yet the intelligence gleaned from researchers on the linkage roles can be used to advantage in helping structure a client for more efficient and effective communications mechanisms and strategies.

New Trends in Network Analysis

External communication focuses of network analysis were new in the mid-1980s. Equally new and particularly significant for counseling firms were the mid-decade breakthroughs in switching from especially laborious hand processing of data to computer programs now available at major universities.

An upsurge of research and development examining such phenomena as interlocking corporate directorates, interdependent health care delivery systems and community development projects was reported by researchers Monge and Miller.[19]

Networks of Public Relations Firms and Fortune 100 Clients Explored   Actually, public relations firms and their *Fortune* 100 clients already had been placed under the research microscope to measure the relation of interorganizational networks to coverage in the *Wall Street Journal*, *New York Times* and 295 trade and professional publications. Moreover, the network analysis focused on how corporations linked by use of the same public relations firms fared in the value of their common stock over a five-year period.

In 1986, three university-based researchers disclosed research findings with major implications for public relations counseling that go far beyond supporting their hypotheses. The following highlights were extracted from the research findings of James A. Danowski, George A. Barnett and Matthew Friedland:[20]

To determine the network relationships of corporations contracting with the same public relations firms, the researchers consulted *O'Dwyer's Directory of Public Relations Firms*. They learned that corporations most linked with other *Fortune* 100 companies by using the same public relations firms had certain common characteristics and shared several benefits:

1. They had more diversified product/service areas.
2. These corporations were more diversified in numbers of organizational units such as divisions, subsidiaries, member firms and other *Corporate Affiliations Directory* listings.
3. The *Wall Street Journal* and *New York Times* not only carried more stories about them, but also devoted more depth to the coverage given over the course of a year.
4. Although to a lesser degree than the *Journal* and *Times*, the 295 publications listed in the *Business Periodicals Index* data base provided more media coverage for these clients.

Danowski and his colleagues concluded that as companies share more of the same service firms—which might extend beyond public relations to accounting, legal, advertising and others—their organizations become similar. To the extent that individual counseling firms have their own style of doing business, clients are more alike in the kinds of public relations activities they implement. But it was the questions the research subsequently raised that offer the greatest implications to the counseling industry:

Do clients with the most in common with other *Fortune* 100 corporations select public relations firms that help maintain their high degree of centrality within a particular network?

Or is it possible that, if a company toward the periphery of the *Fortune* 100 network retains the same public relations firms used by more central organizations, it will become more successful with the media and gain a better image in the stock market?

May there be an indirect causal flow from public relations activities that directly communicate with publics instead of through mass media? "Do media practitioners detect this increased salience to publics' interests and—due to circulation, profit and prestige motives—decide to cover the organizations more?"

What is the potential for extending future research to directly obtain audience image data with use of readily available information from directories, indices and financial records? Understanding what it is and how it works becomes second-nature to those who work with this research, including one of America's largest financial institutions and parts of the federal government.

What useful findings could flow from future interorganizational research to examine retention of other service firms, such as advertising, accounting and legal, and what could be learned about how public relations firm-based networks compare?

How useful would it be to analyze merger and acquisition phenomena with methods such as those used in the 1985-1986 research? When a more peripheral corporation is acquired or merged, does it benefit from the media coverage and image profile of the more centrally networked company?

Would continued studies help convince media and other communications researchers to rid themselves of their "blind spot on the key role that public relations firms play in organizations' linkage through the media to their publics?"[21]

Way Paved for Counselors to Apply Research   Utility of network analysis in public relations counseling should be expected to increase geometrically with the application of computer tools, new formulas for collecting and interpreting data and new concepts for measuring and evaluating the functions of networks and their components.

The leap from a focus on internal organization to an exploration of clients' external linkages opens up network analysis to even broader application, including diagnosis of communication policy needs and trend analysis. Researchers look to a better understanding of communication flow "to make it possible to improve the organization's policies for communication distribution and collection" and provide the basis for routine monitoring of the networks for early detection of changes or trends.[22]

Subsequent research found that new developments in network analysis "would appear to forecast a steep growth curve in the amount of substantive knowledge to be accumulated about the emergence, stabilization and dissolution of networks, and about the psychological, sociological and other factors associated with these processes."[23]

It is in the applied research of psychological, sociological and other factors associated with processes in individual and group decision-making and behaviors that public relations counseling firms began to establish a beachhead in the 1980s.

PSYCHOGRAPHICS

Research Rises to New Level With Application of VALS

In the mid-1980s, Ketchum Public Relations, Hill and Knowlton and Burson-Marsteller began to share intelligence with other counselors on how they capitalized upon computer-aided research that measures the psychographics of segmented publics. This research hones communication for maximum impact on the behavior of individuals and narrowly defined groups by incorporating data on their lifestyles.

The term *psychographics* may be defined as research that develops a psychological portrait of individuals and helps counselors and their clients understand more about how people may think and respond.[24] Psychographics goes back to post–World War II years, but improved research and an increased understanding of its applicability to counseling has contributed to a new surge of popularity. This was evidenced in 1985 when the *Public Relations Journal* called it "the newest wrinkle" in public relations research: "There's no doubt that the language of lifestyles research is going to be an increasingly important part of the public relations vocabulary in years to come."[25]

Values, attitudes, opinions and needs all play an important role in counseling research. It is important to understand how they relate to each other:[26]

1. Values often are held unconsciously. They're underlying beliefs most people learn in childhood, such as deference to superiors, belief in fairness and the work ethic. Values are slow to change.
2. Attitudes often arise out of fundamental values, such as "the poor should not be allowed to freeze." They change only slightly more quickly than values.
3. Opinions are statements about specific issues. They can be volatile as media, speakers and groups change the focus on issues.
4. Needs, real or perceived wants and desires of varying urgency, can be used as the basis of marketing and issues programs.

Psychographics seemed to blossom as a counseling tool with the development of VALS—the acronym for *Values and Lifestyles*—by the university-affiliated Stanford Research Institute and come to full flower with a refinement of that research methodology and its application by the SRI International think tank. VALS has been called "a classic model" and "whole new dimension" for research directors in an *Atlantic Monthly* cover story.[27]

Basically, VALS divides Americans into nine types, clustered in four major psychological groups, each with its own specific lifestyle and each with varying degrees of compliance with the criteria for the group. In an era of fluidity, however, the system takes into account that individuals move from one group to another. The four major VALS groups consist of:

✓ **1.** *Inner directed*: This is the only group expected to grow through the mid-1990s. Within this group are the societally conscious, those who tend to be experiential and others who focus inwardly in an "I-am-me" psychological orientation. The societally conscious, as one example, tend to have strong attitudes on environmental issues and personal health, vote to a far greater degree than members of other groups and represent a higher degree of activism in politics.

 2. *Outer directed*: These outer directed individuals tend to be subclassified as belongers, achievers and emulators. Belongers have ranked as the largest segment of American adults—sentimental, stable, traditional. Achievers respond to certain messages supportive of the current socioeconomic system and tend to be prosperous, middle-aged and materialistic. Young adults trying to break into the achiever level have been identified as emulators.

 3. *Need-driven*: This group includes persons categorized as survivors and sustainers. Sustainers have problems matching income with expenses and have less education. They tend to be younger. Some are members of minorities. Survivors tend to be old with little hope, income and education.

 4. *Integrated*: This fourth classification combines those who are inner and outer directed.[28]

VALS Model Applied to Public Affairs Counsel Industry dialogue on strategies of applying VALS to counseling opened when Ketchum Public Relations Chairman Paul H. Alvarez went public with briefings to other public relations practitioners at invitational seminars.[29] Ketchum proposed to clients that "VALS is rooted in a disarmingly simple concept—Americans' values sooner or later influence public policy."[30]

But it goes further than traditional public opinion research by telling the public affairs professional how different segments of the population with group-specific lifestyles think and feel about issues. As a public affairs counseling tool, VALS can raise important questions, such as: What psychological and informational components should be included in messages for different groups; which groups are more likely to be affected by client actions and communications, and thus where priorities might be attached; and which media would be more effective with given publics segmented by values and lifestyles.

According to John L. Paluszek, head of Ketchum's public affairs division, "VALS and similar approaches help counselors pretest messages in a communications program, test how key groups feel about new issues important to a client, and track societal attitudes on important issues, new and old."[31]

Counseling firms, including Ketchum, use the VALS research model to weave demographics, attitudes, issues, activities, consumption patterns and media patterns into fabrics characteristic of adults with a varied combination of lifestyles and values. By subscribing to SRI's VALS service, counseling firms automatically get results of annual questionnaires aimed at several thousand consumers so they can analyze for clients how they change from year to year.

Paluszek said a counselor can use VALS data analysis to convince a client CEO that to reach certain publics a byline article in *Audubon Magazine* would be better than one in a newsmagazine. Counseling firms commission tailored research for particular clients. "But very few public relations firms are tapping into VALS in the public issues area," he said.[32]

There is value in combining VALS with other research methodologies. Public opinion surveys, for instance, can be made more useful by breaking down the results by lifestyle groupings from VALS data as well as by traditional demographic categories. VALS techniques may help a counselor select media that "achievers" and "societally conscious" groups are likely to use. It also can work well in combination with focus groups or surveys in pretesting messages and policies.[33]

Use of VALS to Target Consumers, Open Markets Impresses Clients Psychographics research also may prove impressive to executives considering what it can do to help open up new markets. As a case in point, before a presentation to the United Dairy Industry Association, Hill and Knowlton President Robert L. Dilenschneider and his colleagues used VALS to help answer the question: "How are we going to specifically target the 70 percent of America SRI identifies as not consuming enough dairy products, but that are persuadable so we can pinpoint your marketing efforts?"[34]

He used VALS techniques to arrive at the "powerful force" of the persuadable 70 percent of the population:

"One group, the Emulators, represent about 10 percent of the population. They're in their 20s, they have reasonably good jobs, they've had some technical training or a year or two at college—and they're still open to the influence of role models. But their role models are not perceived as milk drinkers. That can be changed.

"Another persuadable group includes the Achievers, representing nearly 20 percent of the population. They're upscale, well-educated, tend to be in middle-management. They're potential milk drinkers.

"The Belongers make up roughly 40 percent. Most are past 40, they have a problem of getting the protein they need, and the women in this group are now finding they're not getting the calcium they require. This group should be a prime target of your promotional effort."[35]

VALS Contributes to Marketing in Low Consumption Periods Public relations firms have found the VALS breakout approach useful in support of
other types of marketing campaigns. For example, Burson-Marsteller used
VALS for tailoring strategies to persuade certain types of individuals to eat
turkey during low-consumption periods before Thanksgiving and after
Christmas.

As reported in *Public Relations Journal,* "research indicated that Sustainers and Survivors, the need-driven folks, ate at erratic hours; con-
sumed inexpensive starchy foods, often in front of the TV set; seldom ate
out or entertained; and often bought in bulk. . . . For the need-driven,
Burson-Marsteller emphasized bargain cuts that could be stretched into a
full meal."[36]

Persons in the VALS Belongers typology were found to "make something
of a ritual of eating" with "all family members required to be on hand at
the same time every day, foods served in traditional ways." The message to
Belongers appealed to symbolism of dining on turkey and focused on cuts
that "signaled turkey," such as drumsticks.

"Achievers were more innovative, more willing to try out new foods.
They ate out frequently at a variety of restaurants." Burson-Marsteller
counseled emphasis on use of gourmet cuts in new recipes in publications
such as *Gourmet* and *Food and Wine.*

Not a Panacea, Only a Tool for Selective Application VALS has proven
itself to be a useful tool when applied selectively in public relations research. But it is no panacea. Indeed, it sometimes has been criticized by
some counselors who find the specific VALS categories to be far too limited.

Burson-Marsteller's research director has cautioned account teams to
"use VALS with care—don't design your program as if there were really
people out there who have exactly the characteristics of a given VALS
type. These types are really just composites, averages. Psychographic segmentations tend to be so generalized that sometimes they don't have
direct applicability to specifics of the problem at hand or explain behavior
we're trying to have an impact on."[37]

Atlantic Monthly reported that SRI has sought to strengthen the value
of VALS by including in its services detailed quantification of VALS types
in terms of demographics, attitudes, regional distribution, household in-
ventories, activities, media habits and consumption patterns for over 700
categories; access to VALS on-line computerized data bases; and even systems tailored to specific client interests for classifying people into VALS
categories relevant to a firm's special interests, such as a geo-demographic
breakout by the postal zip codes in which consumers live.[38]

The combination of demographics with values and lifestyles data has
been found of value by both advertising agencies and public relations

firms. But even with this enhancement, VALS and simila
research methodologies represent only part of the mix (
selecting media, targeting segmented publics and designir
messages.

MEDIA MEASUREMENT

Increasingly, counseling firms go beyond just giving clients traditional reports on the quantity of exposure in media campaigns. The demand for more sophisticated systems for monitoring and analyzing media coverage comes from counselors seeking better intelligence for planning and reviewing communications.

The demand also comes from client executives dissatisfied with mere numbers of audience exposure and clipping albums, videotapes of television coverage and simple tabulations of coverage listing media names, audience research and space or time allotted.

Client demand has reached the point that a "measurable return on communications investments is the hue and cry from the board room," according to James B. Strenski, chairman of Chicago-based Public Communications Inc. This requires benchmark studies and analyses by message, medium, audience and frequency. "These techniques provide the basis for value equivalency comparison that can relate quality as well as quantity of exposure to the bottom line."[39]

Tool for Planning Media Relations as Well as Evaluation

One computer-assisted publicity tracking model was cited in one book for opening a new era of campaign evaluation in terms of the amount of target audience exposure received *and* the degree to which planned messages are delivered to target audiences:[40] "Because the Ketchum Publicity Tracking Model requires program performance objectives stated and agreed to by the client in advance of a media campaign, the Tracking Model is as much a tool for planning media relations and publicity programs as it is for evaluating their effectiveness," Alvarez said.[41]

The Ketchum model was credited for helping define the results that a cost-effective publicity campaign should achieve and reporting on how well the actual performance met client objectives.

Media Tracking and Communications Impact Assessment Combined
Media tracking can profitably be combined with other research tools such as with the assessment of impact of coverage on targeted publics. For example, Ruder Finn & Rotman reported that its research division "had designed procedures in the fields of media tracking and communications

impact assessment that hold greater promise as future approaches to quantification."[42]

Media tracking at RF&R not only provided a content analysis of editorial coverage with a rating system based on such factors as communications objectives, frequency and quantity of coverage; positioning of articles and broadcasts; and the number of client mentions but also the relative value of specific media placements in relation to a company's key publics. The complementary communications impact assessment research was designed "to provide quantitative and qualitative reports on how communications are received by specific audiences" and was modeled "on the kind of testing used in planning and evaluating major advertising campaigns."

Media Coverage Data Combined with Interview Research   At Carl Byoir & Associates, researchers measured and analyzed media coverage of the client and its competitors in relation to client objectives and attitudinal data derived from interviews and other research. Such a combined approach provided useful input for Byoir's marketing plan for Glaxo pharmaceutical products.[43]

Byoir's research staff studied journals influential with physicians to measure the amount of coverage given to drug companies in each of the publications. The firm then analyzed the message points and the image conveyed in each of the articles about Glaxo and its competitors. Preset criteria were employed as the research staff measured how many times each company was mentioned; if the coverage was positive, negative, or neutral; and what was communicated.

"Glaxo was seen as a well-run, good marketing company, but essentially, a one-product company. Some companies in Glaxo's field had stories about weakness of management," the Byoir research director said. The focus of research included media coverage of the client and competitors in such areas as management, product effectiveness, innovation and cost. But it's not just what's in the media that counts for a client; of more importance is the impact of that coverage on critical publics.

The research staff for one manufacturing association looked at existing public opinion data about the industry, analyzed media content, and then interviewed people from the Pentagon, Congressional aides and editors of special publications. "What turned up was that most people don't pay much attention to defense issues," the research director said.

Public opinion research for a hospital client concluded that it was being mistaken for another hospital with a similar name that was getting much negative media coverage. Researchers were concerned about how strongly negative or positive the stories were and whether mentions of the client and its competitor were casual (somebody had triplets) or substantive (cancer research). The combination of opinion research and media analysis led counselors to recommend a name change despite the costs involved and a loss of identity.

Media Model Gains Power; Issue Tracking Follows With improvements in methodology and years of actual client-funded experience on top of its own investment in publicity tracking research, Ketchum Public Relations, meanwhile, adopted its own combination approach to media analysis and is going beyond its focus on publicity to long-range issue tracking, according to Kay S. Cushing, senior vice president.[44]

The firm blended computer technology, social sciences content analysis and counseling approaches for setting measurable objectives against which to measure media campaign performance.

The proportion of the target audience reached and the size and position of coverage by print or electronic media can be projected and measured, and actually have been in more than 120 markets. Ketchum built a base to guide setting of communication objectives for clients with a diversity of publics, markets and media needs.

Beyond the quantitative measurements, however, the system also provides for qualitative adjustments based on such criteria as the following for publicizing an event:

How effectively was the event identified?

How effectively was the company identified with the event?

How positive was the tone of the placement?

How well were the date and location communicated?

In a fine-tuned, market-by-market campaign, issue tracking can establish standards by calculating expected performance based on previous programs for this and other clients.

Location of an article in certain media components may be a critical factor to plan and track for the client. In handling the Newport Jazz Festival, for instance, it is important that it be covered in the entertainment section because publics reading those pages are the ones to take the action desired by the client.

In another situation, such as Gulf sponsorship of *National Geographic* television specials, issue coverage on the editorial page would be meaningful. Here, tracking would monitor media coverage designed to generate awareness for Gulf and enthusiasm about the specials themselves. In this instance, winding up on the TV page could be secondary to gaining feature coverage in the business section.

But as important as media and their components may be, the primary concern lies in tracking communications to targeted publics. According to Cushing, "the trick is to use the model as a planning tool in determining how good the given media opportunity is in reaching your audience. For instance, if you wish to reach women 18 to 34, you may discount the opportunity to appear on a public service show that runs at 6 A.M. Sunday."

Counselors tend to discourage clients from aiming at certain media merely because they are prestigious. They are more concerned with the particular audience reach of a medium. Tracking gives a firm ability to be very analytical and selective in the planning stage.

When assigning values to message points covered in the media, criteria are established in advance of starting the research and analysis. Criteria to be rated in identification of a client as underwriter of a public service special broadcast could include indicators of significance in measuring enthusiasm of reviewers. Three points could be assigned to mention of a fact. But if coverage went into the long history of the client in sponsoring a series of specials and what they accomplish, that might be scored five or six.

With help of data from more than 120 markets analyzed by Ketchum researchers, counselors can count on more than their own experience in predicting what may be a tough media market in a particular campaign and what may be needed to get points across to a specific public.

Media tracking continues to show signs of increased sophistication. "We have been giving thought to linking the psychographic research of VALS with the evaluation tool of our tracking model," Cushing said. "We could come up with interesting research methodology for getting into the heads of target audiences. This would be useful in projecting how the media would respond to a given problem, corrective action or the communication generated for a client." The state of the art makes it possible to "literally probe through the VALS research the kind of media your targeted public is likely to see."

The media-tracking model has spawned work on a methodology for tracking issues. Well into 1986, Ketchum researchers were working on concepts and techniques for tracking positive and negative points over periods of time. For instance, "the subject of nutrition was a hot subject in the first half of the 1980s but was showing signs of burning itself out at least temporarily."

Cushing predicted that the publicity-tracking model and its offspring "are going to become more and more critical to practitioners in the future because public relations is no longer an inexpensive tool and management is demanding more and more accountability."

The investment in such research also may be considered from the standpoint of the one-time-only opportunities for media coverage. Burson-Marsteller's Kirban said that "we're becoming more concerned with making an appropriate fit between what we want to say and the vehicles needed to reach target audiences."[45]

Since you can only get one exposure in a particular publication for your client's message, how can you get the equivalent of frequency? You start looking at other communications vehicles and opportunities to tie in to point-of-sale merchandising and to direct marketing. The major thrust now is to find ways of reaching a person using a variety of channels, recognizing you're not going to reach him more than once annually on the same subject through the same channel.

With the expense of reliable data, however, go costs of research that adds the polish, effectiveness and accountability of science to the art of communicating through the mass media and other channels. Although bigger firms and bigger clients seem to have more command of resources and commitment to such research, opportunities also exist for smaller organizations.

If budget is a serious concern, it is possible to set up a reliable in-house reporting and analysis system for measuring the effectiveness of publicity efforts "without paying a fortune for a highly sophisticated data base," said the principal of the Washington, D.C.–based A.J. Barr & Co.[46]

Albert J. Barr recommended a plan for building a media data base, developing matrices for recording coverage and monitoring publicity efforts for clients and refining data management to "provide an efficient, low-cost way of tracking our efforts and ensuring that our communication strategies complement those of our clients."

"ClusterPlus" Market Research System

Clients Given Computer-Generated Map of Best Prospects   The counseling industry has progressed to the point that new research methods, technology and concepts enable it to pinpoint and reach publics through alternative media such as videotape.

Hill and Knowlton's Dilenschneider said that in 1986 his firm was proposing to clients that they put videotapes about their products into the homes of those VCR owners who are most likely prospects. "Using tapes in this way, direct markets can have the persuasive power of television," but more efficiently and economically than through conventional broadcasts.[47]

But to do that requires determining who those best prospects are. "Through a market research system called 'ClusterPlus' we can give clients a computer-generated map telling them where their best prospects are—in terms of lifestyle and market behavior—down to the specific block and household."

ClusterPlus was developed by Donnelly Data Systems, aided by Simmons Research Bureau, a subsidiary of the parent advertising agency,

J. Walter Thompson. Hill and Knowlton, in turn, created its Strategic Information Research Corp. (SIRC) subsidiary to market the system.

"The linkage between persuasive TV materials with these highly refined segmentation techniques can be used in many ways. We believe that this form of direct marketing is more effective than advertising and far cheaper. It is more personal than telemarketing and direct mail. We think it will make direct marketing a major force in global business." Among businesses identified as potential users, Dilenschneider listed real estate companies, retail food outlets, movie theaters, malls, public agencies, national brokers, accounting firms, automakers, home improvement product companies and auto repair shops.

Computer Yields Four Billion Bits of Information   The system works with J. Walter Thompson's Simmons data bank, described by SIRC President Rowan as "a brain with four billion bits of information and total instantaneous recall."[48]

The data bank spews out on command information on how consumers relate to products they put in, on or around their bodies. It processes information on a behavioral level about the material and immaterial uses these products have in life, Rowan said.

> It knows how all of them interrelate or associate. It can tell the relationship of families with dozens of pairs of shoes to the heavy or light use of hair curlers. It has the ability to kick out correlations that might occur in life but which you would never imagine if the computer did not tell you it was so.

The data bank contains information on 38,000 U.S. households, showing product buying, brand usage and media habits "as well as lifestyle characteristics and demography in virtually any data configuration," according to a capabilities brochure.[49] Two examples illustrate how the system has been used:[50]

"Outlining the demographics and lifestyles of U.S. purchasers of French Champagne compared to their investment portfolios so that the French Champagne company, unlisted in the U.S., can approach its users here as a potential stock purchasing market."

"Discovering that Americans who use accounting services, beyond tax preparation, tend to read food magazines more than the financial media as one might expect" (done for a presentation to an accounting firm that wanted to go retail).

"PeopleMeters" Focus on Cable, Independents, VCRs

Portable Device Provides More Identification of TV Viewers   A new electronic device for individuals to record television viewing habits—the

"PeopleMeter"—was tested in the Boston market in 1985 by Audits of Great Britain and found to provide a number of advantages over other rating systems.[51]

Marketing and Media Decisions reported that the portable handset provides "better identification of audiences, particularly for cable, independent television channels, VCRs and new distribution channels like satellites and fiber optics, which are shortchanged by existing ratings. Demographic breakdowns can easily be obtained."

Other "PeopleMeter" features include the ability to remind viewers to record shows by flashing periodically, convenience of touch control through numbered buttons, capability to monitor up to four television sets and VCR units in the same residence and track viewership on as many as 32 channels.

Electronic Mail Analyzed for Content, Network Intelligence

Combination of Techniques Yields Implications for Counseling
One powerful new tool for media analysis was emerging from the academic laboratories, where it was first tested on electronic mail traffic, in1986. Like other sophisticated media analysis approaches, this involves a combination of techniques—computer-aided content analysis and network analysis.

Preliminary research was limited to one statewide organization, its heaviest month of electronic mail traffic and the charting of relations among words occurring in a string of messages, according to lead researcher, James A. Danowski.[52]

The procedures developed, however, may be used on messages transferred via conventional channels of communication, such as face-to-face, newspapers and television; and computer-based communications media, such as group conferencing, electronic mail and computer bulletin boards.

The primary goal was to design tools to analyze the message content of computer-mediated communications. This would enable researchers to:

1. Provide a documented record of all communication transactions
2. Capture actual message texts verbatim
3. Detect and remove unread electronic mail
4. Study communication over a specified period of time
5. Represent concepts with a set of words
6. Analyze relationships between words based on their distance from each other in a message

A review of the findings indicates that the methodology could be put to valuable use by research divisions of counseling firms.

Captured Patterns of Communication during a Crisis
Danowski captured these patterns of communication associated with a crisis—concerning

funding, merger and staff position reductions—that was known to have occurred that month:

1. *Evidenced shape of crisis network*: By examining identities of electronic mail users that month with content related to the crisis, the research depicted the shape of the crisis communication structure in the statewide organization.

2. *Change in communication volume*: A significant increase in the amount of communication that correlated with message content related to what managerial personnel perceived as a crisis.

3. *Change in communication length*: Crisis-related pressures may have been related to findings that messages became shorter during that month and returned to normal later.

4. *Groups came together in crisis*: The individual communication networks that existed before the crisis period became less interlocking internally, and one large network formed. More people used electronic mail that month. But the coalescing effect of the crisis did not last, and group structures returned to normal the next month.

5. *Language patterns changed*: If there had been no executive knowledge of a crisis among branches of the organization, at least the language patterns used would have served to alert communications counselors. There was a significant increase in the use of 27 words; used at least 10 times more often were: cooperative, relevant, increase, forced, decision, funds, federal, legislature, function, finance and potential.

A public relations counselor working with the researcher's interpretation of findings and data from more traditional modes of counseling research would now find this intelligence useful. But Danowski said his procedures were relatively primitive compared to the sophistication he expects in the future.

For counselors, as well as scientists, each advance in the theory and research relevant to the business of servicing clients contributes to answering questions concerning public relations research, program development, follow-through and evaluation. Danowski's union of network analysis, content analysis and electronic mail messages stimulated ideas beyond the questions it answered.

Ultimately, rules may be developed for investigating selected strings of words or phrases to accurately summarize ongoing communication behavior among large numbers of people. This could lead to programming of computer software to report on the main social and cultural trends within an electronic mail or computer-conferencing community.

He said the next stages of research development would be aimed at developing message design strategies useful in communication campaigns. "If it is desired that new concepts be introduced into a community, then word-network analysis may show which other words should be linked to the new word to increase its speed and location of integration into the discourse."

SECONDARY RESEARCH

Secondary research—the use of materials that already have been unearthed and have found their way into computer data banks or onto library, archive or office shelves—is a major tool for contemporary public relations counselors.

As indicated in the objectivity chapter, public relations audits normally start with computer and literature searches for such secondary research data as existing survey reports, other published research projects, government documents, client records, historical perspectives and media reports before turning to primary research.

The technology section of the chapter on planning growth focuses on the profitability of applying electronic data bases for mining secondary research information on clients, markets for public relations firms and counseling practices. This section illustrates the utility of secondary research through the prism of a classic case.

The Road Information Program Case

The 15-year campaign that was conducted by Carl Byoir & Associates on behalf of the nation's roadbuilders is an example of the value of public relations programming built on strong secondary research. It used government data about road and bridge conditions as an integral part of the program to build continuing year-after-year support for legislation at both the state and federal levels.[53]

The campaign began in 1971 at the height of anti-highway sentiment. The construction industry had neared completion of one of the greatest building projects in history—the Federal Interstate Highway System. Although much work remained to be done to complete it, and to maintain the country's vast network of roads and bridges, public opinion didn't see things that way.

"Don't pave over America" was a popular slogan then, and the roadbuilders suffered massive public resistance. Cities opted to use highway funds to build subway systems. In rural areas, even the farmers who relied on farm-to-market roads for their livelihood rejected new taxes and bond issues for road repair.

Trying to create a balanced flow of information to the public was a tiny advertising project dubbed The Road Information Program (TRIP). Severely limited in funds, the organization was able to create and place only one or two full-page newsmagazine ads a year. They were lost in a flood of news-paper clippings damning the pavers.

Late in 1972, following nearly a year of discussions between TRIP direc-tors and Byoir, the public relations firm began a campaign that has now become a model in the building of grass-roots support for one side of a major public issue.

In one sense, there seemed to be sufficient facts at hand to form the basis for a program. Although the Interstate system was not yet complete, some of the earliest of these "superroads" already were beginning to crum-ble due to age and heavy use. Only half of the country's roads were paved. Years of neglect had created problems for bridges, and about 150 were collapsing yearly. Muddy and rough rural roads hampered the movement of coal from mines to railheads and damaged produce on the way to market.

But to a public that was tired of hearing about new superhighways, these points sounded only like the plaintive arguments of contractors trying to preserve their market.

"We had to sidestep the constant criticism of the road program and create an entirely new image and sense of public purpose," said Donald S. Knight, the then executive director of the program. "Hammering home the need for more roads wasn't working. Talking about the joys of highway travel wasn't working. We had to do something to appeal to editors and readers who were bored to death with the news about roads."[54]

Byoir's program was based on two important premises: It had to be factual, and the client's interest had to be communicated in terms of the interests of the target audience.

Using Facts for Credibility   Timothy J. Doke, Byoir vice president who supervised the project for three years, said the organization's ability to constantly deliver credible news about road repair needs was the secret to TRIP's solid reputation among editors as a news source:[55]

> It used to be that we plotted day and night to get our stuff in the papers. But after a dozen years of providing bulletproof stories, facts and analysis to the media, it began to work the other way. Eventually, whenever a bridge fell in or a pothole caused an accident, the reporters called for background. TRIP became a major source for the networks and other news organizations because its facts were correct and accu-rately interpreted.

Used Existing Information on Conditions in Each of 50 States   TRIP's work involved studying existing, detailed information about road and bridge conditions in each of the 50 states. The information was obtained in computer printouts directly from the Federal Highway Administration and state transportation agencies.

Periodically, the organization produced studies that summarized its findings and analyzed road needs in the various states; such information was released through the network of Byoir field representatives, who made personal calls to media people in each state.

Doke said the studies were often frightening and almost always sobering. "We were not trying to make friends among the highway departments in each state, and we were not trying to make people feel comfortable about their roads," he said. "We were trying to explain that maintaining a decent road system is very important and very expensive."

TRIP studies explained that road repairs required in a given state simply to maintain current conditions would cost millions—or billions—of dollars. A similar approach was developed for the need for work on bridges.

TRIP's success was based not only on its accurate analysis of the country's road ills, but also on its ability to appeal to the human interests of people at the grass-roots level. "We translated every fact about road and bridge needs into human values," Doke said. "If roads in Iowa needed repair, we talked about food prices in Chicago—and released the story in Chicago. If bridges were restricted or dangerous in Florida or North Carolina, we talked about what that would do to tourist travel."[56]

We build our cases on the fact that most people want to get to work on time, want to pay a low price for their purchases and want to be safe and comfortable while traveling. They want low repair bills and high mileage on their cars, and they want jobs, prosperity and some degree of economic development in their communities. We trade on those specific needs in our materials.

Typical news release leads would say: "If the state were to spend $89 million on road repairs in the next biennium, as now budgeted, it would mean a savings of $1.41 for every mile you drive your car."

The organization was instrumental in developing major public opinion campaigns for such issues as the five-cent gasoline tax for road repair passed by the U.S. Congress in 1983.

Specific Damage and Per-Citizen Cost Data Effective at the Grass Roots   In one example that won a PRSA Silver Anvil award in 1984, TRIP worked in Washington state to alert publics that their roads were wearing out because of a lack of funds.

Before TRIP could launch a program to combat this problem, it needed to know just how decayed Washington's highway network really was. In its review of published information about bridges, TRIP found that 1,855 spans—or 25 percent—were too old or weak for current traffic demands. More than 24,000 miles of primary roads—half the system—were on the brink of wearing out. The added costs to the state's 2.6 million motorists because of these conditions was $640 million a year, or $245 per driver.

These findings led the Byoir group to the following conclusions:

1. The state's roads were wearing out faster than they could be repaired with tax dollars from the 1977 legislation.
2. A new legislative package was needed quickly.
3. The legislature would have to be convinced that a highway problem actually existed and that the people of Washington understood the problem and solidly supported tax increases to solve it.

Data Converted into Understandable Reports   This project was budgeted by local contractors at $45,000 and ran for one year. The plan was to convert TRIP's data into easily understood reports and to capitalize on the importance of the releases by tying their dissemination to political or legislative events.

TRIP released three in-depth reports over a six-month period. Each analyzed a specific aspect of the highway situation, and each was tied to a major event. As an example, the poor condition of Washington's bridges made news around the state at the start of the summer driving season. And just before the November election, TRIP told voters that millions of dollars could be saved if the most important roads were maintained rather than being left to wear out.

The program worked well. Media coverage was extensive and supportive. Lawmakers were well versed on the transportation issue, and legislation was passed to fund repair of the road system through the highest gasoline tax in the nation. As the chairman of a legislative committee wrote TRIP, "There is no substitute for citizen awareness in shaping public policy. When the public understood what was at stake, it was easier for us to act."[57]

The entire operation for both federal and state programs consisted of six professionals, two from TRIP and four from the counseling firm. Two of the Byoir people devoted full time to research, sifting through federal and state publications and other sources for background and writing research reports to make specific points in the various states. Two others worked full time in the field obtaining data, clearing materials with the local highway industry groups and placing studies and stories with the media.

"In many ways it was a formula program, using the same systems year after year to address the same problems," Doke pointed out. "But it's a formula that works like magic."[58] That formula started with secondary research. But not all questions in such campaigns can be answered with existing data. Some require the kinds of primary research previously reviewed, and others lend themselves to focus group treatment.

FOCUS GROUPS—EMERGING STRATEGIES

One of the more powerful areas of research methodology long used by public relations firms for decision-making and testing comes under the heading of "focus groups." But although the tradition of using focus groups is rooted deeply in counseling history, new strategies continue to emerge as firms experiment with methodologies and techniques, such as Burson-Marsteller's new "Prevue" instrument.

"Prevue" Developed as Message-Testing Vehicle

Tape Recordings of Focus Groups Add to Qualitative Research   One of the principal uses of focus groups has been to test the effectiveness of messages with a panel of individuals typical of the most important segmented publics targeted in a campaign. In one of his interviews for this book, Burson-Marsteller's Kirban disclosed details of "Prevue," a new message-testing vehicle under development in the mid-1980s as a special adaptation of focus group research methodology.[59]

Pilot tests of "Prevue" started in 1984, and Burson-Marsteller continued to refine the instrument over the ensuing years. It was in 1985, for the first time, that Kirban's team began an experimental study of tape recordings of oral reactions from individuals representing target audiences to proposed messages, so counselors could get a qualitative feel for the nature of the responses.

The use of tape recordings gives account people an experience "almost like sitting in on individual interviews rather than watching focus groups," Kirban said. But researchers cut the amount of time needed for this kind of observation when they selectively sample and tape the interviews.

Although interviewees respond to questions that can be answered with a paper-and-pencil ballot, "a lot of questions really are open ended," and, unlike some focus group methodology, they are asked in one-on-one interviews. Both account people and researchers are able to listen to verbal responses and pick up insights from nonverbal cues. The tape recordings allow observers to study responses as a whole or to selectively reexamine portions of the interviews.

The main thrust of "Prevue" at its inception was to expose focus group individuals to both rough and finished renditions of client spokesperson interviews to determine what is really communicated to and what is assimilated by an audience.

"Basically, you're exposing a sample of people to either a print or broadcast illustration of what you're going to communicate and getting their reaction. Without a message testing instrument such as 'Prevue,' you can't be sure the kind of things you're saying are what they will take away from the exposure."

But there is more to such testing than just confirming assumptions made in designing particular messages. Pretesting or field testing a communication with any preview testing mechanism gives counselors an opportunity to discover ineffective communication or unintended effects so they can be changed. And even these modifications can be tested before a campaign goes public.

"You're looking for message point recall. The main idea is to learn whether exposure leads to attention, perception or intention change," Kirban said. "And that's not done after a program already has been executed; it's done before."

A "Prevue" testing of one spokesperson communication, for example, found that audience members got so interested in what the client representative was using to introduce the ultimate issue that they became distracted and lost the intended message points. The spokesperson's opening was found to be a barrier rather than a bridge.

Control of Focus Group Research

Why Researchers Play an Intimate Role in Analysis, Interpretation Although a company may delegate quantitative operations to researchers in the field, some public relations firms' own specially trained personnel do everything but recruit participants in qualitative research.

Kirban supported the notion that public relations researchers should play a more intimate role in analysis and interpretation of qualitative research than they do in dealing with numbers. In quantitative research, the handling of data is standardized for field work and data processing. In qualitative studies, the researcher has to be able to extract information that is not freely given. A person may not want to talk about something or may not really know how he feels about it. "The use of that information requires that your firm's own researcher be more involved in the data collection so you don't lose anything in the interpretive process," he said.[60]

Actually, qualitative research serves two basic roles in public relations counseling, much as it does in other professional practices in the behavioral and social sciences. In the first role, qualitative research is used by counseling firms as a step before quantification—such as in identifying hypotheses or in analyzing the appropriateness of certain language to be used in interviews.

In the second role, counseling firms use qualitative methodology to better understand quantitative results. Kirban said qualitative studies are done after statistical data are reported to pursue issues or results that require further understanding.

If there appear to be anomalies (deviations, irregularities or inconsistencies), "we may choose to look at what appears to be anomalous after we're sure the study itself did not have unintentional defects that contributed to bias of the findings."

When to Buy (or Buy into) Research Services from Others Regardless of their in-house research resources, a number of counseling firms draw the line on doing the research themselves—particularly quantitative—that can be purchased from others. Burson-Marsteller's research director explained why:

> We have examined various kinds of research services and found that where there is compelling need for probability (statistically reliable representation) sampling of publics, one of the more useful tools has been the omnibusiness-type survey underwritten by a major research company. This is a syndicated service which you buy into for your particular questions. The survey is administered to a national probability sample and amortized over several different subscribers. That saves costs that would have been incurred if each firm had done its own survey.

Kirban said "the cost is extremely nominal" to obtain data from a national probability sample broken down into demographic characteristics. Some research services even yield overnight reports on surveys done only several hours earlier. "This gives you an inordinate amount of opportunity to collect from large probability samples timely and highly accurate information."[61]

Trendy but Also Powerful Tool in Focusing on Gut Concerns   Although they may seem appealing in terms of cost and ease of administration, focus groups are not always the appropriate tool. For some counseling firms and clients, the nominal costs of buying into a national survey may be beyond their budget. These organizations may need intensive, first-hand study of perceptions and motives of individuals in a small group, even if they sacrifice some scientific reliability of classic large-scale opinion surveys.

As researcher Jan Rogozinski told Byoir personnel, "focus groups are very trendy, but they are not projectable to just any audience." Individual response may not provide a sound basis for predicting group behavior, let alone a large population. And, yet, such research "can be a powerful tool in focusing in on the gut concerns of audiences."[62]

He credited focus groups with accomplishing three useful missions for counseling firms:

1. "They help us get inside the heads of consumers and other audiences— to get people to provide us with unprompted information we might not think of asking for."
2. "They tell us what people mean by the words they use."
3. "They measure the intensity of public needs and concerns—that is, people may prefer brand A to brand B, but do they care very much?"

Models for Understanding Focus Groups

Such research missions, however, can break down unless clients understand and support the purposes and values of different kinds of focus group research. They also can break down unless counseling firms tailor their research to specific target publics in given situations.

Testing to Explain Why a Strategy Might Succeed or Fail   One model for interpreting focus groups to clients comes from the Washington, D.C.–based Rowan & Blewitt. The firm's research division, the Center for Communication Dynamics, tells clients that focus group testing "will help explain why a particular strategy might succeed—or fail. The research helps reveal probable reaction to different communication options."[63]

In one form of focus group testing, Rowan & Blewitt's research division exposes small groups to actual television, newspaper, radio or magazine reports. Tests indicate positive and negative attitude shifts resulting from the exposure. Sessions involve pretest, posttest and interview formats. Comments are recorded and evaluated to pinpoint why people react to specific messages in specific ways. In another application of the same research methodology, the firm evaluates alternative communications options by testing responses to modified, simulated news stories:

"We reshoot, rewrite and re-edit reports to reflect various types of coverage likely to result from different ways of handling media inquiries. Public reaction to each option (and the reasons why) are measured in these tests with small groups of individuals."

By focusing on what listeners or readers perceive and on audience motivation, the research enables counselors to provide an impact-oriented approach: "By measuring the impact of messages, Rowan & Blewitt provide clients with data to evaluate specific actions, programs and strategies involving their interests."

Counselors Academy Monograph Examines Focus Group Strategies   Decision Research Corp. armed members of the Counselors Academy with a briefing on the "how" and "why"—and the "how not" and "why not"—adaptations of focus group interviews to public relations practice. The briefing appeared in a monograph by Robert S. Duboff and F. J. Baytos.[64]

"While many marketing researchers who utilize the focus group interview tend to concentrate on product and consumer related issues, the application of this tool to a broad range of research concerns is becoming more widespread," they concluded.

"This technique is particularly suited to the public relations field because it provides a forum during which thoughts and opinions about sensitive social, psychological, political, and legal issues can be easily and fully explored." They said numerous counseling objectives can be served, including:

In-depth analysis of a client's image with target audiences

Exploration of critical issues to assess impact and handling

Development of campaign themes

Public reaction to potential promotional literature

Examination of opponents' and proponents' positions and intensity of support, opposition and feelings

Duboff and Baytos cited several advantages that make focus groups particularly relevant to public relations counseling:

"A focus group makes use of multiple interactions to learn about the social dynamics and immediate interpersonal features of the topics at issue. That might include how people talk about a subject in conversation, their vocabulary and phrases . . . as they are informally stimulated."

"Credible sources of information and influence can be elicited and discussed."

"Each group meeting usually develops a characteristic social tone . . . illuminating the subject's significance as a social, political or other type of issue."

"During exchange of thoughts, ideas, and opinions, it is useful to observe whether subject matter promotes apathy or uncertainty, is exciting or sobering."

Members of a group "given different knowledge about a subject will learn from one another and show how information and attitudes are absorbed or resisted."

"The focus group is especially valuable for discussion of trends that are social, economic or style-oriented."

Cabbage Patch Kids Case

Focus Groups, Experts Help Turn Potential Marketing Disaster into Coup Focus group methodology has matured in recent years and proved of particular value in public affairs and other areas of counseling. Yet it remains a powerful tool in preliminary research, field testing and periodic evaluation in support of marketing programs.

Consider the classic example of how Richard Weiner Inc. combined focus group studies and involvement of child psychologists in setting off Cabbage Patch Kids mania around the world. The dolls were created with disproportionate and plain features some might consider ugly and with a concept that could have proven offensive to adopted children, their adoptive parents, their natural parents and special-interest organizations.

The Cabbage Patch Kids media-and-consumer love affair that started in 1983 and persisted past mid-decade had been termed in its early stages as mania, craze and fad. It was not a fluke nor media hype. It was not merely publicity. It was a carefully researched public relations campaign.

And for Richard Weiner, president of the New York–based firm that became the Richard Weiner Division of Doremus Porter Novelli in 1986, "research was the single most important component, next to the product, itself" of marketing effectiveness in the United States.[65]

The campaign created the long-lived Cabbage Patch Kids boom and helped rescue Coleco at a time when the failing of its diversification into computers threatened its survival.

Weiner told a New York University/PRSA seminar that focus group and expert consultant research enabled his firm to tailor marketing strategy for a campaign that *Jack O'Dwyer's Newsletter* said "touched off one of the great product crazes of the century."[66]

"We had serious questions about how to sell what might be seen as an ugly doll. We were worried about potential negatives among real-world adoptive parents and adoptive children, themselves," Weiner said. "The research phase totally turned us around in our thinking."[67]

Research guided the development and honing of strategies that built the overwhelming demand for Cabbage Patch Kids. That momentum continued years past the Christmas season for which the product was rolled out, even after Coleco's failing Adam computer product line siphoned off sufficient profits that the client felt forced to do without external counsel for the Cabbage Patch Kids account and rely on the momentum built by Weiner.

Research conducted by Weiner and Coleco included focus groups with potential consumers, particularly children, and also with parents of adopted children. They also retained two prominent educators and child psychologists and consulted with such experts as a child psychiatrist, pediatrician and doll historian. "From this research came something that would not have materialized if we had only trusted our own judgment," Weiner said.

> The whole parenting theme was very well accepted by adoptive parents. From that understanding we moved to appreciation of the concept that this was not a doll; it was something unique that children look upon as more than a doll, as something loveable, something attachable. To every parent, his or her own child is beautiful. A child looks at a Cabbage Patch Kid differently than anyone else.

The see-through package reveals a doll with arms outstretched. "The torso is shaped so that emphasis is on the body. Everything about it is cuddly. Everything about it is appealing to the child who owns it."[68]

Research Base Expanded in Canada Burson-Marsteller was retained by Coleco Canada to deal with negative reactions by the media and consumers after the dolls were introduced at the Montreal Toy Fair.

The public relations firm reported that some Canadian parents and teachers complained that "the dolls placed overwhelming responsibility on young children and could cause psychological trauma, especially for children who were adopted."[69] The first step in the Canadian program involved developing a survey to gauge consumer reaction, identify concerns and pinpoint potential supporters who could act as third-party spokespersons.

As did Weiner, Burson-Marsteller consulted with experts and conducted meetings with special-interest groups such as adoption agencies. The communications program built upon the research by the client and its counseling firms in both the United States and Canada. In Canada, counseling purposes included pre-empting negative publicity, eliciting balanced reporting and reinforcing that "the Cabbage Patch Kid is an educational and entertaining toy that helps generate positive human behavior patterns in children and that Coleco is a responsible, innovative toy manufacturer."

In both nations, the counseling firms used child psychologists as spokespersons to give positive messages endorsing the Cabbage Patch Kid concept and, as Burson-Marsteller put it, "help demystify the birth/adoption process."[70]

Additional Strategies Prompted by Rioting in Malls *Burrelle's Clipping Analyst* took note of Weiner's "careful market and communications research" in "what started out as a $100,000 PR campaign and quickly ignited into what *Newsweek* described as 'a masterstroke of marketing.'"[71]

Newsweek, as was the case with many media, week after week, month after month, allowed the Cabbage Patch Kids story to take precedence over world events. For instance, a child kissing her Cabbage Patch Doll and the headline "What a Doll!" dominated the cover of an issue that dedicated six pages of the Business section's main story, color photo spreads and sidebar features to Weiner's client. "Oh, You Beautiful Dolls!" the Business section headline exclaimed. The second deck heading captured the essence of the phenomenon: "They're rioting in the malls for the chance to cuddle with the Cabbage Patch Kids."[72]

This research-based campaign included a number of elements that taken individually or as a whole would be impressive. One area of strategy, for instance, helped build sales and public opinion in support of the previously controversial adoption aspect and kept journalists, dealers and consumers from blaming the client when demand became superheated.

The client announced it was suspending the advertising that had started only a few weeks before the riots, rushing overseas production of an additional million dolls and paying freight on intercontinental jet delivery, according to Ravelle Brickman, who was senior vice president at the Weiner firm before opening her own consultancy.[73]

Weiner said that although his firm had only a short-term contract for giving marketing support to the Cabbage Patch Kids, it counseled developing a program in the long-range interest of the client so the product would not appear "faddish or unimportant, but thought of in terms of public service."[74]

Donating 50 to 100 dolls to major children's hospitals around the country and raffling dolls to raise funds for charities seemed to help the client avert any backlash caused by the unexpected consumer and media mania. This public service also helped Coleco weather storms in 1985 when it abandoned its Adam computer line—shortly after denying Wall Street and industry rumors that it would do exactly that after the Christmas 1984 buying season.

But what intrigued the PRSA Silver Anvil judges most, one of them recalled,[75] was the New York City counseling firm's research and counseling strategies for coping with what Brickman called "the volatile issue of the adoption contract" that the inventor had planned as part of the doll's appeal.[76]

Research armed counselors and client to reframe dangerous negatives into strong positives with a communications program that conveyed to children, in essence, "you're not only preparing to take care of a baby, but to learn parenting with commitment, loyalty, dedication and love."

Approaches to Focus Group Studies

Although public relations counselors traditionally have relied in years past on the client (or its advertising agency or marketing research vendors) to do the focus group research, some counselors, including Weiner, had been becoming more and more involved in doing their own studies or overseeing the work of subcontractors. Focus groups generally cost a New York City firm about $2,500 each to conduct. Because they're relatively inexpensive, Weiner said he has frequently scheduled more than one.[77]

Moderators are selected on the basis of their professional qualifications, such as their skills in questioning and in preparing and conducting the sessions; it is important that counselors and clients be provided with the information they need, not with what they or the moderator may want to hear. Weiner counseled:

"It doesn't matter if group or individual interviews are done in person, by phone or through mail: Don't accept any assumptions. Don't accept what the client is telling you. Don't accept your own prejudices or feelings on strong or weak points of product, service, or proposed campaign. Go into this research with an open mind."

Of the $2,500 or so, the moderator is paid $500 to $1,000 for a two-hour session. The firm tends to use psychologists or other social scientists. Many are full-time focus group moderators. Depending on situational variables, the firm may use the same moderator in different parts of the country or hire resident moderators.[78]

Among factors to consider: After conducting the first of a series of focus groups for a given client, the experience may enable a moderator to reduce the time needed to prepare for, conduct and analyze the sessions. Using the same moderator provides a more consistent perspective. These benefits, however, are offset to varying degrees by the amount of travel time and expenses incurred by one moderator.

Focus groups may consist of 10 to 12 persons who frequently are paid amounts ranging from $25 to considerably more, depending upon such considerations as the value of their time to them and their expertness.

Videotaping represents another cost factor. But it is valuable when researchers or members of the account team can profit from replaying segments of special interest in order to analyze verbal and nonverbal communication, interaction of group members with the moderator or among themselves or behavior of panelists when they handle a product or are exposed to campaign themes or materials.

At times, public relations firms go into joint focus group research ventures with advertising agencies and marketing firms. Public relations firms without in-house staff expertness for such research may contract with companies specializing in focus group services. Some large public relations firms, advertising agencies and research organizations have subsidiaries or divisions that are available for referral of, or vending of, focus group work.

Helps Make Case for Client

Helps Client Make Case for Budget Clients often can be persuaded to spend a small percentage of their investment in public relations on focus group research to see how their messages get through. Such research can become the basis not only for strengthening current counseling firm income and client advantage, but also for expanding contact with clients and cultivating future business.

Strenski, of Public Communications Inc., said that the client executive who works with the counseling firm then becomes positioned when "reporting to his boss to discuss measurable results for investments in public relations."[79]

"In addition to other values, such qualitative studies as focus groups allow counselors to demonstrate to clients that these messages do in fact appeal to consumer needs, promise wanted benefits, and deal with real concerns," according to Jan Rogozinski.[80]

When focus group studies are combined with publicity tracking, analysis of sales data and pre- and postcampaign opinion survey procedures, research gains power to produce at relatively low cost the kind of numbers that executives want when they make budget decisions.

Toward Stronger Relations

Consider research and the knowledge it yields, research and the confidence it builds, research and the effectiveness it assures, research and the progress it measures. Such research methods as focus groups strengthen the capabilities of public relations firms. Research for counseling continues to make progress at unprecedented rates of change. Symptomatic of such change is the granting by a foundation of $18,000 in 1985 to Glen M. Broom and David M. Dozier to write a book titled *Using Research in Public Relations: Applications to Program Management.* Tentatively scheduled for 1988 or 1989 publication, that book was planned to explore methods for gathering information, analyzing data and using research results.[81]

Other strategies join those of research in helping clients and their counselors take full advantage of creativity and objectivity. These strategies are intrinsic to building the psychological environment for productive counselor-client relations.

5
CLIENT RELATIONS STRATEGIES

From strategic listening, from a capability to instill a sense of involvement and from a sensitivity to clients'—and their own—psychological variables, counselors can establish effective, lasting partnerships.

To such partnerships come client officers who are willing to reveal vital information about their companies and to share their innermost thoughts and concerns. They are motivated to participate fully in the counseling process. This chapter shows how counselors analyze management psychology, relate to client chief executives and build understanding for their roles through educational and communication techniques.

APPLIED PSYCHOLOGY

Counselor, First Know Thyself

Some Seek Professional Counsel, Including Psychiatric Analysis At the core of a strong counselor-client relationship is an understanding of psychology, starting with its application to one's own needs, motives, attitudes and behavior.

Some public relations counselors profitably adapt to their own calling the biblical enjoinder "Physician, heal thyself" and the old saying that "A lawyer who defends himself has a fool for a client."

It is not a radical idea that counselors should seek counsel. Organizations such as the Counselors Academy and other PRSA sections, Canadian Public Relations Society, International Association of Business Communicators and Texas Public Relations Society help members learn to better understand themselves and their clients and prospects.

The most obvious opportunities for counselors to receive counsel are at seminars and workshops. Less obvious, but more prevalent, is the one-on-

one interaction of counselors among themselves testing ideas, probing for insights.

Some counseling firm executives seek outside counsel when they recognize that they can become so preoccupied with managing the business that they cannot know what's going on in other firms. They have sacrificed breadth of experience for depth.

Counselors may profit from the kind of self-exploration and development sessions staged for their own clients. This approach to learning about inner self draws on concepts involved when a psychoanalyst goes into therapy with another analyst. Even when people are sure they know what ought to be done, they may find it useful to talk to somebody detached from the situation.

One individual recounted going to a psychoanalyst for 25 years and adapting to public relations counseling business techniques learned in the psychiatrist's office. The psychiatrist manipulated the counselor—not in a devious way but by subtle questioning and eliciting self-analysis, much as the counselor learned self-persuasion through self-understanding. The transition from psychoanalyst's office to counselor's practice was "very, very successful."[1]

Another counselor "reached a plateau and got terribly frustrated" in attracting new business and in elevating the level of counseling services for existing clients. A friend advised psychoanalysis. "I tripled my business at the end of the first year. It changed my whole mental outlook," the counselor reflected. "I learned to love my clients instead of seeing them as adversaries."[2]

Dealing with Pressure and Hostility   Not unique to the counseling industry is the type of problem characterized by what one source described as an "immensely capable executive who drives out some of his best people. The better their work, the more competitive he feels until hostility explodes."[3]

For whatever reasons, counselors are expected to take inordinate amounts of stress and even abuse. Many train themselves to have a high boiling point and are able to desensitize themselves to irritants that might cause others to lose their tempers. But a flurry of demands, complaints and challenges may build from client officers, colleagues, media people and even family to the level where the boiling point is reached.[4]

Key ingredients in keeping accounts include recruiting and orienting counselors to buy into their work emotionally and give clients every consideration they expect.

Counselors also are expected to provide client management a first line of psychological—as well as communications—defense when something disturbing looms. "We help provide management an environment of stability and certainty so they can concentrate on their core activities," said Otto Lerbinger, a public affairs counselor and Boston University persuasion scholar.[5]

That environment may be more idealistic than realistic when public relations people—internal or external—find themselves diverted by what may be perceived as threats from competitors.

For instance, a *PR Reporter* poll of practitioners found that management is seen as favoring marketing people over public relations; this has led to resentment against "the invasion" of what some respondents described as "carpetbaggers": "Marketing people were seen as 'trying to keep PR in a second-stringer position.' Resentment has turned defensive."[6]

Resentment and defensive posturing arise when internal staff fear, with or without grounds, encroachment by external public relations counselors, whether it be in areas such as marketing, public affairs or top management counseling.

The psychological insights gained by counselors from analysis may help them in understanding and working with client internal staff as well as the CEO. Davis Young, president of Cleveland's Young-Liggett-Stashower Public Relations, once compared the product of counselors to that of industrial psychologists, lawyers, CPAs and management consultants. "We provide a professional service for our clients in terms of listening to their organizational problems or opportunities and counsel on how best to proceed in the area of communications."[7] The role of the counselor as applied psychologist actually extends into several areas.

Applying Ghostwriting Psychology

Get Inside Executive's Head, Know More Than Person Across Desk Some counselors evolved from speechwriting roots. They not only have worked within the framework that management demands but also have helped shape it. Occasionally, they came up against the immovable object in a client organization. With strategies learned in speechwriting, such counselors have learned how to move the immovable—sometimes.

A counselor, as a behind-the-scenes ghostwriter of speeches, has to help executives understand the processes that produce excellent counsel. The word "counselor" may be substituted for "ghostwriter" in the insights shared with the National Association for Corporate Speaker Activities by James F. Fox, past president of PRSA and chairman of the Counselors Academy. The founder of New York's Fox Public Relations has said that:[8]

Executives do not understand that by definition a ghostwriter has to know his client, has to get inside his head, be able to read his mind. But the common pattern is that the public relations person has to go through layers of management and guess what the executive wants or he will be misinformed along the chain of command.

If you are going to motivate people, you must know their nature, their ways of reasoning, their desires and emotions and search for the arguments that will gain their assent to your proposition.

As individuals, you must accept greater responsibility. Stop complaining about the lack of input from your principals. You must learn to research ideas and then conceptualize in order to develop original solutions to problems. You must not just transmit information. You must create knowledge. That knowledge not only comes from research, but also through analysis and thinking.

Fox counseled: "disperse apathy," "make issues exciting" and learn from this quote of an ancient philosopher:

An Athenian said: "When Pericles spoke, the people said, 'How well he speaks.' But when Demosthenes spoke, the people said, 'Let us march.' "

To create knowledge and earn confidence the counselor must explore to learn as much about the client's corporation and industry as the executive across the desk. As Fox said: "Managements today care little about your opinion or mine. They want decisions supported by facts developed through sound research. They want team thinking from specialists. The generalities of the old-fashioned business speech have given way to the documented position of the Business Roundtable."[9]

Lessons Gained in Interactive Relationships with Executives   In years past, many clients tended to be reactive. The trend has been to become proactive. Contemporary counseling, as speechwriting, has added the dimension of interactive relationships with publics—and with client executives. Advantages of such relationships flow from the following lessons:

1. *Cultivate patience*: Recognize that progress may require a great deal of patience.

Fox's speechwriting and counseling experience, for example, taught him "you have to have patience to argue the case and go away. You plant an idea and come back three months later. If the idea doesn't take by then, come back again three months later until the executive thinks the idea is his."[10] The counselor has to resist temptation to claim credit then or later.

2. *Build alliances*: A counselor, as a speechwriter, can gain support from respected peers of the executive such as the lawyer, head of research or treasurer. "Build relationships so others are saying to the executive, 'that's not a bad idea our counselor had; maybe we ought to go back to him.' "

3. *Learn what's important to executive*: Get to know the executive and what's important to him. "If you relieve him of anxiety and solve a problem for him, he'll love you. If he doesn't see a problem for which you have a solution, he'll think you're foolish."

4. *Persist*: If a vice president acts as a barrier or filter to the CEO and blocks your ideas or counsel, continue to probe.

5. *Use inoculation strategy*: Communication theorists long ago developed immunization theory to explain how to anticipate erosion of commitment to an idea by passage of time, raising of self-doubts or counterpropaganda.[11]

Fox advocated inoculating the client against "taking too seriously 'life and death' adversary relations that may arise under counsel. It's valuable to build a position of trust so that he will accept your vision of this as he does on other things."[12] Inoculation may consist of examples to which the CEO may relate before a situation with negative ramifications can arise.

6. *Know when to refer*: One way to build trust and serve the client's interests is for a counseling firm to recognize its own limits and refer the client to an expert whenever necessary.

7. *Know when to quit*: For self-respect and the respect of clients, counselors have to know when to quit.

An example from Fox involved a client who was "burned by a young reporter and issued an order that no one in the company could talk to him." He argued that this would cause him to continue to write negative stories and that the reporter could be educated. ("I try to get business people to appreciate implications of inhibiting or intimidating the press.") The client rejected the advice. Fox resigned the account.[13]

8. *Adapt self to executives*: Many counselors try to adapt to client executives, just as effective ghostwriters have sought to identify with speakers. But counselors differ on the degree to which they should adapt to executives' personal styles.

One said that if he had a client whose passion off the job was fishing, he would learn to fish. Another took pride in being able to identify and establish a rapport without joining clients in playing golf or in social drinking.[14]

9. *Create close ties*: It is possible to have formal business relationships with executives and yet be intimate enough to understand their thought processes.

10. *Spend time with CEO*: Getting inside the heads of executives also means spending time with them to observe and listen. Some counselors, as speechwriters, do that by traveling with the CEO on the way to meetings. Two examples follow:

One counselor invited herself along whenever the CEO rode in his limousine and gave dictation to his secretary. She did this on the pretext that observation would be helpful in learning his communication patterns. The counselor was able to make the transition from listening to dictation to observing the CEO at policy-making meetings. She said she knew weeks in advance what was going to be discussed at the highest levels of the corporation. She positioned herself not only as a counselor on communications but also as one on policy.[15]

Another worked with a prominent executive who insisted that his counselor had to be at social functions. The CEO frequently entertained people in the news and didn't want to subject them or himself to interviews on personal time. "He felt that if I was there and reporters came to the door, I could get rid of them." The counselor didn't relish the role of doorman to the media but accepted the command performance invitation because he had another agenda: He could see and listen to the CEO in action informally. He heard ideas not related to business. "I was able to study his patterns and really get to know the inner-person, as well as the executive."[16]

11. *Manipulate*: Manipulation through persuasive power is done by effective ghostwriters and counselors. Several persons used "manipulation" in a way that could be interpreted as hardball, but ethical, persuasion. "Some people are frightened by the concept," Fox said. "But I don't see a need for us to exist if we're not a force within client organizations. There's hardly a counselor who wouldn't say he's an advocate instead of a 'communication channel,' and that alone is quite a change in our business."[17]

Manipulation, as other words that have taken on connotations different from their roots, may fall into a semantic trap. Just as some forget that "propaganda" had its roots in church dissemination of information to influence and educate, others may overlook the primary definition of manipulation as "managing with skill."

A Counselors Academy guest speaker summarized several psychological strategies for selling services as "non-manipulative," though students of semantics might accept them as examples of manipulation in the best sense of the term:

Anthony J. Alessandra, co-author of *Non-Manipulative Selling*, recommended use of a typology of personalities. He described four types: "the Director, who gets to the point and is results oriented; the Thinker, who adores details and considers the process as important as the results; the Socializer, who wants the big picture first and is bored with details; and the Relater, who doesn't like being pushed and is concerned primarily with interpersonal relationships."[18]

How to Analyze Psychological Needs of Clients

A typology of personalities can be useful in analyzing counselors, their clients and prospects. Any typology, however, is limited by the same kind of reality that defies a zoologist in trying to classify a duckbilled platypus;

one individual may be a complex creature that fits into more than one classification. There is utility in taking stock of some of the variables that enter into differentiating them among personalities.

In building client trust and confidence, some counselors have discovered it pays to develop ways to gain that intelligence and then put to work the analysis of individuals in firms they represent—or would like to counsel. The mission of counselors may profitably include probing beyond the expressed needs of clients to the underlying, deeper psychological needs.

Visions for Building Clientele   This concept is supported by the principal of E. Bruce Harrison Co. of Washington, D.C., who found that "if we meet only the expressed needs of clients, we may miss satisfying needs far deeper—basic human needs that sent the client looking for us."[19]

Harrison built his practice by creating sharp mental pictures to visualize what he wants to do and how he wants to move toward these objectives. He developed, and each year updates, a book of "Client Goals and Objectives" with succinct but comprehensive, programmed follow-through for his public relations firm's business relationships with prospects and continuing clients. The goals and objectives relate not only to the prosperity of his firm but also to the priorities of his clients.

When he started his company, he disciplined himself to shape and adhere to a vision of the clients he wanted, the services he wished to provide and the criteria his customers must satisfy. He wrote down names of companies that exemplified the kind he would want as clients.

Then, and over the years, Harrison would try to conduct himself, and run his firm, as though he already had those clients. When he recruited new employees he would ask himself, "Are they the caliber of people I'd be proud to present to DuPont?" Similarly, his orientation extended to the professionalism that might be observed by a visitor. For instance, "How would the office look to the chairman of GM?"

A primary question that he has asked of himself and his colleagues remains: "How do we relate to the individual past the client's marketing and issues needs?" Developing intelligence on individual needs has not been a quick process. "It takes hanging in with the client for a long time."

Immediately after spending time with a client executive, he enters on the word processor what the client said about his interests, who he is and what he hopes to do. ("Once I know something about the individual, I'm always running into something that will interest that person.") More important than merely recording and observing is a periodic review of such notes, and he encourages his staff to develop similar approaches. To cultivate such techniques, he tries to arrange quarterly Saturday retreats to talk about client relations. "We visualize. We make our plans and dream a bit."

At the heart of the method is a dedication to following through. "We spend all of our professional lives trying to get clients to confide in us and listen to advice we have to offer. That type of relationship is very fragile. It can be lost through lack of attention, through thinking everything is OK without knowing it is."

What Clients Fear and Love   Harrison reviewed some of the things that are not OK (seven fears of clients) and some that are OK (client loves). Among these are:

"Fear of failing," as in not achieving "an objective tied to the client's personal success."

"Fear of inability to produce a result expected by another person with authority over the client."

"Fear of losing turf."

"Fear of embarrassment or surprise by events the client might have been expected to anticipate or might have controlled if he/she had known in time."

"Fear of losing the edge inside his/her own organization by not having the information or being in on the action in time to stay ahead of peers or superiors."

"Fear of stepping out front and being 'wrong.' "

"Fear of losing control."

"Desire for respect or attention to their view."

"Desire for recognition for their personal achievement in the context of their professional life."[20]

How to Meet Client's Desire for Personal Recognition   Although the desire for recognition of personal achievements and qualities of leadership may be a love of client executives, it has been an unrequited love for many. This challenges counselors to probe into this deeper psychological need and to provide the executive with opportunities to strengthen the organization's reputation through seeking out ways for meaningful public involvement and recognition.

David Finn, chairman and co-founder of New York City–based Ruder Finn & Rotman, said that "even sophisticated and socially minded executives have not been recognized as effective leaders of society." Worse, as a group, top managers are "branded as villains, evil people, even murderers who deserve public retribution for the deaths caused by their products and policies."[21]

In an article for the *Harvard Business Review*, "Public Invisibility of Corporate Leaders," Finn asked why "so many business leaders hide their human qualities behind a mask of corporate anonymity?" He suggested that part of the reason may be that they fear appearing to be on "ego trips."

Finn did not lay any blame at the door of public relations. Yet it seems that part of the problem may lie in too-rigid interpretation of the executives' penchant to hide their human qualities. For instance, he said that rarely are trustees of cultural, social, religious and educational institutions visible to the public as corporate executives. "Nor are they given credit by their companies or stockholders for their accomplishments as citizens who perform outstanding services for the community." Mention is limited to official biographies and obituaries; they are not mentioned in annual reports, articles about the company or communications to employees.

To transform them from anonymous instruments of "impersonal corporate interests" to executives who can find publics responding to their leadership, Finn counseled clients to:

1. Integrate community and business lives so executives gain credit for their public services and are credible when making statements about their businesses.
2. "Develop an appetite for being in the public eye as individuals who represent the character of their companies."
3. "Speak publicly and convincingly about human needs and values, as well as economic benefits when discussing business policies."
4. Exercise courage to initiate company programs that grow out of personal interests, and act as public spokesperson for them.
5. Develop their own sense of style about conduct of business without worrying that they may be catering to idiosyncratic tastes.
6. Persuade stockholders that it is important for managers to be human beings with deep concerns about the health and well-being of fellow citizens.

How to Meet Client's Desire for Sense of Partnership Another deeper psychological need of client executives is a desire for a sense of partnership in which the executive's leadership is acknowledged.

"The best public relations is practiced by people who are partners to clients, rather than vendors," according to the chairman of Harris, Baio & Sullivan of Doylestown, Pa. A *vendor* in Michael V. Sullivan's lexicon means "the client says 'I need work and this is how much I can pay' and the vendor says 'yes, I have that on the shelf and will send it over.' The vendor doesn't bring leadership, aggressiveness, innovativeness to the relationship."[22]

"Both parties need that sense of partnership. If you go in with the attitude that you're a partner and accountable and responsible, then you do better work for your client. If he sees you as a partner, he's more open, more receptive to your ideas, and he demands more of you." Here's how to position counselors and clients as partners:

Refuse an account that just wants a vendor. Insist that the counseling firm becomes "pretty near a full voting member of the marketing team." Understand the executive's environment and

> be candid with him, telling him what you want to do and pointing out the benefits to him of the partner relationship. Public relations is a commodity business. Anybody can write a press release or stage an event. What really counts are the energy, thought, devotion, creativity, accountability, emotion, responsibility that go into what you do.

The psychological values of partnership go both ways. "Aside from the money, it makes me feel wonderful when I feel like a partner in decisions the client makes that yield results," he said.

How to Listen and Develop Confidence

Opportunity to Become Trusted Friend of CEO, Board Chairman   A partnership depends upon trust. Trust depends upon openness of communication and sensitivity to another's interests. That sensitivity depends upon taking pains to discover and verify those interests and keep them in mind. Discovery and verification are based upon astute questioning, observation and listening. Strategic listening requires that the prospective client partner be willing to talk. This willingness to open up depends, again, upon trust.

One of the long-time masters of developing the trust of executives, Chester Burger has counseled many individuals on the listening-centered process. "The counselor has the opportunity to become a trusted friend of the client, a person with whom the chairman can let his hair down and confide with privacy and trust," said the founder of New York's Chester Burger & Co.[23] A number of counselors build this relationship with clients.

Life at the top often leads to isolation and creates a vacuum that trusted counselors can fill. Senior executives like to be with peers, but they may be hesitant to confide in their counterparts from competitive corporations. Even with peers from noncompetitive organizations, opportunities to share confidences tend to be limited.

The public relations executive can bring to a client relationship absolute trust and confidentiality. That doesn't necessarily mean that a CEO or senior officer of a client will perceive the counselor that way. The counselor has to have a fundamental respect for the client executive. Less than that and the danger exists even with the most artful of communicators of inadvertently appearing disrespectful or patronizing, especially with a sensitive client.

Another danger looms if the counselor is seen as seeking to build a friendship for monetary gain. There may be a difference between intention and perception on the part of the client. If the counselor approaches the CEO on a personal friendship level with the thought of developing more business out of it, that self-serving approach will quickly reveal itself, according to Burger.[24] In reality, however, it is the rare counselor who can divorce business opportunities from thoughts related to a client.

Burger's response to this human dilemma: "When you want to sell something to the chairman, understand your strong self-interest and spell it right out to him. Never prevaricate. If he wants to act negatively, at least he knows that your whole orientation is 'how can we help this guy?' "[25]

The concept boils down to establishing dominance in one's own mind of the interests of the client executive above self-interests. Although seemingly idealistic, this can be a powerful, pragmatic strategy for developing friendships that ultimately yield dividends for the counselor's own practice.

How to Improve Listening Skills Burger, management communications consultant to many of the *Fortune* 100 firms and to more than 40 of the 50 biggest public relations firms, provided the basis for tips on how to listen:

1. *Understand the counselor's own need to impress others*: It's endemic to humans to want to impress everybody with whom they come in contact. Some counselors dominate conversations, first for their own psychological needs, second for selling services. They talk about all kinds of success stories about their firms and themselves.

2. *Then understand client's need to impress*: The client, however, has psychological needs of his own. He wants to impress the counselor with how brilliant and effective *he* is, how successful *his* firm has become. This mutual urge to impress can lead to negative vibrations unless the counselor listens instead of talks.

3. *Too much impressing backfires*: One way in which a counselor's efforts to impress can have an unintended negative effect is when the client feels "that's brilliant, why didn't *I* think of that?" Competitiveness and strains in the relationship follow. If the client already feels inadequate, this would tend to make him feel less open to the counselor, even resentful.

4. *Get client to talk—then listen*: Because everybody likes to be heard, pleasantries—even a comment about the weather—can start a client talking. Burger recalled the experience of meeting a board chairman for the first time: "I walked in and he started to talk. All I did was nod. He turned to me and said 'you're the most brilliant guy I ever talked to. Nobody else will listen.' "

5. *Understand sensitivity to criticism*: Verbal criticism or a glance that a client can interpret as critical may dam the flow of communication. Herein lies a dilemma—how can the counselor be honest with an executive without being perceived as critical of the executive's actions or communication substance or style? But that is no dilemma for Burger:

6. *Help client save face*:

A policy that is found to be defective after a while may have worked well when the client started it; obviously, he did it for good reasons. Give him some way of extenuating it. He'll be much more likely to change posture. For instance: "Everything has been great up to now. Now you have a different set of circumstances; now you have fresh time to look at it" vs. making him feel he didn't recognize change.

7. *Use dialogue style*: A counselor can guide an executive through the process of taking a fresh look at something in the form of a planned dialogue: "What experience have you had with this?" "Have you ever done it this way?" "What has the competition done?"

8. *Consider semantics*: Use "we" rather than "I." ("What can we do about this?") The "we" makes it implicit that counseling firm and client are successful because they're working together.

9. *Give—or share—credit*: If the client says "you did a great job," a thoughtful response is: "No, I couldn't do it by myself, but look at what we accomplished together." To say that with conviction so the executive will not perceive flattery, Burger advised "you must recognize you couldn't have done it without implicit or explicit client executive support."

10. *Avoid unintentionally condescending*: Unless there is true respect for the individual, it is easy to unconsciously condescend. Before going to a meeting it might be valuable to pause and reflect on all that the executive has accomplished, what qualities make him an asset to the client company.

11. *Bring breadth to relationship*: A client does not have to get involved in some of the mechanics of services. He may listen politely, but his nonverbal communication may signal the counselor to bring a broader perspective and more substance to their relationship.

12. *Develop substance*: One way to bring substance to a conversation or relationship is to keep away from a technical orientation and be conversant with society trends and how they might impinge on the client.

13. *"Lay it on thinly"*: Some people who gravitate to public relations, as to other professions, may have what Burger called "a compulsive need to be liked." That need can be manifested in fawning over people, "laying it on thickly." That can provoke discomfort.

14. *Listen physically*: For counselors like Burger, listening can be almost physically exhausting. Tips: lean forward, show an alert posture, make strong eye contact, try to hear every word and nod frequently or give other signs of active listening.

15. *Avoid negative cues*: Out of their own insecurities, some counselors give off signs of arrogance or anger. Despite sensed provocation, "that's self-defeating," Burger said.

16. *Look for non-verbal cues*: "Suppose you're talking to a client on a very serious matter, and in the middle of the conversation you notice a smile on his face. That may tell you he's going to say something so painful to him, he's trying to mask the pain."

17. *Ask a friend*: Consider turning to a friend or spouse to find out what cues one gives in a sensitive conversation: The best friend may be an expert in communications.

18. *Hear out and understand*: The active listener not only must hear but also think about and understand the client's points. Understanding also requires homework before a session.[26]

EXECUTIVE-TO-EXECUTIVE COMMUNICATIONS

The fact that client executives like to talk to peers suggests another area of strategy for officers of public relations firms: executive-to-executive communications.

In the full sense of the word, *peer* means a person of comparable rank and ability. For some clients, rank may be important. In some cases, such as in one-person or modest-sized counseling firms, rank is irrelevant. For many clients, an individual's title means far less than the counselor's abilities to communicate at *their* level of interest, respond with effective, reliable counsel and mobilize resources.

How to Start

Basis for Relationship Determined in First 15 Minutes The operational definition of peer depends on how the client perceives a counselor. That perception develops quickly and, not infrequently, is even formed before client executive meets public relations firm executive.

The basis of a strong, enduring relationship between a counselor and a senior client executive happens in the first 15 minutes of the association, according to Harold Burson. The chairman and CEO of Burson-Marsteller took issue with the school of thought that suggests such relationships build over time. "That's rare; it is usually there at the beginning, or one never makes it."[27]

Within the first 15 minutes or so of the first meeting, the client makes an appraisal of the counselor based on what he says and how he presents himself. This doesn't mean some laws of logic are at work. The determination may be at a visceral level.

The heads of large companies normally call on counselors after they have discussed their problems with trusted individuals in their own and other organizations. Before the first meeting, and in its aftermath, client executive perceptions are influenced to some degree by what other people in their peer group have said about the counseling firm. Frequently counselors are put through an internal screening process by subordinates concerned with matching up their qualifications, experience and personality with the perceived needs of their executive. As Burson said, "much of the relationship depends upon how you are positioned by those people."

Preliminary Strategies for Working with CEO   Burson's counsel set the stage for 15 preliminary strategies:

1. *Build psychological profiles*: Develop not only detailed biographical sketches of senior executives but also build multidimensional psychological profiles.

2. *Do network analysis*: Trace (or, if that's not feasible, project from biographical data) the client's network of peers and influential subordinates.

3. *Study own firm*: Similarly, build psychological profiles of the counseling firm's own principals, analyze networks in which they may intersect with the client's peers and anticipate potential matches among individuals in both client and counsel organizations.

4. *Surprise client*: Go in knowing more about the client's business and problems than he would expect you to know at this stage.

5. *Prepare to lead client to own solutions*: Be prepared to respond to a client's questions "in such a way as to lead the other party to continue talking about what his real problems are and to lead him to develop his *own* answers."[28]

6. *Read and adapt*: Read voluminously and adapt findings to specific situations.

7. *Use numbers*: Be numbers-oriented. Nothing is dearer to a CEO than knowing that people really understand his business. Most of what is needed can be found in the annual report. The rest, including 10K reports filed with the SEC, is readily available in computer-accessed data banks.

8. *Open to client point of view*: Cultivate openness and be sensitive to the client's point of view. Counselors can ill afford to be rigid.

9. *Understand client's agenda*: The course of a meeting depends on who calls it. When a client does so, Burson's advice is "to ask right then what we're going to talk about."

10. *Cover points quickly*: When the counselor calls the meeting, it usually is best to make three or four points that need to be made and get those out of the way quickly.

11. *Go with the flow*: "Some clients love to tell stories; some want to get right to the point. You move in whatever direction. However, sometimes it's the role of the counselor to deftly bring the executive back to the point." (Among factors to be considered are who called the meeting, how much time is left and whether the real agenda is to establish a relationship or cover certain points.)

12. *Adapt to reality*: Adapt quickly to what the reality is rather than what another perceives it to be.

13. *Bring back to reality*: Determine if what has been described as "the" problem is really *the* problem. "Most CEOs are not willing to accept that their trusted sources can be highly biased in their favor and tell them what they want to hear." One technique for the counseling firm executive is to say, "I've got to talk to my people and really find out what the problem is; I need to look at different scenarios."

14. *Define role early*: Establish an honest broker relationship at the inception in making it clear that you will counsel, not just reflect the client's thinking.

15. *Use syntax techniques*: To give clients satisfaction of feeling something is their own idea and to reduce chances of resistance, use such syntax as: "You must have thought of this before" and "Could it be possible that . . . ?"

How to Honor Commitment and Still Delegate Contact   When a counseling firm is small, the principal will be involved in practically every contact. That becomes impossible as a firm's size, number of clients and complexity of responsibilities grow.

Burson and his senior executives have developed their own middle course of honoring personal commitments to clients while delegating some of the contact work. He said he goes to relatively few new-business presentations because he feels that his appearance is a commitment to continued involvement. But "if there's a really highly sensitive issue to a client, I will get involved."

As is true of other counseling firm principals, Burson has felt compelled to cater to clients whose businesses have grown up with his. Long-time loyalties that helped build a public relations firm earn interest on that investment. "I realize I'm not an account executive, but all they have to do is pick up the telephone and I'll come."

The policy is to maintain continuity of relationship with client executives through account managers. On occasion they may call in Burson or other officers of the firm. "I may go in for that discussion and may not see the CEO for another year or live with top management for a week, depending upon the situation." Delegation, however, is not a perfect instrument. Good chemistry may not exist between client executive and the counseling firm's contact person.

And, yet, without delegation, growth can founder.

We grew because we were smart enough to delegate responsibility to other people and tell them: "You make your own relationships; I don't have to be part of everything." That takes a lot of confidence in your people, which is why you try to find and bring along good people. The measure of your growth is a measure of your people.

The ability of people to work with top client management is aided by training and development programs, ranging from the creation of policy to the application of tools and techniques.

In client relations, I don't believe in only presenting one person. We emphasize that the client is getting services of a total organization rather than experience of just one individual. The account manager knows she has specialized resources to call on—public affairs, industrial relations, communication training people. The account manager orchestrates the relationship and may do some of the work herself, but she knows she's backed up by other people.

Whoever handles client contact must convey that "you really are interested and that you really care." Burson identified the ability "to say to them, 'it's not you and us, it's *us*' " as one of the most critical elements in long-lasting, continuing relationships.

"This is where you're regarded as an extension of the executive's own organization. Even when you're brought in on a project basis, you're trying to build that long-range relationship."

Analyze Executive's Background, Organizational Environment Building such relationships often begins with a systematic analysis of the chairman, CEO and the people around them. This helps counseling executives plan communications, logic, presentations and services that will be compatible with thinking of top management.

Peter G. Osgood, vice chairman of Hill and Knowlton and former president of Carl Byoir & Associates, advocated exploring the background of executives, with special focus on how they got to their present positions.[29] Tracing career path to the executive suite helps illuminate how the individual approaches decision-making. According to Osgood, "the engineer likes to see summaries with detailed backup. The marketing executive prefers to see a program in bullet fashion *without* detailed backup."

Similarly, in order for public relations firms to position themselves for long-range relationships they must examine an organization's structure and culture, the environment that influences client executive style and orientation. Osgood, past chairman of the Counselors Academy, suggested several questions:

In what kind of organization is the executive working?

What are the organization's idiosyncrasies?

Is it centralized or decentralized in its decision process?

How much authority and responsibility are given?

What is the relationship among executives of the company?

How do they approach the planning process collectively and individually?

How much does the CEO delegate at the various levels of the planning and implementation process? (The parameters of that process help counselors determine whether to start at the bottom of the organization and work their way up or start at the top with the CEO.)

Does the CEO view public relations as policy or staff function?

Who influences the CEO? (Valuable insights could be gained by examining areas of decision-making and specific individuals' influence and asking: with what degree of impact, with what interaction among sources of influence and with what styles?)

Is there a special corporate philosophy of headquarters organization, asset deployment and asset management?

Do senior executives leave planning and operations to divisional and subsidiary heads?

Or do they involve themselves on a much stronger basis in providing oversight of overall services, strategic thinking and day-to-day operations? (To the extent that senior executives involve themselves in the operations of subsidiaries and divisions, Osgood said "it follows to take a harder look and deeper understanding of who most influences them and why. If they're decentralized, however, you deal at the corporate level with corporate issues, and it becomes more important for the counselor to get to know better those heads of business units in which the CEO places trust and confidence.")

Counseling Firm Principals Benefit from Personal Involvement in Audit By personally becoming involved in audit functions, ranking officers of counseling firms can gain strategy-guiding intelligence from prospect or client management. Much can be learned through the interview process, particularly with the aid of advance research.

"You do a lot of homework so you can be prepared when you meet with an interviewee to push certain hot buttons and see how he reacts," Osgood said. Hot buttons include how the executive views CEO roles, board relationships and evaluation of subordinates.

Interface among client and counseling firm CEOs depends on such variables as the nature of work, who brings the firm in, and for what reason. In small to medium-sized public relations companies, CEOs are more likely to be involved in the majority of decision processes than their counterparts in larger organizations.

Developing Sensitivity to Needs

CEO-to-CEO Relations Vary with Crisis Environments If the client CEO anticipates a crisis or if the company already is in crisis mode, interface begins with intense involvement of top counseling firm management regardless of size.

This is exemplified by a defense-industry crisis. According to Osgood: "When clients and individual board officers and CEOs are defending their own credibility and the industry's, you become involved at the CEO level. You're dealing with a situation in which you must take individual charge." He maintained that kind of relationship with General Dynamics during that company's 1984–1986 siege under congressional, Department of Defense, judiciary and media investigation.

The crisis turned a corner in 1986, when the then-new chairman of the board and former president of TRW, Stanley Pace, was cited in such media as the *Los Angeles Times* for his pro-active program to give government customers "what amounts to a money-back guarantee" on value of orders, to "ensure that all employees understand the vital importance of the highest standards of business conduct and put them into practice" and to create a corporate responsibility committee of outside directors.[30]

Pace and General Dynamics were positioned to change corporate posture and public opinion under a softening glare of media spotlights, even as several present and former officers of General Dynamics were under criminal indictment. The Navy suspended new contract awards, and millions of dollars of alleged overcharges were being repaid to the government.[31]

How to Become Sensitized to CEOs Counseling firms, as well as their customers, benefit from an early development of sensitive modes of understanding and meeting the needs of client CEOs. Here are several strategies:

1. *View CEO's perceptual MBO road map*: Beyond sensitivity in understanding the CEO's goals and objectives, Osgood recommended that counselors study how client officers "perceive their road maps for achieving MBO."[32]

2. *Use language of cost/value ratio*: Speak in the CEO's language, not in the jargon of public relations. For instance, strategies and activities programs that are recommended to the CEO are best expressed in cost/benefit terms to him and the client as a whole.

3. *Sensitize to individual's fragility*: As humans bearing their responsibility and authority, client CEOs are fragile. Osgood said:

> We have to be sensitive to how fragile the individual is, how he wants to be viewed by his own board, rank and file employees, his industry, peers, executive team and the media. We have to be sensitive to his

ambitions. We have to know how that person views himself as a public or private person. We need to be sensitive to the role the CEO really wants to play and to his personal values.

4. *Go for private sessions*: There are times when the counselor will wish to assure that sessions with the client officer are private. "You have to be alone with a CEO so he can talk to you in an unencumbered fashion. He may not wish to indicate weakness or concern in front of his subordinates," Osgood said.

Although there are times to involve others in the counseling firm, their presence can inhibit the openness that the client would have in one-on-one communications. A one-on-one relationship with a trusted counselor can lead to a special role:

5. *Serve as confidant*: "A lot of times, I get calls from CEOs who say they're coming into town, and ask if we can get together quietly," Osgood said. "They want to talk to somebody outside their immediate environment so they can test ideas and test their thinking and not be subject to people whom they have to manage on a day-to-day basis. The role of the public relations firm CEO thus can become that of trusted confidant."

6. *Earn trust*: Developing trust requires an ongoing track record of good attention *and* solid performance. "That's performance predicated on solid understanding of what is to be achieved and solid execution and, finally, review of results to show you achieved what you set out to do," he said.

7. *Focus on quality of interface*: In a quantitative business environment, one may be tempted to focus on frequency of interface among executives when the emphasis should be on quality.

8. *Be prepared to be responsive*: Although there are ways to delegate or buy time, CEOs who want to talk to their counseling firms' principals expect personal involvement. That does not preclude a principal from bringing in a team to follow through and evaluate, but it does suggest the importance of assuring that he is well briefed and in position to counsel at any stage. As Osgood said, "If a client CEO calls up midway through an activity and asks how I feel about what's going on, it's awkward if I say that 'I have to find out and get back in two hours.' I have the obligation to say, 'Let's re-think it and see if we're on the right course or in wasteful activity.' "

9. *Communicate as businessperson*: The counseling CEO can best communicate from the perspective of a businessperson. Clients and counseling CEOs have much in common. "I have the same problems and anxieties as many client CEOs," Osgood said. "What differentiates me from my client is that I'm in the business of counseling and have certain communications skills. I see myself and my senior colleagues as having been through most situations that one is likely to confront from a communications standpoint. That means we can bring a variety of experiences to bear."

10. *Help guide CEO on options*: The counseling CEO's role is to help the client CEO arrive at a proper conclusion. Osgood and Burson used almost the same language to make this point:

> But we have to remember that we're on the counseling side, and the decisions are not usually right or wrong. Rather, there are vast shades of gray, and all we can try to do is guide the CEO toward policy decisions, strategies or actions that we perceive to be in his best interests. There is always more than one way to solve any problem. Our job is giving him those options, helping guide him on those options and, if we feel a course of action he's chosen will have dire consequences, our job is to guide him back on the right course.[33]

11. *Emphasize what can be done*: Some client choices may not be feasible. Some may be unrealistic in the degree of achievement sought. Others may be destructive and lead to bankruptcy. There are steel-reinforced brick wall equivalents in the business world too strong to be smashed through and too high and wide to get around economically. But few CEOs warm to a nay-sayer. Emphasizing what can be done is a technique of choice for counselors such as the principal of Epley Associates of Charlotte, N.C. "We approach our clients with a positive attitude of making their objective possible, not of why something can't be done," Joe S. Epley said.[34]

12. *Give benefit of doubt*: Even when in serious doubt, it is possible to approach a client's idea from the perspective that it can be done. Epley suggested: "Look for other ways that may get at some of the client objectives and may be parallel to what the client, publics and you will find palatable. However, reality should not be blinded by optimism."

13. *Ensure client CEO shares agenda*: Sometimes, however, both client executive and counseling executive may give each other so much benefit of the doubt that objectives pursued by the public relations firm may not be what the client really wants. Such a risk underlines the importance of counselor-client communications to assure that objectives are mutually agreed upon.

14. *Cope with impatience for results*: Client executives may be impatient and expect immediate results rather than wait for objectives that take a year or more. Epley recommended breaking down objectives into limited time-frame pieces, such as by the month. "In doing so, you can look at the client and say, 'Here are things we *can* accomplish for you.'" This helps assure the CEO you can work within time requirements that meet client needs.[35]

15. *Anticipate anxieties on capability to respond*: Client CEOs often read or hear about their counseling firms becoming involved in major new campaigns or crises of *other* clients and may be anxious about their capability to respond to their own needs at the same time. Such worries may be eased by assuring that the CEO gets to know and gain confidence in other senior counseling executives. Some find it useful to show clients the depth of their talent. It also pays to assure client executives that arrangements have been made to provide backup with knowledgeable people ready to assume control in an emergent situation. This is similar to lawyers and physicians arranging for other members of their firms or independent colleagues to handle their overload or cover for them when they're away.

Keep in Touch with the Client   The cultivation of long-term relationships also profits from building and maintaining a rapport with clients. It is true, but nevertheless easy to overlook in the press of business, that an essential component of rapport lies in keeping the client well informed.

A number of firms use a system combining oral action reports with a written follow-up. "Routine and significant matters may be reported verbally but should always be followed up by a written report," he said. "The written report goes not only to the client, but also to the client's records and to all key people who may need to know."[36]

Conference reports are used to avoid the need for client executives to have to depend on memories. For example, Epley protocol entails preparing brief summaries of meetings for both client and firm to assure that commitments made by either or both parties are available as part of the record. Both sides have the opportunity to review for accuracy of interpretation.

A case in point involves a client with corporate headquarters in New York City, a plant near Charlotte and operations headquarters in Richmond, each with a need for copies of action and conference reports. As part of the service, and as a way of maintaining and building upon rapport, Epley sees to it that client executives with a need to know about the outcome of programs or meetings involving the Charlotte plant receive copies of conference reports.

As part of regular reporting, he calls for a quick summary of what's been done for a client over the years so executives can readily see progress and be reminded of his firm's capabilities. "They may need an overview of what's been done, not just for understanding the investment made in counseling and services, but also in suggesting to them other problem areas that might be placed on the agenda."

Coach CEO in Recognizing Opportunities and Problems—Early   Another way to build rapport with client senior executives is to position them to be among the first to recognize opportunities and anticipate problems. This can be done by helping executives see parallels. "We may see something happening in California with no direct relationship to North Carolina, but we can recognize and help the client see parallels that may relate to his business. Helping him recognize things that could have impact on his business leads to more business for you in the long run and provides better quality service." Epley recalled "the old adage of management—the boss doesn't like to be surprised."

The CEO and others can be prepared in advance. "If you see something that could impact, start developing dialogue in anticipation," Epley said. That doesn't mean there is only one dialogue. The "something" could be a legal matter that also needs to be brought to the attention of the client's attorneys.

Early warning on potential impact situations "enhances our role in helping meet the client's goals and industry position." And for the client CEO and other officers, "the more knowledge you can bring out, the more comfortable they can feel, particularly when it has significant impact on their own operations."

When Clients Do Not Have Internal Public Relations Apparatus A special case for sensitivity to client executive needs exists when a company does not have its own internal public relations staff. Several techniques apply:

1. *Become part of the client management team*: Although this advice to counselors may be useful in a number of situations, it is particularly applicable when clients do not have their own internal public relations apparatus. Epley, however, cautioned that the counseling executives need to maintain enough of a mental distance to give the CEO "outside, objective viewpoints and recommendations." Once rapport is established and confidence earned, the counselor is positioned to go beyond the technician orientation for which the client may have contacted him.

2. *Develop taste for counsel*: Venturing the first questions and ideas to determine client needs may lead to a partial acceptance of the role of counselor instead of reinforcing a belief that a firm merely provides technical support.

3. *Plant ideas in depth*: Whether the firm starts the counseling relationship with the CEO or somebody else down the line, "ideas are accepted by a depth of people." Epley suggested that the counselor "not depend on one individual to interpret your views to the rest of the management team."

4. *Encourage client CEO to name liaison person*: He adapted several points from a monograph on client liaisons to his own firm:

The client CEO may be the person who decides to have the program but he can't be expected to deal with it day to day. That task is usually delegated to a staff member who is best suited to keep materials and information flowing between the client and the firm. The liaison person, whether the CEO's assistant, the public relations director or another should meet the following test:

Be fully sympathetic to the public relations program and dedicated to its success.

Have ready access to information that may be required to make the program workable and to executives with the clout to move things.

Be authorized to approve most ideas and copy. Precious time can be wasted and opportunities lost, if the liaison constantly needs to get a string of approvals.

Understand the nature of public relations and what people must do to get results.

5. *Bring back to CEO-to-CEO level*: Epley said that liaison problems could merit "going over and talking confidentially to the CEO." This would "keep the account manager from the awkward situation of going over the head of the person he has to deal with." There is no one sure way to resolve problems. "Maybe you improve relations based on your knowledge of how things work within the company."

CLIENT EDUCATION

New Thrusts at Macro Level

Perhaps one of the most important areas of strategy in counselor-client relations for the 21st century will be acceleration of attempts to educate clients. On the global, or macro, level, this is being approached by several new thrusts:

A concerted effort to introduce public relations into the curricula of business schools was launched by the Foundation for Public Relations Research and Education with strong support from counselors on the board of directors. By 1986, the Foundation had invested more than $50,000 in the development of modules that could be adopted in undergraduate and graduate programs. Members of the board had contacted several of the more prestigious university MBA programs to pave the way for acceptance of modules under development by a team of business school researchers.

The Counselors Academy, in 1985, launched an annual week-long management training program for members under the joint leadership of its own executive committee and a faculty organized by a consultant from the Harvard Graduate School of Business Administration.

Counselors stepped up education efforts by writing articles for journals and newsletters and giving speeches at forums for client-side public relations executives and other officers.

Public relations firm officers moved to share with their competitors strategic approaches for educating clients.

A Gradual Process for Sophistication

As the discipline of counseling matures in public relations applications to business, clients, too, gain sophistication. Neither type of growth seems instant or bound by limits.

Increasingly, counselors see client education as a gradual process that begins during the first discussion with a potential client and continues throughout the relationship. By its nature, a process is a systematic series of actions; a continuous, progressive series of changes. It is dynamic. It works best with deliberate, patient planning that includes setting and adjusting to specific levels attained and doing the research and evaluation to keep on target.

From an analysis of how more successful brokerage houses worked with their clients, a veteran of the New York Stock Exchange developed a philosophy and techniques for client education that he has adapted to the counseling field. For Terence A. McCarthy, partner in Boston's Agnew, Carter, McCarthy, Inc., client education works best when it's approached as a qualification process. That is, it qualifies what public relations generically and the firm specifically can do.[37]

Just as Burson has emphasized the importance of the first 15 minutes of CEO-to-CEO relations in developing new business, so has McCarthy stressed the integral role of the initial orientation of prospects to understanding of not only how to work with a counseling firm, but also the very meaning of "public relations," its possible range of applications and the capabilities of the particular firm.

Consider the case of a company besieged by damning and false rumors about its ownership and control. McCarthy's firm had invested in the gradual qualification process. "They knew what our agency could do for them and they asked us how we thought it should be handled" even though there was hesitancy to engage in any program that might seem by its very existence to add credence to the rumors.

The counselors brought in a Tulane University psychologist who specialized in rumor research. Together, they probed the depth of believability, mapped the paths the rumors followed and then developed a multipronged program of working with certain opinion leaders and the media "to absolutely squash" the rumors and put in place a contingency program "should anything ever arise again, to stop it right there and then." The client bought it and it worked. "If they hadn't learned how to use us, this never would have happened."

Twenty-one Techniques for Starting the Process   Here are 21 techniques for starting the client education process:

   1. *Explain at onset what public relations and firm can do*: To follow through on the qualification process, counselors invest time at the onset of a relationship explaining what public relations is. Then they explain what they can do for the client.

2. *Don't take assurances of understanding at face value*: According to McCarthy, a new client will say, in essence, "I know what you can do, I understand your business, and here's an area where I think we can work together." Many a relationship is damaged by taking such words at face value. Too many executives have dated, fragmented, distorted perspectives of public relations, let alone counseling capabilities and services.

3. *Recognize state of flux*: The answers to what may be needed—or accepted—in client education are in a state of flux. An important component of that flux is the rapid increase in utilization of public relations services by younger generations of business executives with different orientations to government, consumers, the media and public opinion in all its dimensions.

4. *Challenge humility "ethic"*: What enters into education is a function of market size and change within it. Once, some consumer product companies disclaimed the need to advertise. Once, medical corporations shunned public relations. As McCarthy put it: "The ethic used to be that 'I don't have to talk about my product.' A relatively new attitude now prevails that to do less is not businesslike."

5. *Take advantage of openness window*: Ideally, a mutual educational relationship, with provisions for the learning process of counselor as well as client, would be implicit in long-term contract arrangements. Practically, a fee-for-service or flat-fee situation may inhibit that. Yet sensitivity and openness to learning normally is at its highest for both parties during the first few months.

If it may be assumed that many enlightened executives understand and expect that their counselors will do sufficient study to tailor even short-term projects to unique sets of client situational variables, it is implicit that these executives would be open to the idea that time must be invested by both sides in the learning process.

6. *Build case for joint management process model*: The process works best when counselors are accepted as part of the client's management process. McCarthy's approach is to tell them that " 'we adopt the model that we're in this together and, in essence, a part of your management process. It behooves both of us to understand how the process works and for you to understand how to use our firm.' "

7. *Motivate with time-saver point*: If the client agrees, the next step involves motivation. One way is to explain that planned reciprocal learning shortens the time of that process.

8. *Help view program as joint product*: As such involvement develops, the client can be encouraged to look upon the program as a joint product (rather than something that is developed independently and then presented for approval in advertising-agency style).

9. *Anticipate risks—either way*: Including decision-makers in the planning stages of a program involves a different set of risks than waiting until action is set to begin. McCarthy said, however, that "if the client's interface person doesn't understand how to use your firm, you may anticipate a lot of defensiveness, lack of understanding about the roles of your firm and the client organization and how they overlap and interact in mutually supportive ways."

10. *Assess if talking out will help*: When faced with a client who lacks understanding of public relations processes and firm capacities and who also seems reluctant to learn, McCarthy supported a reassessment: "If your analysis indicates this is a person who can be talked to directly, suggest, 'Let's talk this out.' "

11. *Use written communiqués at times*: Written reports or proposals may strengthen a relationship with somebody who can't be reached personally. For example, communiqués can review mechanics on how programming works and identify positions that are tenable.

12. *Gauge willingness to invest in MBO process*: Rigorous procedures for defining and programming measurable objectives provide opportunities for in-depth education about counseling. For clients unwilling or unable to invest time or fees in a complete MBO program, an option is to urge them to take partial advantage of the process.

13. *Try doctor-patient model*: When a client, usually smaller, can't employ more sophisticated problem-solving approaches, McCarthy follows the advice of a psychologist who briefed members of the Counselors Academy on a doctor-patient model: "This requires diagnosis and consultation, with a conclusion to the client of: 'This is what you want us to do for you.' " The client has the option of accepting the conclusion or offering the counselor an alternative. Occasionally the alternative may not be feasible, or a client may have difficulty in getting at what is really wanted.[38]

14. *Remove mystique about value, costs of counseling*: Clients and counselors continue to be haunted by vestiges of an earlier era in which mystique shrouded what it is that public relations does, how it's evaluated and how it's charged. In England, the managing director of Daniel J. Edelman Ltd., David Davis, found that a "frank approach and willingness to discuss profitability has been received as a welcome breath of fresh air by potential clients."[39]

15. *Explain how counselors profit*: For some clients, it may even be necessary to make it clear that the counseling firm exists to make a profit. Whether or not anyone doubts that, it does make sense to explain to—if not to remind—clients that profits come from fees charged for the time of qualified, skillful and experienced people.

16. *Explain basis for fees*: Providing a breakout of the basis for fees can be helpful (such as *X* percent for consultant, executive and support staff salaries, *Y* percent for overhead costs and services and *Z* percent for profit before taxes). To this would be added the reminder that client and counselor agree in advance upon production costs and other disbursements that will be charged.

17. *Review tangible values*: Ways of identifying tangible values of counseling are reviewed in the chapter on research and in other books. The Edelman executive saw a dilemma in choosing between the scientific response that couches an answer in research jargon to the client query of "How can I judge you?" and the response that goes "to the pragmatic extreme to provide a thick wad of press cuttings" and calculate what the same amount of advertising space would cost.

18. *Give basis for assessing true worth of service*: It pays dividends to invest in explaining the value of services, including quality of counsel based on experience, research and expertness; creativity and objectivity, emphasizing strategic problem solving; efficient planning and budget control; quality and impact of media results (rather than merely quantity); the firm's level of working knowledge about the client's business; and initiative.

19. *Find out what they think and plan strategy accordingly*: Although Davis said that potential clients often ask, "How can I judge you?"[40] it may be noted that the question is not restricted to prospects nor to interpersonal communication. It may, indeed, be on the minds of well-established clients and newcomers to counseling services. And the answers tend to be filled in by the clients, themselves, often without bothering to raise the question.

20. *Learn how to make decision to cut losses*: Some clients are not open to learning or they make education too costly for a firm. Most counselors understand the concept of "know when to cut your losses." But there's a temptation to persist. This suggests that beyond knowing *when*, there is a need for introspection and development of an analytical approach that can be put in place to help counselors learn *how* to make decisions to cut losses.

The decision to refuse or resign a revenue-producing account usually is not easy. Yet hidden costs of not walking away may include damage to esprit de corps, productivity and creative excitement needed for building and attracting other accounts. An intangible cost may be loss of reputation as the client feels forced to take the step to terminate "because nothing is happening or they're chronically unhappy with anything that is done," McCarthy said.[41]

21. *First give it a college try*: For veteran counselors who have worked at developing and refining education strategies, there have been substantial returns from making at least one try after investing some research and analysis into a client's understanding of public relations functions and counseling firms.

Conditioning Future Clients

Persuasion of any kind, including education, tends to work best when predispositions to behavior—attitudes—are shaped well before the need for the behavior arises. In the case of client education, conditioning may profitably begin before counselors are selected, let alone before relationships are defined. Such persuasion may meet less resistance, take deeper root and pave the way for education to follow.

Use of Credible Literature   One ideal setting for such conditioning is literature that commands credibility from executives, including business publications and trade journals. Counselors contribute indirectly through suggesting articles and providing background materials and leads for other sources. They contribute directly by arranging for their own in-depth interviews or byline articles. Here are some examples:

1. *Business to Business*:

Once you have decided that an agency can help your organization, you have to . . . decide whether or not you are willing to commit to working in harmony with it. Answer such questions as "Am I willing to make the PR agency a part of our company? Am I committed to being open with the agency? Am I willing to risk the openness needed for an agency to learn about our company, our people, our products, our marketing plan?"[42]

2. *The Counselor*:

Although few corporate executives would deny the importance of public relations, even the best of them are sometimes at a loss to know when to seek counsel. The reasons go beyond the ingrained executive notion that "We can handle things ourselves" and the impression that retaining outside counselors must necessarily be an expensive proposition. They are less than fully aware of advantages offered by outside experts or circumstances that make outside counseling particularly advisable. Executives frequently need to be reminded that public relations is more than just those collective techniques we call communication. It is the result of employing those techniques.[43]

3. *Public Relations Business*:

Allow enough time to make the relationship work. You hired the firm to bring other skills and perspectives to your program. With some patience, the firm should begin winning your confidence as it climbs along a learning curve in your industry and with your organization.[44]

4. *Computer & Electronics Marketing*:

Try to choose a PR agency whose people want the company's business to be their business. . . . Once the PR agency has been chosen . . . challenge the agency—but remember to let it challenge the company. . . . Most important, the PR agency should be considered part of the company's team—regardless of whether the team focuses on management, marketing finance or other areas. Let the agency personnel be more than implementers and order takers—encourage them to be strategists and planners.[45]

5. *Public Relations Journal*:

Selecting or changing public relations firms involves critical decisions that cry out for systematic guidelines. . . . If the firm serves as a consultant and not just an implementer, it should not try to fit your programs into existing staff and in-house capabilities, but will recommend and secure the best resources to meet your needs.[46]

Models of Conditioning with Criteria for Counsel Selection   Models of techniques for using "how to" on retaining and working with public relations counsel have come from Public Communications Inc. executives in Chicago and Tampa who have aggressively sought to educate businesses on criteria for selecting and evaluating counsel.

For example, Chairman James B. Strenski arranged to have the *Office Guide to Tampa Bay* publish his "Ten Criteria for Selecting PR Counsel." But some of the most valuable material could be found preceding and following the models from Strenski on how to condition clients. He offered these suggestions to client-side officers and public relations firms they might contact:

1. *Prepare management before soliciting proposals*: "Verification of approval from upper management should be secured beforehand." That calls for doing the fact finding and developing a case to convince top management that outside counsel is really needed.

2. *Explore time element*: To explain to laypersons the essential role of clients in controlling time costs, he said: "Knowing that most firms sell communications talents in increments of time can optimize a company's use of public relations counsel."

3. *Ground clients in time control*: Helping clients understand they can economize on costs of time and speed counseling action was the point when he said: "Counsel's ability to serve you is in direct proportion to how effectively it uses its time and how expediently the resources of your company are available to the firm."

4. *Condition for loyalty to counselors*: His comment after a helpful lesson on criteria for selecting counsel was an example of long-range conditioning strategy: "Both your organization and the firm should question your respective procedures when evaluating programs. It's good business for you to reward your public relations firm with loyalty for successes achieved."

In studying how other counselors do so, one can gain a grasp of primary considerations from the vantage points of both sides of the counseling table.

5. *Condition clients for orientation program*: He illustrated the technique of preparing executives for education: "Both sides have to be committed to spending time and money in achieving and maintaining a successful firm/client relationship. The firm needs to invest its time in thorough orientation."[47]

The following synthesizes Strenski's "Ten Criteria for Selecting PR Counsel" and an article by his firm's president, Richard A. Barry, in *PR Casebook* on "What Every Client Should Know":

1. *Overall profile*: What types of accounts does the firm have? Who are the firm's active clients? What are its annual fee billings? How many employees? What is the firm's record in maintaining accounts? Where would you rank as an account?

2. *Financial stability*: How does it check out with such credit ratings as Dun & Bradstreet and with major suppliers? Has it experienced steady growth? Is growth balanced between new clients and expansion of programs for continuing clients? Is there adequate profitability to sustain growth? Does it pay its bills on time?

3. *History*: Does the firm's growth correlate with your own? What is the frequency of account turnover? Why? What is the frequency of staff turnover? Why? What do other agencies say about the firm? Why? How is the firm or its affiliates positioned to help in other parts of the U.S., Canada and other countries?

4. *Professionalism*: Are key people actively involved in professional public relations organizations such as PRSA? One could add: Are principals or senior officers involved in the Counselors Academy or other specialization organizations? Have members of the firm earned accreditation in PRSA or IABC? What professional education and experience do they have?

5. *Client referrals*: What is the firm's record on behalf of clients? Are past and present clients willing to recommend their services or capabilities?

6. *Specialization*: How does the firm match its areas of expertness and experience with corporate needs? Is there adequate specialization or affiliation to refer client to specialized service as needed? One could add: Is there also general expertness a client may need, much as a patient may look for a physician who can treat the whole person or serve as a quarterback when specialists are called in?

7. *Reputation with media*: How do editors of media important to the client perceive the public relations firm? Especially, how do business-financial editors or other gatekeepers of essential sections view the firm? What is the nature of the firm's credibility with special interest media, such as trade publications?

8. *Account team*: Who are the people who will work on the account? How do their personalities match with those of client executives and staff? What backup exists in areas of strength needed, either within the firm or affiliates? What is availability of management for evaluation of activities or review of strategies?

9. *Programming and measurement logic*: What is the philosophy toward research? Objectives? Programming? Evaluation? What are its accountability procedures? How does it check and report progress?

10. *Interaction*: Are they responsible for leading or following your lead in areas of public relations? How will they stay in communication? Will they anticipate the client's problems?[48] Add: Will they feel free to question potentially harmful client policies, procedures, actions or communications?

Condition First-Timers with Special Guidelines

Model Cuts Complaints up to 20 Percent, Reduces Tampering with Writing 70 Percent Such systematic guidelines also are important for effective postcontractual relations with a public relations firm, particularly for clients with little or no experience in using outside counsel.

But instead of placing responsibility for developing guidelines on normally overtaxed members of management, the founder of Chicago's Bernard E. Ury Associates developed his own copyrighted guidebook for new clients. It is part of an educational system that uses face-to-face communication and reinforces that with periodic newsletter-style memos.[49]

This approach may be particularly valuable for counselors with client loads similar to Ury's. About 85 percent are first-time users of public relations firm services. Most don't have internal staff. Some have used advertising agencies to issue personnel releases.

Although guidebook components, interpersonal sessions and follow-up materials would benefit from rigorous testing on areas that need changing or strengthening, Ury has found through several years of trial-and-error experience that they have been helpful in preventing friction generated by misunderstandings. Moreover, he said they have helped client managers understand public relations and the roles they should play in working with his firm.

"This is all the result of bitter experience, getting into client expectations you can't possibly meet and what public relations can or cannot do.

Why get into a situation where irreconcilable differences arise a few months into the contract?"

The system has not been a panacea, but he estimated up to a 20 percent reduction in negative client questions and challenges since instituting the system. There may be a hidden factor at work: Use of such a system would tend to generate increased consciousness of the importance of open client-counselor relations on both sides.

One of the more tangible results was sharply reduced counseling staff frustration achieved through cutting the time needed to get written communication into production. The number of problems his firm encountered with client officers "tampering" with writing dropped 70 to 75 percent: "They're more reserved in taking pen in hand and slashing up copy. Now they have far more understanding." And when there are differences, they discuss questions or suggestions in person.

The system also has eliminated sources of friction on billing. Clients tend to be more mindful of what's in the budget, how charges are incurred and how they're billed. More consciousness tends to correlate with more understanding.

How Guide Is Used to Teach Management about Public Relations, Their Roles   Here are examples of how the client guide is used to teach management about public relations and their roles:

1. *Initiate before signing stage*: The firm usually gives the guide to clients in the prospect stage "so they know what they're getting into." It's not only a way of conditioning them for a contractual relationship, but also for weeding out those with whom there might be irreconcilable differences. There is no simple cause-effect relationship between making the guide available and clients using it, however. "Some read it, some brush it aside. Most welcome the opportunity to use it, but others say it's 'too academic; let's get on with the job.' "

2. *Offer to go over guide in person*: The reading barrier often is overcome by the offer of the firm to review the guide's points in person. More important, the personal presentation facilitates questions and prompts discussion on factors of concern. For the counselor doing the briefing, written guide materials provide a checklist of points to cover. For clients with some public relations experience or limited patience, a quick review of the table of contents and a few key points may suffice.

3. *Make copies available to others*: Without going over the head of the client's contact person, Ury tries to get guides in the hands of decision-makers and resource persons. If the initial contact is the chairman or CEO, additional copies are offered.

4. *Chart capabilities—and limitations*: A simple matrix labels areas of public relations concern (public policy, marketing, executive participation, employee relations, etc.) alongside concise columnar descriptions of

"What Only the Company Can Do" and "What a PR Firm Can Do." Before developing this tool, Ury recalled such problems as having a client who wanted speaking engagements but declined to make people available. Here's an example from the chart on customer relations: Company only— "Develop programs for good customer relations; take action to remedy product and service deficiencies." PR firm—"Carry out communications programs with customers and prospects; determine areas of dissatisfaction; advise remedies."

5. *Review where billable time goes*: The guide includes a two-page summary of 17 time elements with explanations such as:

Developing story material for the client may involve "personal interviews, further research and validation, writing, editing, re-writing and planning for illustrations. Depending on the accessibility and responsiveness of persons or other sources required to contribute to a story. . . ."

Ury's firm used to have problems with clients who didn't understand, for instance, why it takes so much time for a media release. The guide attempts to get at the "nine tenths of the iceberg the client can't see." In it and in face-to-face communication, "we explain the hidden time they don't see when glancing at an annual report or brochure." The formal presentation even anticipates such newcomer "time-saver" misconceptions as using off-the-shelf formats for product features.

6. *Suggest client protocol after contracting*: The Chicago counselor's guide uses two single-spaced pages to recommend how and why the client should, among other things:

Appoint a coordinator

Supply background information

Send routine and confidential management reports to the firm

Brief entire organization on the public relations program

Respond promptly on proposals and copy

Provide approvals in writing

Allow sufficient time for results

Keep employees informed about public relations results

Instruct employees to alert firm on media contacts

7. *Review operating procedures*: Particularly for the newcomer, a review of procedures can be useful in helping understand the processes involved in working with a firm. The guide covers how to work with an account executive; the role of principals; approaches to media selection; considerations in scheduling; and quality-control checks on programs, materials and progress.

8. *Develop insight on writing techniques*: The "Why We Write the Way We Do" component begins the education of client executives and employ-

ees whose cooperation is needed by counselors in the research and development of written communications. It's a to-the-point primer that explains
such considerations as differences between advertising and public relations style; techniques to assure credibility; structure of news stories;
wire service style; problems with superlatives, qualifiers and puffery; readability elements; attribution requirements in writing for news media; need
for substance; need to anticipate media gatekeeper questions on details;
and anticipation of outdated information in published reports.

9. *How to use questions to teach*: Ury's 30-question "P.R.I.Q." component of the guide is a testing instrument that does more than test a client's
"Public Relations Information Quotient." It actually is a teaching instrument for both client officers and Ury's more than dozen staff members
when they observe verbal and nonverbal reactions. Whether or not a client
bothers to take the quiz, either a look at the questions or a glance ahead at
the answers will serve several purposes. He said P.R.I.Q. "wakes up" people at a presentation and provides an opening for discussion of potentially
dangerous misconceptions.

It also may be ventured that the very act of considering the existence of
the questions psychologically predisposes a client to give thought to the
issues. There also may be a predisposition to become more personally
involved later when similar questions arise in the actuality of public relations proposals and follow-through.

Here are some examples of true-false questions from the P.R.I.Q.:

"If a publication writes about a competitor, you should expect the publication to publish the same kind of story about you?"

"If you make a not-for-publication statement to an editor, you should
expect the statement will not be printed?"

"The best way to deal with unfavorable information that must be disclosed is to bury it in the last few paragraphs of a news release?"

"Complaining to a publication about unfavorable treatment is a good
way to get better treatment next time?"

"If a reporter or editor tries to reach you by telephone for commentary,
and you're unavailable, you should expect the editor will wait for you to
return the call?"

The answers beyond the simple "true" or "false" are as provocative as
the questions.[50]

Counselors who obtain the copyrighted P.R.I.Q. from Ury may wish to
consider not only adding of other pertinent questions but also whether all
existing questions lend themselves to the simplicity of true-false choice. It
also is recommended that such instruments be field-tested, perhaps with a
focus group.

Newsletter Gives Prospects and Clients Continuing Education One way to keep in communication with clients and even educate former clients and prospects is through a vehicle such as a newsletter. Ury's *PR Memo* provides readers some of the same kind of substance subscribers to professional newsletters find in the sections discussing techniques.[51]

He leans over backward to keep the publication from appearing commercial. In sample issues analyzed nowhere was to be found an article about his firm. The only Ury identification appeared in small type font in a "published by . . ." insert at the bottom of page 1.

Another strategy: The simple, clean format with capitalized lead-in headings and underlined key phrases is not unfamiliar to readers of the more popular business and public relations newsletters.

But the most effective aspect may be found in the subtle teaching in articles appealing to persons concerned about corporate public relations. The reports deal with a variety of topics such as citations of new perspectives from national business and trade publications, recastings of the basics of public relations and useful tips.

Examples include concise reports on: When Does a Company Outgrow Its Need for PR?, Why Certain Executives in Any Industry Are Quoted, Traps for the Unwary Executive, Do You Have a Crisis Plan?, Ask Your Prospects and Customers, Among the Many Myths, Mouth Go Dry Before Speech?, Know the Gatekeepers, A Good Liaison Person Is. . . , Newsletters Are Excellent Vehicles, Using Advertising Pressure, Where Do People Get Most of Their News?, No Comment May Be Best Response, Set Up Your Own PR Department, People Who Like People Not Necessarily Good at PR, Should Doctors and Lawyers Promote Themselves?, Readability Formula Interpretations, Tips on Language, Fundamentals vs. The Big Idea and Chicago Area PR Salaries to Increase.

Ury supplements his newsletter mailings with reprints of articles from such publications as *Public Relations Journal, Fortune, Forbes* and *Chicago Tribune*. Beyond choosing articles that are relevant to a particular client interest, he adds a cover note that goes beyond the traditional FYI or colored highlighting to explain how to use the information. The cover note technique is used by a number of internal public relations officers who have found over the years that executives often heed what third-party experts have to say. Inviting clients to professional society seminars on particular areas of public relations is another way of exposing executives to the influence of third-party experts.

Educate Clients with Visions of Future, Lessons from Past

One Model Uses Scenarios to Drive Home Moral When Hill and Knowlton's president and CEO spoke to the 1985 convention of the United

Dairy Industry Association, he illustrated a client/prospect continuing education strategy favored by some of his peers around the country. Much as old storytellers used parables, he gave a speech to deliver a moral.[52]

In the case of his dairy industry speech, Robert L. Dilenschneider first eloquently identified with his audience's deepest concerns:

Today, American farmers are in a deadly conflict.

For decades you fed the world—and now many of you are worried about feeding yourselves.

For decades, the sons of rural America have gone off to fight wars— and now many are fighting for their financial futures.

For decades, American farmers have stood for stability and hard work—and now statistics tell us suicide rates. . . .

The first moral of the parable was not long in coming: "Unity is the engine that drives any successful organization through stormy times. And yours started picking up speed in recent months." The second took time to build upon the first, but followed logically and inescapably: "Now in suggesting a better relationship with the media, I'm suggesting that each organization should speak the same message."

Dilenschneider outlined the components of an effective communication plan, including scenario development, as he led the audience from the importance of monitoring media through marshalling of resources to "focusing on one issue that can turn a situation around." Then he focused on a different scenario for what *could have* been done when a *Time* magazine article "savaged your industry."

If there had been a media monitoring program in place, if a networking system had been in place, if a scenario had been developed, if allies had been lined up to speak as one, if the dairy industry had focused on one issue—*if*—and then he read the statement that *could have been* the thrust of *Time*'s story.

The scenario reached deep into the emotional and mental core of his audience by speaking not about generalizations but about specifics, by offering a glimpse of a different reality than the one uppermost in their minds, by dwelling not so much on the damage done as the possibility of using public relations strategies and methods to minimize future damage, maybe even to make gains. "That's the message of a united group, an organization that knows that unity is strength. If you don't get that message out, many of you may share the misery of the crop farmers."

He didn't promise that the American government would act in any way, just that the dairy industry could have its message heard in the court of public opinion and that it would be a message that would be heard by consumers and elected representatives who might share their concern that the supply of milk as well as a vital industry could be jeopardized "through the brutal, quick elimination of price supports."

Backcasting Process Used to Help CEOs, Boards Buy Future Similar to Dilenschneider's building of scenarios, but with an added strategic fillip, the adaptation of management consultant James Kingsley's backcasting concept helps prepare client CEOs and boards to accept counselors' projections and buy into new or modified programs.

Kerry Tucker, executive vice president of the San Diego–based counseling firm of Nuffer, Smith, Tucker, and Robert F. Smith, president of Strategies & Teams, said that in their work with backcasting over a several-year period, they found that the process "can provide public relations practitioners with valuable cost-benefit data for program evaluations and readjustments made necessary by resulting emerging threats and opportunities."[53]

And in so doing, the process provides a data base that makes changes in program direction easier to sell to chief executives and boards of directors. Smith and Tucker defined backcasting as "a process of clarifying for yourself and others program impact versus manpower and out-of-pocket expenses in each of the areas in which you do business" and of spotting program trends.

Basically, it involves a systematic review of an organization's history—focusing on public relations roles and activities—as the foundation for making projections for the future. In its more sophisticated mode, counselors graphically chart statistical data from a three to five year period. When it's not feasible to assemble the numbers, an optional mode calls for backcasts of results to be described in a narrative account. "Narrative backcasts can often lend perspective beyond historical facts by including organizational values and attitudes."

Nuffer, Smith, Tucker documented three cases demonstrating the value of backcasting in client education and persuasion:

The CEO of a client was positioned to convince her board to adopt a significant budget increase at a time when economic conditions predisposed them to slash expenditures for public relations.

Another client board with strong commitment to continuing its traditional promotion program gave a unanimous vote of approval for a new publicity thrust when "backcast statistics made it clear that an expanded publicity program would significantly multiply audience reach while decreasing expensive man-hours."

The counseling firm was alerted by charting coverage of its news releases in metropolitan dailies to a serious decline when the year under study was contrasted with a four-year backcast. Before patterns of media usage of news releases could harden, the firm intervened with a plan to increase personal contacts with key editors.

Although the counseling and management consultant firms found backcasting helped convince management when it became necessary to counsel action plans to change client organizational culture, Smith and Tucker recommended that "strategies for selling organizational change should be designed to reinforce rather than differentiate from an organization's culture."

Dealing with "Mental Indigestion" and the "Judo" Approach   Favoring adjustments that reinforce corporate culture over more drastic change fits with a body of persuasion theory and research that says that people with strong commitments are far more prone to accept that which seems to be in harmony with their convictions than to undergo conversion.

This tends to be particularly true when an executive has taken actions or made statements in support of those convictions. Persuasion scholars use the term *cognitive dissonance* to describe the mental turmoil that arises when an individual is forced to contradict his or her own beliefs, behavior or public utterances. Cognitive dissonance basically amounts to "mental indigestion."[54]

When conversion doesn't work (in the sense of accepting abrupt change or swallowing unpleasant "realities" that contradict one's own), other strategies may be tried. An example of a strategy that may work has been borrowed from the martial arts by Nager and has been named "the judo approach."[55]

A martial arts analogy is used to teach the judo approach to persuasion: If a diminutive person attempts to match force for force with a towering hulk, odds are against moving the other individual. Translate physical bulk into power and position, and it also is clear that it may be futile to get in the way of the executive's momentum or to contradict a belief in the hope of changing the executive's course.

Judo and other martial arts operate on the principle of moving with the momentum; moving with the other person, in the same direction. Then when the other creates an imbalance, it is possible to redirect the momentum and change its direction.

Going with the momentum, and in the same direction before changing course, begins with seeking to understand the values, beliefs and behavioral pattern of the client. The joining of counselor and executive in moving with the CEO's mental force field continues with accepting the goals, objectives, strategies and priorities that are in the client's interests. In some cases, there may be hypothetical or conditional acceptance for purposes of persuasion. Imbalance in an individual's beliefs is best brought about by that person, alone. The perception of being thrown by a tricky maneuver may be acceptable in a martial arts gym; it is not, in the executive suite.

Self-induced imbalance followed by an openness to ideas that can help restore a sense of balance (what physical and social scientists call a homeostatic state) can be brought about in several ways that usually involve getting individuals to raise their own questions.

The modes of doing this are not new to many lawyers, physicians or public relations counselors. Questions that do not deny the person's beliefs but do require some introspection to develop a response may be asked. Fresh evidence may be introduced, not laid out as contradictory, but offered in a supportive manner. The client is placed in the position of choosing among options for which pros and cons have been helpfully placed side by side.[56] Other modes include the scenario building of a Dilenschneider, backcasting of a Tucker and Smith and illumination techniques of an Edelman.

Helping Client Learn from Past Problems   Daniel J. Edelman, president of the Chicago-based public relations firm that bears his name, demonstrated a strategy for educating clients who need to learn from unpleasant episodes in their own histories. This case relates to development of new product lines as well as the programs to bring them to market.

Edelman illustrated how to anticipate client or prospect defensiveness and deftly educate executives for increased sensitivity to media, government and major special interest group concerns in an educational speech to a _Fortune_ 500 company's officers.[57]

The company had come under the harsh glare of the media's spotlight and had incurred the wrath of anti-war demonstrators during the Vietnam war; it later found itself the target of environmental and consumer special interests, legislators and investigative reporters.

Edelman dealt with the negative aspects of the issue only after laying a positive foundation, by citing experts respected by his business audience and sharing his own perspectives on the theoretical and pragmatic aspects of product marketing. As part of that groundwork, he reviewed cases in which other clients were positioned for new product roll-outs and continuing publicity campaigns in situations that could have been threatening to buyer and stockholder confidence. Then he reviewed in detail the then-current and the recent achievements for product promotion for his audience's company.

About three quarters through his presentation, he diplomatically broached the subject of the manufacturer's problems in an increasingly complex society in which "companies like yours find themselves in situations involving a variety of issues, audiences and problems."

Then he reinforced their consciousness of the company's visibility to consumer groups, media, Congress, state legislatures and governmental regulatory agencies as backdrop for bringing up the problems they encountered over the years due to public perceptions. He balanced his review of negatives with a discussion of positive image components related to corporate strength, financial stability, innovativeness, research and "exciting new ideas in products that make life better for Americans and people around the world."

With this buildup, he primed his audience for greater awareness of the interests of publics that have "a stake in your company and who want to voice their opinion about it." After reviewing the diversity of influential publics he stressed the need for sensitivity "as you develop new products and prepare to introduce them."

The illumination strategy of Edelman would tend to elicit openness, rather than defensiveness. It would tend to open an audience of executives to the understanding that public relations counsel begins with decisions on product development rather than with tacking on of a publicity campaign to marketing programs.

A Teacher's Model for Motivating to Learn and Change   As indicated by the examples of Dilenschneider, Edelman and Tucker and Smith, counselors, like teachers, can use the lessons of history to establish credibility. Counselors, like teachers, can guide an audience of one, as well as a full auditorium, to learn from history and to consider scenarios for the future.

Most important, counselors, like teachers, can help plant the seeds of motivation to learn. And that motivation, more than any technique dependent upon it, lies at the heart of change. It lies at the heart of changing attitudes toward the media, government involvement, public opinion, the engines of the marketplace. It lies at the heart of changing attitudes toward the principles and pragmatics of public relations counseling.

6

CLIENT-SIDE
PERSPECTIVES

Public relations counselors, along with attorneys, physicians, architects, management consultants and accountants, are learning that quality of service should be a negotiable item between client and professional firm. Terms usually applied to client relations, such as "quality service," tend to hold different meanings for each individual. This chapter acknowledges that the link between a professional firm and its client almost always is fragile, complicated and in need of strengthening.

The focus is on client-side perspectives; the insights come from counselors who role-played professional firm clients during a seminar and from former counseling firm executives who made the transition to internal public relations positions, past corporate public relations officers who became counselors and career client executives who shared their criteria for quality service.

COUNSELORS AS CLIENTS

What Professional Firms Share in Common

Role-playing is an imperfect instrument because no human ever really can effectively clothe himself in the framework of reference gained in another's lifetime. But it does help open the mind to fresh insights about oneself, other individuals and relationships.

At their 1986 Spring Conference, members of the Counselors Academy learned to look across different professions and draw upon their collective experiences to see themselves as clients. In interaction with David H. Maister, management consultant and former Harvard Business School professor, and among themselves, they agreed that the "quality" of the firm-client relationship must be negotiated.[1]

171

By the end of their seminar, the counselors concluded that the biggest problem in client relations is not improving quality by increasing technical competence but understanding the psychological experience the client has in using professional firms.

Through their role-playing experience, they learned that in most situations, clients would rather not have to turn to a physician, attorney or public relations counselor.

It is apparent that "quality service" reflects neither only the "client is always right" nor the "I know what quality is" orientation of the counselor. Instead, it requires a shared definition based on an understanding of both the client's and counselor's needs, interests and psychologies.

But those factors are in flux on both sides of the relationship, sometimes because of environmental forces. That dictates recognition of the fragility of client-firm relations. As Maister put it, "quality needs to be constantly renegotiated." Defining service excellence means going back to verify if firm and client still mutually agree on roles they expect each other to play.

What Clients Want   In role-playing as clients of members of other professions, counselors said that they looked for solutions to problems. While role-playing clients of attorneys, counselors said they sought "solutions to problems I can't solve myself," "something you can't relate to but that he has in his bank of knowledge," "something solved the same day" and "excitement that you're going to win."

From management consultants, seminar participants said they wanted "free advice," "an education" and "quick and free answers." As the clients of accountants, counselors looked for "reassurance," "the promise that I'm going to save money" and "high expectations for help in getting me out of a tax bind."

One member of the seminar audience said that in visiting physicians, "it's a relief that you're going to get help." Another said, "a doctor is somebody to give problems away to." A third said he looked to his doctor for "supersolutions."

The executives and members of public relations firms attempted to put themselves in their own clients' shoes and determine what it is that they're trying to buy from counselors. Among the answers:

results

reinforcement

comfort

confidence

security

solutions

skilled help

objectivity

authority

understanding of my problem

understanding of me

discretion

to give the problem to someone else

to share the problem

to make money or not lose it

a defender

objectivity in my favor

empathy or sympathy

make me look good to others

peer acceptance

competitive advantage

experience to inspire confidence

ability to deliver what you promise

a quick fix

"Clients expect professionals to 'fix' problems, and you and I know that's not possible," Maister observed. He said 90 percent of all misunderstandings over service quality arise when professionals "don't have courage up front to say what's achievable, what's not."[2]

Insights from Exploring What Disturbs Clients Irritability, discomfort and other factors that bother clients of professional firms affect those who go to public relations counselors as well as lawyers and doctors. Probing this area is of value.

In role-playing patients, seminar participants said they would see doctors with fear, apprehension, anxiety, "awkwardness because of the personal nature of the visit," concern over expense, distrust because "they can't fix your problems" and a sense of confusion over medical knowledge to which one might not be able to relate.

Going to lawyers for help would bring out vulnerability in "having to confess to weakness," frustration in revealing a problem "you can't solve yourself," impatience in wanting a problem solved "right away," anger at "contracting with a principal and ending up with other members of the practice" and anticipation of high fees.

In role-playing clients of accountants, counselors saw themselves de-

pressed, confused, worried about charges as well as financial losses, and resentful to have to ask for outside help.

Other significant revelations with a bearing on understanding counselor-client relations came out of role-playing clients of professional firms, including public relations:

"They exacerbate problems by finding more complications than the client thinks are there."

"They never return calls."

"They bill for every second."

"They either use jargon or talk down to you."

"They're arrogant."

"He doesn't understand my real goals and priorities."

"It's intimidating to deal with someone who lacks knowledge of my business."

"I don't want to pay for his time to learn my business."

"It seems he should be giving more; what's he doing for me that I couldn't do for myself?"

"He has no initiative; he does what I ask but no more."

"He makes decisions without consulting me."

"He patronizes me—tells me what he thinks I want to hear because he's so worried about losing the account, or maybe just to make me feel good."

"They're rushed, never have enough time for you."

"Delays, delays, delays!"

"He says 'no'; he says I can't do things; and he is negative rather than facilitative."

"He's more concerned with the past and much less focused on the present and future."

"His errors are very costly, and that makes me nervous."

"You don't feel like you're Number 1."

"He acts like *he* is the professional."

Counselors around the country, as well as in a management seminar, can strengthen client relationships by seeking greater understanding of what clients want from the professional firms they retain, what bothers them, what barriers emerge on both sides, how executives want to measure success and judge quality of service and how individuals vary on their perspectives of quality service.

FORMER COUNSELORS' PERSPECTIVES

Transition Radically Alters Perspective

By making the transition from counseling firm careers to positions as internal public relations executives, some individuals have walked in the shoes of counselors and then clients—literally. Such persons can offer precious insight to their former colleagues in counseling on how to relate to clients. The transition can radically alter their perspectives.

When Thomas E. Nunan headed the Southern California regional offices of Burson-Marsteller, fees clients paid to his and other firms seemed relatively modest for the caliber of services provided. Nunan was frustrated because some clients wouldn't invest more in sophisticated research and counsel. He was frustrated when some clients took a short-term view and only wanted limited projects.[3]

But after Nunan became vice president of communications at United Technologies' Mostek Corp., he developed a radically different orientation to budgetary concerns and counseling services.[4] A vacuum in public relations counsel was filled by Nunan at a time when Mostek had barely any product publicity—let alone more sophisticated communications programs.

Mostek, Dallas-based manufacturer of computer systems, components and software for civilian and military markets, had no budget for retaining counselors when he was hired away from Burson-Marsteller in 1982. "There was no public relations to speak of." There also was no budget for an advertising program. What Mostek did have was a brand new CEO, described by Nunan as "always available, involved, a believer." It also was a time when the United Technologies subsidiary was besieged by rumors it was going out of business.

Within three years, Mostek was positioned as the eighth largest U.S. manufacturer of integrated circuits and the first to reach the billion-dollar mark in 64K dynamic random access memory hardware.

With the help of Nunan and his supportive CEO, Mostek built and funded a diversity of communications programs, reflected in the glow of *Business Week, Wall Street Journal* and *New York Times* front-page treatment. More important, top management correlated public relations achievements with corporate profitability.

Although Mostek contracted with a London-based public relations firm and retained services of counselors in Belgium, West Germany and France, the corporation tended to look to its vendors "only for limited, defined needs, such as media projects, special events, international representation, and one-time speaker training, sales meetings, audio visual creative services and problem solving."

Nunan found himself operating from "a perhaps strange perspective for one with 17 years of public relations firm experience and three years of corporate"—restricting use of outside counsel to short-term services that his own staff couldn't cover (primarily in Europe) and objecting to "the tremendous size of fees."[5]

Counsel from Corporate Perspective

Another counseling firm executive gained a new perspective on financial matters after he became group vice president for corporate communications of American Medical International (AMI).[6]

Peter J. Dowd rose in counseling to head West Coast operations for Hill and Knowlton and to co-found Haley, Kiss and Dowd (New York, Washington and Los Angeles) before his 1983 move to the client side with the second largest health care services company in the world.

This move reinforced some of his convictions about the advantages counseling know-how would give him in working directly for a company such as AMI. But he was surprised by the gaps left in his education during his career with counseling firms. Advantages outweighed disadvantages, but there were lessons to be learned from both.

Advantages of a Counseling Background

1. *Take confidence in crisis management*: Dowd learned that the depth and diversity of experience in working for hundreds of clients in dozens of industries positioned him well for crisis management. "I was quite comfortable when the first thing I had to do was live through a nationally important negative story that started on CBS news. It was the first time AMI had something that major and negative."

2. *Take pride in grasp of electronic*: With his counseling background, Dowd was able to help AMI gain new dimensions in developing electronic communication capabilities. He introduced broad-scale television and teleconferencing and created a new video studio. His experience made top management comfortable, and it made him confident in counseling new directions.

3. *Contract for contacts*: Unlike some of his former client public relations executives, he didn't have to go to a firm and ask procedural questions: "I can direct agencies; I don't have to go to New York and ask, 'what do I do in this case?' I learned to use counseling firms for their contacts, such as when we needed to work with the governor of Oklahoma."

4. *Be sure of leadership knowhow*: "I knew how to lead and get the most out of staff, thanks to what I learned in counseling."

What Counselor Can Learn as Client Executive   There is a great deal that a counselor can learn from his colleagues on the client-side if the right questions are asked. Dowd, however, learned the hard way—through on-the-job experience after he left counseling. Here are lessons to be gained from his experience:

1. *Respect client budgeting process*: "I never realized how complex corporate budgeting procedures could be for a department head." He had developed program budgets for many clients, but that was much simpler. "Here I'm concerned with not only staff and benefits, but also internal programming costs, external costs and interaction with the marketing budget."

It doesn't stop with budgeting for a program or a year's operations: "Once a quarter, you have to review budget with your superiors. It's a whole intensive process and you need to be pretty much in control." His own budget runs several million dollars.

2. *Learn clients' budget processes*: The implications for counselors who tend to be essentially idea persons as they move up the ladder in counseling firms are: learn, know and coach account teams on the concerns of client CEOs and public relations officers.

3. *Learn business perspective of corporate officers*: "In corporate, regardless of whether you're a staff or line officer, you have to operate more as a business person." Dowd realized it would pay for counselors to emulate internal counterparts who strive to understand the business perspectives of other corporate executives.

4. *Assure that ideas are precise, relevant, feasible*: "When I was a counselor, I could go in and present ideas even when they were not right-on because I didn't have to worry about them unless they were adopted. Now, when I go into the CEO's office, I have to give ideas that I know relate and are very precise."

5. *Think like general operations officer*: He also learned that it's not enough to frame ideas in a language the CEO understands. "He expects me to think like a general operations officer of a business. I have had to learn much more about operations and straight business planning to do my job well." That kind of understanding also would be useful for an external counselor in dealing with client executives, including sophisticated public relations officers.

6. *Consider MBA training*: "An MBA helps anybody, but it's even more necessary for a corporate public relations person than an external counselor." He didn't say so, but a counselor who has an MBA or other postgraduate business training would find it advantageous to help internal staff make the kind of transitions that Dowd had to make, as well as useful in analyzing and working with CEOs.

7. *Learn when to slow pace*: He had to learn to adopt something different than "the hyper pace of counseling." Aside from pacing for survival is a consideration of significance for both external counsel and internal staff:

"If I tried to push projects or programs through as hard as I might have in my agency days, I would not get as much done."

8. *Know when to back off*: Persistence may be considered a valuable trait of an account executive—to his own firm. But Dowd learned on the inside that because other things occupy the minds of corporate executives, "you're going to damage your credibility if you're not aware of when to back off. Your timing, like your pacing, has to be informed."

9. *Think as part of the team*: "You're not only supposed to know your own job, but how to fit what you do into the overall corporate team effort." That means the counselor, like his inside colleague, can benefit by taking cognizance of what client officers—including the CEO—are doing.

"In the agency business, I was always firing out new ideas for new and continuing clients. I wasn't expected to know the business to the depth I do here. You can't come in with a totally inappropriate budget or recommendations if you're part of the organization."

The following is an example of timing and pacing. In 1982, Dowd foresaw the need for creating a studio "right away" for video and teleconferencing. "If I had still been with Hill and Knowlton, I would have said, 'you need a TV studio now.' " He didn't. Because he found media relations tended to be reactive, his first step was to start a news bureau—primarily print oriented—to do proactive stories on wellness. "Only in late 1984 did I introduce budget and concepts for television services. The timing was right." In mid-1985, he planned to have AMI's first teleconferencing and video studio. "I was adapting to the general pace of the organization."

10. *Go beyond traditional orientation*: He advised,

> When you get any new account, especially a major company, don't stop with identifying the client and the person you report to, getting to know your direct contact and the CEO and learning all about the program objectives and the business objectives for the short term. Find out about internal budgeting and political and personnel pressures under which the public relations person and program operate. Try to learn about the emerging areas of importance in the company.

11. *How to get into the client's board room*: One of the factors that keeps a counselor out of the board room is "a tendency to respond to things that are now, rather than things that will be a year from now." He said that counseling firms used by his company are "aware of where we are, but not where we're going." It's a problem of oversight rather than lack of capability. "They don't call up to ask." In reflecting on what he learned on the client side, he said that "I would be asking, 'where are you going a year from now?' "

12. *Do research and thinking client doesn't have time to do*:

> We have eight agencies under contract. The ninth resource is a coun-

selor in Washington. He doesn't do government relations. He's been with AMI on and off for 10 years and we're only one of four accounts for him. He reads all the trade publications, goes to all the conventions, goes to lunch regularly with all of the association representatives in Washington.

But what he really does to command loyalty and respect is "come up with ideas that I don't think of; he's doing all the background research I don't have time to do."

13. *Do more industry issue tracking*: He encouraged counseling firm officers to find a way to have account executives and staff do more tracking of industry issues for clients.

14. *Do homework on client PR officer*: "I'm most impressed by those counselors who do their homework and know how to work with you."

CLIENT-TO-COUNSELOR TRANSITION

The insight gained in the switch from a senior counseling firm position to the client side is only matched by the transition in the other direction.

Observations from Industrial Executive-Turned Counselor

David Ferguson, 1985 PRSA president, gained his insights through contrast and comparison after moving from the executive suite at USX (then, U.S. Steel) in Chicago to a senior consultant position with Hill and Knowlton.[7] "The wise corporate person's familiarity with culture, politics, traditions, personalities and policies of the company helps him make public relations decisions." On the other hand, "the sharp counselor brings a broader range of experience into play.

"In the corporate world, some public relations executives have never had to make a formal proposal. In the counseling field, proposals are very important." He said that he was more in the position of having U.S. Steel superiors evaluate him personally instead of evaluating his ideas and programs.

Staff Acts as Internal Counseling Firm   Over the years, many client public relations executives have sought to adapt external counseling procedures to internal operations. Ferguson, for instance, said he became aware of the cost to his former employers—and to other corporations—of sacrificing the advantages of counseling firm concepts. "We suffered because we weren't obliged to do proposals and reporting. Corporate staff would be better if we had to do this."

He had advocated creating separate public relations profit centers within his former corporation. His concept called for a nationwide public relations network with the corporation guaranteeing to employ his staff for five years. "After that we would have had to compete for that business, even though we were in the company, and go out and sell other clients. Profits would have gone back to the company, despite the additional risks. The idea wasn't new, but it also hadn't flown well before. GE tried something similar to that once, but it didn't go." USS/USX rejected the proposal.

How to Capitalize upon the Differences Analysis of counseling and client-side practices led to the following ideas on how to capitalize upon differences:

1. *Respect corporate counterparts*: "There's a tendency among some people in counseling firms to not give corporate public relations people enough credit for having knowledge in the field. Give client people credit for being very knowledgeable," Ferguson said.

2. *Respect what counselors bring*: To former colleagues in industry, he recommended recognition that counselors bring to the business relationship experience and talent corporate officers don't have. "There's a problem in preconceived notions on both sides of the table."

Research and analysis of such notions could arm counselors for planning strategic educational campaigns to modify preconceptions on both sides.

3. *Bring in internal person when dealing with CEO*: "If the firm is dealing with the CEO, I suggest they ask to talk to—and get to know—the public relations people. Although it's often not possible, it would be a good idea to invite the public relations officer to sit in on discussions with the CEO and the counselor."

Normally, such an approach would help cultivate internal support, reduce defensiveness and encourage teamwork, although there are a few situations in which it might inhibit the CEO.

4. *Examine pollution of environment problems*: His experience and study of other corporations taught him that "nothing has acquainted industrial management with the need for sound programs as much as environmental problems they now face. That's caused lots of interest in public affairs and public relations."

5. *Recognize crises as keys*: Crisis situations tend to strengthen management commitment to public relations. "Unfortunately, it often takes a major crisis to convince an organization that it needs a strong public relations program," he observed. "It may not be a physical tragedy such as Bhopal, Tylenol or Three Mile island; it often could be financial or environmental problems. It's during crisis times that organizations realize that they need credibility based on solid public relations programs."

One implication of Ferguson's advice is that counselors educate clients on the risk/benefit equation in investing in research and counsel to prevent and minimize the impact of potential crises. The veteran of the foreign import, antitrust, labor strife, automation and other crises that befell the steel industry said: "I think that an alert counseling firm can see crises arising for potential clients and can make proposals that help prepare them for necessary actions."

He said that is one way to "build client credibility very fast."

Former Coca-Cola Officer's Insights on How to Be Credible

Another way to build credibility, as American Medical's Dowd and Mostek's Nunan concur, is for the counselor to analyze client finances and budgetary factors.

William Pruett brought other ramifications of that lesson with him to Atlanta's Pringle Dixon Pringle when he took an early retirement in 1984 from a 25-year career with Coca-Cola. Pruett built his credibility to be elected to a senior vice presidency and to become assistant secretary of the Coca-Cola board of directors.

Before he joined Pringle Dixon Pringle, Pruett used to ask both public relations firm and advertising agency people how they perceived their own careers. The answer he sought was not that they considered themselves expert practitioners at their communications companies; instead, the client officer within Pruett longed to see them identify with the success of their clients.[8]

"People sometimes think that public relations as a function is important. What is important is the product or service of the client you represent. Techniques are only important so far as they can help the client build his firm or sell his products or services."

That is particularly applicable to advertising agencies. It's clear, however, that public relations firms have other important agendas, such as positioning clients and their industries to appeal to the investment community, live with government and have support of internal and external publics they need to survive and thrive.

In his observations of the various advertising and public relations companies that approached Coca-Cola over the years, he found that relative newcomers to counseling tended to "spend more time worrying over techniques rather than what the client was trying to do. The ultimate function of the outside firm is to help the client grow in any way it can. The only reason a business-conscious client is willing to put out money is the belief that the outside firm can help make it profitable and help solve its problems."

Understand and Work with Client Finance—Internal as Well as External
Among the recommendations made by Pruett, or implicit in his observations as a client executive-turned counselor, are several that underline the value of understanding and working with corporate finance—internally and externally.

1. *Recognize differences in financial control systems*: "All corporate entities—at least, those that are successful—have very well structured financial control systems, unparalleled for the most part by professional firms."

2. *Know when, how public relations budget processed*: He recalled that at Coca-Cola and other companies he knew, public relations executives had to justify expenditures at least twice a year in thorough budget reviews.

> *Typically, the annual budget review process starts toward the end of August and we feverishly work on projections for the next year so we can come before the board when it meets in November or December. At that point, the internal public relations executive says, "We require X dollars of which Y percent goes to outside counselors." Some controller will ask: "How can you justify that kind of expenditure? Why spend all that money externally?"*

3. *Anticipate rejustification challenges*: External counselors and their internal liaisons should anticipate challenges for rejustification of expenditures, particularly if there are cost overruns, but also as a matter of course in some companies that have midyear reviews of progress and spending.

4. *Help client liaison justify expenditures*: Counselors must bear in mind that the client's liaison officer normally has to justify to other people, "sometimes a lot of other people, almost every dime we spend." It's in the counseling firm's interest to help the client's representative present the program in such a way as to accomplish that. "Any counselor who tries to appear heroic while the internal person struggles to justify may find the future of the account doomed." The idea is to make the client representative look good with his own top management.

5. *Give confidence and pass the statistical ammunition*: The internal officer

> *has to be made comfortable and confident in saying not only why he believes it's important to spend X dollars for outside counsel, but also why it's a tremendous bargain: "And for $100K what we're getting is $1 million worth of service. If we had to staff up ourselves, it would cost us $280K." It's up to the public relations firm to provide the kind of ammunition the client officer needs.*

6. *Brush up on finance*: If an intense course in finance was not part of formal education or on-the-job development, it's clear that it pays to learn. Even for the veteran counselor, it probably pays to brush up on old lessons. "It's one thing to be interested in the back pages of the client's annual report and those of competitors; it's another thing to understand the business and public relations implications. That takes a working knowledge of business."

Many senior counselors take the pains to understand client finance, even if they're not doing financial public relations. PRSA, the American Management Association and the American Marketing Association are among organizations that sponsor courses in finance. Most major cities have evening or extension school programs with financial material for persons who are not financial specialists. Major brokerage houses have useful brochures.

Build Client Relations through Learning and Follow-through   Pruett's analysis of his Coca-Cola experiences and the perspective gained from moving to counseling yielded fertile ground for other recommendations to strengthen client relationships, including studies and attention to following through:

1. *Temper creative impatience and probe*: When a lawyer sits down with a client,

> *he will be excruciating in asking questions to make sure nothing is left unknown. Some public relations people tend to be impatient: we're creative, we don't like to be detailed. The client starts to go into detail— and it may be tempting to allow yourself to get impatient and signal— if not say outright—that "I know all that" or "I got your point; I'll come back with a program."*

2. *Study specific facets of client business*: Many clients welcome the counselor's interest in learning more about specific facets of their business, such as looking into shipping or observing certain aspects of sales. "They welcome that interest unless they perceive you're just trying to put in time for which they'll be billed," he said.

A counselor may be able to have both the benefit of the kind of study Pruett recommended and the fees to pay for counseling firm costs in doing it. It is possible to propose formal miniaudits of specific client activities. The precedent has been established by legal and financial firms to charge for time spent in studying operations. And many clients pay for time of their own officers to do on-site studies in other departments. Such study can help counselors pinpoint specific opportunities for improvement.

3. *Plan maintaining communication in writing*: One of the factors that builds confidence in counseling firm executives and makes it easier for client staff to ask advice has to do with how diligently counselors report to clients. For example, monthly, written status reports kept Pruett thinking about a firm. How those reports were written, beyond actions and progress summarized, was important to him. Telephone calls from counselors were welcome, but he was more impressed by those who sent along written follow-up communiques that documented what each party was going to do.

4. *Stay in touch:* Even when a client is down the street or in the same building, out of sight can be out of mind.

> *Counselors get so busy that when a client doesn't call and ask for specific work, they get immersed in other accounts. Then the client will realize "it's been about six weeks since I had a call from the agency; I wonder if I really need them?" You may have been working on that client's needs, but unless the client sees fairly regular reminders of valuable work going forward on his behalf, he begins to get uneasy. And somebody is looking over his shoulder and saying, "we need additional funds for another purpose; what difference would it make if we slice $10K or $50K from your budget?" If you're paying the bill, the cumulative effect of hearing from the counselor on a regular basis ultimately persuades you that you can't do without the public relations firm.*

WHAT CORPORATIONS, INSTITUTIONS WANT

It doesn't take a conversion to or from counseling for a client executive to be able to develop valuable insights on what public relations firms can do to make corporations and institutions view them as worth the fees, let alone as indispensable.

A lifetime on the client-side and an analysis of the strengths and weaknesses of a client-counselor relationship can yield intelligence on what it takes to attract, hold and build business.

Industry Looks to Buy Specialized Knowledge

North American industries have witnessed a surge of toughened overseas competition, stricter environmental regulations, increased labor costs, unprecedented expenses in keeping pace with the technological revolution and rising costs for increased quality of products.

It has become a time when some survival-minded industry leaders have felt forced to acknowledge that they could buy quality raw materials cheaper than they could produce them domestically, that their future lay in concentrating on value-added product lines. The resultant restructuring of industries often brings with it trauma to workers, communities and even whole states and provinces. That's a challenging setting for the application of internal and external public relations know-how. It's also a setting in which cost controls for public relations may be equally unprecedented.

Two conflicting trends seem to have been at work, one for a greater utilization of external firms to shape internal public relations operations, the other for internal operations to become self-reliant once given the advantages of general outside counsel.

Implications of New Marketplace Force at Work   Joseph F. Awad, corporate director-public relations, Reynolds Metals Co., has traced a new, third, trend with important implications for counselors and clients alike.[9]

The past PRSA president said that although he and the public relations function at Reynolds benefited from auditing and counsel in getting started, "we have not retained general public relations counsel for a number of years." But there appears to be a new marketplace force at work. Here are the implications.

1. *Cater to geographical coverage and special program needs*: Awad said that Reynolds has used counseling firms at various times either for geographical coverage or for special programs. He predicted this kind of usage will increase significantly in the years ahead as companies strive to reduce and streamline corporate staff and come to rely more and more on outside services as needed.

2. *Market specialization expertness*: "When corporate public relations people call in an agency, they usually are looking to buy either their special knowledge of a clearly defined geographical area or their expertness in some specialization such as financial or marketing or legislative public relations."

3. *Offer local assistance*: "In most instances, a company will have a well-thought-out corporate strategy and program already in place and is simply looking for specific local assistance in its implementation. This can be frustrating to counselors, as it does not allow much room for new creative concepts and program planning."

4. *Explore history vs. reinventing the wheel*: "Yet some firms will sometimes insist on reinventing the wheel, attempting to sell a whole new 'from the ground up' approach. Some of these plans sound great but, because the agency has not been privy to the long history of research and discussion that went into the corporate program, they can miss the mark." Awad recommended that counselors who "disagree completely with a corporate plan or feel that it simply won't work in their area should be up front about it and probably not accept the assignment." Alternately:

5. *Follow client's work style*: Counselors "need to follow the 'style' of the company in the work they do as its representative, even though it may not be their preferred style."

6. *Encourage client to be specific:*

Usually a company with its own public relations staff is seeking a clearly delineated package of services from the public relations firm. In fact, my experience is that the more specific the client can be in outlining what is expected from the agency, the more satisfied both parties will be with their relationship and the more effective will be the results.

Social Services Perspectives

New Business Trends Identified   In her two terms as head of PRSA's Social Services Section and in her Houston and New York City senior vice president posts with United Way of America, Sunshine Janda Overkamp gained perspectives on how counselors can get access to a burgeoning market in the human services, health and welfare spheres.

The 1986–1987 member of the PRSA board of directors has had liaison with dozens of public relations firms, including most of the largest, in serving as internal consultant to what amounts to a trade association of 2,200 United Way chapters and in her responsibilities over the years for the Texas and Tri-State headquarters operations. She has observed several trends with significant implications for counselors and their clients in the social services:[10]

1. *More will pay for external counsel:* "Even now, social services agencies actually are hiring firms and paying them. There is a growing understanding of public relations and its importance."

This happens despite—and maybe in part because of—the shrinking of the tax base and threats to reduce breaks for philanthropy. When taxpayers receive smaller deductions for donations, more public relations counsel is needed to persuade donors. When the tax base shrinks locally or concern mounts over the federal deficit, government grants fail to keep pace with rising needs and costs.

2. *Opportunities increase in government relations:* Boards and staffs of not-for-profit organizations increasingly will turn to outside experts with government relations and lobbying strengths as they perceive the increasing need to be a part of the public dialogue on issues such as tax reform. "And we are becoming more and more part of that dialogue," Overkamp said.

3. *Corporate volunteers give impetus:* Volunteers from the board room and executive suite who are involved in social services organizations recognize "we can't do the job they'd like us to do without correct underpinnings, without the right tools. A lot of impetus for new communications and action planning comes from executives who volunteer their services.

Sometimes they will try to help find the resources and expertness our own staffs can't provide."

4. *Corporate executives part of decision process*: In the identification, development of funding and retention of public relations firms, volunteer executives tend to play a key role. Overkamp said that successful firms have approached social services organizations with sensitivity, seeking to assure that their paid staff and volunteer leaders are consulted and involved in the decision-making process despite their different roles. This is similar to counseling approaches to trade associations.

5. *Window for exposure*: Counseling firm executives are increasingly active with nonprofit organizations and are gaining visibility in an arena in which they did not have much exposure.

6. *Helps with business prospects*: It can be predicted that exposure of sophisticated counsel and bottom-line-oriented services in the institutional sphere will gain the favorable attention not only of media and government people supportive of a particular cause but also of prospects in other organizations. That includes the profit-making firms of volunteer executives.[11]

7. *Business clients benefit more*: Public relations firms have been accelerating the trend to bring social services organizations into mutually advantageous joint programs with their private enterprise clients. "As public relations firms get more involved with social services, they're discovering that in doing good, they're also able to do good for other clients," Overkamp observed. As head of the honors and awards committee for PRSA in 1985, she said she was surprised to learn how great a role the public service component played among so many of the Silver Anvil winners. "Doing good can have bottom line impact for other clients."[12]

What Social Service Clients Look for in Counseling Firms First, however, comes satisfying the special bottom-line needs of the social services clients.

1. *Bottom-line orientation*: The bottom line of social services organizations is determined by community needs, as interpreted by board officers and staff. "We determine how much money we have to raise by how much we need to do in the community," Overkamp said. "The bottom line can be how many homeless we get off the street or how many children we get off drugs—and get to stay off." Or it can be how many qualified volunteers are attracted and retained.

2. *Approach as any other client*: She said that "sophisticated counselors approach United Way or other social services organizations as any other client, with the same in-depth analysis, audits and background research."

3. *Invest in learning period*: Many public relations firms that win social services contracts first gained experience in learning about operations as volunteers. "It's very important for a firm to have that learning period," Overkamp said. The investment of voluntary service often pays dividends in bringing in business.

4. *Give most prized value—objectivity*: Overkamp had this one-word answer when asked what she and others in her field find especially attractive when working with or selecting external counsel: "Objectivity!" She explained: "You work for a social services organization so long, you don't see things the way a firm would."

5. *Offer specialized resources and depth*: Most social services agencies have one person on staff for all internal and external public relations, media relations, government relations, publications, video, films, etc. "When you have a generalist like that, the depth of a firm's expertise is a real added value."

6. *Anticipate openness to research*: Increasingly, social services organizations are using research and evaluation. Staff may be more open to such proposals because they come from an academic background in which research is emphasized, she said. They also learn evaluative techniques in dealing with agency clients. Overkamp, who conducts workshops on how to do marketing research, said there is strong demand "to learn how to do valid research that is less costly."

7. *Demonstrate creative commitment*: Among the most important values sought by social services clients is that of commitment. "We look for firms that will take the time to understand the organization and then unleash their creative resources. One reason why counselors like such clients is that it gives them the opportunity to do fine creative work that they couldn't do somewhere else."

8. *Don't underestimate willingness to buy creative*:

> *Although some would ascribe to us a reputation for not taking chances, most social services organizations are more than willing now to take chances with very creative public relations programs. We have come to understand that if we want anybody to listen to us, it's important that we cut through the clutter of communications out there.*
>
> *We know people don't go around looking to give away their money. One of our problems is in asking for funds for causes that wouldn't win a popularity contest. Some social services provide for major needs that don't have the emotional pull of diseases. It's getting easier, but it's still hard, to raise funds for battered women's shelters, for instance. You have to stand out or you won't get attention.*

And one could add that even if you get attention, you have to make the case salient enough to alter behavior of individuals who can make gifts or grant decisions.

9. *Sell crisis communication skills*: It's advantageous to familiarize social services prospects or existing clients with crisis intervention and prevention resources. "We have crisis situations just like any others, but we don't always turn to public relations firms. Public relations firms would be wise to start selling crisis communication skills to social services organizations."

10. *Offer contacts and networks*: Counselor membership in a communications organization or network is valued by clients. This enables counselors to refer specialists and vendors, not just in the headquarters cities of national clients, but also in different parts of the nation or in other countries.

Non-Profit Clients Want Respect for Business Acumen From the clients' perspective, the stereotypes of their field serve as one of the greatest barriers and discordant elements in relations with counselors, particularly at the initial proposal stage.

Leaders of non-profit organizations expect respect for their business acumen. "One of the biggest problems occurs when counselors don't understand that many social services organizations are run like a business by competent, capable people," Overkamp agreed as she reviewed several suggestions.

1. *Rethink perception of charity*: "Some think of us as charities. We are, but we're not ashamed and don't want sympathy. Some need to change their perception of what a charity is."

2. *Check first if action already taken*: Because there is a tendency to underestimate the professionalism of charitable organizations, some individuals give counsel too quickly without giving staff or volunteer officers credit for brainpower. "Some say, 'this is what you should do' and find out it's already been done."

3. *Carefully assess client resources*: Frequently, a counselor who is a newcomer to the social services sector can overestimate the resources available. He can come across as "too used to working with organizations with a great deal of funds or resources"—even if that is not so—and be considered careless when proposing projects beyond an organization's means.

Conversely, but with less frequency, a counselor will underestimate the resourcefulness of an organization that can draw upon in-kind gifts and even the financing of entire operations by corporate friends. To avoid either extreme, Overkamp recommended a study of the different modes of funding and resource gathering systems as well as the specific finances of each organization.

4. *Understand volunteer roles*: Counselors benefit when they understand the role of volunteers in the client approval process. Just as their counterparts in trade associations do, some social services executives report to volunteers at the policy level and welcome help in selling proposals to them.

5. *Understand autonomous and affiliate relations*: With organizations such as the Red Cross, Girl Scouts and United Way, the challenge is not only to convince national voluntary leaders, but also affiliates or autonomous organizations, such as local boards.

6. *Understand change is a constant*: "Counselors need to realize we have changed and we are changing."

7. *Look to where they are and who "they" are*: "We're better managed than people expect us to be. We have in place our management systems, computer systems, human resource training and development programs. Most people want us to be run like Exxon, American Express, J.C. Penney, Prudential. Our major volunteers *are* 'they.' "

What a $10 Billion Corporation Expects

Increased understanding of client perspectives also may be gained from in-depth probing of how an internal public relations executive of a large corporation views the use of counseling firms and what he expects from counselors in services and relationships. For example, take the case of the corporate vice president of a $10 billion firm.

Next: More Precise Objectives, Measurement, Internal Communications   In the 1990s, Eastman Kodak Co. expects public relations firms with which it will do business to "define program objectives with more precision and provide quantitative, as well as qualitative, measurement of results," according to David J. Metz, vice president in charge of corporate communications.[13]

In the last decade of the 20th century, Metz projected that "internal communications aimed at employee involvement and commitment are going to receive great emphasis. Most companies are going to pay a lot more attention to two-way communications."

Now: Aggressive Balance and One Voice Around the World   Toward the end of the 1980s, he expects Hill and Knowlton, Rumrill-Hoyt of Rochester and other firms that service the client to provide counsel and services that would produce "aggressive balance." Aggressive balance translates into effective efforts "to balance Kodak's internal resources and staff with those of national public relations firms and smaller agencies and suppliers."

Aggressive balance fits with Kodak's "one-voice" policy, which insists that messages sent to a variety of audiences be timely, properly representative and consistent from one audience to the next.

Of the 125 public relations staff members at Kodak headquarters, about

75 are professional. That means that they can be spread thinly in taking care of ongoing projects, let alone in attempting the scale of roll-out that introduced Kodak's disc photography to the world, in managing public affairs campaigns such as the 1985 effort to get the U.S. government to stabilize the overvalued dollar or in handling the crises that arose in 1986 when the courts found for Polaroid in ordering Kodak to quit the instant photo business and pay reparations to its competitor.

Metz said the first role of public relations firms is "to extend our geographical and editorial reach." In the disc camera launch, for instance, Kodak split up contacts on its trade, special interest and news media lists and turned to counselors for media training and help with regional press conferences.

Although a large corporate staff such as Kodak's prides itself on building close relationships with major business and financial media and trade publications, it can't have that kind of contact with youth, leisure and other specialized media. "We depend on agencies with contacts in vertical media to look for opportunities, such as to tell readers of *Seventeen* of a terrific camera for teenagers."

Kodak does not maintain public relations staff in major U.S. cities but relies on public relations firms "to do for us what we cannot do ourselves in terms of reach and efficiency," Metz said. To retain outside services, he must be convinced that counselors "can do something more economically and with greater impact than we can."

To help provide a unified sense of direction, Kodak retains national firms for corporate counsel, publicity and promotion of consumer products. A local Rochester firm helps publicize a full range of nonamateur products. Other firms are retained on a need basis for special projects.

How to Reach Client-Counselor "Intimate Partnership"   In selecting counsel and in inviting more involvement, Metz has insisted upon a number of conditions for what he has termed "intimate partnership" between corporate staff and counselors:

1. *Be willing to share experience*: "You have to start with a mutual willingness to share experience." He acknowledged that public relations firms "bring a broader range of experiences with other clients than we can normally find inside the company. We are looking to draw ideas from those experiences."

2. *What counselors should expect from client*: In his more than two dozen years with Kodak, he learned that corporations owe their counselors "ready access to information within the client organization," "solid direction in terms of client objectives and motivations," and "realistic expectations on our part."

3. *What clients should expect from counselor*: "We expect professionalism and performance. We expect them to provide creative skills. We expect them to be cost competitive relative to our own internal capabilities and to be competitive in the qualitative sense."

4. *Develop reciprocal candor, openness*: An intimate partnership requires "a great deal of candor and openness on both sides." That translates into openness, not only on strengths but also areas of weakness: "We expect them to be completely honest with us." An example illustrates the value.

An external investor relations counselor finished a year-end review of his services to Kodak and concluded: "There's nothing we can do for you next year that you're not already doing." Metz remembered for "a long time" that the counselor made a candid assessment rather than an impression "of being out for fees." If he had said much else, "I would not have had much respect for him or wanted to find ways to continue our relationship."

5. *Challenge "quick fixes"*: It takes an understanding on the part of the client that "years, not months, may be required to reach peak agency performance" in developing a thorough long-range program. To both counselors and colleagues on the corporate side, Metz had this common sense advice: "Don't look to quick fixes."

6. *If client buys into first team, deliver first team*: He described occasional situations in which "an agency rolls in with its first-string team to get an account" and then brings in the second team. "When you base your initial approach on the experience and expertness of your principal or other top executives, the client rightfully expects to have access to these people" and will be primed to look for another firm if disappointed. Here is a lesson to be derived from Metz's point: If it is not feasible to deliver on what appears to be an implicit promise, make that clear at the onset.

7. *Make success stories relevant*:

> You expect an agency to share their success stories with you, but some people don't seem to worry enough about whether they're applicable to your own goals and projects. There's nothing worse than a misrepresentation of what an agency can really do for you. If performance falls short of expectations, you can be sure the public relations director will never forget it, and the business relationship won't last long.

8. *Stop prospecting after sale is made*: Once a client has contracted for service, the time for selling additional services "should proceed only with great care and selectivity. Good ideas will mean good business. Redundancy will lead to business losses."

9. *Inform staff before prospecting*: He was typical of client executives interviewed in expressing strong distaste for "end runs" to the head of marketing, CEO or board. "There's no better way to build animosity than to go prospecting without informing us."

10. *Know corporate policy on contracting*: Any Kodak division or subsidiary that plans to retain counsel is required to alert central corporate communications. "We will assist in screening and selecting agencies and will try to produce economies of scale. We will help formulate programs. We will make sure billings are in line." Thus, it would help to look for ways to fit a proposed project in with on-going client programs to achieve economy of scale and to investigate corporate headquarters criteria and interests.

11. *Probe for information, insights*: However, persistence may be warranted to access information and insights on problems and opportunities from the client. "If your agency is left entirely to its own devices, you and we are going to fail."

12. *Emulate "silent service" approach to media, VIPs*: Just as Metz has viewed internal public relations staff as "sort of the silent service—telling the company's story through its management people"—he said he prefers a similar approach from firms that represent Kodak. "Journalists and security analysts always prefer contact within the company rather than the agency representing us."

13. *Silence should not extend to costs*: Although counselors appear divided on strategies on how best to incorporate cost elements in proposals, Metz said that he and colleagues in most corporations have no equivocality on the subject. They become irritated when in-depth cost information is missing from proposals or reports. "We want quantitative analysis beyond itemization of costs and results. We want to know the value of benefits produced for dollars we spend."

14. *Look beyond project to sustained support*: Although there are indicators that a trend has been at work in the other direction, a primary criterion of Kodak in selecting external counselors is "not what you can do for us in an isolated short-term sense—it's easy to announce, introduce, launch and market a clearly superior product." Instead: "We're looking for agencies that can sustain support when the product no longer has the attraction of newness to it."

15. *Be precise on planned impact*: While quantitative precision is becoming increasingly important on the client side in both objectives and reports, Metz included in his definition of precision the use of qualitative analysis. "It's not enough to know how many media impressions were made at what cost. We need to know what certain kinds of impressions in specific media really do for us."

16. *How to gain a holistic perspective*: Counselors find it beneficial to establish the kind of relationship with internal contact officers that will help them gain a perspective of the corporate whole into which particular counsel and services will fit. For instance at Kodak, public relations staff sits in on meetings between marketing executives and the product advertising agency, even though Metz has no direct responsibility in advertising. "We know taboos, we know objectives, we know how markets segment themselves, we understand how critical publics will react to any significant announcement."

17. *Take advantage of staff access to CEO and board*: In some client organizations, public relations staff officers command access to individuals and intelligence data that may be needed to provide sound counsel. Metz, for instance, begins almost every day with a half-hour, or longer, session with the CEO and board chairman.

How Corporations Review Counselors

It also is important to understand how corporate clients review public relations firms in selecting counsel to represent them. Robert L. Lauer brought to his analysis perspective gained as vice president-corporate affairs for Sara Lee Corp. and, before that, from his experience at Johnson Wax, Clorox and Harshe, Rotman & Druck.

Criteria for Developing New Business In a speech to the Counselors Academy and a subsequent interview, he reviewed "Lauer's Laws" for developing new business:[14]

1. *"What the agency says is what the client ought to get."* Actually, Lauer's first "law" revolves around listening, not just by the counselor, but by the client as well. "The core of the problem is that neither of us listens very well. You're usually not listening when you're trying to sell me a new proposal or program. You're usually not listening when you're counseling." He recommended: "Start each client meeting with these questions: 'What do you want to tell me today? What do you want me to know?' " At the end of each meeting, "insist on reviewing with the client what you think you heard. This will force the client to analyze what he thinks he said."

Ironically, both client and counselor view themselves as professional communicators and, as such, may take it for granted that the other party, as well as they, themselves, are listening.

2. *"A little knowledge is a dangerous thing, but. . . . "* Not just the head of the counseling firm and account executive, but also "everyone you assign to the account should know the client's business, its people and what its competitors are doing." Lauer acknowledged that this is easier said than done, unless the client cooperates. He said that such cooperation may depend on the counselor helping to "teach the client how to be a client."

With or without cooperation, many counselors do become familiar with all public knowledge about a company, how competitors position themselves and the products or services. But there are exceptions. "One agency came in with a tremendously creative idea. The only problem was that our competitor had been doing it for five years."

3. *"A client/agency relationship is like a loaf of bread—no matter how you slice it, it's going to get stale."* The staleness of a relationship is correlated with one party taking the other for granted. Lauer raised these questions:

"How often do you sit down with the client—at your initiation—and assess where things are?"

"Have you taken time to explain your billing system to him again?"

"Have you reminded him of what you've been achieving? (It's almost like married people who become critical of each other without taking stock of strengths both bring to the relationship. That can lead to misunderstandings and can cause relationships to go sour.)"

4. *"Make sure your act is together before you take it on the road."* He asked:

"Do you know the kind of performance your people are turning out? (Once a relationship gets going and a person is not performing, why should the client have to be the one to point out that somebody is not right for the job? You need to be on top of the quality of work being performed" and intervene before it becomes an issue.)

"Do you train your people on how to supervise others before you promote them to a supervisory position?"

"Are people expected to learn at the client's expense—at the risk of losing the account?"

"Do your people understand and support your organizational culture" in representing the firm to clients?

5. *"If an idea is worth doing, it's probably already been done."* "We clients are always looking for something original, something that's never been done before. Your job is to come up with that new idea, that new variation on an old theme." He asked:

"Do you engage the client people in a planned dialogue to involve them in creating the new idea?"

"Do you go back and call a meeting of the creative team?"

How Executive Selects Public Relations Firms The Sara Lee vice president reviewed several client strategies for selecting public relations firms:[15]

1. *Ask peers for success stories:* "The first thing I do is call peers in other companies and ask who they think the really good people in product PR are. I will start looking around for success stories. The counselors don't necessarily have to specialize in product PR, just have demonstrated the ability to effectively do it."

2. *Talk with media friends:* They may have the vantage point of observing the caliber of public relations firm-produced materials and seeing the style of counselors' media contact work.

3. *Interview former, present clients*: He places "an awful lot of importance on talking with people who are present or former clients to get a first-hand appraisal" of firms he is considering.

4. *Pay for substantial presentation*: As an acid test, he calls for proposals from two or three firms, but he doesn't believe in asking them to do research, development and presentation at their own cost. He got to that point because he felt "free" presentations were largely "boiler-plate" in which the name and a few factors of his company were substituted for those in the proposal to the last client.

> *As a client, I don't want anything superficial. I've already checked them out to find out how well they can do. I want something thoughtful to measure or judge their creativity. I want to see something of their people. I realize this costs time and that has value to an agency. My conclusion was that we would just pay them for the time it would take for them to put together a knowledgeable proposal. We will pay them so that we can see how their better people do research on the company, issues and competition. I would expect something out of the ordinary. If it works, we get a better proposal. If it doesn't, that makes it easier to choose another agency.*

5. *Assess planning, creativity*: In written proposals and oral presentations, he seeks to judge skills in organizing the proposal and the logic of the plan: "I look for signs of creativity that tell that they have some good talented, skilled people."

6. *Analyze counseling firm members' interaction*: He found it useful to observe how well a firm's people work together and to sensitize himself to signs of "inner conflict among agency people."

7. *Look for pride in selves and employer*: Professionalism and motivation can be manifest in the way individuals and a team make a presentation. "Other than the quality of material they're showing you, the way they appear can tell you whether they're professional," Lauer said. He has advised client-side colleagues that because "every agency comes to you with its best sales people and best presenters, try not to be overwhelmed. Look at more subtle things, signs whether people enjoy working for that agency. See if they reflect pride in themselves and in their employer."

8. *Do on-site observation*: Counselors might benefit from anticipating what a client executive such as Lauer might actually see—or think they observe—in a visit to a public relations firm's headquarters. "You can walk in the door, and you can feel the personality of the agency, from the moment you arrive. Sometimes it's as easy as asking the receptionist if she likes to work here." (Some have actually said "no!") He has trained himself to observe the bearing of the people as he passes their offices. "Discerning they're harried or laid-back suggests the need to check it out further."

9. *Review diversity of writing examples*: With an eye to quality and creativity, he looks at a diversity of writing products, "from speeches to corporate capabilities brochures" to determine:

"Is the writing clear and simple, or convoluted?"

"Is it articulate?"

"Does it reflect creativity rather than a me-to approach?"

"Is there evidence of thoughtful research and thinking?"

"Is it interesting to read?"

"Does it seem to communicate well?"

"Do they have a good understanding of graphics?"

"Does it appear to be supportive of objectives?"

10. *Consider smaller firms*: "There's a good chance you can run into a representation conflict, particularly with all the mergers that have taken place. While I have no trouble with an agency doing corporate PR for a parent company of a direct competitor because I respect the ethics of most counselors, many marketing people have no comfort with that at all. That's one reason for looking into smaller agencies. Sometimes you can get better attention and a spark of creativity that goes with being hungry. Smaller agencies also don't have as much overhead."[16]

However, a client also may want to consider that in a larger consultancy there may be economy of scale and specialized training and supervision to motivate attention and instill creativity. It also is true that a specialized counseling organization with expertness and a record in a given area, regardless of how small or how large the firm, may provide the creativity, resourcefulness and value needed.

This principle was illustrated in 1986 when the New York Boat Show contracted with Miami-based Bruce Rubin & Associates. A New York City public relations firm president asked: "How could a small firm 1,500 miles distant walk away with such a lucrative contract?"[17] Rubin said:

It would be tempting to say we stole this from all the big New York firms that could have gone after the business and didn't. But the real reason is that we know boat shows. We've done the Greater Miami Boat Show for years. We know the people in the boat show business. We have people on our staff who are immensely competent at this kind of thing. In the end it didn't matter to the client that we were in Miami or how big we were as much as that we could do a reliably excellent job. We couldn't have competed with the New York firms for a New York client in the high-technology area or in investor relations. But we sure can compete in boat shows. And that's a good way for smaller firms to compete—by being indisputably superb at one thing and marketing it all around the country.[18]

Client Identifies Factors to Consider at First Meeting

Charles C. Dayton, director of corporate communications for Perkin-Elmer Corp. of Norwalk, Conn., shared with other client executives elements to consider in choosing a counseling firm. The veteran of three decades with the billion-dollar corporation included in his basic criteria a match of specialization of counseling firm and client and a match of corporate style and culture: "Do they have the right personality and quick read ability to get management's respect? Remember, you'll want to use them as an advocate." During the first meeting between client officers and prospective counselors, he recommended that corporate executives consider such factors as:

"Are they ready for you when you arrive, or do they have to scramble to get people and materials together?"

"Is the meeting well-organized and smooth, with a crisp presentation of agency credentials?"

"Is the meeting structured to allow ample time for you to play an active role in questions and give-and-take?"

"Are the people who will actually work on the account present and do they play enough of a role in the presentation and discussion for you to get a feel for how they think and work?"

"Do all the people present demonstrate that they have done their homework on you, probe, ask intelligent, pertinent questions?"

"Are they candid on finances and where you would fit in their client base, on account management, planning and reporting?"

"How does the agency follow up on the meeting?"[19]

Client Executives March to a Different Drummer

In Hartford, Conn., the senior vice president for corporate communications of Emhart Corp. noted that although counselors may feel an urgency to initiate programs, that sense of urgency frequently isn't matched on the client side and may even backfire.

But when client executives are primed to move full-speed ahead, resentment can arise if counselors are in the midst of other business and don't keep pace, John F. Budd told *PR Reporter.*[20]

Frustrations arise because counsel's urgency to initiate a program isn't matched by company's appetite. Deadlines are painful to executives asked to take "unaccustomed initiatives." Approvals come grudgingly. And when counsel goes back to the office, a subtle counterattack against "change" is waged behind the scenes.

When management gets involved in a project, they literally get involved and they stay with it until it's completed. They also have other things to do, but they give priority to the immediate. The necessity of PR counsel to juggle many balls at once tends to break the concentration on any one client's project and stretch out the gestation period unreasonably.

Budd said that on-the-scene involvement of counselors, close communication, and carefully planned follow-up activities help alleviate such problems.

Intertwined with client-side perspectives as an integral part of counselor-client relationships are considerations related to the marketing of public relations firms and the additional strategies needed to move clients to accept, seek out and seize the proposals and presentations of experts in communications, experts in solving and preventing problems and capitalizing upon opportunities.

7

MARKET DEVELOPMENT

As the public relations counseling business grows and broadens its qualifications by introducing new services and capabilities, the job of marketing them and the firms themselves takes on new significance.

It used to be that opening a new office would be sufficient to bring in adequate business, particularly in the case of an already well-known practitioner. But the emergence of strong public relations capabilities in specialized areas means that firms now must project individual identities. The potential for opening new markets provides opportunities. Proliferating public relations firms and fresh competition from attorneys, management consultants and others create marketing challenges.

This chapter reviews ways in which counselors market their capabilities to prospects and to existing clients, focuses on strategic market research, examines presentation techniques and explores how counselors cope with conflict.

MARKETING STRATEGIES

Setting the Stage for Professional Firms

The taboos against members of long-established professions engaging in public relations programs to market their firms or themselves were deeply entrenched into the mid-1980s. Simple advertising or public relations activities, let alone more sophisticated programs, sometimes were prohibited by law and often were damned by old-line professional societies.

Even when legal restrictions were lifted, strong peer pressure persisted to enforce them as part of a so-called ethic that indicated it was acceptable to appear in the society column but not be covered elsewhere.

The professional marketing sphere has opened up a cornucopia for counselors, with special strategies to deal with such clients' relative lack of public relations understanding. Increasingly, public relations counselors have been overcoming the barriers and educating their legal, medical and accounting clients while helping them improve their business, government relations and public reputations.

200

Counselors have adapted to professional firms many techniques that have been proven of value for corporate and institutional clients. The importance of market-creating strategies was reinforced by the founder of Regis McKenna Inc., in California's Silicon Valley. McKenna said that for contemporary managers "the emphasis is on applying technology, educating the market, developing the industry infrastructure and creating new standards. The company with the greatest innovation and creativity is likely to win."[1]

Counselors May Be Like the Shoemaker's Children Ironically, however, some counselors have been slow to treat their own firms as clients, at least not with the systematic, strategic, long-range perspective and commitment of resources that they would counsel for others.

A *Public Relations Business* article has likened this phenomenon to the saying about the shoemaker's children:[2] "Like the shoemaker's children, PR agencies are all too often barefoot when it comes to publicizing their own businesses," wrote Robert G. Wilder, chairman and CEO of Philadelphia's Lewis, Gilman & Kynett. He advocated that counseling firms systematically communicate "why our particular talents are worthy of client consideration."

Most public relations firms,

> *despite our rankings in the trade magazine listings, despite our prominence in our communities, despite the prizes and awards, are still nowhere as well known and respected as we may think. Only a few of the very largest firms are household words in this industry, and they compete amidst a sophisticated and knowledgeable business community for the biggest accounts.[3]*

Certainly, some firms take out institutional advertisements in professional rosters and journals; compete vigorously for professional recognition and client respect they gain with Silver Anvils, Gold Quills and regional association awards; issue announcements on new accounts and personnel changes for the trades; invest in educational speeches and articles; and involve their principals in civic, cultural and social service causes, just as they counsel their clients.

But there has been a tendency for counseling firms to relegate public relations to secondary-objective status, something that can be done on a piecemeal basis when the pressures of servicing accounts allow and the budget permits.

Strategies for Public Relations Firms

A trend in which public relations firms handle themselves as clients seems to be emerging. Some organizations, such as Hill and Knowlton and

Burson-Marsteller, assign marketing responsibility to a vice president. Most involve their principals to varying degrees.

To extend the analogy, it could be said that when "the shoemaker's children" walk around in well-crafted shoes, the demonstration of product value and pride might be a factor in persuading customers to buy the same quality for their own children.

Program Marketing as Part of Ongoing Business Development   A growing number of counseling organizations have developed carefully planned marketing programs with specific activities for each year as part of ongoing business development operations. The model of Boston's Agnew, Carter, McCarthy Inc., illustrates how.

1. *Explore avenues open to professional firms*: The principal architect of the Boston program, Jack F. Agnew, sought to "explore all the avenues open to professional firms and assign the same priorities to marketing support that we do for our paying clients."[4]

2. *Move toward quantifiable business objectives*: As other clients, the firm is moving toward more quantifiable objectives. He said the programs for attracting clients and retaining business do produce measurable results, but that planning needs to be more specific in projecting the exact percentages by which business should increase.

3. *Target*: Specific markets are identified.

4. *Set dollar budget*: As in any businesslike marketing program, there is a need for a financial commitment and budget.

5. *Budget top management time*: Agnew, Carter, McCarthy assigns a given number of hours for an account executive to devote to the firm as a client. Members of top management, including the partners, also allocate hours they will account for in servicing their own firm. They then decide upon and execute a well-defined and clearly assigned agenda of tasks.

6. *Call for year-end review of task performance*: Such a program works best when provision is made for a built-in review of performance to determine what is achieved. If, for example, it's budgeted that Agnew give 10 major speeches, a fiscal year-end review examines how he did in accomplishing his tasks. More importantly, it checks if business increases, especially in the areas targeted.

7. *Exercise flexibility as other client needs warrant*: There has to be some flexibility if contractual client needs are to be met. "The difference between servicing our own account and those of other companies is the option to be more flexible and, dependent upon needs of other clients, we can have a different ebb and flow as we change assignments of our people by moving them on and off our own account."

8. *But insist on equal priority, quality, evaluation*: Some things may be deferred or rearranged in deference to external accounts but, "basically we're the same as any of our clients and should be treated accordingly—with the same priority, commitment to excellence and measurement techniques to evaluate effectiveness," he said.

9. *Select services for marketing focus*: Just as a client would want to concentrate efforts on marketing support for certain services or products, so should the counseling firm develop and review areas for focus of its own account activities. Agnew, Carter, McCarthy, for example, shifted focus with the 1985 start-up of its new public affairs and issues management division.

10. *Encourage others in industry to market selves*: On the surface, this may appear to be idealism carried to extremes. But, as Agnew said, when firms in the communication business "put the same kind of vigor into marketing themselves as they do for their clients, we will be a far more successful industry."[5]

This fits with counsel given by public relations firms to trade associations—recognize that the parts of an industry tend to be interdependent. The reputation and marketing success of members to varying degrees are inextricably linked to those of the industry.

11. *Depend upon professional associations*: In anything requiring tremendous breadth, depth and duration of campaign, such as changing business attitudes toward public relations, he advocated that individual firms operate through professional organizations including the Counselors Academy, PRSA, IABC, Canadian Public Relations Society and regional associations instead of taking fragmented approaches.

12. *Divide responsibilities among principals*: This tends to strengthen marketing efforts by matching expertness with areas of need.

13. *Make feasible marketing plans*: Gerald S. Schwartz, who founded New York's G.S. Schwartz & Co. in the midst of the early 1980s recession, stressed the importance of creating feasible marketing plans. He said that although some marketing plans and specialization look good on paper, it's more important to have "a simple list of things that are 90 percent do-able."[6]

Marketing Support Activities and Strategies Activities in support of marketing objectives vary with the size, resources, objectives and management philosophies of counseling firms. Here are some areas of activity in Boston together with strategies that were suggested by field research in other parts of the country.

1. *Newsletter*: Agnew, Carter, McCarthy partner Lewis A. Carter assumed responsibility for the firm's quarterly newsletter, which is targeted to existing and prospective clients and community and government leaders. The 2,000-circulation publication is designed to increase awareness in various target markets of the firm's particular strategic capabilities.[7]

Just as professionals counsel their clients that newsletter articles be salient and relevant, so, too, is there a need to assure that articles be chosen and edited for marketing support and readership appeal rather than be merely ego boosting.

All the newsletters sampled showed a conscious effort to keep them timeless so that even back copies will have fresh appeal to clients with particular needs.

2. *Publish or perish! Publish and thrive!*: More and more firms emphasize article writing as a marketing activity. Analysis yields insights on how and why counselors do this for themselves. They have the well-established precedent of ghostwriting for traditional client executives as well as the experience in preparing byline pieces for lawyers, physicians and accountants.

Several basic types of articles seem to appeal especially to counselors:

Articles that share tactics with other counselors may lead to referrals or joint ventures and also may enhance the reputation of authors and firms in their own industry.

Think pieces that offer philosophy or analysis help prospective and existing client executives understand public relations functions and approaches. Some of these articles are directed to the working level of staff public relations officers, others to marketing or advertising vice presidents, and yet others to board members, CEO's, and other line officers. These articles establish authors—and their firms—as helpful, thoughtful and capable of counsel.

Articles on trend projections or current issues establish the expertness of the authors and serve as samplers of the depth they have to offer. Articles range from implications of changing demographics to political processes for dealing with foreign trade imbalances.

How-to stories may cover such topics as how to give testimony before a Congressional committee, appear on television, respond to queries by investigative journalists, build a coalition, develop venture capital, open a new industrial development or ward off hostile takeovers. Such articles display the know-how that may persuade executives to turn to the author's firm when situations arise or awareness mounts of the need for upgrading internal capabilities.

Case studies serve as illustrations and evidence that a counselor can effectively deal with real-world opportunities or problems and offer something special in giving clients an advantage.

3. *Speeches to business groups*: Agnew said the purpose is to expose a principal of the firm to the business community and help audiences understand "what PR is, how it works, and why it is of value to them."[8]

Parallels may be drawn between writing byline articles and giving speeches in terms of kinds of topics addressed and purposes served for counselors and audiences. The biggest differences lie in the far greater reach of the printed article and in advantages derived from interpersonal, small group communication when audiences get to see and hear counselors and, most important, interact with them afterwards.

Some counselors, as many university-based authors, develop their speeches with future articles in mind. They also plan byline pieces to elicit interest in expanded oral presentations. This model works for public relations counselors as long as the redundancy is limited to the theme rather than to detail.

Agnew, Carter, McCarthy is an example of firms that aggressively market themselves and don't wait for invitations but actively seek out speaking forums such as Chambers of Commerce, Rotary clubs, trade associations and university business schools.[9]

This does more than demonstrate professional commitment. Tangible benefits flow from building confidence in the leadership of counseling firms, reaching persons who eventually will influence decisions important to existing clients and setting in motion phased outreach for long-range client recruitment.

Agnew said that occasionally members of the audience come up to the podium after a speech and ask about counseling services. During new-business presentations, prospective clients sometimes mention that they remember hearing a counseling firm principal speak months or years earlier.[10]

So there may be a sleeper, or delayed reaction, persuasion effect as well as more immediate responses.

4. *Speeches to communications organizations*: Opportunities also exist to address professional communications organizations, particularly those in the public relations sphere just as there is a market in writing for *Public Relations Journal*, *Public Relations Review*, *PR Reporter* or the *Journal of Organizational Communication*.

But counselors also may find the program chairs of media-centered communication organizations (press clubs, professional societies) receptive to speeches related to breaking or building front-page, top-of-the-prime-time news. Beyond the obvious advantage of strengthening a firm's media relations, consider the bonus that some speeches to media audiences are given extended reach through mention in newspaper columns and the organizations' local or national publications.

5. *Be available for quotation by media*: When a scandal rocked a major New England financial institution, one of the counselors easily accessible to media for comment on public relations implications was Terence McCarthy. Agnew pointed out that his partner commented on the case for the *Boston Business Journal* "because he had made a conscious decision to be available to the media on anything that has to do with the public relations business."[11]

In representing other clients, some counseling firms develop and distribute media guides with names, credentials and phone numbers of experts on different topics who are available to field media questions. This is done for trade associations, medical centers, universities and individual corporate clients. It would make sense for counseling firms to develop their own media guides that include similar information and how to secure the help of counselors on stories involving their clients.

6. *Generate publicity*: Most firms do issue routine news releases on themselves ranging from personnel announcements to client acquisitions. *Jack O'Dwyer's Newsletter* presents many pages of counselor and client items and exemplifies the initiative of firms in helping chronicle business and personnel happenings. Other public relations, marketing and advertising newsletters use such items.

Some firms do advance publicity on their own speaking engagements, but it seems that relatively few arrange for media coverage of the substance of these speeches.

Most seem to target business pages or other components (real estate, food, sports) read by prospective clients. Few, however, target business components of broadcast television news or take advantage of the proliferation of narrowcasting opportunities presented by cable television.

A growing number of firms select vertical trade publications in the markets in which they do—or seek—business, such as technology, health, environment, agriculture, trade association, entertainment, food products and leisure.

7. *Client publications and podiums open*: Speakers from counseling firms contribute to client annual conferences, seminars and retreats discussing topics that are salient to their business practices and do not appear self-serving. This is in addition to seeking program time to review public relations progress and plans.

Agnew, Carter, McCarthy, for example, found client publications an open market for stories quoting, or bearing bylines of, their counseling firm executives.[12] Editors find psychological readership value in the expert, third-party endorsement implicit in comments of counselors about client activities or policies.

8. *Advertise beyond listings*: The Boston firm budgets limited advertising, but does not restrict itself to mere listings in directories, business magazines, and advertising and public relations publications. A firm can buy space in a directory for institutional advertising for its strengths and capabilities, Agnew said.[13]

9. *Join boards and civic old boy/old girl networks*: All three principals of the Boston firm volunteer service on civic boards of directors. Agnew said he served on the boards of the Big Sister Association, Salvation Army, Boston Harbor Associates, Art Institute of Boston, Jobs for Youth, and Boys Club of Greater Boston. Beyond the firm's belief in its "obligation to the community," he agreed that marketing purposes are served by being exposed to other business leaders on these boards.[14]

"In business, the old boy/old girl network does exist. It helps you expose yourself as a person and as a professional in ways that you can't get across when you're directly selling. You can demonstrate and teach PR approaches, philosophy and pragmatics without being seen as 'selling' them." This is another instance, as Agnew put it, "of assuring that this 'shoemaker's kids' wear shoes." He and his colleagues counsel their clients to be similarly involved.

10. *Be visible in professional organizations*: The primary motivation, altruistic or otherwise, may be helping the profession. But counselors are conscious that their involvement helps cultivate business referrals and occasional invitations to join in a new-business presentation.

In Boston, for example, Agnew, Carter and McCarthy partners are active in the Counselors Academy. McCarthy became secretary-treasurer in 1986 and chairman-elect in 1987.

The firm advertises Academy membership in the Greater Boston Yellow Pages.[15] The apparent implication to executives using the Yellow Pages is that affiliation evidences professional caliber.

In California's Orange County, Jacqueline Schaar found that although she opened a firm with herself as the only full-time counselor, the visibility she achieved in progressing to president of the local PRSA chapter and then to the national board of directors helped her build her practice. She said that even after becoming well established, "my designation of APR and interpretation of it to clients in literature and presentations provides another, valuable dimension of professional respectability."[16]

11. *Invitational forums for executives*: Some counselors, such as Washington, D.C.'s Ernest Wittenberg, organize forums on selected public relations aspects and invite prospective and existing client executives. Wittenberg's public affairs forums, for instance, feature headliners including U.S. Senate and House of Representatives leaders and Cabinet officers.[17]

12. *Train firm's staff to anticipate marketing opportunities*: Account executives and other employees may profitably be trained to anticipate marketing opportunities and maintain the interest of prospects. A useful model of such training programs was developed at E. Bruce Harrison Inc., in Washington, D.C.[18]

Harrison coaches officers and account executives to anticipate meeting a person at a business event or party who will ask them to explain what their public relations firm does. To provoke more curiosity, his strategy calls for employees to keep the communication open by responding to a question with another question.

His staff learned that a response such as "We're a specialized consulting firm" usually is followed by "What do you consult about?" or "Who do you consult?" That can be "the opening through which we can probe the interest of the other person and have a conversation about our firm in the context of the questioner's interest."

13. *Build on existing client relationships first*: It's easier and more cost effective to continue momentum for building on an existing client relationship than to go prospecting. David Maister, former Harvard Business School researcher who designed the Counselors Academy Management School programs in 1985 and 1986, supported this concept when he said that although "we all know the best marketing you can do is to obtain repeat business or generate referrals from clients, we fail to operate as if we really believed it."[19]

To keep the momentum after contracting, Harrison's counselors learn that marketing efforts must continue with planned steps to keep bonds strong and avoid losing touch with client expectations and interests. As an example of steps to maintain strong relationships, Harrison teaches counselors to gather insights on client executives where they work: "Visit the client's library, look through open shelves, files, etc., to see what they're interested in or doing that you may not otherwise pick up on."[20]

14. *Opt for quality rather than quantity of clients*: Some executives in counseling and other industries have learned the hard way that it's the quality of customers that's important, not the number of new-business leads they develop. Moreover, they have learned that lower quality markets sometimes cost considerably more to maintain and even dilute the effectiveness of profitable markets. As Maister said, a major challenge to counseling firms is "not getting more clients; it's getting the right clients. Not all new business is good business. Don't fill the factory with junk work."[21]

15. *Concentrate on strong suits*: Not only is it important to concentrate on markets to pursue but also to focus narrowly on the major strengths that are being marketed. It is necessary to break out and narrow the scope of what is offered to what market experts refer to as a firm's unique selling proposition.

Professional firms, according to Maister, do best when they concentrate on their expertness, experience and execution capability. Moreover, he noted that "clients increasingly demand specialists—by industry, type of service, size of company" and that "specialization is no longer an option; it's a necessity." To be successful in a competitive marketplace, a firm must convince clients "it is one of the very few to turn to with complex and critical matters."[22]

STRATEGIC MARKET RESEARCH

Critical Component of Marketing and Sales

Technological Revolution Opens New Vistas   Departing from historic precedent and building unique selling propositions require the development of a marketing machinery fueled by research and facilitated by the application of strategies of the technology era. Actually, research, when combined with technology, may be identified as a critical new component of marketing.

Many of the principles and strategies that are developed in this book's research chapter apply or may be easily adapted to the marketing of public relations firms.

Not everything that works for physicians, attorneys, or accountants can be—or should be—applied to public relations firms as their own clients. But many of the strategic innovations, as well as some of the more traditional approaches, may be used to develop areas of specialization.

The technological revolution has opened new vistas for research into client industries as well as into demographic, psychographic, and behavioral data on their customers—information previously unavailable or beyond the means of most counseling firms. Technology useful for doing relatively inexpensive, fast, and simple research for developing markets, prospecting and new-business presentations is reviewed in the next chapter.

It is in planning new-business presentations that a diversity of counseling firms are investing research, technological and creative resources in an unprecedented sophistication of sales methodologies.

The place of new research strategies in the marketing process was emphasized in the sequel to *Megatrends* when John Naisbitt and Patricia Aburdene told readers of *Re-inventing the Corporation* that although it's important to understand trends, that is no longer enough.

You must also discover the specific way that your company fits into the business environment. The company's vision becomes a catalytic force, an organizing principle for everything that the people in the corporation do. . . . The new information society has created new markets and new-business opportunities. And in this new environment, individual entrepreneurs hold a key advantage over corporations: They can act faster.[23]

Research Positions the Counselor, Assures the Client   Research oriented to maximizing new-business opportunities tends to be underwritten by public relations firms' own budgets for the most part, although more clients are recognizing the value of paying at least part of the costs of presentations.

One market research model in the industry is provided by Burson-Marsteller. Its international research director, Lloyd Kirban, said the firm continues to invest in basic research to better position itself in the marketplace, and the state of the art allows counselors to prepare written proposals and sales presentations with far greater confidence than before.

Research should be used to make presentations more effective and demonstrate our knowledge of the client's problem. There's also a psychological value in using expert knowledge of business and product in new-business presentations. Clients are impressed by the initiative an agency will take to demonstrate its interest in obtaining the business.[24]

But research, of and in itself, does not sell anything. It provides a knowledge base from which a program is presented.

New-business development relies primarily on secondary research with the burgeoning of data bases. Secondary research for marketing a counseling firm includes such simple, but essential, tasks as examining a client's or prospect's annual report, reviewing new accounts or looking up what has been filed with government or private agencies on a company and its competitors.

The combination of a number of secondary and primary research approaches are "part of an array of techniques available for program development, refinement, and evaluation—all of which help" build more client confidence in following public relations counsel and buying into new programs, Kirban said.[25]

"It is becoming relatively rare that our new-business teams go into brainstorming without situational analysis that describes in terms of the target audience all those factors that bear on the client's problems." He divided such problems into those arising from external or environmental conditions and those developing from within the client organization and immediate sphere of control.

Prospects and Clients Expect Completed Staff Work in Proposals For the most part, secondary data is used to gain a commanding understanding of a prospect's or client's circumstances. Less of that data now comes through print library operations of counseling firms and more is accessed through electronic data banks.

Low-cost office and personal computers, modems for computers to telecommunicate via phone lines and popular subscription services to data banks have become great equalizers in the secondary research capacity of the largest and smallest firms. Today, a counselor working out of his home can have a computer capture in minutes an array of information from data bases all over the continent without even paying for long-distance phone calls.

The importance of such research was made clear by an executive of Honeywell and also by the HRN counseling firm executives who wrote the handbook *Leveraging the Impact of Public Affairs*. Honeywell's James Reiner told consultants at a client conference that he expected people who presented proposals and reports to him to do "completed staff work," interpreted as thorough scoping of a problem or issue, laying out of alternatives and delineation of action steps.[26]

Reiner would "listen carefully during the first five minutes of a report to determine whether the person really had done his staff work adequately" and then ask a question to determine the level of preparation and expertness. If satisfied, "I'll then participate as vigorously with full attention for as long as it takes." If dissatisfied, "I'll tune out after the first five minutes and think about more pressing business until the person leaves."

Trend Research Maps Where Markets Will Be

Implications of Naisbitt's Report on New Economy   The staff work to scope a problem or issue and find alternatives for a business presentation to an outside client is similar to the research of the sociosphere, the economy and trends needed by public relations firms to do their own long-range marketing and business plans. There are lessons to be gained from the trend analysts.

For example, John Naisbitt said that 1985 was positioned as a watershed, the year in which business was set to discover what a handful of companies already knew—"to survive in the new information-electronics economy, they must re-invent themselves." In a report from the Washington, D.C.-based Naisbitt Group, he looked past the confusingly overlapping cycles of recovery and recession to predict:

> This entrepreneurially driven, information-electronics economy is moving powerfully into place and will serve us well for the balance of this decade. . . . In this new economy, successful companies must acknowledge that their primary resource is information. . . . We are not in a recovery and we are not in a recession. What is occurring is much more important: We are changing economies. Economists ignore the entrepreneur as they continue to rely on irrelevant industrial indexes and irrelevant notions of recession-recovery cycles.[27]

The entrepreneurs of public relations counseling have found that it pays to keep their own business operations at least abreast of their clients' in studying trends—to verify that innovations and departures suggested actually are needed, workable and adaptable to their marketplace.

How to Compete with Superspecialists   As indicated earlier, specialization and focus, indeed, are important to the marketing of public relations services. But in the competition to guide today's and tomorrow's executives to a new sociosphere, a new economy, a new environment in which to do business, too much specialization may get in the way.

In the marketplace, it is not so much the competition among counselors that keeps business activity from reaching aggressively developed objectives. A key factor lies in the competition of hardened ideas about the roles and limitations of public relations in the minds of prospects and existing clients. But there is a booming market that will dramatically increase as client executives continue to look outside for more resources to meet challenges they identify.

Marketing efforts to seize the business opportunities presented by dynamically fluid trends are not confined to public relations counselors. The competition includes counseling practices in law, industrial relations, industrial psychology, management development, marketing and the like.

One area of specialization that has strong marketability, in addition to narrow areas of client services and counsel, is that of a public relations firm's capability to bring it all together, to look upon a client's "reinventing"[28] or "adaptive"[29] needs and then to provide counsel that copes with not only highly specialized fragments but can also deal with the entire system.

An analogy can be drawn to the specialist in internal medicine who may have a patient with interacting health problems that extend beyond the sphere of any one area of medicine, such as a combination of heart disease, ulcers and arthritis. Another person may see an ophthalmologist, orthopedist, gynecologist and ear-nose-and-throat specialist during the course of a year but occasionally needs somebody concerned with the whole human system as well as its parts.

An internist may deal with his own area of specialization and—at the same time—coordinate and keep track of the work of other experts. Physicians and their patients have learned the hard way that seemingly innocuous medications can interact dangerously with other specialists' "perfectly sound" prescriptions or have side effects on other parts of the human system.

The public relations firm may both specialize *and* play the critical generalist role of looking to the systemic needs of the whole client and follow what the other players inside—and outside—the organization are doing to pursue goals and achieve objectives that cross lines between areas of specialization.

Perhaps that is one of the strongest unique selling propositions counselors can bring to the new-business presentation.

PRESENTATION STRATEGIES

"Pitching" Clients: Dangers of Semantics

If Language Structures Thinking, It May Be Time to Change Language
With the maturity of counseling and the sophistication of its practitioners, it is ironic that the language of old-time, somewhat less-than-classy press agents persists at the end of the 20th century.

It is the word *"pitch"* in all its variations that typifies the throwback to an earlier era. Field research found "pitch" used in professional seminars, brainstorming sessions, meetings for developing client proposals and re-hearsals for new-business presentations.

At best, phrases such as "pitch letters," "pitching a client," "the pitch" and "pitch strategies" may be innocent expressions that lost their root meanings and remain as an archaic remnant of jargon passed on from generation to generation. Perhaps the slang, for some, connotes something other than the *real* meaning of "pitch"—high pressure sales, the style of the "pitchmen" at carnival concessions.

Judging from the contexts in which "pitch" is sometimes used and the diversity of individuals whose vocabulary it has invaded, there probably is, indeed, sharp variance in the intended meanings. Even the *Public Relations Journal* as recently as November 1985 carried a workshop feature on "How to Make your New-Business Pitch." The article concluded: "Re-member, you won't win all the competitive pitches you take part in. But if you're not hired, it means that it wouldn't have been a good match be-tween your firm and the prospective client in the first place, and you're probably better off putting your energy into the next pitch."[30]

It is possible, however, that the semantic and psychological meanings carried by "pitchmaking" get in the way of establishing a good match with some prospects. At worst, the concept of "pitch" colors the perceptions of some individuals engaged in developing programs for clients and influ-ences to varying degrees motivations for proposals, their substance and the manner in which they are presented.

Language structures thinking and thinking structures behavior, accord-ing to many a communications researcher, from the late Marshall McLu-han ("The Medium Is the Message")[31] to modern day semanticists and social scientists.

In his 1986 persuasion book, Herbert W. Simons wrote,

Language is in some respects constitutive of reality, rather than merely reflective of it. Who we are as individuals and as people, how we understand ourselves to be joined together in time and space, what we consider to be problems or non-problems, all depend on the language we select to "create," as it were, the world we inhabit.[32]

Replacing Ambiguities with Spark for Imaginative Problem Solving Could ambiguity of such words and concepts as "pitch" impair, instead of aid, the thinking about problems and opportunities in selling services and counsel as well as in developing concrete proposals to meet the needs of customers?

It is possible for reality, such as the development of new business, to exist independently of the language used to characterize it. But Simons said: "The job of the problem analyst, then, is to characterize problems and their causes accurately and unambiguously. This requires that language be used 'correctly'; that the language user 'discover' the 'right meanings' of the words to be employed and then 'tell it like it is.'" This could lead to more imaginative thinking about problems and solutions as well as more sensitization to dangerous ambiguities in language used by others—and self.

Newcomers to a field tend to pick up the jargon, if not the style, of their seniors. That's part of the socialization involved in public relations counseling and other disciplines.

It has been observed in university public relations seminars that students operationalize in their projects a hard-sell, seller (instead of buyer)-oriented, occasionally gimmicky approach after first hearing about "pitches" from guest lecturers. One counselor, for instance, used "big red tomato" to denote flashy appeals in "pitch" proposals. The next week, several students went to extremes in developing what they proudly referred to as "pitch tactics" and "big red tomatoes" in inviting corporate involvement in a seminar project.[33]

Few counseling firm executives would welcome the notion of being "pitched" by their own employees or family members. Of course, the framework of reference of both parties to a sales situation is more important than the vocabulary. Yet, it is apparent that "mere" words have powerful impact upon users as well as readers and listeners. For example, "Black is beautiful" helped alter the self-perceptions of a people as well as the perceptions of other sectors of society as they changed from "Negro" to "Black."

As the last vestiges of the hard-sell, hype approach to public relations sales are rooted out of the thinking of counselors and prospective clients, individual firms and the counseling industry as a whole will tend to gain more confidence in the marketplace.

Positioning Client Public Relations Executives as Counselors

Extend Model for Internal Public Relations Management to External Counsel Memphis counselor E. William Brody, president of the Resource Group, has advocated to client organizations "the consultant model of public relations management" for developing or redesigning internal functions. In his 1987 book, he called for recasting public relations divisions as profit centers.[34]

Presumably, they would charge the rest of their companies for time and other cost elements rather than just absorb them into overhead. Brody limited the purpose of his model to "generate greater effectiveness" in internal corporate operations.[35]

But the model could be extended and adapted to work for external counsel.[36] The authors envision counselors helping to position client public relations executives as internal consultants. This would help them—and the executives to whom they report—identify with the value of increasing utilization of external counseling resources.

It would contribute to educating other parts of management on the values—and costs—of internally provided services as well as those purchased from counselors. Public relations firm fees would not seem quite so high to client marketing and industrial relations executives, for example, if full costs of doing business internally were passed on instead of loaded into corporate overhead.

This envisions that costs for internal public relations payroll, fringe benefits, facilities, depreciation of equipment, phone bills, expense accounts and costs of vending printing, graphics and the like would be prorated and built into charges to "client" divisions.

Because an internal fee-for-service arrangement would tend to emphasize measurable achievements and even shed more light on the actual costs of the public relations function, some inside operations would tend to become more accountable and credible in the eyes of top management. That would help divisions secure more resources—including counseling firm services.

Scenarios Provide Insights on How Process Works   Several scenarios provide useful insights into how the process of converting the internal public relations function to the counseling firm model works:

1. *It didn't work at U.S. Steel*: As indicated earlier, David Ferguson, had a vision for such a profit center at U.S. Steel before he moved to Hill and Knowlton. That management did not buy the proposal—and even slashed the public relations operation after he left[37]—indicates that more persuasive power may be needed to drastically redirect the mode of handling public relations costs and functions. Perhaps respected objectivity of outside counsel might help. Certainly other variables have to be weighed. It is feasible.

2. *How insurance company created consultancy*: In 1985, *Jack O'Dwyer's Newsletter* reported that a Pennsylvania insurance corporation, Colonial Penn Group, accepted the proposal of its senior vice president for corporate affairs and created a new firm, Communications Services Corp. of Philadelphia.[38]

William Bennington negotiated a two-year contract after helping his former employer see that it could save a quarter of a million dollars in internal overhead the first year and up to a half million the second year. "It no longer made sense to keep a high-priced executive like me to lead a small staff," Bennington said.

3. *Health complex set up in-house firm*: The head of corporate marketing and community relations for Baptist Hospitals and Health Systems of Phoenix stayed inside the organization but set up a separate in-house firm to serve affiliate hospitals and some other health interests in Arizona. *PR Reporter*, however, reported that the operation hadn't proved profitable in its initial phase "because it needs more commitment from upper management."[39]

Ironically, Cherie Grigas said that although the move did increase credibility with top management, the in-house operation lacked a primary advantage of external firms and, at the same time, confronted an attitude outside counselors sometimes face when clients have to consider the real costs. "The dilemma is that if consulting comes from outside, it's better—even though they're saying the same things you are," Grigas said. "If you're independent, maybe they'll have more faith in you."

A problem that may—or may not be—peculiar to the not-for-profit sector developed when clients began to consider the actual costs of public relations. Grigas found that some executives who used public relations support before the billing policy was initiated became resistant to paying for services and opted to do without expert help.

4. *Land developer goes external—with own vice president*: A large land developer/agricultural complex in Southern California went external for the first time by becoming the first major client of its public affairs vice president, C. Thomas Wilck, when he left to create a firm.[40]

Wilck Associates of Newport Beach continues to do "much the same" community relations and public affairs for the Irvine Co. that the principal oversaw when he was on staff.

5. *Blue chip corporation changes policy on consultants*: Sometimes corporate reorganization or layoff situations can provide a catalyst for change. This happened, for example, about the time GE began to acquire RCA and engaged in restructuring itself. O'Dwyer reported that "GE in the past has not allowed ex-employees to become consultants to the company, but has made an exception in the case of the 14 news bureau professionals who received notice."[41]

They founded Masto, Dagastine & Associates in Schenectady, N.Y., and High Technology PR in Westport, Conn. GE officers said that company units themselves have control over their own public relations budgets and that the new policy represents an opportunity for marketing-oriented firms to call on individual GE businesses.[42]

6. *Placing firm employees in client offices*: Another scenario has called for placing public relations firms' employees in client offices as mini-branch operations to make them readily available to clients, position them to strengthen relations and develop new-business opportunities.

In an interview with *PR Reporter*, Truitt explained why some firms, such as Byoir, had dropped the practice: "It hampered the flexibility of our people, committing them to work entirely on one client." Physical proximity to client operations has advantages, but he said that objectivity is sacrificed. "Some people say you shouldn't be too close to your client because you soon become fully equipped with the reasons why things can't be done."[43]

There's another trap involved in too much identification with clients, said S. Judith Rich, Chicago executive vice president of Ketchum Public Relations: "You have to keep enough distance to be a good consultant. It's easy to catch yourself saying something to a client like, 'That's my opinion because I know you and understand you,' when you should be saying, 'Here's the reality.' "[44]

Shaping the Presentation Team

Considerations in Selection and Preparation of Team Members Selecting and preparing members of new-business presentation teams bear importantly on effectiveness. Consider the following:

1. *Choose those who understand business and personal needs*: There is more to selection than matching people on the team to fit psychologically and in terms of credibility with individuals in the client's company. They must be capable to "really understand the client's business and personal needs," Rich said.[45]

2. *Select those who like individuals, product, company*: In field research on new-business presentations, the word "chemistry" arose frequently in interviews. Rich, who was national creative director for Daniel J. Edelman before her 1985 move to Ketchum, goes further. She concerns herself with how team members feel about the prospect's officers. "If they don't like people they're going to be working with, they may not have as good a product to present."[46]

Distaste for client officers, products or the company itself will tend to be sensed during the course of a relationship, if not during the initial presentation.

3. *Analyze degree of liking*: The best course of action may be to encourage people to recognize any dislikes they have and communicate reservations to the person organizing the team. Rich believes in a frontal approach by the person in charge—asking: "Were you comfortable with them, did you like so and so?"[47]

4. *Sensitize to personality matching*: She recommended sensitivity to the comfort factor of the client with different types of individuals. That may be oriented to such simple demographic factors as age or sex or more complex psychographic considerations, such as degree of personality intensity—in the vernacular, whether a member of the team could be perceived as too "uptight" or "laid-back."

5. *Try diversity approach, then observe*: If the client's comfort index can't be assessed before a presentation, she suggested bringing a diversity of people and observing with whom the client executives like to talk and how they seem to relate to each other.

6. *Coach on style*: Rich coaches her own teams: "Basically, you're nice and warm and friendly. Don't try to be something you're not. Don't pretend to have knowledge you don't have. Recognize there's nothing wrong with asking questions."

7. *Anticipate bizarre communications*: "There always are some clients who put you on the spot with weird questions, such as, 'can you put me on the cover of *Time* like the last agency promised?'" One went beyond weird: "I think advertising is slime and PR is lower than slime." The prospect was asked, "So why are you here?" His response: "To have you convince me that you're not."

8. *Make sure you have a chance*: Although such a situation may seem to pose a challenge, it can, and in the above case, did, "eat up a lot of new-business time." A familiar lesson comes to mind: Know when to cut your losses. "There's a necessity to make sure you have a chance rather than staying involved in a public relations hunt that takes a lot of money and ideas" and robs a team of spirit.

9. *Beware of speculation*: Speculative proposals for which clients pay nothing continue to be a problem in the industry. More sophisticated clients do pay all or some costs. But Rich noted that when a promising new account is attainable, "if one major contender gives free proposals, it seems nobody can afford not to."[48]

10. *Test client's seriousness*: Veteran counselors often outline proposals until they have reason to be confident enough to invest time and ideas in filling in the details.

There's no panacea, but here are some modes to test a prospect's degree of seriousness: Check out the company with people who know it. Do a credit rating. Observe if a client answers openly when asked for information a counselor would need to do the job. Ascertain how negative findings will be received.

Establishing Right Level of Contact

Attention to factors involved in the level of contact within both the counseling firm and the prospect's organization is integral to the effectiveness of presentations and long-range relationships.

Beware of Misinterpretations and Conflicts at Lower Levels People at the lower levels of a client organization and a public relations firm may agree—but on the wrong solutions. For instance, they might agree that publicity will be "the" answer even if it may create more difficulties than it's worth.

Sometimes the problem lies on the client side of the relationship, particularly in the designation of a liaison person who may not have capabilities, access to information, confidence of his executives or strength of motivation needed.

"There are too many companies in which the public relations responsibility is foisted upon somebody," Rich suggested. "The client contact may not get respect within his own company. That means you have to be able to work at the highest level possible."[49]

Although much of the relationship in developing new business can take place at lower levels, sometimes a person acting as the client's filter may— from lack of understanding of what the CEO or chairman of the board wants to achieve—give a counselor his own point of view in trying to solve a problem. A breakdown may occur in the very process of filtering communication down through the various levels, much as rumors are distorted as they're passed through several individuals.

Charles Lipton, New York-based vice chairman of Ruder Finn & Rotman, gave an example of a client's problem and its solution.[50] A company in the pharmaceutical industry was conducting test marketing to determine the relative success of a drug.

The client's public relations people made the interpretation that they had to raise awareness of the manufacturer as leader in this particular area of the industry. The CEO, however, said there was only one degree of success or failure and, "that's whether or not we outsell the sales quota we established." The guy paying the bills said it wasn't awareness but simply a matter of how many pills are sold.

Three months were wasted until the marketing executive dressed down everybody. As a result, biweekly meetings were organized for all the people involved.

At those meetings, "the senior marketing guy sits there and listens and makes sure that the campaigns for which they're paying are on target."

The level at which public relations services are performed can surface as a major source of problems at any stage of the client relationship. "If the public relations activity is somehow or other not cued into the thinking of the top level of executives in the company, you can have 'excellent' results from your point of view, but the relationship may be doomed to failure in the eyes of the client CEO," Lipton said. Shifting level of contact, however, can be fraught with problems.

Some internal public relations staff may perceive external counselors as disruptive. Even when a counseling firm is sensitized to working with internal staff and helping place them in a favorable light with their own top management, all it may take is a CEO teasing a staff officer with a

comment like, "Why didn't you come up with that idea?" to set in motion
antipathy toward external counsel.

This may lead to efforts to interfere with counseling firm access to the
highest level. Lipton said that insecurity-motivated interference with executive access is not restricted to internal public relations staff. "It happens within public relations firms themselves."[51] On the client side, it also
may exist in legal, accounting and advertising areas when outside experts
are brought in.

A key strategy is to help public relations officers be confident that no
attempt will be made to undermine the internal function and that special
efforts will be made to help them receive the resources and recognition
needed to do their jobs.

That way, instead of running into interference from those who may be
insecure about meetings between their executives and counselors, one
may encounter "public relations directors with enough confidence in their
CEO and enough trust in you that they'll facilitate access rather than
worry about either of you undermining them."[52]

The ideal time to establish the appropriate level of contact is at the
beginning of any relationship. An initial audit provides an opportunity to
meet the CEO and other senior officers and bring up the level of contact
with them. Lipton's approach: "I might say something like, 'I presume
we'll be presenting the program to you personally and be meeting with
you at least quarterly to review it.' "[53]

Groom Staff to Relate to Client Executives   It also is important to establish contacts at different levels between the prospective client organization and the counseling firm. Counseling firms have found that professional development of junior account people concerning the corporate
milieu and specific business functions spares them, and client executives,
anguish. Education on complex interrelationships that can exist within a
company helps junior staff work their way through the corporate maze
and gain confidence and stature in developing the business.

For example, Lipton said, "you often find the broad field of financial
relations segmented, part of it under investor relations, part under public
relations, with PR doing the annual report, quarterlies and media relations. The junior person may be confused about who's saying and doing
what."[54]

One way to avoid this quandary is to assure that staff know how to
proceed within the counseling firm or the client organization to the level
responsible for overall program or specific aspects.

How to Script a Presentation

Criteria for Effective Dialogues in New-Business Development Meetings
Once a team has been selected and prepared to approach a serious prospect

for new business, it concentrates on scripting the actual presentation. A number of points may prove valuable.

A review of some of the more salient criteria may be found in a monograph for the Counselors Academy by the management consultant who founded New York's Chester Burger & Co.:[55]

1. *Keep it short*: Many presentations may be written in the belief that sheer length will impress the prospect. But most executives lack the time, interest and patience to read them.

2. *Let problem analysis speak for counselor qualifications*: A description of a firm's qualifications and experience should be reserved for the end of the presentation. Most prospects are far more interested in "your analysis of his problem and proposed public relations solutions." If they are sound, Burger said "you will already have succeeded in establishing your professional competence."

3. *First, state the problem*: Beginning with a statement of the prospect's problem—as studied by the counselor—demonstrates an understanding of the client's needs and sets the stage for the rest of the presentation.

4. *Next, offer analysis*: A presentation that offers solutions without first analyzing the problem may lead the prospect to believe that the solution is not tailored to his company or his needs.

5. *Then, give solution, not details on techniques*: Itemizing techniques tends to bore executives who really want "the certainty that you offer a solution."

6. *Risk by outlining good ideas*: Although some counselors "worry that a prospect may simply appropriate your ideas," he said "it happens so rarely that you can safely delete it from the list of perils. Further, there's a big difference between your good idea and someone else's ability to execute it successfully."

Burger also warned counselors that their meaning of the words "presentation" or "proposal" and the client's interpretation may differ.[56] That implies the need to do enough questioning or restating to verify what is expected before anybody goes off on a tangent that can cost counseling time and credibility.

Strategies in Dealing with Client Expectations

Realistic Expectations Predispose Healthy Relationships The expectations of prospective and existing clients extend to critical areas beyond what they look for in a "presentation" or "proposal." Too high expectations of what public relations or a counseling firm can accomplish can arise during—and often, long before—the first meeting.

To Paul Alvarez, chairman of Ketchum Public Relations, "one of the great problems that has plagued the public relations business has been overpromise," a problem compounded by "agencies on the fringes of the

profession that may promise undeliverable products to get a client's business."[57]

To foster healthy relationships, counselors use a number of techniques
before, during and after new-business presentations. But the emphasis
tends to be on "before." The reason was well stated by Michael Campbell,
chairman and CEO of the Toronto, Ontario-based Continental Public Relations. "Expectations can't be changed afterwards; all explanations on why
an expectation was too optimistic or couldn't be delivered will sound like
excuses."[58] Here are approaches favored by American and Canadian counselors.

1. *Define and adjust expected results—together*: Although client and
program objectives frequently provide a reference point they may be too
general or long-term to serve as appropriate measures. Consultant and
client, therefore, work together to define specific results expected and
adjust their thinking or action as needed.

2. *Tell it like it is on capabilities*: Corporate executives are helped to
understand the true scope of public relations and the counseling firm's
ability. Campbell said he couldn't recall ever hearing of a client changing
consultants "because the supplier confessed to not having the expertise
required for a particular assignment." But he could cite "numerous examples of firms being fired because they could not deliver what they had
promised."[59]

3. *But don't promise too little*: Some people promise less than they
know they will deliver on the premise that shaping client expectations
they will surpass, rather than merely meet, will promote more client
loyalty and larger projects. Underestimation, if *perceived* as a sales trick,
can cause terminal damage to a relationship. Underestimation of results
also may convince an executive to look for a firm with more confidence in
its capabilities.

4. *Watch own non-verbal signs*: An example was furnished by Alvarez:
"What may be an innocent, but misleading reflex, can occur when a client
says, 'I'm sure you can do this,' and the counselor shakes his head up and
down."[60] A client may infer from such a gesture that the counselor is
saying: "I can do that and more!"

5. *Go for specificity*: Sometimes allowing unreasonable expectations is
not so much a matter of overpromise but of client and counselor lacking
specificity in what is expected and what can be delivered. The responsibility for being specific may belong to both sides, but it's in the counselor's
interest to take the initiative. Alvarez said such initiative will help establish a favorable reputation with the client's peers in other businesses as
well as with the client organization.[61]

6. *Take into account intervening variables*: Intervening variables are
those realities that, beyond a simple causal factor, actually influence a

result. For instance, what may appear to be a simple cause-and-effect relationship between a public relations campaign and a spurt in product sales may be the result of other causal factors or a complex combination of causes.

Variables that intervene between what appears to be the cause (publicity, for instance) and the effect (sales increase) may include sales promotion, advertising, point-of-purchase factors, relaxation of efforts by the competition, something in the product itself or even degree of shoppers' confidence in the economy.

7. *Use case studies carefully*: Case studies are valuable in presentations but also can be dangerously deceptive. As Alvarez said, make sure "you realistically show what has happened to other clients; don't let them think they're going to have a Cabbage Patch Doll phenomenon every time they use public relations. Show them other examples of work that parallels theirs and what comes out of it." This means not only bringing out "case histories where promotion was successful," but also those "where it was a dismal flop, too."[62]

8. *Help understand down-side possibilities*: A surgeon discusses the chances of complications and risks with a candidate for an operation. An attorney tells a client what the other side's counsel, witnesses, jury or judge might do to cause an unfavorable decision. Similarly many a counselor is not only concerned that clients have realistic expectations of what goes right, but also what could go wrong. This can be ticklish because, as Alvarez said, "often a new client is very concerned about what could go wrong."[63] So is the client of an attorney facing a seven-figure law suit or the patient considering open-heart surgery.

In some cases, discussing down-side possibilities could relieve some of the worst anxieties, fears that might be greater than realities warrant. In other situations, the client may not like to hear of down-side risks, but may have more respect for and confidence in the counselor. Certainly, that client will not feel later—if anticipated things do go wrong—that he was deceived.

9. *Condition expectations on size of bills*: It also is ticklish, but rewarding, to make sure that a client is conditioned for the size of bills that may be incurred.

In Canada, as in America, Campbell found that prospective clients "need to understand differences between a consulting firm's approach to income vs. an advertising agency's mix of fees and commissions on sales of media space and time."[64] Executives may think of public relations firm charges as high compared to agency fees because they overlook commissions usually paid by the media to agencies. Such commissions are passed on to clients by the media.

Some counselors approach conditioning of clients with a technique epitomized by the style of Michael V. Sullivan, chairman of the marketing communications firm of Harris, Baio & Sullivan in Doylestown, Pa. Right after contracting, he tells a client: "Six to eight months out, you'll dislike me; you're going to be very upset after looking at my bills. After one year, you're going to be very happy."[65]

Alvarez said "people like Mike help their clients understand that counseling is a pipeline business; that is, it takes a lot of work before things come out well at the other end."[66]

Overcoming Bill Barrier to Proposal Acceptance

How to Get Value Concept into Minds of Prospective Clients   Field research indicates that one of the greatest barriers in the early phases of client relationships, even before a company considers approaching a counseling firm, relates to the question of fees. One technique some counselors find effective in overcoming this barrier involves positioning a value-added concept in the minds of client executives.

It seems basic for members of a discipline so little understood as public relations counseling to invest effort in teaching prospects and clients about the economics of what they pay for. Here are some steps that could be taken to educate executives on the value of counsel.

1. *Sponsor an industry-wide value education program*: Through their trade associations, *other* industries retain public relations counsel to develop educational programs on the economics of rising costs and values. At the macro level, this presents opportunities for a counseling industry-wide sponsored program for corporate, institutional and governmental executives. At the micro level, more concerted efforts by individual counselors and their firms could be orchestrated.

2. *Teach actual value of hours charged*: Some executives look at hourly fees as they look at hourly pay rates. Whether a firm charges by the hour or by the program, there is still advantage to be derived from educating executives to shed their perception of public relations as an expense rather than an investment.

As Lipton said, "a client can be charged $100 or more an hour but the counsel emanating from that hour can be worth a veritable fortune to the company!" He illustrated the point with the following case:

"The Wall Street community thought that because it manufactured garments, the client was a textile company." Counsel helped the client understand why and how to position itself so that Wall Street conceived of the company as a service-type industry. "Without anything changing but the communication and the perception, the price/earnings ratio increased from 7 to 12. For that hour of counsel, the result was worth millions to the client."[67]

3. *Use physician or attorney billing models*: There is already in the industry some billing for actual value, but it may be too early to say that this is a trend. Clients who pay such fees learn they pay for the value of ideas and programs instead of time. A parallel may be seen in a heart surgeon charging $10,000 or more for an operation rather than billing for hours in the operating room. Different types of fee-for-value arrangements may be found in the legal profession.

Some law firms work on a contingency basis that specifies a percentage of what is awarded to the client. Others work on a retainer but really are not on budget. Lipton said: "They throw in lawyer after lawyer to win a case" rather than worry about accounting for each hour spent by partners and other members of their firms.[68]

He recalled a meeting on merger and acquisition activity with a client and representatives from two proxy firms. Ruder Finn & Rotman was represented by two officers, the law firm by two partners and nine other lawyers. "The client asked the senior partner, 'what are the nine junior people from your firm going to do?' Before he could answer, he said, 'better yet, don't tell me what they're going to do and don't charge me for it.' But most clients never even challenge a legal firm on resources and costs involved in an important case."

4. *A matter of timing*: Changing attitudes about public relations fees, just as modification of behavioral patterns in a client's publics, may require patience, continuing education and a sense of timing. Progress has been made, however.

Opportunities for charging for the value-added products of public relations will tend to increase as more business executives gain experience in using public relations counsel, as business students are required to learn more about public relations roles in such areas as public affairs and marketing and as more are helped by their peers and consultants to understand what counseling accomplishes.

5. *Differentiate between routine and problem-solving charges*: This has to be done before charges are incurred, with a clear understanding of procedures for determining what is "routine" and "problem solving." Lipton recommended that "when you're talking to executives of major companies, you can help them understand that if you really help solve major problems, clients will have the obligation to pay more."[69]

6. *Innovate with base charge plus bonus fee*: Although public relations firms have shied away from the legal profession's precedent of contingency fees, there is the possibility for innovative adaptation. A client could contract for a base fee and agree to pay a bonus fee on top of that for certain results. The challenge is to be able to ascribe success to public relations activity. But with the trend to measurable results, that is becoming feasible.

For instance, Lipton said a firm could arrange for bonus scales for investor relations counsel. He said this would be more likely to be adopted by clients or in situations in which public relations is a major force. Bonus fees are "a foreign concept in public relations, but it is something that could be done."[70]

7. *Charge more to remain competitive*: Counseling firms will have to pay—and charge—more to recruit and retain top talent. Traditionally, counseling firms charge considerably less than counterparts in other disciplines, perhaps because of prevailing rates or the consideration of competition for accounts by others willing to charge less. A new and larger factor looms on the horizon: the increased competition with advertising, marketing and other fields to recruit and retain talent. And as clients begin to recognize the value of internal public relations officers and pay more for their skills, there will be more pressure to increase compensation for counseling personnel.

8. *Charge for value of preparedness of expert team*: There also is a trend for public relations firms to charge for preparedness, not just services rendered. This seems particularly applicable to industries where sudden moves by corporate raiders or government can do serious damage, if not threaten their survival, unless there is an expert public relations team in place.

Sometimes the threats to survival—or opportunities to capitalize on an opening in the marketplace—can arise and demand instant responses. The effects on the investment community confidence can be long lasting and deeply felt, despite a transitory crisis or the shallowness of a rumor. Whole lines of pharmaceutical products, such as pain capsules; and of computer hardware; and even foodstuffs can crash from sales leadership or rise from relative oblivion depending on preparedness to make sound decisions and implement new programs quickly.

Preparedness, however, means more than contracting for a team of experts or a program off-the-shelf. Normally, when a team of experts is hired, they must invest time in the learning curve. This includes time to do trend analysis and projections, to know the inner workings and objectives of the company, to develop with the client working relationships that operate efficiently under the worst of circumstances and to learn how an emergent situation involves the client's competitors.

Handling Embarrassment of Too Much/Too Little Time   Charging on a cost-per-hour rather than value-delivered basis poses problems that can embarrass the firm if not misguide a client about the worth of public relations ideas and services.

Management consultants Chester Burger and Peter Brooks dealt with this issue in a crosscontinental, tele-computer conference that linked public relations practitioners at home and office computer terminals in their first live seminar.[71] Excerpts from the computer transmissions follow.

BURGER: There is a tendency in the business . . . to exaggerate [in time sheets completed by employees of counseling firms] time spent on a particular project. If we have a hard time of it and spend too much time, we are embarrassed to say so. Or we are so efficient that we accomplish something very important with a couple of calls. . . . I think the best way to handle this is to record the truth. Then management can decide whether to charge more or less, but it will know what it actually and truthfully cost to do the job.

BROOKS: He mentions accomplishing something very important with just one or a few calls that took little time and is not very billable. In that case, however, the quickness with which the job was accomplished may be due to the expertise or the contacts—or both—of the consultant and thus has much higher value than the time it took to accomplish. Therefore billing on the straight time may not accurately reflect the value of what was accomplished, and one could justify billing at a higher rate for that job.

NATHAN J. SILVERMAN, Chicago counselor: What alternatives are agencies using to the flat fee method for bidding on special projects? Due to the unexpecteds and uncontrollables, many of us routinely run over budget.

BURGER: The best way is to give an estimate and state at the beginning that if it is to exceed that amount, you'll advise the client in advance so they can decide whether they want to spend the additional money. Another way is to set a flat amount for a highly and sharply defined series of activities and specify extra costs for anything beyond that. . . .

BROOKS: Many attorneys will bill for some of the so-called direct costs in addition to their time. . . . If your attorney takes a trip on your behalf, he will bill you for all the direct expenses and for his time. . . . Most of the firms I have worked with and most of the attorneys I have talked to do it this way.

BURGER: The most common [budgeting practice] is automatically to include 10 percent for contingencies. . . . Let me emphasize the value of time record-keeping [and analytical projections]. Our fees are approximated on the following basis: We know from experience that one of our partners can do four average-length interviews of corporate managers per day. And our time records have told us that for every day we have spent in interviewing, we spend three person-days in discussing, analyzing, writing, reporting, etc. So if the company tells us we should interview 15 people, we can reasonably well estimate our labor costs. And if they reduce the number of required interviews, our fees drop, and vice versa. It's in their control.

BROOKS: The big eight accounting firms have another way of dealing with this problem: They will quote a job in advance and establish an hourly billing rate for it. If they go overtime or incur other unanticipated expenses or are asked to do new jobs not originally agreed to along the way, they track all that time. The billing time agreed to as part of the contract is called "above the line"—"below the line" [represents] the contingency costs. They don't expect to recover all [below the line costs] but will negotiate with the client for some percentage at the end of a job and use the time records for justification.

Some Firms Institutionalize Value-Added Policies One way to demonstrate the value of public relations services, build client loyalty and condition executives to want to buy more is to deliver more value than the client pays for. On the surface, that seems contradictory, if not radical. But on closer inspection, the concept has heuristic value in suggesting ideas for increasing the appeal in client presentations and relations. Two examples of firms that institutionalized value-added policies are E. Bruce Harrison and Burson-Marsteller.

Harrison adopted a policy that requires his Washington, D.C., firm's employees to "purposely over-service every client by at least 5 percent and often up to 10 percent more than they pay." He supplied examples: A client paying $5,000 a month gets $5,500 worth of services, a difference of five hours of an account executive's time. A $20,000-a-month client gets an extra 20 hours of time spread over the billing period.[72]

"The effect is that only the accountant and I know that we're lowering the rate. Nobody in our firm ever has the feeling of any sacrifice, just that we're all well paid and we deserve it. But the client knows he's getting more value. It shows up in the quality and quantity of the work, in the attitude of service and overservice." He said that he sees this as an investment in his corporate growth. "We're going to get what we need to the extent that we give clients what they need."

In an introspective review after a dozen years in business, Harrison said that the overservice policy assuring clients that they receive more than their money's worth "is a strong developer of staff pride" and helps motivate the spirit that attracts new clients and cultivates more business from existing clients.

William F. Noonan, vice chairman of Burson-Marsteller, briefed some members of the Counselors Academy on his firm's formal "Value Added" program, ostensibly an internal-competition program modeled in part after PRSA's Silver Anvil awards. The "Value Added" competition was field tested in the United States for three years before Burson-Marsteller expanded it to its international offices.[73]

"This program is not just to showcase good work. It is to recognize work that goes the extra mile, that gives the client something extra. The 'training' element is to build client leadership among our staff. We promote it aggressively internally, and we give the winners a lot of visibility. The judges are a peer group of middle managers" who, presumably, are motivated by their participation to instill more of the value-added spirit in the people they manage.

Turning Mistakes That Lose Clients into Value-Added Positives

A *Public Relations Journal* article by Los Angeles counselor Renee Miller on "How to Keep Clients: 11 Mistakes to Avoid" cites a number of West Coast public relations firms' executives on mistakes that have cost them business.[74] Chief among them seem to be taking clients for granted. The negatives are reframed in this book as value-added positives.

John Margaritis, vice president, Fleishman-Hillard: "Work terribly hard" to service the account with the same degree of effort invested in winning it.

Roger S. Pondel, principal, Rifkind, Pondel and Parsons: In developing bids, compensate for the normal tendency to under-estimate the time (and cost) that a project will demand after it's started.

Ron Rogers, past president, Rogers & Cowan: "Be convinced that the job they are asking for can be done . . . we can make a profit on the business [and] the clients have the potential to become long-term accounts."

David H. Simon, principal, Simon/McGarry Public Relations: Principals of smaller firms should be more attentive to the details of running a business and assure that all charges in the bills are explained and accurate and that invoices are sent out quickly.

Betsy Berkhemer, principal, Berkhemer & Kline: Demonstrate a commitment to the product and to the client.

COPING WITH CONFLICT

How to Manage Potential Conflict of Interest

Loyalty and commitment of counselor to client and of client to counselor fit with the ideals of a golden rule for developing mutually advantageous client relationships and capitalizing upon business opportunities.

Perhaps that's why the reality or the perception that either side is withholding something vital from the other or otherwise violating the golden rule can damn a relationship, hurt a corporation and those associated with it or lead to a court battle.

Janet Laib Gottlieb, partner in New York City's Edward Gottlieb Inc., said that investigation of potential conflict of interest and candor on that sensitive topic should be at the top of a checklist of "some of the things that should be on your new-business agenda."[75] First, however, there is a need to clarify what a client or counselor might interpret as "conflict of interest."

What Is Conflict of Interest?   "Conflict of interest" means different things to different individuals. As more noble expressions, such as "democracy," or more common labels, such as "liberal," the meaning is clouded by semantics and dependent upon context and source. Whatever the meaning, the term *conflict of interest* is laden with highly charged overtones by its uses and abuses by politicians, journalists, orators and lawyers.

Dictionary definitions only help somewhat. For instance, the following definitions appear in one unabridged dictionary.[76]

> *"The circumstance of a person who finds that one of his activities, interests etc., can be forwarded only at the expense of another of them."*

> *"The circumstance of a public office holder whose private financial interests might benefit from his official actions or political influence."*

In counseling, the term usually applies to perception by the client, counselor or both that the counselor's representation of one particular organization or stand on a given issue conflicts with the interests of another client, past, present or future.

At one extreme, it is possible to rationalize anything by claiming that there is no conflict or that the ethics and fair-mindedness of an individual or firm make it impossible to even suggest a breach. At the other extreme, it is possible to figure that all causes and organizations compete for certain stakes or even the attention of the counselor and thus stand in conflict of interest.

Even the internal public relations officer may look upon providing counsel or services to one company division as being in a conflict of interest with the others, each competing for scarce resources, each with its own agenda.

For counselors, the possibilities for overlapping or competing interests would seem to increase geometrically with the number of clients, particularly when they are in like industries or want scarce resources, such as government funds, media coverage or market share. On the other hand, sheer size of a counseling firm and diversity of organizations represented may provide a checks-and-balances safeguard.

Do two health care or food product clients in the same market represent conflict of interest? Or could an argument be made that representing more than one manufacturer of computer hardware or pharmaceuticals benefits all such clients as long as the firm makes painstaking efforts to identify the interests of each and avoid getting placed in a position of doing damage to one to make a greater profit from the other?

Would it depend upon size of market, degree of scarcity of resources sought by the clients, nature of the conflict, and, most of all, candor of counselors within their own firms as well as with their clients in raising and responding to questions of fair representation?

PRSA Code of Ethics Articles Bear on Conflict of Interest   The Public Relations Society of America, with strong leadership from its counselors, wrestled with such questions of conflict of interest—client interests and public interests—in shaping its first code of ethics in 1954 and in strengthening it through four revisions over the next three decades.[77]

The most pertinent article on conflict of interest in its Code of Professional Standards for the Practice of Public Relations is the fourth:

"A member shall not represent conflicting or competing interests without the express consent of those involved, given after a full disclosure of the facts; nor place himself or herself in a position where the member's interest is or may be in conflict with a duty to a client, or others, without a full disclosure of such interests to all involved."

Article 5 protects the confidentiality interests of clients:

"A member shall safeguard the confidences of both present and former clients or employers and shall not accept retainers or employment which may involve the disclosure or use of these confidences to the disadvantage or prejudice of such clients or employers."

Articles 8 and 9 serve to forbid hidden or deceptive representation to publics:

"A member shall be prepared to identify publicly the name of the client or employer on whose behalf any public communication is made." And: *"A member shall not make use of any individual or organization purporting to serve or represent an announced cause, or purporting to be independent or unbiased, but actually serving an undisclosed special or private interest of a member, client, or employer."*

The other articles deal with conduct in the public interest, fairness to clients and publics alike, protection of the integrity of government and channels of communication and accuracy and honesty.

Techniques for Managing Potential Conflicts   Many firms, particularly those with multiple offices, have created ways to keep conflict situations from becoming even potentially dangerous to the clients.

At Carl Byoir & Associates, counselors were faced with a conflict that the firm had no way of avoiding and no way of reporting to the two client companies, Honeywell and Eastman Kodak.[78] Within a period of about seven weeks, executives of both clients called on top management supervisors at Byoir to report that each company shortly would be announcing a new product that had been in development for some time and that would represent a major advancement in consumer photography. In each case, the product was identified as the first practical, consumer-oriented, auto-focus camera lens.

The case illustrates the first five of the following conflict management approaches:

1. *Internal silence to safeguard trade secrets*: Although development details differed between the companies, the products were similar. Each Byoir supervisor, knowing he possessed a significant trade secret, kept it from the other, but proceeded with plans to use the firm's resources in a major announcement.

2. *Essential personnel involved with each client's OK*: The announcement dates were to be within a month of each other. The problem came to light as executives began to bring other essential Byoir personnel—with each client's permission—into the loop.

3. *Each client kept in dark on other's secrets*: But Honeywell and Eastman Kodak were kept in the dark on each other's secrets because neither Byoir supervisor could ethically return to his own client with news of the competing development.

4. *Offer to bring in non-aligned firm*: It was decided that one of the clients would be asked to seek help for this assignment from another public relations firm "because of a product conflict that exists within the firm." Executives of both Honeywell and Kodak demurred, however, saying that they had faith in Byoir's ability to cordon off the project within the office and keep things confidential.

5. *Large firm can divide itself*: With remarkably little leakage between account groups, the twin projects proceeded, media coverage received for both announcements was good and the Byoir teams demonstrated that building a wall within a large firm to divide two competing projects could work, at least for a short time.

6. *Team may go into seclusion from rest of firm*: In other firms, such as Burson-Marsteller, field research found that an account team with information that could compromise one client's trade secrets if it reached other clients would go into seclusion at a rented, remote suite of offices. Individuals were briefed—and sworn to secrecy—on a need-to-know basis as the nucleus of such a team had to be increased in size as launch time approached.[79]

7. *Use a geographic dispersion strategy*: Public relations firms with multiple offices often can take advantage of geographic dispersion to separate client account activities and defuse any questions of conflict that might arise.

8. *Divide account activities among subsidiaries*: Firms that maintain a degree of independence for subsidiaries they acquire in other cities sometimes hand over potentially conflicting business to a wholly-owned subsidiary.

9. *Option—refuse the business*: Although this can be traumatic, especially for a firm without strong financial reserves, the option to decline a business or resign an account is exercised occasionally when other courses do not appear available and when to do otherwise would jeopardize the reputation of the firm.

10. *Option—broker mutually acceptable arrangement*: It is possible for a firm of any size to approach the parties to a potential conflict and explore modes of maintaining integrity without losing either account.

For example, Epley Associates in 1985 had one chemical company under contract when it was approached by a second. Both companies manufacture dyes. The prospect was told Joe Epley's firm was working for a competitor that had to be consulted first. The existing client was given refusal rights if he felt there was a conflict of interest, but he approved with one caveat: The firm had to stop short of providing any market support for the competitor.[80]

11. *Avoid even the appearance of potential impropriety*: Davis Young suggested that public relations people "place the same emphasis on full, accurate and understandable disclosure as we do on timely disclosure" and "go out of our way to avoid even the appearance of potential impropriety." The president of Cleveland-based Young-Liggett-Stashower Public Relations said: "If ours is a business of enhancing trust for other people, products, services and client organizations, then our effectiveness is in direct relation to whether or not people trust us."[81]

Coping with Deceptive Clients

How to Protect Counselors from Deceit   Perhaps another item under the heading of conflict that belongs on any checklist for new-business development is a client's reputation for dealing with counseling firms as well as media and stakeholder publics.

How does a public relations firm protect itself from innocent and not-so-innocent deceits, ranging from clients "forgetting" to pay their bills or hiding their financial shakiness to executives making false denials that a product line is being abandoned—or worse?

Because the reputation, financial health and very survival of a firm may be threatened in the future by client deceit, the question must be raised.

There are no pat answers. But there are ideas worth review and steps that can be taken, such as the following:

1. *Beware of "it-can't-happen-in-this-industry" thinking*: "Everybody knows there are a great deal of lies, distortion and deceit in certain political campaigns or areas of business, but they don't think of that being true in other industries," according to the president of New York's Richard Weiner Division of Doremus Porter Novelli.[82]

2. *Recognize roller-coaster industry influences*: "Certain industries— toy, entertainment, fashion, beauty, apparel, new high-tech ventures—may experience seasonally heavy successes and failures, sometimes in the same year." An item in a trade publication or the financial pages can make "the difference between a hit and a bomb."[83] The roller-coaster syndrome may condition a few executives to do anything to build the momentum and say anything to avoid precipitous drops.

3. *Intense ego involvement may be warning sign*: At the same time, some people who become most visible at the heights of the roller-coaster ride "get their egos pumped up with the fame that magazine cover status brings. You may see it more in industries with youthful entrepreneurs, millionaires in their 20s who become—or feel—omnipotent."[84] And it would seem that the protection of ego, as well as of business solvency, may act as a powerful motivator for a relative handful to breach ethics, if that's what it takes.

4. *Ideal is close relations with management, but . . .* : It can—and does—happen that a counseling firm is not allowed to become involved or become privy to secret planning or negotiations. There are headstrong clients who sometimes engage in wishful thinking, and sometimes are intentionally deceitful. Sometimes public relations people learn through the *Wall Street Journal* that what a client says is not true.

5. *How likely is it client can bring product to market?* Weiner observed that one of the more common examples of wishful thinking or deceit occurs at trade shows, where a client may show prototypes of products not even in existence. Initially, the "product" may be "highly publicized, highly applauded." Then the criticism starts: "Where is it?" "Why the delays?" And when the product does appear on shelves: "Why the failures to perform as promised?" "Why the bugs?"[85]

A counselor may have to be conversant with technical and production considerations to ascertain if a company really knows it can bring out a product in its promised form and time or whether eagerness to corner the market may lead to overoptimism or intentional withholding of information about problems.

6. *Instill confidence to consult principal*: "The Number One principal of an agency may not be aware of what is potentially going wrong," Weiner said. There are times when a counselor can state reservations and "the client or your boss overrules you; so you shrug it off and say, 'so be it.' At other times, the level of hysteria escalates and [the inference drawn by the counselor may be] 'either do it my way or you're fired.' "[86] That suggests a need to train account team members to feel confident in raising questions and, when in doubt, in consulting with the principal.

7. *Raise level of client contact*: If a firm deals with a client on a lower level and there is a hint of possible deceit, it's to the advantage of both client and counselor to raise the level of contact.

8. *Consult with client's legal counsel*: Dealing directly with a company's law firm may help when other efforts seem futile. Sometimes legal and public relations counsel can triangulate to influence a client to adhere to ethical and legal norms.

9. *Develop intelligence and ombudsman apparatus*: Weiner once recommended that PRSA or the Counselors Academy "try to set up some kind of ombudsman operation to address itself to ethical-legal problems on the agency side of the business." In recalling and refining his recommendation, he suggested: "When anybody would have a bad client experience, he should be able to inform the ombudsman office. It shouldn't make any difference whether a firm was fired or resigned from an account; if the ombudsman group thinks the problem relates to integrity, it should investigate and at least put out a listing to alert other public relations firms."[87]

It is of interest that some medical organizations have developed electronic data banks their members can use to gather intelligence on patients with an abnormal pattern of suing physicians.

10. *Put it in writing*: There is a tendency of some counselors to avoid using legal forms when they compete for business and worry about such precautions as appearing unprofessional. But surgeons and anesthesiologists execute a legal contract with their patients. Attorneys draw up contracts with their clients.

One public relations counseling practice is to ask a client for a letter of agreement. But Weiner said that in some cases "by the time the letter of agreement is sent back, you may be in the second or third month of servicing an account."[88]

Advertising agencies tend to be more prone to call for formal contracts than public relations firms. Perhaps the trend to mergers, acquisitions, and affiliations with advertising agencies may lead to more use of contracts by counselors, including independent firms.

11. *Get protection of indemnification clause*: One of the legalities to build into a contract is an indemnification clause to hold the firm harmless if it is ever sued or charged with liability for damages arising out of its representation of the client.

A panel of public relations legal experts recommended adoption of "hold harmless" agreements but warned members of the Counselors Academy that such a clause does not guarantee immunity from legal actions by parties other than the client. In their 1985 session on "How To Protect

Yourself and Your Client," counselors were advised that "hold harmless" releases should be written with a built-in expiration date because courts have ruled that such documents cannot be in force indefinitely.[89]

As Weiner suggested, there may be a benefit beyond protection in an indemnification clause: it reminds client executives that they bear responsibility for information and actions and that the firm is concerned about the legal ramifications for both parties.[90]

12. *What you don't know CAN hurt you in court*: The example of President Nixon's press secretary emerging legally unscathed because of his ignorance of cover-up crimes should furnish no comfort to counselors in the post-Watergate era.

The Counselor reported in 1986 that "counselors are not absolved automatically if they don't know the facts in a contentious information atmosphere. There is an obligation to check."[91]

A Washington attorney specializing in corporate and securities law said that "a public relations firm is obligated to conduct reasonable investigation to determine truth of information supplied by a client for dissemination." Alan J. Berkeley, partner in the law firm of Kirkpatrick & Lockhart, cited legal precedents and a 1984 Securities and Exchange Commission statement reminding those who speak for companies that they must take care that "'all statements that can reasonably be expected to reach investors and the securities markets adhere to the facts.'"[92]

13. *Consider policy to require client review and approval*: In 1984, the Counselors Academy's firm management committee chairman, Bernard E. Ury, released a report on the legal dangers for growing firms. He said an increasing number of counselors have a policy of requiring their clients to review and approve written materials distributed to the press, analysts and the public.[93]

Weiner agreed with having such a policy but said that frequently there may not be time to get approval in writing "in fast moving situations when an agency has to get out information quickly over the Dow Jones or PR Newswire," for instance. At such times, he has relied on phone approvals.[94]

But there is a strategy to document such calls and remind the client of the importance of verifying information. A memo can be sent to the client with a copy to file. Although without legal strength of a signed release form, a memo does allow the counselor to put on record such stipulations as: "We have questioned the following things and the client assured us the information is valid and accurate." This memo would include the time and date of the phone conversation and the name and position of the client executive who gave approval.

14. *Closely monitor payment of bills*: Some public relations firms have carried temporarily strapped clients, but Weiner suggested that "if you see a client two, three or more months behind, it really may be time to quit the account." Another signal is a check—or second check—that bounces or a caller who promises for several weeks that the check is in the mail.[95]

15. *Payment up front vs. 20 cents on the dollar*: The vast majority of clients may be honest and deal fairly with their counselors, but Weiner advised that "if you're dealing with a high flier, even if the client is listed on the New York Stock Exchange and doing millions of dollars of business a year, it's a good idea to ask for a deposit for expenses and payment as expenses are incurred.

"It's important that the deposit be replenished," he said, recalling one case in which his firm did receive a $10,000 deposit. "Because we were moving so fast and the client had initially paid our fee on time and had given us the initial deposit, we got lax. We were financing that client for nearly nine months."

Some firms charge interest on overdue payments as an incentive to pay on time as well as to prevent money market losses incurred in the kind of "financing" Weiner described.

"The iron test of whether a client should be retained is if you get money in advance and promptly in accord with your original letter of agreement. There's not a firm I know that hasn't had a client go bankrupt," Weiner said. "You get 20 cents on the dollar after all the hard work and great emotional hassles. And usually the firm is the last to know."

16. *Research a client's financial situation*: There are at least four reasons to do research on an existing or prospective client's financial strength—and problems:

A frequent precursor to serious client breaches of ethics and the law is financial trouble.

Financial problems, such as difficulties in raising capital or slowness in paying suppliers, borrowing to meet payroll, lack of cash liquidity and the like may signal cash flow troubles that could result in lateness in paying the counselor, efforts to challenge some charges and even bankruptcy.

Knowing the financial posture of the client helps put in perspective plans for new product lines, capital improvements, acquisitions and honoring commitments.

Such research can position the counselor to be more effective in helping the client develop objectives, priorities and programs and to make proposals consistent with budgetary constraints.

The state of the art of technology facilitates that kind of factfinding as well as the research to take advantage of market opportunities. And such technology is one of the major resources of counseling firms in an era of growth.

8

PLANNING GROWTH

Is bigger better? Many of the most distinguished counseling firms that happen to also be one or two-person organizations would maintain that it is not.

Nevertheless, as advertising agencies continue to pursue public relations capabilities and purchase firms of all sizes, as firms themselves merge with each other and as affiliations and networks are formed to link firms from different cities and countries together, most counselors agree they should plan for growth.

As they strategize, many counselors find that expansion must not only involve a growth in size but also in the harnessing of technological resources some of their clients already have put to use. How the burgeoning use of those tools helps firms maintain a competitive edge is examined as a part of this look at growth.

THE VALUE OF BEING BIGGER

Counseling Industry at Watershed Stage

Through the 1970s, only about 1 out of 20 public relations firms succeeded in staying in business beyond the retirement or death of its founder. Counseling had grown up as a cottage industry. The vast majority of firms had staff in no more than a single city, and only a handful were able to offer regional, national or international clients more than limited services.

The 1980s served as a watershed decade marked by a surge of entrepreneurship, increased commitment to technology, more intense concentration on applying corporate financial and managerial strategies to the public relations business and a new thrust to provide clients not only greater geographic reach but also a broader and more sophisticated range of products.

Strategic growth did not begin in the 1980s, but it accelerated at an unprecedented rate as segments of the counseling industry positioned themselves to grow, acquire, be acquired, merge and join forces in formal and informal communications-industry consortia.

The momentum of change seemed to feed upon itself: The more strengths strategic growth brought to counseling, the more clients seemed to demand. Symptomatic of that demand were findings released in 1986 from the Cantor Concern's Forecast of Public Relations Trends. The New York City executive search firm found corporations increasing their use of public relations firms rather than adding staff. Of greater significance, companies were extending the function beyond communications to strategic planning, issues analysis and assistance to senior executives on special problems.

The PRSA Communications Technology Task Force-commissioned survey at the November 1985 National Conference found that 89 percent of respondents expected counseling to continue to grow at least through 1987.[1]

Of the 431 PRSA survey participants, 46 percent opted to "continue to grow substantially" when asked to respond to the statement, "Public relations counseling has expanded significantly during the past few years. How much do you, personally, think counseling will change in the short term (the next two years)?" Another 43 percent said counseling will "continue to grow somewhat." Most of the remainder (8 percent) saw "little or no change" ahead. Only 3 percent expected counseling "may shrink somewhat" and nobody selected the "may shrink substantially" option.

The O'Dwyer's Directory of PR Firms reported that the 40 largest counseling firms experienced a 423 percent increase in net fee income between the end of 1974 and 1984. During the same decade, the number of employees for the 40 firms increased by a little more than a fourth of the rate of income increase (109.9 percent).[2]

Another indicator of increasing attractiveness of the industry has been the trend by advertising agencies to acquire counseling firms. Three-fourths of the 12 largest public relations firms were affiliated with advertising agencies by 1986. An unusual sign of the times occurred in 1985 when the London-based Saatchi & Saatchi Co. paid more than $10 million to buy an independent American counseling firm, Rowland Co.

Three principles of business management seem inextricably bound together in the fiber of the strategic growth and alliances trends: critical mass, economy of scale, and synergy.

Applying Critical Mass Concept

Flow of Business as Chain Reaction   In the public relations business, as in physics, the law of critical mass governs the forces that determine if power can be generated in a chain reaction-like process.

In physics, the critical mass is the amount of certain radioactive material required to sustain a chain reaction at a constant rate. In counseling, the critical mass is the combination of volume of business and the breadth and depth of strategic resources required to maintain a constant flow of account activity and to replenish and modernize the resources.

Those resources include geographic reach of offices, the new technology, the capabilities for research, and the executive, managerial, specialized and other personnel to support the needs of a growing clientele.

Those resources also include a less tangible, but equally vital, diversity of experience and expertness, the spark of creativity and the systems for execution and follow-through to energize and direct the chain reaction.

An example of that chain reaction was reflected in the 1986 Hill and Knowlton moves to acquire the then-third largest U.S. counseling firm, Carl Byoir & Associates, and the eighth largest, Gray & Co. Worldwide Communications. The chain reaction actually had begun years earlier in the building of critical mass in each of the three firms.

From the perspective of Peter G. Osgood, vice chairman of Hill and Knowlton and former president of Carl Byoir & Associates, the critical mass of a larger public relations organization provides an advantage. Some firms, like Byoir, built it through growth and acquisition, others achieved it through formal and informal affiliations. Osgood, former chairman of the Counselors Academy, said: "Being in a larger organization means having around me and at the disposal of our clients, a critical mass of people with different sets of skills and perspectives to bring to bear in problem solving and implementation."[3]

He started his counseling career with an eight-person firm and compared the capabilities engendered in building that organization: "In a small firm, one cannot afford to have units of people skilled in high-tech marketing, data processing and research. But development of a critical mass allows a firm to take technology beyond typical applications to management and development of business."

With such massive resources, a firm can bring to client service and staff development different points of view, knowledge bases and skills. In working with smaller firms, Osgood remembered he lacked "the critical mass to have quality research people on staff." A critical mass of researchers on staff provides the capabilities to teach the value of research to executives, how to sell that research and how to apply it as a tool of communications, "omnipresent throughout the organization."[4] That doesn't mean necessarily that the bigger, the better.

Some firms may do better by controlling growth. In business, as in nuclear physics, it is known that once a critical mass is set to start a chain reaction, too much of a good thing or less than expert handling can trigger an explosion instead of a smooth flow of power, and there may be no reversing or stopping an out-of-control process.

This does not contradict the value of building a critical mass, but it suggests that developing it requires incorporating early warning systems and fail-safe mechanisms.

Building Economy of Scale

Volume and Size Place Expensive Resources Within Reach Similar to the concept of critical mass, the business law of economy of scale fuels the engine of successful public relations practice.

1. Economy of scale means cost sharing that enables a corporate division or member of an alliance to use the buying power of the parent organization or of other members of an alliance.
2. Economy of scale makes possible volume purchasing of services, equipment and supplies that generate discounted vendor prices.
3. Economy of scale makes possible volume borrowing at lower cost per dollar or volume investment of capital at a higher return than would be available for those who deal with smaller amounts.
4. Economy of scale means pooling resources and curbing wasteful duplication.
5. Economy of scale suggests the capability to supply services that still cater to the individual needs of clients but capitalize upon the savings inherent in establishing standardized systems.

One way to build economy of scale is through systematically adding new clients and areas of business. "New clients offer opportunities for a public relations agency to take advantage of economies of scale," according to Dana T. Hughes, president of Boston's Public Relations Consultants Inc. "As the firm grows larger, specialists can be economically recruited to handle projects requiring a high level of expertise."[5]

Standardizing Economy of Scale But which comes first, economy of scale or attracting more business? For some firms, the two are considered interdependent. And standardization plays a major role.

For Harold Burson, chairman of Burson-Marsteller, economy of scale has meant developing, "within a single organization, the ability to fulfill all our client needs, wherever they may exist, with consistency in message, consistency in delivery system and administrative ease and efficiency in execution."[6]

Such organization and ability don't come without strategic planning. Burson wrote his long-range plan to achieve that economy of scale for large client organizations around the world in 1960, before he had done a million dollars worth of business. A quarter-century later, he said his firm could offer clients an "integrated organization—seamless around the world, which is the same thing our customers are trying to give their customers."

Economy of scale enables a firm to make a multimillion-dollar investment in communication technology. Burson planned that by 1987 each member of the professional staff would be able to communicate by computer with colleagues around the world and draw on a data bank in which thousands of programs are stored.

In his seminal article on "The Globalization of Markets" in the *Harvard Business Review*, the head of marketing at the Harvard Business School said that "the powerful force of technology ... has proletarianized communication, transport and travel." Theodore Levitt explained its significance to market-conscious, growth-oriented executives:[7]

"The result is a new commercial reality—the emergence of global markets for standardized consumer products on a previously unimagined scale of magnitude. Corporations geared to this new reality benefit from enormous economies of scale in production, distribution, marketing and management."

Levitt said that the low costs made possible by economies of scale are not incompatible with high quality. "The truth is that low-cost operations are the hallmark of corporate cultures that require and produce quality in all that they do. High quality and low costs ... are twin identities of superior practice."

An advocate of Levitt's thesis is Robert L. Dilenschneider, the president of Hill and Knowlton, who said that public relations firms can adapt the model of globalization of markets for standardizing services for clients in the U.S. as well as around the world.[8]

"We've set up an enormous distribution network among 56 offices to put out public relations products that have the same pricing, same standards and same training of staff all over the world. It also brings economy of scale into play."

Dilenschneider tended to concur with the perspective of Levitt that customization is possible within the framework of global standardization.[9] Levitt wrote that large companies operating in a single nation

> *don't standardize everything they make, sell or do. They have product lines instead of a single product version, and multiple distribution channels. There are neighborhood, local, regional, ethnic and institutional differences, even within metropolitan areas.*
>
> *But although companies customize products for particular market segments, they know that success in a world with homogenized demand requires a search for sales opportunities in similar segments across the globe in order to achieve the economies of scale necessary to compete.*

Moreover, Levitt said that differences in the requirements of markets should be accepted and adjusted to with customization "only reluctantly, only after relentlessly testing their immutability, after trying in various ways to circumvent and reshape them."[10]

Public relations counselors, however, also operate during an era in which micro-marketing strategies temper standardization. Despite the pressure for standardization, Philip Kotler, Northwestern University business professor, said that "marketplace segmentation is one of the most powerful forces going on in marketing. In the 1980s, we are in the age of micro-marketing."[11]

Micro-marketing strategies, adopted by some counselors as well as a number of large corporate clients, may be counterproductive in taking optimal advantage of scale of economy through standardization. "In forcing large companies to abandon their shotgun approach to selling, consumers are raising the stakes in a marketing contest that has grown increasingly complex and expensive in recent years," the *Los Angeles Times* reported in 1986.[12]

For counseling firms, the new technologies not only make standardization possible but also require targeting communication and providing counsel in an environment where "research firms fill an information gap by tracking consumer buying patterns more accurately." This computer-assisted tracking "uses census data to segment the country into micro-geographic communities averaging 340 homes."

As reviewed in the research chapter sections on methods for segmenting publics, micro-marketing can extend beyond demographics into psychographics. Economy of scale applies when such public relations research-based services are brought to a number of markets in standardized form, even though style and substance of communication may vary. Some of the world's largest firms, however, have discovered that size of enterprise alone does not necessarily produce economy of scale.

Alvin Toffler cautioned executives of the era of *The Adaptive Corporation* that there may come a point of diminishing returns, when too big can cause as much harm as too small, when improperly planned growth can lead to "'diseconomies of scale'—barriers to communication, lack of maneuverability, stifling of innovation, impersonality, loss of motivation."[13]

Economy of scale works for smaller counseling firms, although perhaps to a lesser degree. That depends upon a number of specifics related to their own operations as well as to the situations of their clients. That's why it's important to consider the synergy involved.

Combining for Synergism

Interaction among Communication Disciplines *Synergism,* a doctrine with roots in chemistry, physiology and theology, may be seen as a systems concept that basically says two or more elements may work together to produce or enhance an effect.

On an interdisciplinary or large-scale (macro) basis, public relations and advertising can be seen to have synergistic effects when combined to support the marketing of a product.

On an intradisciplinary or micro basis, when two public relations firms combine different resources and approaches, such as coalition building and grass-roots support building in the public affairs arena, each may work to strengthen the impact of the other.

In a broad sense, synergy can be likened to the systems term of interaction. Synergy fits with several systems notions that have been identified as relevant to public relations firms: "the whole of any system is greater than the sum of its parts"; "the parts, working together, create a dynamic whole;" and "you can never do only one thing in a system without affecting other parts of it."[14]

An example of synergism at work in extending the horizons of public relations counseling was described by Dilenschneider. In discussing H&K relations with its parent advertising firm, J. Walter Thompson, he said:

> To the degree to which we emphasize marketing, that linkage will be enormously profitable for us in 1986 and 1987—we're getting a lot of business from JWT. While that's an important linkage and we should exploit it on both sides, the synergies to be brought about through the practice of public relations in JWT-H&K joint client ventures are much broader.[15]

He contended that if a public relations firm is managed profitably, it can produce a better percentage of profit for a communications conglomerate than the advertising agency component on a proportionate basis. "A well managed firm ought to be able to make a minimum of 12 to 14 percent pretax profit." That may not compare favorably with management consultants that make 30 percent before taxes or with some public accounting firms "that do even better," but it is a multiple of the 2 to 6 percent profits generally earned by advertising agencies, he said.

As public relations firms become increasingly attractive properties for acquisition—or as some counselors build their own conglomerates, it may be well to heed lessons learned in corporate America's rush to acquisition and merger. For instance, the quest for the ideals of synergy in acquisitions and mergers may prove elusive.

In *The Takeover Barons of Wall Street*, Richard Phalon recalled a "big acquisition binge" in which "conglomerates, in search of the supposed 'synergism' to be found in a blend of unrelated businesses—the old 'two plus two equals five' syndrome—were buying up everything in sight." The contributing editor to *Forbes* and former *New York Times* financial writer, cautioned that growth—or the appearance of growth—is part of "an ideology that may explain why so many acquisitions that look good on paper prove to be so painful in practice. The ideal of synergy—two plus two equals five—has a perverse way of becoming two plus two equals three."[16]

Strategies for Expansion

Fifteen Considerations to Incorporate in Long-Range Planning The more successful counseling firms emphasize as integral parts of strategic long-range planning for growth such factors as goals and objectives, research, alertness to change and opportunities, human resource development, adaptation to long-range client needs and a mix of globalization and specialization.

1. *Start with questions on purposes*: Strategic growth normally starts with analysis by a firm on what it's doing, why it's in business and where expansion fits into the market plan. This applies at the macro/big-picture, long-range level of planning and also in micro/smaller-scale adjustments to a plan.

2. *Check fit with objectives*: To achieve harmony and a minimum amount of dislocation during growth, plans need to be readily adjustable to meet conditions. Hill and Knowlton's Peter G. Osgood suggested asking: "What markets do you want to serve? What industries do you want within that market? What types of services do you want to provide?"[17]

3. *Check fit with resources*: In a people-centered service industry such as counseling, expansion requires a knowledge of skills that are going to be needed. The planning process takes into consideration requirements in human resources, funding and marketing.

4. *Incorporate research*: Counseling firm executives build research into the growth planning process. This includes investigation of economic indicators, corporate tendencies, trends in similar disciplines, and trends in existing and prospective client industries such as patterns of declining or accelerating growth rates.

5. *Determine value to firm*: Counseling executives examine the values of growth options to their firms in terms of where research and analysis indicate energies should be invested in developing and marketing particular services.

6. *Ascertain long-range implications*: "Firms should avoid fads and opportunistic and short-term hits in favor of solid development to serve steady clients with good service and strategic counseling on an ongoing basis," Osgood said.[18]

7. *Analyze price/value ratio*: As their clients, counseling firm executives are increasingly sensitive to the relationship of price and value in public relations services in planning for change.

8. *Analyze potential as well as risk factors*: This is illustrated by the kind of analysis involved when firms added capabilities to service the technology sector.

"High-tech business sectors will go up and down," Osgood observed.

Mini-computers were leveling off in 1985. Just because they were leveling off and having problems, we did not lose interest in that industry. Technology is global; it is with us and will have its ups and downs, just as any growth industry. Small companies, especially with rapid change, will be subject to dislocation from time to time. IBM can close down its entire PC Jr. operation and it is unlikely that it would make any significant difference in earnings for IBM in that year. As industries grow and mature, there will be a number of companies that will be less vulnerable to swings relative to economic impact on the industry as a whole.[19]

9. *Plan to avoid obsolescence*: Ongoing research and periodic assessments of changing needs of the marketplace are needed to keep a firm current and its services in demand.

10. *Develop staff for growth*: The most critical element in strategic growth is a firm's human resources. That requires planning to incorporate attention to the skills people will need and the recruitment, retraining and continuing education involved.

11. *Consider engaging external counsel*: Strategic growth planning may necessitate external counsel on business development and use of new tools. Public relations firms, like their clients, also benefit from the objectivity external counsel can provide.

12. *Consider resources of parent corporation, affiliates*: A parent, sibling or subsidiary company in the same communications corporation or in a network affiliate may have resources worth exploring and applying to a public relations firm's own development.

13. *Challenge relevance to clients*: It is one thing to consider a new capability and another to examine growth activities in respect to their relevancy to clients and their needs. Such challenging contributes to a firm's long-range economic health.

14. *But be open to pacesetter role in client service*: Taking the pacesetter role distinguishes a firm from its competition. Thornton Bradshaw, RCA board chairman who positioned his corporation for its 1986 acquisition by General Electric, said a firm has to have a philosophy for the kind of business it's in and why, and of being in industries that it understands and in which it's a market leader.[20]

The work being done in counseling needs to be both relevant and visionary to help clients maintain their market leadership and financial community position, to be effective with employees and to establish government relations that will be perceived positively by regulatory and legislative bodies.

15. *Emphasize strengths, not merely size*: America went through a long phase in which size was equated with success. It was a time in which corporations, not-for-profit organizations and government agencies built campaigns around being biggest or among the mighty. To a degree, there is still some preoccupation with size among counseling firms, as well as their clients. Yet values of business executives, consumers and the media have changed.

Thus, larger firms do better to emphasize strengths gained through size, rather than size itself. And there are strengths to emphasize that have absolutely nothing to do with size, strengths that make certain local or regional firms attractive to clients and strengths of specialization and quality of service that make the relatively small so-called boutiques of the industry so successful.

Expansion through Acquisition vs. Affiliation

Cases may be made for expansion of service capabilities and economies by either mergers through acquisition or formal contractual affiliation. There is a third option of growing through adding or bolstering capabilities internally. And there is a fourth option, as reviewed in the next chapter, of networking. But it is not necessarily a matter of choosing one of the options: Some firms effectively combine elements of two, three or all four ways.

This section focuses on the case for acquisition, as illustrated by Ketchum Public Relations, and the alternative of contracting between two firms through the example of the relationship of H&K and an independent consultancy in San Antonio, Texas.

The Case for Acquisition Ketchum Public Relations acquired three other firms in 1984 and 1985 alone as it continued to extend its geographical reach, build its client base and capture specialized resources. By 1985, it had increased its income, partially through acquisition, partially through internal growth, to move into the ranks of the 10 largest firms.

Given the choice between acquisition and developing affiliations, however, Chairman Paul H. Alvarez is solidly on the side of acquisition. There are reasons Alvarez and other executives favor acquisition.

1. *Avoid acquisition just for raising the number of offices*: He said he believes in adding offices only when it's absolutely necessary for the strategic development of Ketchum's client service/marketing strengths. By 1986, after Ketchum acquired The Bohle Co., Ketchum had nine offices. Although Alvarez said geographic reach is important, he said he was mindful of control and economics involved in adding offices. "I recall a colleague saying, 'if you only have one office, you don't have any losing offices.' "[21]

A management consultant's analysis of the earnings of public relations firms found that some with only one or a few offices showed a particularly high profitability compared to larger firms. The principal of Daniel H. Baer Inc., Sherman Oaks, Calif., attributed this to specialization and "excellent management."[22]

2. *Acquire services that would take too long to develop*: Over the years, Ketchum has moved into the technology and venture capital areas of client business, not through internal development but through acquisition. Alvarez weighed the length of time and costs of in-house development and opted for the advantages of instant access to tested operations through acquisition.

3. *Acquire for expertness*: For example, John Paluszek owned a firm in Washington, where Ketchum needed stronger public affairs capabilities. "Even though we had maintained our own Washington office for years, Paluszek had a larger office with additional specialized expertness." The firm was acquired, and Paluszek assumed responsibility for Ketchum's public affairs.

4. *Acquire for geographical reach*: "There is a recognition that public relations is such a service-oriented business that people prefer to be serviced where their offices are, or at least within a reasonably short plane ride," according to Alvarez.

That was one of the reasons Ketchum negotiated with Sue Bohle. The new Ketchum/Bohle Public Relations office provided the firm with not only additional specialized expertness in such areas as marketing and technology but also a presence in one of the nation's major markets— Southern California. Ketchum instantly acquired the roots and reputation of The Bohle Co. Also, there was no time loss or risktaking in creating an infrastructure in Los Angeles.

5. *Acquire for total control*: Alvarez said he had considered network affiliations in which Ketchum would assign work to firms in other cities. But that consideration was short-lived. "From the Ketchum perspective, you want to have complete control of offices."

Ironically, one of the greatest champions of network affiliations among independents was Bohle as she built her firm before its merger with Ketchum. The Bohle Co. had been one of the fastest-growing on the West Coast.[23] Bohle credited her association with her affiliates for helping her and the executives of the other firms "pursue market dominance in their own metropolitan areas or states."[24]

Following the merger, she shifted that part of her focus to Ketchum's pursuit of national market positioning. She also became part of the Ketchum "total control" of Southern California-based operations when she was named executive vice president of Ketchum/Bohle and a member of the parent firm's operating committee. That control is important to Alvarez because:[25]

Total control of all its offices enables the firm to "sell multioffice service to national and regional clients with the assurance that the people on the account will be our own."

"Complete control gives you a strong coordinated posture for dealing with a national client project."

Complete control "gives you the posture to send reserves from one office to another, or to get a person with a particular kind of expertise from one office to another. You need to have the ability to shift and prioritize resources to meet specific client needs."

Total control "assures integration of thinking throughout the firm. Ketchum has an approach and philosophy that are hard to match in a network situation. We have certain standards that are uniform throughout the corporation."

Owning vs. affiliation "positions you to be better at getting good productive work out of each office and every staff member."

Loose affiliation may help counselors establish a less localized marketing posture "but does not tend in many cases to lead to much business referral or additional income." By contrast, "part of every Ketchum office's income is developed through interchange with our other offices."

Another Perspective: Affiliation without Acquisition When Hill and Knowlton approached San Antonio's Sharp, Gossen & Associates at the end of 1984 for merger/acquisition talks, the Texans opted instead for affiliation while retaining their independence.

Ron Gossen, 1985–1986 president of the Texas Public Relations Association, said he and his partner, Kay Sharp, knew that H&K wanted a stronger presence in their Southwestern territory, and the merger was one of the bigger firm's preferences.[26]

The alternatives included building and staffing a separate office, expanding H&K Dallas-centered operations, or, in the vernacular of President Dilenschneider, "parachuting in people," flying in corporate staff for short-term stays in the several Texas counties served out of San Antonio.

Sharp and Gossen did not want to sacrifice their identity or entrepreneurial interests in owning the firm. At the same time, they found it appealing to associate with a corporation with the international reputation, resources and clients of H&K. They negotiated for affiliation as an independent associate.

From Dilenschneider's perspective, "most companies become successful because of internal growth and the ability to provide a sameness of standards, practice, culture, products and services to the marketplace." Although his firm had placed "a lot of emphasis" on internal growth, it also had been willing to acquire other companies when that suited their purposes.[27]

Economics for H&K, as for other counseling firms, has been a major determinant. As Dilenschneider put it, "if it costs $2 million to acquire an existing firm, it's better to invest $1 million in internal growth and develop your own capacities."

The decision to grow from within or to acquire also has been influenced by Dilenschneider's belief that "most acquisitions don't work. You go through a classic honeymoon period; then through a period of 'it's great working together, but these guys aren't getting involved; let's exercise more control' and, then, through a third phase of 'let's spin these guys off.'"

On the other hand, the costs of servicing a client with one's own staff may be prohibitive in terms other than economic. For instance, "if you parachute into a city to have a working relationship with the power structure in 20 days, it's not going to happen. You need somebody there who knows the power structure for 20 years, not 20 days. That's one of the things affiliation can bring to the party."

He subscribes to such affiliation, particularly if the prospective affiliate offers "a public relations delivery system that is sophisticated in public affairs or in the local market for a national product or idea."

The question of control of affiliates is not as much a concern to him as it is to top management of some other major public relations corporations. "You do have control. You're dealing with integrity: if a guy takes a job, he will do it right. You have a budgetary control." The supervisory mechanisms of the parties to affiliation "will assure you get value if you position them well." Gossen reviewed ways both local and national affiliates can benefit:[28]

1. *Local affiliate's costs may be significantly lower*: "We analyzed the cost of 'parachuting' and the relative chances for success. San Antonio is the 10th largest city in the nation but we're still a relatively provincial town. We could accomplish all of their needs locally. But we bill at our rates—significantly less than those of our New York affiliate."

2. *Local affiliate offers expertise*: "We've consulted with them on areas in which we have experience and expertise, such as water conservation and tourism in our region." For example, H&K Texas operations were invited to submit a proposal to an international farm irrigation association. Gossen said that "they would have had to pass on that opportunity if we were not involved." The San Antonio firm brought to the proposal its experience from an earlier campaign for a water district in the five-county area of South Texas.

3. *Local affiliate offers establishment and media identity*: When a national issue involves local media and prominent figures from that area, the affiliation can prove advantageous. For example, the town attracted H&K national client executives and financial media when it was learned that the state district judge who ruled on the $12 billion Texaco-Pennzoil judgment was from San Antonio. The vice chairman of Texaco came from White Plains, N.Y., on a media tour to explain its position as employer of 12,000 Texans.

4. *Local affiliates join forces*: An affiliate from another region can find support in an unfamiliar market in handling a national campaign. For example, H&K's Miami affiliate, Hank Meyer Associates, coordinated with the San Antonio affiliate in bringing to South Texas the Burger King "Herb" campaign of 1985–1986. "We were given a budget to develop a local plan to exploit peaking public interest on 'who is Herb?' and 'what is he doing?'"

5. *National affiliate gives local USP edge*: For the local affiliate, the known association with the national counseling corporation "gives us a competitive edge over the largest PR firm in town even though they are more than twice our size. Our affiliation gives us a USP (unique selling proposition)." For example, H&K executives in Dallas joined Sharp and Gossen in making presentations to local clients with national or regional interests. "Clients really appreciate the national credibility and recognition our firm gained."

6. *National affiliate extends local's reach*: When a local account needs support elsewhere in the country or world, the national affiliate provides the geographic reach. For example, "we used them in New York and Washington, D.C., for our Witte Museum client's special exhibit." That saved the museum the cost of developing East Coast contacts and of travel in servicing national publications, such as *National Geographic, Smithsonian* and *Science 86*. The coverage was arranged for the archaeological dig of the longest continual culture in the Americas, the Indians of the Lower Pecos River Valleys who existed for 10,000 years before they disappeared in A.D. 1000.

7. *National affiliate reinforces USP*: Sharp and Gossen clients joined H&K guests in private receptions with Board Chairman Loet A. Velmans in 1985 and with Dilenschneider in 1986 as part of the reinforcement of the San Antonio affiliate's USP.

8. *National affiliate shares educational resources*: The San Antonio firm has been able to take advantage of professional development resources of its affiliate through continuing education materials from New York and through H&K seminars.

9. *National affiliate expertness available*: "We can plug into resources—their research company, travel and tourism division" and experts or materials at New York headquarters or other offices.

10. *National affiliate provides resident expert*: Although the need for "parachuting" no longer exists in San Antonio, H&K assigned a member of its staff to that office to participate in joint proposals and work with Sharp and Gossen on certain projects.

11. *National affiliate invites local consultation*: Gossen said the national firm issued network-wide requests to find out what affiliates know about a particular area of expertise when special client needs arise. "When they get a job that fits our expertise, such as water resources management, they ask us to consult and plan with them."

Charting Future of Independents

Important Place for Firm That Retains Own Identity There is an important place in the counseling industry for the independent public relations firm that retains its own identity. As a matter of fact, the industry was so attractive that in 1985 alone at least 200 new public relations firms were opened.[29] But there are some challenges as well as opportunities for development and growth of firms beyond the merger-and-acquisition trend.

Here are some trends and forces identified by counselors:

1. *Few larger independents will remain*: Although "there are not that many other big independents left—Ruder Finn & Rotman, Fleishman-Hillard, Booke, Rogers & Cowan," the founding chairman of the Chicago-based Daniel J. Edelman Inc., predicted "a number of firms will remain independent."[30]

2. *New independents will move up*: New consultancies are coming up, including regionals and even new national firms. Edelman said to look for mergers of smaller counseling organizations in New York, Chicago and Los Angeles as "some of the young people who have operations doing six-figure annual business continue getting together."[31]

For example, former PRSA President Jay Rockey could have operated with one office in the Pacific Northwest but acquired an affiliate that placed him in two nearby but distinctive cities in Washington and Oregon—Rockey/Marsh Public Relations in Oregon and Jay Rockey Public Relations in Seattle. "We saw a lot of business needs and realized that although we technically could handle accounts from one or another community, we couldn't do as competent a job as if we operated in both cities."[32]

The principal of the Seattle-based Rockey Co. also looked to the needs of Pacific Northwest clients elsewhere in the country and of corporations with interests in his region but with bases on the East Coast and in Southern California. So he joined forces with Harry Carlson, president of Carlson, Rockey & Associates.

3. *Incentives include entrepreneurial rewards*: A major incentive in operating an independent firm is the entrepreneurial spirit characteristic of American and Canadian business of earlier eras and rekindled in the 1970s and 1980s. "Independents in public relations are no different than independents in any other business. Not that it's the only way to do counseling better—but, like any other business, those who choose to be entrepreneurs have ways of realizing special rewards," Daniel J. Edelman said.[33]

One of those rewards is independence to build specialized capabilities; another is independence of judgment in running a firm. As an example of specialized capabilities, even after the Saatchi and Saatchi communications conglomerate bought the Yankelovich organization, an independent—Ruder Finn & Rotman—still was able to lay claim to the largest research firm in the business through its Research and Forecasts Co. subsidiary.[34]

David Finn, chairman of Ruder Finn & Rotman, emphasized the value of independence of executive judgment in business operations: "If you're an independent, you have more flexibility and can make judgments without having to worry about monetary pressure from the parent organization. Sure, we want to have good earnings so we can reward our employees and make a return on our own investment, but we prefer to run our company without having that pressure."[35]

4. *Cost effectiveness with personal service*: Although there may be economy of scale for advertising agency-related firms, Edelman said he believed "we're more cost effective. We don't have to share in a parent company's big overhead. We don't have to give profits to shareholders or pay into a corporate parent. We're able to deliver more value to a client than we would as part of a big public company. There's more of a personal service thing, too."

5. *But competition is tougher*: Executives of independents argue that there are disadvantages as well as advantages in resisting acquisition by advertising companies. The reality of the aftermath of acquisitions and the growth of a number of former independents, however, heats up the competition. "It's all done by sweat of brow. It's not always easy for us to compete," Edelman said. "It's easier for a Burson-Marsteller with Young & Rubicam or a Hill and Knowlton with J. Walter Thompson to open an office in any city around the world."[36]

The budgetary power of advertising agencies creates a powerful difference in doing business. "In advertising, they have budgets of $50-180 million on a particular project," Finn said. "Our budgets are miniscule in comparison. We can spend half a million or a hundred thousand dollars and not have tangible evidence in some cases. You can have an enormously successful program with little specific to point to compared to an ad campaign."[37]

6. *In pursuit of different objectives and values*: Independents emphasize the different objectives of public relations firms compared to their perceptions of advertising-dominated communications corporations.

Edelman said independents are better positioned to preserve their corporate culture: "We have 'management by walking around,' as they say in

Search of Excellence. We have hands-on management. And our individual identity is maintained." His own firm has become "a little bigger, but we're functioning much the same as we were 10-15-20 years ago in terms of our corporate culture and relations with clients. We think we have a better ability to retain our special corporate culture. There is a difference in being institutionalized as part of a bigger company."[38]

Finn said that the orientation of public relations firms to professional counseling and service time contrasts sharply with the emphasis in advertising agencies that derive much of their revenue from buying space and time. "We might worry about pressures brought to bear by agencies for their public relations subsidiaries to become more profitable, to make more money and to think less of abstract and elusive values as compared to advertising, which tends to be more visible."[39]

APPLYING TECHNOLOGY

Significant Trends for Technological Applications

Regardless of reasons behind merger and acquisition, internal growth, contractual affiliation and networking, it is clear that the structure of the counseling industry has been undergoing strong waves of change. As documented earlier, the structure of the market for public relations services also is fluid and changing rapidly.

According to a business management expert's 1985 assessment, a change in *either* industry *or* market structure presents an opportunity, if not a demand, for innovation and entrepreneurship.

Peter F. Drucker stipulated "four near-certain, highly visible indicators of impending change in structure":[40]

1. Growth of an industry faster than that of the economy or a country's population
2. Rapid doubling in volume of industry growth making traditional perceptions of its services and markets no longer appropriate
3. Rapid change in the way an industry does business
4. Convergence of previously distinct technologies[41]

Public relations counseling in both America and Canada reflect all four indicators of new waves of impending change.

Technology has been part of the public relations industry and marketing structure problems—in the classic sense of "problem" as a question involving uncertainty or difficulty, as a challenge giving rise to opportunities.

Technology also is part of the solution. It is the kind of solution that is as dynamic as the problems confronting counselors. It is the kind of solution that fits into a mosaic of management strategies and operates as a tool, rather than as a panacea. But it is an increasingly important tool.

Surveys Find Strong Rise in Involvement by Practitioners, Publics PRSA's Communications Technology Task Force found a significant involvement of counselors and other public relations practitioners in the use of technology in a survey conducted in November 1985.[42]

Altogether, 491 practitioners at the PRSA National Conference responded to the survey. Almost a fifth identified the Counselors Academy as their area of primary interest.

83 percent said their public relations-related offices had computers

42 percent had personal terminals that were not shared with others

34 percent had purchased home computers for use in their work

They were asked to project how close they were to using technology in their work on at least a daily basis and rank such technologies as computers, online data bases and videotex services on a scale of 1 to 10. An answer of 1 signifies "very far from daily use." Here are the mean scores: personal computers—6.04; videotex services—3.6; online data bases—4.5; video cassette recorders—6.0; cable TV—5.8.

Strong Rise in Public Use of Data Bases Projected Another survey found that by 1990 the public's willingness to make use of new information technology would increase by:

21 percent in use of cable TV

60 percent in use of video cassette recorders

85 percent in use of personal computers

111 percent in use of computer online data bases

135 percent in use of other videotex services[43]

The rapid rates of increase represented the acceleration expected in a few years by a panel of 100 communications industry leaders organized by United Video in 1985. *Video Monitor,* a newsletter that reports on new technologies for public relations and advertising, advised communicators to consider the findings in planning long-range campaigns and information strategies.

Electronic Data Bases Capture Client, Market Intelligence

Now in Book Form: Strategies for Using Computer Data on Competitors Before Leonard M. Fuld, president of Information Data Research, wrote his 1985 book *Competitor Intelligence: How to Get It; How to Use It,*[44] a growing number of counselors were using such strategies for doing their homework on clients' competitors—as well as for research on prospects and existing customers.

Kari Bjorhus of Hill and Knowlton reviewed Fuld's work as "a mother lode of sources for communicators who need business information not readily available" and "a gold mine of leads for public relations professionals who need to do substantial research to design and implement appropriate communications programs."[45]

Competitor Intelligence identifies hundreds of electronic data bases as well as resources in print—ranging from *The Directory of Obsolete Securities* to *Area Business Databank*, which includes financial and trade publication, government, industry and even business school reports.

Disclosure II: SEC Documents Now at Counselor Fingertips   One of a number of electronic data bases used by counselors is Disclosure II, a service that allows subscribers to such computer networks as CompuServe to punch in a few numbers and view on their computer monitors a diversity of company records—some only hours old.[46]

Documents are collected daily from such organizations as the New York Stock Exchange, American Stock Exchange, National Association of Stock Dealers and state agencies. The service also provides updated composites of financial and textual data required for filing by the Securities and Exchange Commission (SEC).

Users of Disclosure II can access data on more than 9,500 companies. Among the SEC documents transmitted through such services are:[47]

Registration Statement: Document filed registering securities for public sale

Prospectus: Final versions of registration statements including final offering prices

Shelf Registration: Document filed registering securities expected to be sold within two years

10-K: Annual document summarizing company's management and financial position

10-Q: Quarterly document providing continuing view of company's financial position

20-F: Annual document equivalent to 10-K filed by companies headquartered outside the U.S.

8-K: Periodic document reporting events deemed to be important to shareholders or the SEC

Annual Report to Shareholders

Proxy Statement: Official notification to shareholders of matters to be brought to a vote

13-F: Quarterly report of stockholdings filed by institutions

13-D: Document recording sale, purchase or change of intention by 5 percent owners of a company's stock

13-G: Annual report of stockholders filed by 5 percent owners of company stock

14D-1: Document filed by those making tender offer that would result in 5 percent ownership of company stock

13E-4: Document filed by company offering to repurchase its own shares

13E-3: Document filed by company offering to repurchase its own shares for the purpose of going private

Form 3: Initial statement of ownership by officers, directors or 10 percent principal stockholders

Form 4: Statement of change in ownership by officers, directors or 10 percent stockholders

An individual caller with a computer and modem can use a service like Disclosure II to get such information as a client's or competitor's acquisitions during the past year, names of all subsidiaries, salaries of its top five executive officers, names of owners and issues scheduled at the annual stockholder meeting.

But it's more than a computer spewing out reams of information; the counselor can be selective and specify parameters in searching for companies that meet certain combinations of characteristics.[48]

New and Traditional Market Research Tools Online   CompuServe's Micro 10K Plus program serves as an example of a search mechanism that can supply a counselor with data for pinpoint market identification or for analyst and investor relations strategies.[49]

This system permits an individual to screen a number of data bases in one operation, such as a search for all companies in a particular industry with a given annual sales volume. A counselor also can research a corporation's sales and stock figures, projections of earnings, capital structure and measures of growth.

Similarly, counselors have found it fast, easy and relatively inexpensive to use their computers and telephone lines to access traditional data bases such as Standard & Poor's or Dun & Bradstreet.

There are additional advantages of going online instead of doing literature research. For instance, a counselor can summon to his computer screen or printer from Standard & Poor's Compustat Services the names of all persons holding a particular office in certain kinds of companies within a given geographic area. Then he can check for interlocking directorates in which the same individuals serve on multiple corporate boards or identify companies that are poised for merger or acquisition. At his fingertips are a diversity of facts and figures on 6,000 publicly held and 39,000 privately owned companies and their quarter-million officers and directors.[50]

How Counselor Builds Business with Nexis and Dialog   The diversity and profitability of computer data bases is illustrated by six case examples from a Denver counseling firm, William Kostka & Associates:[51]

Case 1. *How to do research, prepare for presentation in two hours*: William J. Kostka Jr., chairman, remembers when he used to send staff to do a library search for a day or two just to develop basic intelligence on a prospective client—"and even then, maybe, we couldn't find out all we really needed to know." That was before he discovered such electronic data base services as Nexis and Dialog.

"Now we get the data we need in minutes." He has demonstrated capability to make use of remote data bases the equivalent to a much bigger corporation's large, modern division of research experts.

For example a prospect called and said he would arrive in two hours to discuss Kostka's capabilities for handling his company's account. The counselor got on the computer terminal and connected his firm to the resources of Nexis and Dialog. Long before the executive arrived, Kostka had in his hands "a complete file on the company."

From Nexis, he found out what general, financial, specialized and trade media had reported about the organization and relevant matters bearing on its industry. From Dialog, Kostka got the benefit of a quick in-depth study of salient business and financial data. He had access to more than 200 different data bases.

"We did market research on the industry and took a close look at the company's management team. We looked at environmental and energy problems. We got what amounted to a preliminary briefing on the client's positions, probable priorities, finances and public relations situation before the two hours had elapsed."

At that time, he had a staff of eight professionals and three support personnel, but his firm was as prepared as if it had considerably more resources. The prospect was impressed by the levels of intelligence, perception and attention reflected in the questions raised and in the understanding of the executive's business and concerns.

Case 2. *Saved month of critical research time*: The Denver Partnership, a group of metropolitan businesspersons, wanted to know what corporate executives across the country thought of the city's downtown area. This time, Kostka tied in with a national survey organization and a New York-based public relations firm to develop a presentation of a national campaign to attract investment and corporate facilities to his city.

But first, he went to the Standard and Poor's, Dun & Bradstreet and Moody's data bases to do his homework. Then he developed a national sample of corporate executives for the image study from the Dun & Bradstreet data base, with the computer programmed to search through 125,000 records of companies with a net worth of $500,000 or more and draw a sample of 1,500 executives.

Among the various data bases, Kostka was able to assure that the sample met client criteria for sales volume and standard industrial code (type of business). The sample went beyond those criteria to develop intelligence on such factors as principal officers, directors, legal and accounting firms and number of employees. From the initial cluster of 1,500 executives, he had the computer programmed to draw a narrower, but scientifically representative, sample of 600.

"This saved us a month at a time when it was critical to move quickly in responding to the Denver Partnership's request for a reliable study as the basis for a proposal."

A sample such as this one could cost almost $3,000, but Kostka said that the total spent on data bank searches for all clients normally costs his firm $500 to $1,000 per month. "You bill it just like any other expense. It's invaluable."

Case 3. *Trademark search back into 19th century no problem*: Another Colorado client had accidentally given his newsletter the same name as a North Carolina bank publication. Kostka was able to do a search on trademarks back into the 1800s and discovered that the bank had registered the name. Research didn't solve the problem. But the counseling firm found an appropriate name and was able to assure the client that it was not trademarked by another company.

Case 4. *Land developer client struck toxic waste—and gold*: One client was interested in developing a large piece of land but lost interest when it was discovered that an old waste dump uphill from the property was leaking toxic fluids.

Kostka used electronic data bases to do research on the company that operated the dump, "an outfit none of us had ever heard much about." But his findings revealed that the same company was involved with Times Beach and other toxic waste disposal sites. "We also found out that it was doing $2 billion in annual sales, much of it unrelated to dumping. That gave us a better picture of the ability of that company to close out the dump, and it positioned our client to effectively deal with the situation."

Case 5. *Checks on advertising and what other counsel did*: A prospective client was impressed when Kostka wove intelligence on the company's advertising and media coverage into the presentation.

He used Dialog, which keeps track of 150 consumer magazines, to see what kind of advertising the prospect had been doing and to estimate how much it was spending.

Kostka found it took very little additional time to check on who might have been named counsel for the prospect in earlier years when he used Nexis data banks to search *O'Dwyer's* publications.

Because *Business Wire* and *PR Newswire* also are in the Nexis data bank, he found he could get copies of any releases they put out for a particular company. But more than releases is available. He discovered he could order abstracts on any stories dealing with the company or its industry in any of more than 400 U.S. and Canadian magazines and trade publications.

Case 6. *Electronic directory for prospecting*:

One data base lists every company with 10 or more employees or $1 million or more in sales. You can ask for all companies in certain types of businesses that meet that criteria by ZIP codes in Boulder, Colo. You know before going into a presentation what percentage of sales growth they're experiencing; who their bank is; whether they're a subsidiary and, if so, where their headquarters is located; and the identities of their principal owners.

How Technology Gets Firms around Profit Squeeze

Billing Clients for Activities, Not Just Hours   Many public relations firms have been caught in a profit squeeze because they can't raise their per-hour billing rates for professional and support personnel time fast enough.

The challenge in the 1980s has been to develop a way to get a certain amount of income without a rigid hourly system, a way to charge for the activity the client gets. According to Sue Bohle, that way was through a strategic application of technology.[52]

She started the Bohle Company in her Los Angeles area home and was positioned to make the leap to a Century City suite of offices and a ranking among the 50 largest firms in America by taking advantage of the new technology in almost every facet of her business. And in 1985, the client roster and productivity of her firm helped attract acquisition by Ketchum Public Relations. Here's how she and other executives have approached adapting technology to business operations.

1. *Start by buying computer time*: "I'm a fanatic about productivity and technology," said Bohle, executive vice president of Ketchum/Bohle Public Relations. "I started when I opened my office by buying computer time. Now every person who composes anything has a terminal at his or her desk." She had started, as most offices, with automation in accounting and word processing.

2. *Executives on computers—productivity up, payroll down*: "Then we required executives to use formatting. That allowed us to cut the support staff in half. We did this in three months—and we also achieved a higher productivity level."

3. *Build technology into all operations*:

Our next step was automating a lot of operations—from little items such as rolodexes, through getting into computerized account program planning systems, to providing reports to supervisors every Monday showing time spent against budget for every program or account. We're able to evaluate productivity on a project-by-project basis rather than just the macro basis of the past.

4. *Develop an internal expert*: The most effective word processing person was sent to additional classes in computer systems and then named to manage the firm's computer operations, including a computerized print center that saved additional executive time.

5. *Bill for activity*: A computer accounting system enabled Bohle and her staff to bill on a "piece basis rather than charging for secretary time; we bill for generation of documents—regardless of who does the documents—plus executive time."[53]

Michael V. Sullivan, chairman of Harris, Baio & Sullivan in Doylestown, Pa., uses several methods of applying technology to internal monitoring of client cost control.[54] "Budget considerations have a direct influence over all other marketing activities. The success of any total marketing communications plan is heavily dependent on efficient budgeting and cost control monitoring systems," he said.

One of the more distinctive methods involved his firm's computerized telephone system. Account executives use a special client code when making all long-distance phone calls. At the end of each month, the firm receives a tabulated bill that classifies each call by client. This assures that a client pays no more and no less than phone costs incurred.[55]

6. *Maximize support for firm's executives*: Technological applications make possible a high level of support for executives.

"It's a moving target because we have different types of employees who keep a firm young, innovative and productive if they're given the right kind of support," Bohle said.[56]

Technology had made the public relations members of the staff at Basso & Associates, "33 to 50 percent more effective with less administrative support personnel needed," said Joe Basso, principal of the Newport Beach, Calif., communications company.[57]

His system helps with everything from sales forecasts and spreadsheet analysis through customized news releases to national and regional trade and consumer research. "We spend 80 percent of the time researching, 20 percent writing," Basso said. "If we didn't have our integrated computer system, clients couldn't afford the service we give them."

This not only aids counseling profitability, but also contributes to market development as illustrated by the way Cleveland's Young-Liggett-Stashower has capitalized on its use of technology. "Brainpower, experience and skills are the major marketable assets of a public relations firm. That is why we place such a high premium on having an environment where our professionals can focus on client needs, not the details of our business," promotional literature assured clients.[58]

The firm tells clients that its computer system makes unnecessary manual generation of paperwork and enables counselors to concentrate on professional work. It gives them "the data they need to enhance their productivity and do what they do best: creating." A 201-page document summarized a key advantage for clients of such technology: "Everything in the system is designed to help professionals make better decisions faster."[59]

7. *Challenge executives to look at computer as their tool*: Requiring executives to use computers without special motivation or psychological support may be counterproductive, according to some principals of counseling firms. Despite the recent surge in computer use by counselors, field research indicated a strong residue of resistance, apparently because some felt that their existing work patterns were efficient and that computers were the tools of secretaries and bookkeeping personnel.

Bohle approached the problem after reflecting on her own perspective as "a journalism/magazine-trained person" who was "used to creating, building and administering an agency and servicing accounts" and doing all her writing, mostly at home, on a legal yellow pad. When she had computers placed on executives' desks and wanted them to do their own typing, she convinced them to regard the computer as an executive's tool. Her strategy included abandoning her yellow pad and serving as a role model. She reasoned that "if the top executive was not willing to sit down at the computer and use it, then there would be a rebellion."[60]

Charles Lipton, vice chairman of Ruder Finn & Rotman, said that senior staff "on the upper side of 45 or 50" sometimes require special incentives and assistance to make the conversion to using technology as executive tools.[61]

"Senior people may have to cultivate appreciation of technology in their own work." He said mature counselors face a different situation than recent college graduates, who often come to counseling firms with an understanding of how to operate a computer and work with videotex, satellite communications and narrowcasting.

An appreciation of technology normally comes with hands-on experience, Lipton said. Beyond the economic value to his and other counseling firms, this is necessary if senior staff is to be "compatible with what our clients are doing." He said that when the system really works, the firm operates on the same footing as its sophisticated clients—with savings in time and operating overhead.

Chairman David Finn serves as one of the role models by operating his own word processing terminal. But the firm has gone beyond leaving the adoption of technology to osmosis or choice. "We explain to our people that it's a matter of economics." To back that up, the use of technology is shown to dovetail with profit-sharing incentives. "Peer pressure and pocketbook concerns basically make it a question of: 'Do you want money to flow into your pocket or into clerical payroll?'"

After "almost everybody was trained in word processing, we started going to higher applications, including budgeting and time allocation." He found this especially valuable in being alerted "if somebody is exceeding budget or if an account is not getting its proper share of effort." It also helps in crises when "we punch in to see who has available time to help the group."

At Simon/McGarry Public Relations of Los Angeles, each person in the firm—"without exception"—has a computer terminal, according to the president, David H. Simon. That allows an executive to call up a document that an account person has written and to quickly review the status of a particular client. "We put a lot of emphasis on the way our firm is managed and that includes analyzing projections, costs and financial controls."[62]

8. *Use portable computers, modems, electronic mail*: Because a computer contributes to productivity and innovativeness of executives at the office, some firms have decided that those who work away from the office should have their executive tools with them.

Bohle, for example, began acquiring portable computers for senior executives to use at home, on planes, or in hotels. She furnished them modems and a special phone line to an office computer that operated around the clock. She and her staff were able to use the "electronic mailbox" at the office for sending or receiving messages no matter where they were working.[63] All five offices of Simon/McGarry Public Relations are linked by computer modems.[64]

Computer modems give a firm with multiple offices special advantages over the once preferred, traditional voice conference calls. Modems enable a print-oriented individual to contemplate ideas as they appear on a screen or printer before interacting in a conversation. If somebody is unable to participate in a conference, the person can engage in the communication from a remote location or call up exactly what was covered from the data bank, even at night.

Earlier in this book, a Catch-22 question was raised about conflict between the need for written client approvals on sensitive public disclosures and the deadline pressures that often make that impossible.

Darryl R. Lloyd, president of the Los Angeles consultancy bearing his name, found that electronic mail between counselors and clients helps alleviate such problems. For instance, it enabled him to speed up the approval process by having a copy of a statement for a *Wall Street Journal* interview on the client's desk a few minutes after it was drafted. Electronic mail also is useful for clients who need to modify copy.[65]

Using Technology to Strengthen Media Services

Beyond client research and counseling firm business applications, one of the more valuable uses of technology is in making possible media services that would be too slow or costly if provided by conventional means.

In 1985, Simon estimated that a dozen to 20 U.S. public relations firms had sophisticated computerized media information systems. By 1989, he projected that hundreds of firms would have such applications as the industry experienced a proliferation of use of computer technology in media relations.[66]

How to Use Media Computer File for Clients, Counselors   Examples of how to create a media information system to be used by counselors and their clients is illustrated by model applications of technology that could be adapted for any kind of client from community hospital to smokestack industry to aerospace company.

Bohle built on concepts and practices shared with her by Simon. He, in turn, was stimulated to further refine his system.

1. *How and why to start the system*: Over the course of servicing one fast-growing client—Epson—and getting into daily calls on "all kinds of intricate details" about the company, Bohle designed "a data base system as the master file of any kind of information that any media person could ever want." This served as a library of key business publication articles useful to client and counsel.[67]

> *Now, whenever an executive goes into a business meeting or an interview, that person has a briefing on articles that have positioned Epson, expressed executive views or contained key data. An executive can ask for any data base statistics on market share, unit sales, and the like and have it appear on a computer terminal or printout at any Epson America office.*

Essentially, the Ketchum/Bohle-Epson data base becomes "a file drawer which you can access with any number of criteria for fields of information." This required several steps.

The first task was to figure out everything counselors or client executives might want to access.

The next task was to determine how they would want to access it. Bohle said the concept was to "make it so simple that a secretary in a client office can get out any data needed."

Then the challenge was to identify a software package powerful enough to store all data.

This demanded finding a hardware system on which all this would run—"powerful enough to store lots of information, fast enough to provide very quick access and capable of access from different geographical locations" of client and Ketchum/Bohle offices.

2. *Basic information to access*: "This really was a new way of filing all information generated on a client," Bohle said. "Not all information needs to be in the electronic data base, but there should be easy library access to fact sheets, corporate information, spokesperson information and facts on persons who have written about the client."

3. *Identify what kind of coverage by whom*: The Ketchum/Bohle model also incorporates data on the author of an article and on the focus and negative or positive indicators.

4. *Include analysis of editor and publication criteria*: The next logical stage is a master storage system that analyzes what each publication and/ or editor wants in different kinds of stories or interviews, the level of information about the product or technical understanding the journalist already may have and other editorial criteria.

One distinct advantage for client and firm is that even if an individual leaves the counseling firm or a writer moves from one publication to another, the facts remain accessible.

5. *Keep current with notes on media observations*: Bohle added to the system notes on conversations counselors have with the media. "We're looking for analytical information as well as descriptive." One value of such notes is that only the first counselor to contact an editor "goes in cold." The model also helps orient junior staff.

6. *Keep track for consistency and anticipation*: The Ketchum/Bohle approach calls for keeping track of information passed on to the media "so that we're consistent and can anticipate that which may be combative, such as printed errors of fact, interpretation or analysis by media persons."

For example, she recalled a major piece in *Fortune* that said two cousins in the Seiko organization were on a collision course. Because such an article appeared and was being accessed by other reporters in their research, "whoever writes about Seiko next, *Fortune, Business Week* or *Forbes*, is going to ask about conflict between the cousins, regardless of the reality of any rift."

7. *Build in possible tough questions*: The model also may include information to remind counselors and client executives of any tough questions they may wish to anticipate based upon past coverage by a business publication or on a writer's particular style or background.

Among the techniques Simon incorporated are the following:[68]

8. *Tie in with electronic mail and use for media tours*: By 1986, Simon knew he would have the capacity to incorporate electronic mail notes on specialties and interests of each of the editors in his system and make this intelligence available to counselors working on media tours in the field. Similarly, his creative staff would be able to continuously update the data base from remote locations.

9. *Build in exchange of ideas*: Computer communications seem to be more effective when an interactive capacity is introduced. Simon built into his editorial data base system the opportunity for interaction among the members of his firm.

For instance, a counselor filed an electronic note that he had just talked to a reporter who would be in Los Angeles on June 14, four months in the future. "A note is going out by electronic mail to all professional members of the firm." The implicit message:

You can take appropriate action personally to schedule your preparation for the visit.

You can program the computer to give you a reminder of the visit and on a certain date.

You can append an electronic note to the appropriate part of the file on the visit, for instance: "Because I know this reporter and he's especially interested in 'X,' or because the reporter used to work for 'Y' publication and has such and such background, it might be a good idea to set up these types of interviewees and stories."

You can order a visual display or hardcopy printout of everything in file about the reporter and his visit at any time.

10. *But provide for data accuracy*: Simon wants widespread participation in the system by members of his firm and encourages them to share information and ideas, but he recommended that a mechanism be built in to assure consistency and accuracy when adding electronic notes to the files. That control comes from designating only one person to merge those notes into the files. "When you change the data, it's easy for a person who confuses names of publications, spells an editor's name phonetically, or doesn't understand the format of the software program to corrupt the files."

11. *Who reaches out-of-town publics and uses a certain angle?*: The creation of a comprehensive editorial data base material is useful in planning interviews or news releases at the Los Angeles base of his operations and "particularly valuable when you're on a media tour."

Simon's editorial data bases not only generate names, addresses, and phone numbers, but also information about what kind of stories editors use, who their publics are and what kind of angles they like. With a few keystrokes, a counselor can have a printout or display of all Boston area publications that cover types of stories relevant to a client's needs. "The point is that you can search the data base to help the client no matter where the counselor and client executive may be."

12. *Assuring roundup article opportunities not missed*: Some vertical trade publications use a class of article called a roundup that doesn't get scheduled frequently. But it can be vital for a client to be included.

A roundup looks at a segment of the industry such as floppy disk drives in March and dot matrix printers in May. To get the client in a story scheduled for next March, you begin to plan the previous June. Or you start by finding out who has roundups planned in the printer area, what kind of printer area you should go after, and which editor will be responsible for the roundup.

This can be used as a selling point in presentations. Simon said that

telling a client who's in a certain line of business how you organize to keep on top of roundups, plan media tours or match corporate needs with media criteria is so valuable in new-business presentations. And it's also impressive when you're reporting to your client. It's not the methodology that really impresses the client, but how the methodology improves results.

The Special Advantages of Smaller Consultancies

Firm size should not serve as a barrier to applying of technology to the creative and business aspects of counseling. "The smaller the firm, the more important it is to automate—more automation allows the one-man agency to achieve more, if the practitioner looks at it as a total tool to relieve him of the more mundane tasks of the profession," according to the principal of Nigberg Associates of Framingham, Mass.[69]

Mark Nigberg suggested that heads of smaller firms "look at automation not as a big crazy, unknown vista, but as a business decision which will give them the most for the money." Simon recalled

a time when a smaller firm couldn't look as sophisticated in a new-business presentation as the giants, which could have their New York or Chicago research departments run reams of data on growth rate, rankings of major companies in a field, what's appeared in the media, trends—things the average counselor couldn't possibly do. Nowadays, anybody with a computer and a modem and access to commercial data bases can do the job very quickly.

Loet A. Velmans, then chairman of the board of Hill and Knowlton, one of the "giants" to which Simon referred, told *MBA Executive* that the most dramatic impact of computers on the counseling business was still to come.

Computers will impact our business even more dramatically in the development of proprietary data bases. Two of our pharmaceutical clients already have set up data bases. The advantage is that we now have instant access to everything in world literature and medical literature about certain illnesses and the drugs used to treat them. This helps immeasurably when responding to a crisis or simply developing stories for our clients.[70]

Counselors' Resources in Technology Era

An information explosion, almost an overload, has packed public relations journals and technology trade publications. Voluminous materials are provided by hardware and software manufacturers. Reams of material are available from vendors of electronic data base, news wire, film and video services.

Several succinct, well-organized collections of print and electronic data of relevance to counseling firms may prove most helpful to those who wish to develop or improve their technological capabilities to take advantage of the new-business opportunities.

Dorf Monograph Tells How to Computerize Counseling Firms

In a Counselors Academy–published monograph, Bob Dorf, chairman of Dorf & Stanton Communications of New York, developed a series of guidelines for computerizing public relations counseling organizations.[71]

He reported that within four years of installing his first computer, billings increased 400 percent, but automation held down the rate of growth of support staff to a fourth of that level. Dorf detailed findings and recommendations on why and where to computerize, word processing, reporting, agency marketing, accounting, payroll, copying machines, telephone systems and time analysis.

He said the "rapid-fire pace of new product introductions shows little sign of slackening," and even if an executive waited five years to bring his operation up to state of the art, "two weeks after you sign your purchase order, someone will introduce a better, cheaper, faster, prettier, more appropriate piece of hardware or software."

Research and Education Foundation Funds Book-Length Study

It is not essential, and probably not desirable, for public relations counselors to become technology experts. "The real need is to put the technology at the service of the practitioner in his frame of reference," said Merton Fiur, president of the New York-based Center for Public Communication.[72]

To that end, the Foundation for Public Relations Research and Education in late 1986 published a book-length study "to make it as easy as possible for practitioners to use these tools efficiently and effectively."

The Foundation published results of the study in workbook form to allow for updating and expansion and reserved the option of later placing findings and recommendations in an electronic data bank.

The Foundation study includes:

evaluation of products and services

index of suppliers

examples of how the new technologies are being used

review of factors involved in selecting and using technologies

analysis of related security, legal and human resource problems

Online with Public Relations Special Interest Group Similar to the use of citizens' band radio, public relations practitioners send out signals over their home and office computers to post information for each other on electronic bulletin boards, share special data bases, "meet" in continental tele-computer conferences at set times and have small group sessions. The Public Relations and Marketing Forum provides a range of services for subscribers to the national CompuServe videotex service.

The data bases include reviews of articles of interest to public relations practitioners, bibliographical listings, commentaries, and electronic abstracts and original articles prepared by the members of the Forum for one another. These can be accessed around the clock.

Members have large-scale forums in which experts on topics make brief presentations and then field live questions typed on subscriber keyboards and transmitted via computer modems. Impromptu and scheduled small group conferencing make possible an intimate discussion of various concerns, including, and at times going beyond, things technological.

Once a person buys a CompuServe sign-up kit at a computer store, several hours of free online time is made available before he pays for actual time. Computer-generated calls are placed through local access phone lines and charged at about a dime a minute for evening and weekend time and double that for business hours.

Once the subscriber has a CompuServe identification number and password, he can go online with other members of the Forum by keying in a computer command.

PRLink, which was founded in 1985, was merged into the Forum in January 1987.

According to past Technology Task Force Chairman Ronald D. Solberg, the following special PRLink features were added to the Forum in 1987:[73]

1. *Live forums and seminars*: Members can ask questions and record what others offer on either computer disks or printers. Among counselors who led forums one year were Patrick Jackson, president of Jackson, Jackson & Wagner; Kent McKamy, president of McKamy and Partners; Tom Harris, president of Golin-Harris Communications; Don Levin, president of Levin Public Relations and Edward L. Bernays.

2. *Eleven data bases*: These electronic files offer information and services tailored to the interests of public relations persons. Subscribers can view the information on their computer monitor screens and also use their printers as teletype receivers to transcribe selected portions. Data bases include:

Regularly updated news and feature articles

Summaries of Silver Anvil Award winners and other cases

"The Professional Connection," an electronic bulletin board of PRSA's job-referral service with weekly listings

Calendar of PRSA and public relations industry events

PRStore, an electronic shop-at-home service for professional development resources and other products

EJ (Electronic Journal), a monthly electronic "publication" of articles on new issues and trends in public relations

Activities bulletin board with information on programs and materials for PRSA members

3. *Message center*: An electronic mailbox is provided for Forum members to leave notes, drafts, and other communications for colleagues.

PRSA Creates New Technology Section   In 1985, PRSA organized its 14th professional interest division, the Technology Section. It was convened by Joel A. Strasser, senior vice president of Dorf & Stanton Communications and head of the New York firm's technology division, who said one of its goals would be "to help section members understand and keep up with technology and communications advancements in the industries they serve."[74]

Among services planned for members were a newsletter distributed electronically and by mail, professional development seminars and workshops, a speakers bureau and computer online meetings.

Beyond exploring technology applications, public relations counselors have examined the added strategic resources available by joining forces with advertising agencies (either in their roles as parent organizations or as collaborators), creating consortia of independent public relations firms for joint proposals, developing affiliations in other cities and countries and combining forces into various kinds of networks.

9

ALLIANCES

The clear-cut trend to networking and other alliances among counseling firms seems to have been spurred by the same forces that have influenced expansion of the industry's larger firms along geographical, size and specialization dimensions.

The thrust of both advertising agency-affiliated and independent public relations companies into new markets has been matched by a related move on the part of smaller firms to participate in ever-broader networks that, in some instances, extend around the world.

The new alliances can give instant market access to even the smallest firms and those in remote locations. Networks make available the geographical reach and specialized expertness of other member firms. This results in more emphasis on counseling skill—and less on size—in new-business presentations.

Alliances with advertising agencies have made it possible for many firms to offer a wider variety of services than they could previously. This chapter devotes a major section to advertising agency alliances and counseling firm strategies to handle control by conglomerates, capture resources and cultivate cooperation.

THE TREND TO NETWORKS

Forces and Processes of Alliance Building

Economy of scale, critical mass and synergy join in varying degrees as counselors build and refine networks for the marketing and delivery of public relations services, and, in some cases, for the sharing of competitive strategies and systems for doing business.

The very existence of networks in their area may ignite the spark of competitiveness of counselors to create their own. In part, the networking trend springs from the demands of the marketplace and the perceived needs of clients. The trend's acceleration signifies protective alliance building on the one hand and aggressive pursuit of business opportunities on the other.

The use of networking extends from limited advertising of affiliations to development of infrastructures to improve the product and profitability of individual members and the whole network system. Geographically, networks range from the melding of a handful of one-person consultancies in a single town to the forging of alliances that reach into major markets on several continents.

Networking overlaps other strategic modes of growth and alliances with some firms combining two or more of the following: internal expansion, acquisition by an advertising agency or communications conglomerate and affiliation in the sense of subcontracting relationships.

One way to illustrate the benefits and considerations involved in such alliances is to examine the implications from the perspectives of member firms in different kinds of networks, starting with a relative newcomer, the Public Relations Exchange Network.

Newcomer—The Public Relations Exchange Network

A Minnesota Firm Finds Itself Able to Compete with Major Corporations The Minneapolis-based firm Padilla, Speer, Burdick, and Beardsley is smaller than some of the far-flung field offices of major competitors from other metropolitan areas, but President Lou Brum Burdick said that her network affiliation "permits firms of my size with much less resources to compete with firms the size of Burson-Marsteller and Hill and Knowlton."[1]

Burdick acknowledged that "unless you have impeccable sources of financing, it's extremely difficult in this day and age to build an international firm of any size with branch offices around the world."

Yet, she and some of her colleagues aspired to build such an operation, at least initially in major markets in the U.S. and Canada, but with an intermediate goal of servicing "the top 20 markets in North America, Europe and the Far East."

So, in contributing to the well-developed trend to networks, Brum & Anderson Public Relations (which Burdick chaired before its merger with Padilla and Speer) united with firms based in other cities to found the network. By 1986, their roster included:

United States

Akron—David A. Meeker & Associates

Baltimore—Earl Palmer Brown Companies

Boston—Cone & Co.

Chicago—Janet Diederichs & Associates

Coral Gables—Bruce Rubin Associates

Dallas—Pharr Cox (from which C. Pharr & Co. sprang)

Los Angeles—Berkhemer & Kline

Miami—Woody Kemper & Associates

New York—Makovsky & Co.

Philadelphia—Spiro & Associates

St. Louis—BHN/Public Relations

Canada

Toronto—Marshall Fenn Ltd.

England

London—Extel Public Relations Ltd.

Some of these firms, such as the Canadian, were tied into other networks, further extending the reach.

Considerations of Clients and Counselors The network trend stems from several prime considerations on the part of clients and counselors, as supported by comments from Burdick and executives of other firms:

1. *Clients seek multimarket coordination*: "Clients really do prefer to have counselors with whom they work managing their business and coordinating with firms in other markets; the clients really don't have time to interact with a number of firms in other markets," Burdick said.

2. *Survival in a multimarket environment*: "As the world shrinks, as communication becomes more national and global, smaller regional firms operating individually could not begin to service clients."

3. *Strength in problem solving*:

Cooperating with each other and solving problems facing one or more of us is as important—or more so—than gaining business. We have the opportunity to come together and share common problems and work out our own business problems with counsel from other people who have been through—or are facing—the same thing. That's very attractive and, in the long term, contributes to the professionalization of counseling.

4. *Mutual commitment from friends in the business*: Burdick observed, "you get a level of commitment when doing business with a network friend you meet several times a year and with whom you communicate more often than you do when giving business to somebody that does not know you."

Sue Bohle, who together with Kenneth D. Makovsky and Burdick, was one of three co-founders of the network, cited several other purposes:[2]

5. *Keeping competitive in face of affiliation trend*: Surveys of counselors indicated that one-fourth of all firms in the early 1980s were part of national chains or members of networks. "We had the combined billings, expertise and other resources to be competitive," said Bohle, who became executive vice president of the merged Ketchum/Bohle organization in Los Angeles.

6. *Bringing together growth firms, new leadership*: "We wanted to put together a network to represent the largest or second largest independents in each market," she said. "At the same time, our founders tended to represent an emerging new leadership in PRSA, people between 35 and 55, executives who wanted to run growth agencies and pursue market dominance in their metropolitan areas or states."

7. *Creating ties to end top management loneliness*: Earlier, Chester Burger, New York management consultant, was cited for his point that client CEOs occupy a lonely position and have a need to communicate with peers. Bohle observed the same kind of need among top executives of public relations firms.

> *Being a manager is a very lonely job. You're expected to be an expert on everything. You're put on the spot by staff members. Very often, it's only with a peer from another counseling firm that you can get a line on shared experience to solve problems or just have open communication. Some may consider us too competitive to do that. But when you build a network, you have to develop an enormous amount of trust in each other. Your formal network has a personal network built into it. Before, some of us had nobody we were comfortable to bounce ideas off of.*

Bohle recalled "seven of us sitting around a hotel lounge discussing the problems of one individual's account," impromptu day-long meetings of network members when they traveled to each other's cities and weekend phone calls "when we felt like talking to somebody else who understood our business."[3]

What It Takes to Build and Maintain a New Network   Building and maintaining a network requires a great deal of work and some compromises as field research on the Public Relations Exchange and other networks indicated. Here are some examples:

1. *Limit to one firm per city*: This initial consideration in the founding of the Public Relations Exchange sounds logical and simple, but as counselors expand their own operations into other cities, become involved in acquisitions or mergers or are confronted with requests from colleagues in different firms in one city such a restriction can become troublesome.

2. *Budgeting time for communications, travel for meetings*: The PRSA

National Conference in Fall and the Counselors Academy Spring Conference allow two occasions for network members to get together. But that usually implies a need to come earlier or stay later. Some networks, such as the Public Relations Exchange, require additional meetings. It would seem that electronic mail, conference telephone calls and the computer equivalent to conference calls might ease some of the problems of staying in communication.

3. *Determining who contributes how much commitment*: Burdick said her network members were "wrestling with the appropriate level of commitment to expect from firms in other countries" once the network expanded beyond its base in the U.S., Canada and England.[4]

Entry in Global Market—The Pinnacle Group

Six-Figure Accounts for Some Individual Firms Another perspective can be gained from examining an established network that already has gone global, the Pinnacle Group. Even within a city, let alone a nation, differences in standards apply. When a network goes international, those problems tend to be compounded by distance and cultural and business differences—despite the so-called global village. A similar problem exists for the large multinational counseling firms, but they do not have to deal with an added layer of independence of each member of a network.

But problems tend to be outweighed by the advantages. For instance, Darryl R. Lloyd, past president and chairman of the board of the Pinnacle Group, said the international network "really makes us competitive in being able to do a multimarket roll-out of a new product."[5]

Moreover, "six-figure accounts for individual firms have developed out of our relationship." The president of Darryl Lloyd Inc. of North Hollywood, Calif., said that new business grows out of combined presentations, subcontract relationships and referrals.

By 1986, the Pinnacle Group had reached into markets from Edinburgh to Tokyo and included among its members:

United States

Atlanta—A. Brown Olmstead Associates

Boston—Agnew, Carter, McCarthy

Chicago—Selz Seabolt & Associates

Denver—Servoss-Barnhart

Houston—A. R. Busse & Associates

Kansas City—The Boasberg Co.

Los Angeles—Darryl Lloyd Inc.

Minnetonka, Minn.—Northstar Counselors

New York City—Lobsenz-Stevens
St. Louis—Clayton-Davis & Associates
San Francisco—Amidei and Co.
Seattle—The McConnell Co.
Tampa, Fla.—Roberts & Hice
Washington, D.C.—E. Bruce Harrison Co.

Canada
Toronto—Public & Industrial Relations Ltd.

Australia
Melbourne—Consolidated Royce

Denmark
Copenhagen—Public Relations Konsulenter

England
London—Kingsway Public Relations Ltd.

France
Paris—Project Group

Germany
Frankfurt—Kauders International

Italy
Milan—R. P. Partners
Rome—Studio Italiano PR

Japan
Tokyo—Japan Counselors

Netherlands
The Hague—Beauchez BV

Norway
Oslo—Intervaco Norge A.S.

Scotland
Edinburgh—Dunseath Stephen Partnership

Spain
Barcelona—S.A.E. de Relaciones Publicas

Pros and Cons of Networks vs. Independence or Acquisition Some of the
advantages and problems in working with a network such as the Pinnacle

Group instead of remaining independent or becoming acquired by one of the large corporations include:

1. *Management tool for members*: Beyond its use in new-business development, one of the primary benefits of membership in a network is its application as a management tool. "We help each other with presentations and organize seminars, much like the Counselors Academy's, except that ours are tailored to the particular needs of the group and its members. We spend a lot of time on business strategy and how to sell in particular markets," Lloyd said.[6]

In doing that, the Pinnacle Group draws on the expertness of member counselors who have strong experience in a particular market area.

2. *Reciprocity*: Even without the kind of control a megacorporation has over its branch offices, Lloyd said individual members find there is a spirit of reciprocity that "assures return of support for support, service for service, referral for referral."

3. *Not able to marshall forces in one structure*: "We still don't have the clout of marshalling forces as one does in a single firm or going after a chunk of business that is only available to mega-agencies. Being able to administer operations in one structure has many advantages."

4. *Specialization helps and hinders*: Although specialization in certain areas contributes to network needs, sometimes "there's a problem if an agency doesn't have depth in other areas within its own geographical market."[7]

The tendency of networks to limit membership to one firm in each city thus may act as a barrier when both intimate knowledge of a market and expert skills or experience in a specific segment of business are required.

5. *Draw upon each other's fortes*: Not all members are full-service firms, but they can draw upon the fortes of their affiliates. Lloyd noted, for instance, that the Washington link of the network offers "a reservoir of public affairs and lobbying opportunities that no other firm within Pinnacle would normally have the chance to cultivate."[8]

His area of specialization in technology allows his firm to help identify business opportunities, supply advice on proposals and structure programs for affiliates. In some cases, parts of projects too technical for another firm may be subcontracted to Lloyd.

6. *Save on costs of logistics*: Just as a large firm with branch offices or affiliates in key markets enjoys savings of time and travel costs, so, too, do networks.

Lloyd gave this example:

When Lobsenz-Stevens set up a media tour for us in New York, they handled all the logistics. They also had a lot more clout in getting appointments than we would have had.

We put an L.A. person on the plane with our client, but we didn't

*have to send anybody there in advance and spend all the time getting
to, from and around airports; flying to and from New York; checking in
and out of hotels and finding his way around unfamiliar offices. In
other cases, we don't even have to have anybody accompany the client
representative; the affiliate provides all tour liaison services.[9]*

7. *Members pay fees and percentages*: In Pinnacle's case, "a significant
fee is required, as well as a stringent review process," when a firm applies
for membership. Members also are required to pay into the network a
percentage of income received as a result of inter-agency transactions. A
third form of network income is generated by periodic assessments for
major projects.

8. *Network budget covers meetings, promotional activities*: These
funds are used for administrative, seminar, meeting and promotional expenses. The latter might include such items as a convention hospitality
suite for prospects, brochures or institutional advertisements.

9. *Camaraderie and sharing among benefits*: At quarterly Pinnacle
board meetings,

*We do things social as well as business; there's enough opportunity to
develop friendships. Because we're non-competitive, people never seem
to hesitate to share things that normally have proprietary sanctity
when you're an independent operator outside of a network. Camaraderie and opportunity to share with people who have gone through positive or negative experiences are among the most valuable benefits; you
can't buy that.[10]*

10. *Executive professional development*: Smaller firms, as well as larger
counseling corporations, invest to varying degrees in professional development. But there may be special benefits for network participants from the
crossfertilization of ideas that do not emerge as hybrid or inbred products
of a single company.

"At any meeting, you'll find at least a dozen agency principals there and
involved with specific topic areas, as well as committees concerned with
specific areas of focus," Lloyd said.[11]

One gathering each year includes a two-day seminar as well as a half-
day or longer business meeting. Typical topics are how to determine a
firm's worth, effects on counselors of new tax legislation and setting up
stock plans as a viable alternative to giving equity positions to staff members.

A quarterly newsletter and special bulletins fill gaps between meetings
with educational articles by members. Issues sampled included reports on
such subjects as understanding of Far East client background, Canadian
findings on special events marketing, strategies for placement of articles in
national magazines, financial relations counsel for companies going public
and counseling services for overseas high-tech clients.

11. *Risk of sharing vs. risk of not sharing*: There is a risk in any network because of unknown factors. Professional peer pressure would seem to serve as a deterrent to violation of confidences, if not as an incentive for sharing, however.

"But we've so carefully screened people, and each of us has made such a commitment, that the risk is very low. Sharing of systems and expertise can place you at risk. But that risk is certainly much lower than risks you'd face in not having any affiliation."[12]

12. *The push for multinational markets*: Lloyd credited Amelia Lobsenz, 1986 president of the International Public Relations Association and CEO of Lobsenz-Stevens, for lining up international members of Pinnacle. "With the world getting smaller, the need for global activities and resources is becoming more critical to the growth of public relations capabilities. There will be distinct advantages for independents who are capable of participating in international operations," he said.

Pinnacle has conducted once-a-year international meetings with specific topics on cultivating new business in other countries and on supporting each other's marketing areas.

One of those marketing areas, Canada, has operated with models somewhat similar to U.S.-based networks in the face of increasing competition from American firms and international networks.

Canada Faces Competition with Own Networks

Canadian Network with Continental Reach   In Canada, as in the U.S., some firms are involved with advertising whereas others are dedicated exclusively to public relations. Some are affiliated in loosely connected organizations or join forces for particular projects with firms in other cities.

Canada's largest network in the mid-1980s was Continental Public Relations Association, formally registered in 1986 as Continental Canada Inc.

The Continental Canada network is differentiated from U.S. counterparts because firms have bought equity in their association rather than pay membership fees or commissions on business, according to Michael Campbell, president of Toronto-based Continental Public Relations Ltd.[13] The concept behind its substantial investments in networking is to encourage referral of business to member firms and participation in joint projects. The network reaches from coast to coast:

Halifax—Saga Communications Ltd.

Montreal—Relations Publique Continental Inc.

North Bay—Continental Public Relations Ltd.

Ottawa—Continental Public Relations Ltd.

Regina—Roberts & Poole

Saskatoon—Roberts & Poole

St. John's—Saga Communications Ltd.

Toronto—Continental Public Relations Ltd.

       Continental Strategies (marketing subsidiary)

Vancouver—MacFarlane Morris Peacock Ltd.

Winnipeg—Continental Public Relations Ltd.

"We have structured Continental Canada so it will be a profitable company," Campbell said. In 1986, the network's board of directors retained a full-time business development staff that would report to it rather than to any individual member firm.

Continental Canada moved to extend its reach abroad by purchasing an equity position in an international organization being organized by Ketchum Public Relations. "We're using the network corporation as our shareholder in the Ketchum international operation. This gives us an international scope of service."

The Canadian-based network also was considering making other investments as a group, "such as buying into other companies that could help all of us." He said the network's purchasing plans could extend to outright acquisitions of other firms. In a sense, then, it combines the advantages of network affiliations with the power of a single corporation to grow through acquisition as well as expansion.

Autonomy of member firms, however, has been preserved in what Campbell described as "a very complex and detailed shareholders agreement. We're still autonomous except when we're working on a common account."

Coca-Cola is an example of a common account that Continental Public Relations Ltd. opened for the network. "Coca-Cola now has requirements extending beyond the reach of my firm's offices, so it made sense to designate it as an account of Continental Canada." But each member firm has the option to withdraw from a common account because of a potential conflict of interest with one of its own clients.

The network extends beyond business development. "We're increasingly looking to where we can provide assistance to one another—staff training programs, information sharing, research projects, common data bases, use of technology and innovations that may help all of us be more effective and profitable."

Canada, U.S. Networks Similar, but Autonomy Is Canadian Hallmark Luc Beauregard, 1984–1985 president of the Canadian Public Relations Society, said there are a number of similarities between networks in Canada and the United States. One key difference may be an emphasis on autonomy for Canadian counselors.[14]

The U.S. acquisitions/mergers trend has not moved across the border with any significance, according to the president of the Montreal-based firm of Beauregard, Hutchinson, McCoy, Capistran, Lamarre et Associés. "There have been no major developments in advertising agencies buying public relations firms."

The number of firms with national reach in Canada are few. "We have not more than four or five firms and two or three loosely linked organizations working on a national level." The reason for the relative paucity of national firms and networks is that "there is little national business in Canada," although there are large corporations.

One source of national counseling business that is different from their neighbor to the south is Canada's federal government. "Because of how our country is built, even large multinational corporations give their regional offices a lot of autonomy. The eastern region of a client company, for example, will handle its own marketing."

One of Beauregard's partners, Robert J. McCoy, said that the firm had joined the Continental network for the better part of a year to extend its reach into the major English-speaking markets in Canada. In 1986, however, Beauregard, Hutchinson, McCoy, Capistran, Lamarre et Associés opened a new Toronto-based subsidiary, National Public Relations, to handle such accounts as Apple Computer and Canada's Molson Brewery and return to the autonomy the firm had before joining the Continental network.[15]

"The networking concept is still viable," McCoy said. "We just felt that for our interests we would do better by opening our own Toronto office and contracting with other independents to service client needs in other cities."

Tokyo-Founded IPR Network Reaches 43 Countries

International Group Emphasizes Indigenous, Independent Operations For a perspective on a large, long-established, multinational network, consider the International Public Relations Group of Companies. IPR sprang out of the Orient to become the world's largest public relations network. Its uniqueness extends beyond its reach into six continents and 43 countries and its founding by a Tokyo business executive, Taiji Kohara.

Davis Young, 1986–1987 IPR world director for the Western Hemisphere, characterized it as an international network with strongly independent and locally indigenous staffs in the 98 offices it had opened by 1985. Young, president of Young-Liggett-Stashower Public Relations, said the role played by IPR in servicing the clients of his and other firms has been "invaluable" in terms of the relationships and business development derived from the network.[16]

He cited the example of how IPR enabled his firm to handle a sudden assignment in Korea.

It wasn't a really major job, but it was certainly important to our client that we be able to handle it immediately and effectively. If we had not had our network affiliate's help, the deadline would have passed before we could have come up with a solution.

Now, we're setting up something in Singapore. And we're involved with the Paris Air Show. And we have something with a British client coming our way. . . .

He described the founder of IPR as a counselor "who as early as 1967 sensed the Japanese economy was going to take off and that we were heading for a global economy. Kohara had a concept for coming forward with a network of locally owned, locally managed firms whose personnel would be indigenous rather than imported."

Young became involved in IPR in 1981 "after learning first-hand of the advantages of networking through the Counselors Academy." He rose to head the Counselors Academy in 1984 and became IPR's vice president for the Americas in 1985.

Our job is not to do things, but to know how to get them done. If that means some other firm gets the bulk of the money from an account, well, that's in the client's interest. And that focus on service creates a comfort level that the client couldn't get anything better. That places us in the best light and comes back many times over in business referrals.

Some people are skeptical about networks vs. a single company with branches. Theirs work for them; ours work for us. There is enough out there for all of us.

Ours [networks such as IPR's consist of] independent entrepreneurs, who have worked at our own enterprises and have the flexibility to move quickly and make our own decisions. You know the sun does not set on your capabilities; you can reach anywhere with confidence. You're dealing with established capabilities with people native to their areas, who have built their own business there. They speak different languages, but they do the same things, share the same kind of values. The fact they're indigenous to the areas in which they're operating means they're well connected, they're not subject to transfer and they know what's going on.

The diversity of areas of specialization ranges as wide as the geographical reach of the network. "The fact that we have a connection in Italy or Australia really shortens the process; it means we're working with a known quantity—and quality."

For the most part, he said that working with other IPR firms is like using a branch office. "These people are executing the program at a distant point. They report back to you, not to the client."

When he had a need for information gathering and media relations advice in India, "it was awfully nice to know somebody in Bombay." And when Queen Elizabeth came through Vancouver, British Columbia, and inspected a piece of equipment made by a Young-Liggett-Stashower client, it helped to have a Canadian network affiliate.

A single firm may have branch offices and affiliates around the world but it takes a great deal more resources to have in place the bases of operation of a network such as IPR. In early 1986, the participating IPR partners in North America included:[17]

Canada

Calgary—Francis, Williams & Johnson Ltd.

Edmonton—Francis, Williams & Johnson Ltd.

Halifax—J.J. McKeage & Associates Ltd.

Montreal—Les Consultants PS LTEE

Ottawa—John Doherty and Co. Inc.

Saskatoon—Parry Martens Public Relations Inc.

St. Catherines—Ontario Editorial Bureau

Toronto—Ontario Editorial Bureau

Vancouver—International Public Relations (Canada) Ltd.

Winnipeg—Wordsnorth Communication Services Ltd.

United States

Anchorage—Murray/Bradley & Peterson Inc.

Atlanta—International Public Relations Co. Ltd.

Baltimore—Wills & Darcy/International Public Relations

Boston—Clarke & Co. Inc.

Charlotte—Epley Associates Inc.

Chicago—Public Communications Inc.

Cincinnati—Adams, Gaffney & Associates Inc.

Cleveland—Young-Liggett-Stashower Public Relations

Dallas—Howell-Fournier Communications (Garland)

Denver—Darcy Communications Inc.

Detroit—PR Associates Inc.

Fort Lauderdale—Gary Bitner Public Relations Inc.

Hilton Head—Darcy Associated Counselors Inc.

Honolulu—International Public Relations Ltd.

Houston—Churchill Group Inc.

Jacksonville—Fey & Associates Inc.

Los Angeles—International Public Relations Co. Ltd.

Louisville—Jack Guthrie and Associates

Miami—Bennett & Co. Public Relations Inc.

Minneapolis—Padilla, Speer, Burdick, and Beardsley

New Orleans—Bauerlein Inc.

New York—International Public Relations Co. Ltd.

Philadelphia—The PR Co.

Portland—Rockey/Marsh Public Relations

Raleigh—Epley Associates Inc.

Salt Lake City—Darcy Communications Inc.

San Francisco—International Public Relations Co. Ltd.

St. Louis—Drohlich Associates Inc.

Seattle—Jay Rockey Public Relations

Tampa—Public Communications Inc.

Tulsa—The Blakey Group Inc./IPR Tulsa

In the Latin America/Caribbean region, IPR network affiliates were in Buenos Aires, Caracas, Lima, Montevideo, Rio de Janeiro, Sao Paulo, St. Michael and Trinidad. In Africa, IPR was represented in Cairo, Harare, Lagos, Marshalltown and Nairobi.

European affiliate bases included Athens, Barcelona, Bonn, Brussels, Copenhagen, Dublin, Geneva, The Hague, Helsinki, London, Manchester, Milan, Rome, Vienna, Zurich and Istanbul.

The network's reach in Asia and the Pacific region extended to Bangkok, Bombay, Colombo, Jakarta, Hong Kong, Karachi, Kuala Lumpur, Manila, New Delhi, Seoul, Singapore, Taipei, Tokyo, Adelaide, Auckland, Brisbane, Canberra, Melbourne, Perth, Sydney and Wellington.

Florida, Ohio Networks Serve Statewide Needs

But not every client operates on an international or even a national basis. Some need to have public relations firms that can concentrate on markets within a single state, such as Ohio or Florida.

Florida Public Relations Network Avoids Down-Time, Coordination Problems   James B. Strenski, past chairman of the Counselors Academy, had introduced Cleveland's Young to IPR. Young reciprocated by sharing insights with Strenski on the operations of Ohio's statewide network.

Although Strenski, chairman of Tampa-based Public Communications Inc., had linked his firm to others across the country and abroad through IPR, he felt something equivalent was needed within Florida itself to reach into any or all of that state's markets.[18]

He primarily modeled the Florida PR Network's goals and system operations concepts after IPR and also adapted Ohio's model to the special client, counseling firm and marketplace characteristics of his own state.

Strenski was not alone among principals of Florida firms in believing that a single project in a particular market or a statewide campaign could be conducted more efficiently without down-time normally required for an out-of-town consultancy to know—and establish itself in—a new community.

The Florida Network was established in several state markets:

Fort Lauderdale—Gary Bitner Public Relations

Jacksonville—Fey & Associates Inc.

Miami—Bennett & Co. Public Relations Inc.

Orlando—Public Communications Inc.

Tallahassee—Stan Tait & Associates

Tampa—Public Communications Inc.

They provide a presence in every major community for out-of-state or Florida clients who want breadth or depth of focus, whether it is in providing market research and strategy development, public issue campaigns, fine-tuned publicity into specific neighborhoods or other elements of public relations counsel. Strenski said that by 1986 three types of campaigns had emerged as best suited for the network.

1. *Issues*: "A network like ours is positioned well to sell concepts to the legislature, media and voters."

2. *Multi-faceted corporate clients*:

For a corporation that is multiofficed or multimarketed and wants entry into key markets, it helps to offer the coordination of well-established firms throughout the area. There's a fair amount of work among our members to cultivate clients with corporate marketing thrust who are trying to penetrate the state.

3. *Trade associations*: Although Florida's trade associations are headquartered in Tallahassee, their members, their members' customers and the legislators whose support they want are located throughout the state as well as in the capital city.

An alliance like Florida PR Network works well in a bellwether state like ours. Because of the rapidly growing economy, Florida requires rapid growth in its infrastructure to support the increasing population and market. Add to that picture the issues such growth brings with it and the expanding opportunities for support of trade associations.

Ohio Model May Work for Other States   Young, 1985–1986 president of PROhio Inc., predicted that other states would follow the lead of the networks in his state and Florida and said that the model is available for study and adaptation.[19]

A statewide network can be "very impressive from a new-business standpoint. If you need something in another city, you can have great confidence that your colleagues will get it done right and on time."

He recalled the irony of the 1984 luncheon meeting that led to the creation of the network. David Meeker, president of David A. Meeker & Associates, and Young are separated by 35 miles of highway. The first time they met, however, was at the 1979 Counselors Academy Spring Conference in Arizona. The second time was at the 1980 Counselors Spring Conference in Florida. Those early meetings among professional neighbors paved the way for the 1984 luncheon.

Although there are several major markets in Ohio, they found that no public relations firm had an office in more than two of those areas. They reasoned it would be useful from a competitive standpoint to have representation in all seven markets, and to that end they sought involvement of other firms that could help them meet that goal.

By mid-1986, these firms were covering the six markets:

Akron—David A. Meeker & Associates

Cincinnati—Penny/Ohlmann/Neiman

Cleveland—Young-Liggett-Stashower Public Relations

Dayton—Penny/Ohlmann/Neiman

Toledo—Fluornoy & Gibbs

Youngstown—Farragher Marketing Services

In a statewide network, as in a national or international one, it helps to have different areas of specialization. Young said: "Most of us are generalists, but among us, we are strong in such areas as high-tech, public affairs, community relations."

PROhio created a funneling point for circulation of information on joint new business opportunities and other intelligence by designating a counselor from the member firm in the State Capitol of Columbus as executive director.

Interpersonal communication is enhanced by meetings (every six weeks the first year, semiannually beginning in 1986) to review network finances and relationships; new business projects or campaigns and joint marketing opportunities.

Beyond those meetings and talks at semiannual Counselors Academy conferences, "we call each other quite frequently." That frequent communication helps bring to bear combined expertness on problem solving. It also enables "realistic expectations when we get into joint service to a client."

For Young, if such a statewide network "can serve clients better just once, it's worth all the time and effort—but we've been able to do it a number of times already."

Extra Business Generated Is a Dividend on Top of Other Benefits   When the network was formed, the members felt that any extra business generated by the affiliation would be more of a dividend than the primary return on their investment because they sought other benefits, including:[20]

1. *Advantage in presentations*: "Even in individual presentations that have nothing to do with statewide operations, a network is a good thing to talk about; it impresses clients."

2. *Helps professionally*: Although the principals of the several firms do belong to the same national organizations, the example of Meeker and Young not meeting in the state until the network was started suggested another advantage. Others thought this would be a good group of people to be able to network with on a professional basis, not just on a business network basis.

3. *Crisis potential*: The network was considering developing a crisis team that would be available to clients of any member. This would involve pooling of resources. Specialists from the firms would be designated to be in position to support any client.

4. *Pool mind power*: There also is the potential of bringing to bear the collective and individual strengths of the several firms' executives in giving counsel on a client's problems or programs, at least for limited projects, if not on a sustaining basis.

5. *Media placement edge*: Statewide networking can make local media placement more effective because affiliates tend to know their immediate markets and media better than outsiders. Established counselors in a particular city know where best to target a story, which television and radio programs would like spokespersons and which editors would use a certain kind of story.

6. *Link up with out-of-state firms*: Because each of the member firms is involved in its own informal networking, as well as in formal systems, it's possible for an executive to call on behalf of a PROhio colleague and secure support in another state.

City Networks Serve Smaller Practices

If networks could improve business and client service at the state, national and international levels, it stands to reason that smaller counseling practices could be served by different forms of alliances. Three models are reviewed.

Joint Bidding Helps One-Person Firms Become More Competitive In the Houston area, a number of senior practitioners who are independent counselors, including one-person consultancies, have joined in bidding projects.

"One of the ways we become very competitive with larger firms is by joint bidding and assuring our clients that they will be dealing with senior talent, with each of us an independent principal with different areas of expertness," according to the principal of Sally I. Evans Public Relations Counsel.[21] A consortium may be flexible and able to shift its composition from presentation to presentation.

Houston area practitioners who have participated in this form of network affiliation included Evans, who has specialized in helping corporations position themselves to go public; Margot M. Dimond, 1985 president of the PRSA Houston chapter, who has expertness in the not-for-profit sector; and Sabra H. Gill, executive director of the 1986 Texas Sesquicentennial Commission for the Houston area, who also brought to the consortium employee communications and marketing skills.

Beyond the joint bid benefit, the Houston consortium, like bigger networks, meets a special need of the individuals. "The biggest difficulty as a small-practice counselor is the lack of contact with others to do brainstorming. It's so easy to get isolated," Evans said. The city network helps fill the void together with her active membership in the Counselors Academy and PRSA.[22]

Richmond, Va., Principals Form Network Partnership In Richmond, Va., four counselors with their own independent practices created a network called The Public Relations Council and made it stronger by becoming affiliated with a Virginia advertising agency.

Kenneth A. Murphy, president of Public Relations Operations, heads a minority-owned counseling firm with an emphasis on special events, foreign manufacturer client representation and handling of government accounts.

David M. Clinger, chairman of The Boardroom, brings to the network a full-service financial public relations operation with additional specialization in legislative and public issues campaigns and graphics and publication design.

William M. Dietrick, president of Media Consultants, emphasizes his expertness in such areas as battling tax legislation and his academic base at the University of Richmond. Benjamin J. Pope, president of Pope Public Relations, specializes in such areas as product promotion, employee communication, audio-visual programs and sports special events. Finnegan & Agee is the advertising agency member of the alliance.

In their joint prospectus, they used this appeal:

> *Just as organizations come in all sizes, so do their public relations requirements. The Public Relations Council was created to custom-fit such diverse needs. It offers the advantages of a large firm and its resources along with the personal attention of a "staff" executive. The Public Relations Council blends the talents and experience of four individuals, each distinguished by independent careers in the field. Their professional skills, depth of experience and versatility [documented in the prospectus] are rarely found outside the nation's largest public relations firms.*
>
> *With professional careers spanning almost 25 years on the average, The Public Relations Council is geared to producing results through solid, business-like planning. Its partners have spearheaded strategies that have resulted in some classic marketing stories. The affiliation with Finnegan & Agee sets the stage for some of the most comprehensive public relations programs in the region.*[23]

Another Model: Professional Independence with Cost Savings   Another networking model seems to borrow from affiliations formed by independent physicians and lawyers in private practice, but it stops short of incorporation.

E. William Brody, president of the Resource Group in Memphis, described the networking model for small counseling practices in a *Public Relations Quarterly* article.[24]

"It consists of a group of individual practitioners who agree to co-locate their practices in order to economically share facilities and, to a greater or lesser extent, professional support as well. . . . Each may enjoy the economic benefits of shared spaces and services without regard to the degree of further professional involvement."

Aside from arrangements for lease or purchase of facilities, equipment or services, the basic professional association model has no legal requirements. As independent physicians or lawyers, members of such an association, however, may make agreements "to support one another during periods of overload, illness or vacations."

Or they may set up joint billing procedures as another mode of achieving economy of scale and critical-mass benefits. Such procedures might cover compensation for services provided by colleagues and how remittances are to be made.

Brody recommended exploring longer-term arrangements in which "the association also can provide for the continuity of service which, especially in one's later years, can become a point of significant vulnerability to the individual practitioner."

Regardless of the mode of establishing such an affiliation, it, as the other kind of networks reviewed, can provide a psychological environment "in which those involved can exchange ideas and provide for the mental stimulation and informational exchanges which otherwise may largely be denied the 'solo consultant.' "

Another model, which can be used by counseling firms of all sizes, but which could fit well with Brody's professional consortium concept, involved some of the giants of the public relations industry. In 1986, 20 communications industry corporations, including Burson-Marsteller and Hill and Knowlton, announced the creation of the Professional Services National Credit Association to exchange information on bad credit risks.[25]

That model could be extended into other areas in which counselors could pool resources for data bases, joint purchasing power or even self-insurance.

Counseling from Main Street

In Era of Global Village, Counselors Go Back to Roots Something of a trend appears to have developed in the era of the global village, despite the clustering of public relations firms in metropolises—the movement of counselors to small towns. One counselor, Patrick Jackson, calls such a base "Main Street" and another, James Little, terms it "the heartland."

Jackson and Little serve as prime examples of counselors who established successful counseling practices in the countryside. Both commanded sufficient respect of their colleagues in major cities to win election as presidents of the 13,000-member PRSA.

Both discovered that networking is even more important to the counselor on Main Street than to practitioners in metropolitan areas. It can mean the difference between thriving and merely surviving. Some may have marveled that counselors in small towns could do well at sites remote from media centers, cities filled with mega-corporations, financial districts, seats of government and all the other amenities that practitioners can count on in a New York, Los Angeles, Chicago, Dallas, Atlanta or Washington, D.C.

When Little presided over PRSA, he would introduce himself to audiences or individuals as "Little Jim from Friendly Findlay, Ohio." Findlay, about an hour south of Toledo and north of Columbus, had only 35,000 population at the start of the decade.

"Maybe 20 years ago, you couldn't have done what I'm doing now in

Findlay; you couldn't have run this kind of business except in major cities," said Little, the president of Diversified Communications Inc. "Clients were caught up with transportation and proximity. There may have been some bias against folks in a small city. You had to be from Chicago, New York or L.A. to be believed."[26]

Jackson, senior counsel of Jackson, Jackson & Wagner, founded a practice that has clients throughout the U.S. and also in Canada and overseas. He does have offices in Grand Rapids, Mich., and Albuquerque, but his headquarters are on Front Street, Exeter, a New Hampshire town with a population of about 7,000. That's nearly five times the size of his previous base of Epping, N.H.

The former PRSA president practiced in New York City and Chicago before he moved to New Hampshire in 1962. He said that practices such as Little's in Findlay and his own are proving a theory.

You don't have to be right next door to your client if you're really counseling instead of providing routine services. What's important is that you have to have a close relationship between your client and you or your staff—but not in geographical terms. You don't have to be there all the time holding their hands.[27]

Using Burson-Marsteller and Hill and Knowlton to illustrate a point, he said, "you can't practice just from a metropolitan base—look at how many offices they have in smaller cities."

How to Do Well on Main Street or in the Heartland Jackson and Little have developed a number of insights and strategies to make counselors from small cities effective and credible:[28]

1. *Take advantage of networking*: The networking that ultimately brought Jackson and Little to the presidency of PRSA reflected part of each of their business philosophies. It's at least as important on Main Street, as it is on New York's Madison Avenue, L.A.'s Wilshire Boulevard or Chicago's Michigan Avenue.

"It's how you position yourself. That's why participating in a professional society not only helps you keep up, but also positions you to develop your own network," Jackson said.

"While it's very important for all people to be involved in continuing education through seminars and professional organizations, it's even more important for those of us not based in major cities," Little said. "As you become more involved in professional associations and networks, you no longer need to be in a large city."

2. *Capitalize on referrals*: Because counselors in small towns may experience difficulty in marketing services in traditional ways, referrals take on more importance in getting business. So do professional credentials.

3. *Systematically develop contacts*: The counselor who wishes to do well in a small city needs to systematically develop contacts. One of the models Little cited is his predecessor as national president of PRSA: "Pat Jackson is one of the top lecturers in the United States. Marketing his business may not be his purpose in giving speeches all over the country, but it does establish his credentials and it does make a lot of contacts for him."

4. *Locate strategically*: Successful Main Street counselors find their communities not only idyllic, but also strategically located.

Counselors such as Jackson and Little have not been alone in recognizing the lower expenses, higher productivity and lifestyle benefits of relocating from big cities. It is advantageous to position a counseling firm where corporations are likely to cluster headquarters operations or branches.

Jackson noted a trend on the part of companies to move national and regional facilities to smaller towns. "A counselor can find clients spread across the landscape—not just corporations, but also hospitals, public service organizations, universities . . . ." In his case, that's true of such clients as Coors, United Way of America and Los Alamos National Laboratory (site of the Strategic Defense Initiative/Star Wars planning).

Another part of strategic locating has to do with vendors upon whom public relations firms depend, ranging from phone company service centers to printing establishments. "It pays to locate near major corporate operations because vendors tend to move near those facilities and you get better service than you could in the average small city," Little said.

5. *Use the environment as a USP*: Counselors can capitalize on the advantages of living and working with people outside big cities and use it as a unique selling proposition (USP) rather than be defensive with prospective metropolitan clients.

Operating a counseling firm in a place like Findlay is important for the client who wants counselors who can identify with customers in the heartland, according to Little. It's not just living in middle America; "we can get out on Main Street much quicker than those people in major cities."

"In New England, we're equidistant from Montreal and New York," Jackson said. "We're sitting in the middle of great research, educational, manufacturing and cultural institutions. We live a more normal life; we're closer to the great majority of American people who live in smaller cities of 100,000 or less."

Jackson said that "if you're not practicing in a big city, people tend to look at you differently—'You're from Exeter? What are you doing *there*?' " His counsel: "Exhibit self-confidence right off." He said that counselors who get to their offices "without tremendous hassle" and who live outside of metropolises "tend to be more in control of their lives. It's natural to be very self-confident."

6. *Let distance help clients adapt to counseling role*: Distance can work for a counseling firm, if a counselor recognizes the implicit advantages and lets them work for him.

Jackson said geographical distance from clients helps foster reliance on "very capable internal staffs of well-managed organizations" for day-to-day activities. The distance factor and an emphasis on internal staff for ongoing functions may enhance understanding of the role of outside practitioners as management consultants who specialize in objective third-party counsel.

7. *Differentiate between media and relationships*: Distance alone does not do the job. Jackson said that positioning a firm on Main Street to move from routine service to counseling sometimes begins with education of clients "to the true role of media relations.

"Many of the fiascos in the history of public relations have come from the old-fashioned view that working with media is most of what a counseling firm should do," Jackson said. "For us, it's 10 percent of our work at most. Sure, New York is the media center of the world, but we put out material that would be good across the country."

He said the emphasis should be on "the personal media used in the building of relationships—working with and training the client's people" to understand what they need to do in directly relating to significant individuals and segmented publics.

8. *Start with getting to know staff and doing workshops*: In overcoming the geographical barrier and helping clients make the shift from short-term use of counselors for routine activities, Jackson recommended starting relationships with a combination of conducting workshops and getting to know client staff.

"We tell our clients that we're public relations educators," he said. "We're not academic educators; we're training practitioners on the job or with seminars. We tell clients that 'our goal in working with you is that you and your people will know as much as us.'"

9. *Take advantage of lower overhead*: Communications and travel may represent additional expenses, but overhead costs a great deal less than in major cities.

Jackson, Jackson & Wagner operate out of an 1809-vintage, federal-style mansion on the town square in Exeter, "a heck of a place to do business!" Jackson also maintains an office in an Epping farmhouse that was built in 1713.

Little's firm is based in an old mansion with marble fireplaces in the offices. Yet, he said "we spend considerably less on cost per square foot; we can invest our capital more in things other than land, lease or rental."

Jackson said counselors best capitalize on low overhead by charging clients less.

10. *Count on travel*: Operating from a place like Exeter or Findlay means traveling to where the people are. It means going to big cities and other small cities. "You can't do enough business in Findlay alone," Little said.

11. *Use the phone*: Phone conversations can create the feeling of closeness between counselor and client and allow for maintenance of communications between trips. "We could have offices on the moon as long as we had phones," Jackson observed.

12. *Harness technology*: Distance factors can be offset by technology. "We're working our way through technology now," Little said. "We've purchased computer systems for word processing, typesetting and graphics. We're looking to link our offices with other cities through modems. That will be another way of making the small city part of any larger community."

13. *Attract creative talent at lower cost*: Some creative people, as principals of firms, look to the amenities of moving back to their—or their parents'—roots. Because the cost of living "is not so atrocious," Little said, "we can be competitive with metropolitan areas and pay well by the standard of the community."

14. *Make environment conducive to productivity*: Staff can rusticate or become more productive when they move away from the big city. It depends to a great deal on the principal.

"Today's a Saturday," Little told an interviewer. "I have a couple of my people with me who will get out a project for a client over the weekend. Nobody minds. We have people come in at eight and leave at five-thirty—they're not commuting an hour to get here; they're not running to catch a train in the evening. An earlier start, a longer day and less stress in commuting provide more productivity."

For the principal in such an environment, however, Little pointed out the danger of allowing the surroundings to deter from "paying enough attention to the business side of running a firm."[29]

That business, if trends continue, may include developing more strategic relationships with advertising agencies.

ADVERTISING AGENCY RELATIONSHIPS

Understanding Mergers

Differences of opinion exist within the ranks of advertising agency executives, as well as among management consultants and public relations firm officers, about what has caused the rush to acquire counseling firms, but nobody disputes the existence of the trend.

Understanding the purposes of advertising agencies is the first step in developing strategies for counselors. Those who are parts of total-communications companies must plan to take advantage of the resources of their parent firms as they build their businesses and cultivate new-business leads.

Attractiveness of Counseling Firms to Advertising Agencies Counseling firms are attractive to acquisition-minded advertising agencies because of the public relations industry's strong growth, ability to refer clients to their own counselors, the competitive edge it gives to have in-house counseling capabilities and the opportunity to compete with other joint advertising-public relations ventures.

Profitability of counseling firms ranks high. There is a special attractiveness to building a conglomerate that offers an integrated communications package from a total-communications company. There is also the desire to be positioned to fill unmet public relations needs of agency clients, particularly in areas of special counseling competence. Agencies also seek to buy into the credibility and special marketing support of counselors. These factors are supported by a diversity of experts.

1. *Growth industry appeal*: "We believe PR can grow faster than advertising," an executive of the largest advertising agency told an audience of financial analysts. Glen A. Dell, executive vice president of the JWT Group (J. Walter Thompson), told a Paine-Webber audience about one of the factors that explained the rush of advertising corporations to acquire public relations firms. In reporting the statement from the parent firm of Hill and Knowlton, *Jack O'Dwyer's Newsletter* noted that "many PR firms are reporting gains of 20% and 30% for 1985."[30]

2. *Able to refer to own counselors*: One of the motivational factors may be the ability to refer to another part of the house communications work that advertising people can't handle. Kay Berger, executive vice president of Manning, Selvage & Lee, cited the case of "a CEO of a major advertising agency who said that it's conceivable that his company would recommend that clients not advertise but rely on public relations and other strategies."[31]

3. *To compete with joint advertising-PR ventures*: Although he predicted the trend toward acquisition will continue, perhaps "at a far slower pace than in recent years," a Southern California management consultant, Daniel H. Baer, said some advertising agencies were asking him "to investigate such opportunities because they feel they simply can't compete with agencies that already offer the two services."[32]

4. *Money only one factor*: Yet, Chester Burger, New York management consultant, said he has "yet to find a situation where a public relations firm was acquired to make money—that's just a secondary or tertiary consideration."[33]

5. *Profitability ranks high*: Edward Gottlieb, principal of the New York City counseling firm of that name, said that although profit may not be the primary motivation, it ranks highly with advertising agency executives: "Ad agencies want their PR function to be as profitable as possible and that's why so many of the deals have profit incentives built into them."[34]

Robert Pfundstein, executive vice president of Doyle Dane Bernbach, said "the only legitimate reason for any acquisition is to generate good profits."[35]

6. *Integrated communications package advantage*: Jack Bernstein of *Advertising Age* contrasted the views of those who favor and challenge advertising-public relations mergers and concluded that "ad agencies that have acquired PR companies see their ability to offer a fully integrated communications package as an important plus. The theory is that any communications need or opportunity that may arise can be dealt with effectively in one shop. They view this as an enhancement of their competitive position."[36]

7. *Total-communications company drive*: "The leaders in the advertising industry are acquiring resources to become total-communications companies," said Jean Schoonover, chair of D-A-Y, O&M, the public relations arm of Ogilvy & Mather after its acquisition of Dudley-Anderson-Yutzy Public Relations. "They want our business because it complements theirs," particularly in client problem solving, but also in communications, Schoonover said.[37]

8. *Ad agency clients have unmet needs*: "The reason advertising agencies want to acquire PR firms is that clients have needs that do not get met by advertising agencies alone," according to the founder of Chester Burger & Co.[38]

9. *Agencies buy competence*: Agencies often want public relations competence because of the nature of problems Burger said "they may feel unequal to meet, such as public policy—regulatory and legislative, financial issues, community relations problems and crises."[39]

10. *Want credibility*: A key element that influences acquisitions is frequently the unique difference in effectiveness they achieve by capitalizing on the credibility of public relations. That credibility can be particularly important in product claims.

11. *Want marketing support*: Advertising agencies also have learned that public relations marketing support can be as subtle as impressing media reviewers of new products to help them gain ready access to corporate executives. A case in point involved a journalist who complained that he placed more than 40 calls to an advertising agency-advised client before he could talk with someone in authority. He did not have the ease of access counselors help assure.[40]

How to Handle Control of Counseling Firms by Ad Agencies

Some public relations counseling firms and advertising agencies have grown up as siblings. Others have been brought together recently through acquisition and merger. Yet others are—or soon may be—in the process of negotiation.

Regardless, the most important consideration remains the "how"—how the public relations component is assimilated or controlled, how the conglomerate deals with questions ranging from structure through budget to interaction of the discipline with advertising in client programs.

Factors to consider before, during and after acquisition range from involvement in the acquired firm's strategic planning to a leave-them-alone policy. This is related to a concern over consequences if the public relations function is made subservient. Advertising agencies are well advised to involve counselors in presentations related to marketing and public relations strategies.

To assure the integrity in the public relations areas of expertness, several techniques are useful. Advertising top management must be educated to help them understand why and how to value public relations products and to change their attitudes toward budgeting for counseling services. Public relations as well as advertising executives benefit from learning how to remove barriers to working together in the client's interest and how to establish interdependent, mutually supportive roles for the two disciplines.

There are opportunities to help advertising executives appreciate why counseling firms must maintain separate, as well as adequate, budgets and why advertising personnel can't be substituted for public relations people in a particular job or in a client presentation.

Models from advertising agencies that effectively integrate public relations firms are of value. So is the use of third parties to negotiate mergers and recognition. It is important that top management help bring together the disciplines. Some CEOs, however, advocate another alternative—retain independence. Following are some considerations:

1. *Preserve autonomy but provide interaction*: The CEO of an investment banking house specializing in media and communications businesses said that agencies have three "options" in handling the merging of acquired public relations firms into their organizations. John Suhler, president of Veronis, Suhler & Associates discussed these alternatives:[41]

"Bring the PR unit into the agency's mainstream and ruin its independence. It becomes subservient and loses its credibility."

"Buy it and do nothing. There's no interaction, no involvement of the senior guys, no benefits."

"Care must be taken that the PR firm does not lose its own client base to the point that its autonomy is jeopardized. But there should be sufficient interaction in the strategic planning process for clients that additional business can be pursued independently."

2. *Leave them alone*: "Our office has said in each case to advertising agencies, 'if you don't keep your fingers off your PR firm, you're going to wreck it,' " Burger said, citing historical precedent. "With few exceptions, the parent advertising agencies leave the PR firms alone."[42]

It is said that there are extremes to everything and exceptions to almost any rule. One firm was allowed to drift aimlessly "to the point where they almost ran it into the ground." But his counsel to advertising clients usually is to maintain "arm's length distance." He said he has told advertising executives: "These are two different professional disciplines, and your people don't know public relations."

3. *Avoid subservience*: In one firm, the public relations function became an integral part of the agency. Burger said that for any one client there would be a supervising advertising account executive and a public relations person.

> *If one of these persons has a $50 million budget, and the other has $50,000, you can guess who calls the shots. In such a case, public relations has been reduced to supplemental publicity in the most pedestrian way, backing up marketing needs of the moment, but never used in terms of strategic or tactical applications to marketing thrust.*

4. *Strategic decision maker needed for PR presentations*: In another case, an advertising agency invited the counseling firm to join in a presentation to the client vice president of advertising or marketing. That was an improvement over an era in which the agency's public relations department wasn't even involved.

But the change may not go far enough. Burger said "a lot of problems faced by the client have nothing to do with advertising or marketing. The person presented to has no real understanding of public relations capabilities and utilization. The president, chairman of the board or other persons making strategic decisions need to be there for public relations presentations."

5. *Integrity in area of expertness*: Schoonover said "it was very important in joining any advertising agency that we would be able to assure continued independence and retention of our identity—the D-A-Y name and reputation. We're experts in public relations, and we wanted to make sure that nobody would tell us what to do in that area."[43]

6. *How to preserve independence*: "We've been a subsidiary of H.B.M.

Creamer for more than 30 years in which we've been a distinct public relations firm and a distinct advertising company operating under the same roof," said Mitchell C. Kozikowski, president of Creamer Dickson Basford. Here's how it works:[44]

> "We measure professional independence and how well it's working by how well we grow, how well we keep good professionals and how well we attract and keep very good clients."

> "Demanding the very best—and that sometimes means expensive—talent in your staff begets very good client work and that, in turn, generates respect for independence and integrity from your advertising colleagues. If you have a solid standard of excellence in the public relations part of the company, you will continue to have the freedom and resources to get the job done."

> "You do not allow out work that is not sound from the public relations point of view and you stand firm against such work being forced upon people to execute."

> "You make sure that there is no temptation to throw in 'PR' discounted at rates less than the services are really worth."

7. *Value product professionally*: The throwing in of "free PR" with advertising is anathema to Alan J. Jacobs. The chairman emeritus of Bozell & Jacobs offered the combined disciplines perspective of a principal who headed the American Advertising Federation and of a Counselors Academy member who built the public relations component of an agency. "If PR is thrown in free, it's probably not very good. And if it's good, it's probably not appreciated."[45]

> What firms should do is hire good people, charge professionally for their services and deliver a product that has value. "It's only recently that the giants of advertising have wakened to the fact that they have to treat public relations with respect."

> By bringing together both sides of the house in client meetings and agency seminars, Jacobs said the barriers to understanding and valuing of public relations products can be lowered.

> "In many cases, advertising executives learn that the product in those 'smaller' PR accounts will produce more measurable results for both the client and the agency than some advertising budgets. A good solid business-to-business PR marketing program is not fantastically expensive. But advertising rates are so high that you have to spend a considerable amount before you start getting results."

> Part of the problem is that some advertising executives "may regard themselves as highly professional people in an industrial business, but

may not extend the same attitudes to PR people in building something worthwhile in their firms."

8. *Change budget thinking*: "Most advertising agency people are used to dealing with bigger budgets and operate on the basis of commission dollars vs. fee arrangements," said David R. Hoods.[46]

The president of Southern California's Geneva Marketing Services gained perspective on advertising-public relations budgetary differences in earlier positions with Doremus and Ayer.

"If a client had a million dollar ad budget and $175,000 for public relations, you could have a real problem in trying to convince the ad account executive to be willing to reduce his budget and go along with a shift of needed resources to the public relations side."

But it can be done. Here is one approach: Patiently educate agency management that $100,000 in public relations budget represents real dollars of fee income, and that a million dollars in budget for advertising only means a commission on that amount.

9. *Knock down barriers before acquisition*: Part of the control problem in acquisitions may lie on the public relations side of a communications conglomerate.

Jacobs said many are "so fearful of being dominated by an agency that they construct huge, artificial walls to protect themselves. It's clear that's a terrible mistake." His counsel:[47]

Most executives running major agencies today are very, very astute and sensitive business persons. They have sensitivity to concerns of any acquiree. You want them to be strong, secure, independent and you really don't have the time to run their businesses for them. Some PR people are not taking advantage of opportunities in access that could be extremely helpful. You always have the opportunity to reject an idea or suggestion. But first listen.

10. *The client needs interdependence*: This point was supported by Kozikowski when he said:[48]

If a professional service firm has the skills that encompass advertising and public relations techniques, the client doesn't necessarily want to get caught up in distinctions that may exist between the two disciplines. Clients don't have a problem in understanding that the two come together at least at the chairman level and that they need to be brought together within the agency.

Clients are going to let agencies run their own shows, but they are not going to stand for anybody wrapping themselves in a cloak of professionalism and saying they won't have anything to do with the other discipline.

It's not just good business relationships from the agency point of view to bring together the two disciplines, but the driving force behind all this is our clients. They're pressing for advertising and public relations people to work together for common client objectives.

If we follow a joint approach, the client should benefit. Granted, we're two distinct elements and the client still gets an ad agency and a PR firm. But with very close coordination, the client also gets reduction of waste, duplication and inefficiency.

For instance, targeting of audiences for the client is very easy when both of us are under the same roof. We reach one audience through advertising and reach other audiences through public relations because this is the most efficient way to do it.

But that takes some control mechanisms:

In Kozikowski's company, coordination becomes part of the whole process early in auditing and planning for the client.

Internal and external audits are done jointly.

Although the two account teams draft separate techniques, they coordinate presentations.

It's policy for top management to share client activity reports "unless we're working on competing accounts."

"We have rather frequent interchange on what's happening at management meetings at different levels in various offices across the company as a whole."

H.B.M. Creamer and Creamer Dickson Basford also encourage information exchange in person and through reports and newsletters.

The interdisciplinary approach is prompted by responsibility to stockholders of the communications corporation as well as clients.

"To our stockholders, we're one entity. It's in the interest of every professional that we make a greater profit for the whole. We've had years where our income was up and advertising down and vice versa. We gain greater respect of the whole of the company by balancing for the lower profitability in one area at any given time."

A similar viewpoint was voiced by Gerald J. Voros, president of Ketchum Communications Inc. in Pittsburgh, who offered some solutions in an article in *Madison Avenue*:[49]

"The two disciplines can no longer afford to operate in a vacuum. Clients need a comprehensive, interdisciplinary approach to their marketing problems."

Public relations counselors take the initiative in clearing up misunderstandings "because they frequently know more about advertising than [their ad agency colleagues] know about PR."

Client marketing directors should "not only be able to call on objective counsel for a particular problem [from an agency's advertising and public relations managers who] understand and respect each other's capabilities . . . but also count on joint programs with unified themes, complementary strategies, and coordinated message directed to the same target audiences."

"There will always be rivalry between advertising and public relations as each tries to convince his client that his ideas are the best. . . . But once the plans are set, it's essential that the two teams put the contest aside and start working and living together. Better still, they should get married."

11. *Don't subordinate one to the other*: This point received support from David R. Drobis, New York–based president of Ketchum Public Relations, when he spoke to members of the Association of American Advertising Agencies (4A's). "PR people should report to PR management; ad people to ad management."[50]

12. *Keep budgets separate*: "If PR's appropriate, it deserves not only its own budget, but also a big enough budget to do the job right," he said in calling for an end to "throwing in some PR money as part of an ad budget."

13. *Don't substitute across discipline lines*: "Don't ask an ad man or woman to fill a slot on the PR side because it seems a convenient way to do it," he told the 4A's. "And don't shift a PR person into advertising. The two skills are different."

14. *Let each side speak for itself*: "If there's an advertising new-business presentation and interest in PR has been indicated, include the PR people. That, of course, goes both ways," Drobis said. "Don't try to speak for each other." The cost is "the absent side never having a chance because it didn't have an opportunity to sell on its own terms."

15. *Advertising agency model of giving independence*: John Becker, senior vice president for international communications of the advertising firm of D'Arcy MacManus Masius, credited J. Walter Thompson's top management for smoothly integrating Hill and Knowlton into JWT by giving the public relations firm a high degree of independence. Becker, a JWT-H&K liaison during the merger, warned that without such independence and special attention to building bridges, "antagonisms have a tendency to develop quickly" with "danger that tensions will escalate."[51]

16. *Use third party to negotiate merger*: Acquisition negotiations are best handled by an attorney, financial adviser or other outside consultant rather than risk misunderstanding and acrimony between principals of the two parties.[52]

17. *Top management takes the lead*: For example, Young, whose firm is affiliated with Liggett Stashower Advertising, said the CEO and executive committee must set the path for the corporate culture in bringing together the disciplines. Establishing mutual respect and teamwork is aided by getting advertising and public relations people "to sit down together, look each other in the eye and talk about how they can bring interdisciplinary benefits to bear."[53]

18. *Another point of view—stay independent*: The founder of Robert Marston & Associates of New York represented a minority viewpoint among CEOs of the 20 largest U.S. firms when he offered another option on control, in essence: avoid being acquired.[54]

Marston gave as one reason the threat of impaired counseling objectivity, regardless of the nature of the controls. "I'm not saying it would happen, but the fact that it could represents an impediment that no independent PR counselor needs to confront."

Capturing Advertising Agency Resources

Public relations counselors may face certain dangers in acquisitions, but operating as part of a communications corporation with a strong advertising component can yield a number of advantages.

Availability of those advantages often depends upon more than the control mechanisms implemented. Some advertising resources and strengths may fall into place automatically; others require strategic initiatives to capture.

Many counseling executives enter acquisition with plans to gain infusion of capital and resources for expansion. Advertising campaigns are designed to reinforce and enhance public relations. Other firms find they can remain independent but still take advantage of relationships with advertising agencies.

Executives of firms that do merge learn to exploit new-business leads but recognize that some leads can evaporate in the trade-off of independent status.

Counselors can capitalize upon some of the richest resources of agencies, including research and computer systems, intellectual strengths, advertising know-how, ties to advertising associations, audiovisual sophistication and creative stimuli.

Here are some points for counseling firm executives to consider:

1. *Infusion of capital*: This is one of the primary motivations for public relations firms to merge with advertising agencies. For example, Robert Schwartz, chairman of Manning, Selvage & Lee, recalled that before acquisition, "the need for capital was becoming more urgent." Infusion of capital from Benton & Bowles, however, "accelerated the company's penetration of the international scene." And, "through equity positions and joint ventures, the agency is now quite active abroad."[55]

2. *Resources for expansion*: For a counseling firm oriented to expanding both its geographical reach and bolstering existing operations, acquisition can supply the resources. This was the case as Dudley-Anderson-Yutzy merged with Ogilvy & Mather.[56]

"While we were growing 25 to 30 percent a year before the merger, we really were losing ground in terms of our ranking in the industry because normally same-level competitors were merging with other public relations firms or ad agencies," Schoonover said. "As an independent we had limited resources, and it was hard to dedicate them to new areas that might eventually lead to new growth. It was hard to think in terms of an international network or satellite offices."

"It became extremely valuable to have Ogilvy & Mather with its terrific potential in place in all its offices." The agency brought to the merger 16 public relations offices in 12 countries. It also was operating in cities where it was considering developing public relations capabilities. Although the foreign offices were not placed under D-A-Y management, "we now have linkage and meet with public relations affiliates around the world. This brings the potential of new business from overseas."

With the widened base of operations came the economy of eliminating duplication of effort along with the power and flexibility of having resources that could be moved into campaigns as needed.

3. *Ad campaigns can reinforce, enhance PR*: That's true in Canada as well as the United States—when the two disciplines are engineered into mutually supportive roles.

Michael Campbell, chairman and CEO of Toronto's Continental Public Relations, cited Wendy's "Where's the Beef?" campaign as an example of the synergy created between advertising and public relations.[57]

But "unfortunately, this 'total communication' strategy of interlocking public relations and advertising in a marketing plan and assigning to each discipline a distinct role, is too seldom used," according to Campbell, whose company became the largest in Canada in 1985 with acquisition of Tisdall Clark & Partners.

A decreasing number of products can be sold with a message that simply says "try it, you'll like it." To public relations falls the task of filling in the gaps; supplying that additional information the consumer needs before making a purchase.

Public relations strategies parallel and complement the advertising, which often sets the stage but can't close the deal in conveying large amounts of information and using a diversity of modalities from spokesperson activities to point-of-purchase activities.

4. *But it doesn't take acquisition*: The founding chairman of Daniel J. Edelman Inc. heads one of the largest independent counseling firms in

North America. He acknowledged the value of interdependence of advertising and public relations in a marketing campaign, but said it works without acquisition:[58]

"Advertising creates a mood. Public relations provides the prelude to awareness and then authenticity for the advertising with more details, background, depth."

Although he has resisted being acquired, Edelman said he believes in working with advertising agencies. "We work with agencies as closely as some public relations subsidiaries work with their parent firms. We have a close relationship with about a dozen ad agencies: We share ideas. We have to know what's been done or planned in an ad campaign, just as they need to understand the fit of public relations.

"There's no lack of cooperation—Kentucky Fried Chicken is a Young & Rubicam advertising account. We do the public relations. They're extremely reinforcing of us.

"Leo Burnett brought us into the 9-Lives account. The Morris the Cat commercials were terrific, but they had a problem: Not everybody recognized Morris as the 9-Lives Cat." Edelman was asked to develop that association.

5. *Source of new-business leads*: One of the more valuable resources can be new-business leads an advertising agency can provide.

Dana T. Hughes, president of Boston's Public Relations Consultants Inc., said association with an advertising agency should provide a valuable source of prospects. "Maintaining regular communications between offices, including at the branch level, regarding new-business opportunities should be a top priority throughout the organization."[59]

6. *Some leads evaporate in trade-off*: When Dudley-Anderson-Yutzy was merged into Ogilvy & Mather, the counseling firm "had to weigh the advantages of new-business referrals and growth opportunities against disadvantages of some people not calling on you because you're no longer an 'independent,' " Schoonover said.[60] "But the strong ties with your new advertising affiliate get you referrals that offset any drop-offs in new-business opportunities."

7. *Capitalize upon research resources*: Methodologies and systems for research and evaluation in planning and executing campaigns represent a powerful area of agency resources.

Burger advised counselors in advertising agency conglomerates to "get access to whatever research capabilities that are available and try to identify components that are applicable to your work."[61]

With the media becoming increasingly fragmented in terms of segmentation and narrowcasting, "the media departments of advertising firms have a tremendous advantage in being able to develop so much information on how to reach audiences segmented by demographics, behavior and other characteristics." He said help with such methodologies is usually available from parent firms for the asking.

Schoonover agreed that "being part of the family gives you priority. You become a key research client overnight." She listed several research strengths available from the parent advertising agency, including:[62]

"Tremendous knowledge resources" in areas of clients, industries and products

Expertness in advising on research needed

Special research groups, such as Ogilvy & Mather's Hispanic unit

Research methodologies and data banks on communications effectiveness

Perceptions of the advertising industry and the company itself

Prospects by the 1990s for computer access from remote offices to the research capabilities of the entire organization

8. *Tap into computer systems*: Because of their critical mass, advertising agencies often have larger, more sophisticated computer data systems.

Burger said that such systems can be used for public relations as well as advertising cost analysis, time reporting, invoicing and client data and for accessing or entering research data.[63]

Hoods recalled the efficiency of the BBDO and Doremus advertising computer assistance available to the public relations side of the house: "Push a button and you'd have printouts on everything mattress companies have done over the past five years."[64]

9. *Mine intellectual strengths*: Some resources are less tangible, such as the creativity within advertising agencies. For example, Cleveland's Young said that one of the most impressive resources of large communications conglomerates is "the brainpower for bringing interdisciplinary task forces together."[65]

10. *Employ advertising know-how*: Intellectual strengths, as a resource, subsumes the advertising know-how agencies bring to mergers. The chairman emeritus of Bozell & Jacobs said that the mix of advertising and public relations strategies and techniques is one of the more resourceful areas of joint operations. "My public relations executives said they get amazing ideas from the advertising side when they sit down together to develop strategies for clients."[66]

Advertising ideas particularly provocative for counselors pertain to measurement techniques, media capabilities, art direction, marketing, sales promotion and issues advertising.

11. *Use ties to advertising associations*: With merger and acquisition, counselors are brought into the professional networks of the advertising agencies, and that represents distinct advantages.

Hughes said that advertising agency relationships "allow a firm's name to be known among a wide group of agencies, companies and prospective clients" through the affiliate's membership in such organizations as the American Association of Advertising Agencies, Affiliated Advertising Agencies International, Business/Professional Advertising Association and American Advertising Federation.[67]

12. *Capture audiovisual sophistication*: For some public relations firms, resources to capture include the skilled personnel and special facilities for satellite video transmissions and production of sophisticated film and video communications.

13. *Take advantage of creative stimuli*: As developed in the creativity chapter, counselors found advertising experts contribute to professional development workshops and infuse staff with stimuli for fresh approaches to campaign themes and message development.

How to Cultivate Cooperation and Confidence

Whether a public relations firm remains independent but joins advertising agencies in certain campaigns, is acquired by a company controlled by the advertising contingent or is involved in a formal partnership with an agency, it is useful for counselors to understand some of the strategies for cultivating cooperation and confidence. Some of the same principles may apply to building cooperation and confidence when two public relations firms merge—without any advertising agency involvement.

To cultivate cooperation and confidence on the advertising side of a relationship, counselors find it of value to become more oriented to bottom-line results rather than techniques, to take advantage of equivocality in the ways advertising agencies define public relations, to separate marketing and corporate public relations functions and to become more of an integral part of the marketing process.

Counselors position a public relations firm in a conglomerate through exemplary management, creation of profitable lines of new products and services, development of a common language, encouragement of joint agency-firm meetings and bringing together of branch operations into a unified whole.

Public relations firm executives learn that their advertising agency counterparts often respond warmly to help in gaining access to clients' senior executives, briefings on the plans of clients and efforts to better understand their discipline and business.

A number of misconceptions by advertising agency executives can be eliminated through public relations education. Similarly, education can help lay groundwork for the understanding of the finer points of counseling philosophy and methods. Counselors can learn in the advertising agencies' training programs and become part of the faculty for advertising personnel.

In the long run, counselors can have great impact on advertising agencies' thinking by educating the next generation of their management and working with business school curricula.

Several techniques help the two disciplines improve mutual understanding. Moreover, advertising agencies, themselves, can become clients of their own public relations subsidiaries. There also are opportunities to condition the advertising side of the house in order to build business together. Finally, it is advantageous for clients, as well as advertising-public relations relationships, to examine when it is best to work together or apart.

Here are some recommendations from public relations executives who are experts in several types of advertising affiliations:

1. *Become end-result vs. technique-oriented*: The chairman of Burson-Marsteller advocated "total communications" strategies in which "advertising and public relations can be coordinated to the client's advantages."[68]

Harold Burson's experience with advertising agencies predates his firm's merger with Young & Rubicam; it started in 1953 when he joined forces with Marsteller. His counsel:

Recognize that "advertising is a technique, public relations is a technique, merchandising is a technique, sales promotion is a technique. Bring them together and motivate people on what you want them to achieve. The client doesn't care how you do it, he just wants to see it get done; he's much more objectives oriented."

Anticipate that "the process of strict goal and objective orientation will increase as segmentations of audiences increase. Because we can pinpoint audiences better than we could 10 years ago with cable and research on interest groups, it's easier to identify segmentation than ever before."

This means "a lot of things are coming together increasingly to achieve objectives. Some clients are taking the lead in saying they don't want to look at what you do as advertising or public relations, but as problems and results and they're saying, 'You tell me what combination of disciplines should be brought to bear.' "

2. *Take advantage of equivocality in PR definition*: The vast leeway for interpreting what public relations actually is and what firms do is evidenced in the many, differing definitions that still exist. That uncertainty, however, can be used to advantage in broadening or deepening the public relations function. Burson said:

My experience is that we bring a broader understanding to the prob-

*lems than any of the other disciplines. Because public relations means
many things to many people, we do not have parameters that limit us
as an advertising agency is constrained. We're better positioned for a
holistic approach than other disciplines that are more narrowly defined. The broadness of the definition of "public relations" is an advantage. The equivocality in that definition serves to our advantage.*[69]

3. *Separate corporate and marketing functions*: Although the distinctions between advertising and public relations may be blurred at times,
Burson said "we have to separate corporate and marketing functions." This
may entail:

Helping the internal public relations officer who also has responsibility
for advertising see the differentiation of corporate function requirements
and the special role counseling firms can play in meeting them.

"Look at what the market is, particularly the enormous needs in which
we have not been traditionally involved, in which we can use our talents and thought processes." For example, Burson said "one of the greatest opportunities for motivation of people, productivity and reduction of
turnover is in employee relations, an area in which public relations
firms have not had as much of a role as they should."

"Look at what the market needs rather than what we have to sell. One
such area that is becoming a specialty is in working with companies in
self-generated cost-containment programs."[70]

4. *Become an integral part of marketing process*: In marketing, advertising agencies tend to be the dominant part of the process with public
relations providing support. But public relations can become integral to
marketing:

"To make ourselves more important in marketing, Burson-Marsteller
has gotten deeper into product promotion and merchandising. If public
relations is to bring about changes and motivate people through modification of attitudes to buy products, I see merchandising as a complementary tool."

Burson said his firm has never made any attempt to say that a client can
use public relations as a replacement for advertising, "only that we can
make the selling job more effective."[71]

5. *Position firm through exemplary management*: One way to build
confidence and cooperation within a megasized communications corporation is through exemplary management.

The goal should be "to become the best managed firm in the business,"
said Hill and Knowlton President Robert L. Dilenschneider. That includes

watching overhead and management of people plus producing a high volume of business.[72]

When the public relations component of a business excels in its managerial and financial strength and "when your people are of such a stripe as to have a real sense of their job," the Hill and Knowlton CEO said that neither they nor the integrity of public relations are about to be compromised. Dilenschneider stressed that such strength acts as an effective deterrent to threats to professional integrity and independence.

6. *Create new products, services*: The Hill and Knowlton CEO said that the profile of a public relations firm aggressively positioning itself in the marketplace, including the global market, builds confidence of top executives in a parent organization and "encourages investment of money to develop your new products."

For example, he said that Hill and Knowlton's marketing of health services "will add to the mix when we have a breakthrough" in providing "health care public relations all over the world with a sameness in all the different quantifiers of effectiveness and the strategies for product differentiation."[73]

7. *Develop a common language*: When advertising and public relations components of the same organization do not understand each other, the seeds for dissension are sown.

Dilenschneider recommended additional concentration be placed on not only "starting dialogues with the truth," but also "dealing with a sameness of language so everybody understands what everybody else means."[74] The initiative in developing that sameness would tend to fall to the public relations side because of its experience in implementing strategies for listening and interpretive communication.

8. *Encourage joint meetings*: For example, Hill and Knowlton and its parent company, J. Walter Thompson, initiated a program of monthly visits between senior account people of both organizations. In addition, whenever a major account is presented, joint strategy meetings, as well as joint presentations, are planned.

9. *Gain prestige, power through worldwide company*: Dilenschneider was speaking of strategies for unifying the offices of Hill and Knowlton around the world into a powerful whole, but the concept he described[75] also might be applied to position public relations in a coordinating function within the parent organization.

Even if restricted to just the public relations component, there is prestige and power to be gained within a conglomerate through the kind of unification advocated by Dilenschneider:[76]

"Until recently, we had offices around the world but they were more oriented towards local markets. . . . It was Hill and Knowlton, New York; Hill and Knowlton, Chicago; Hill and Knowlton, London . . . and we saw communication in local or regional terms, not in a worldwide perspective. . . . We realized that if we were going to grow as a company, we would have to regard our resources around the world as belonging to one company, not 56 separate offices. We realized that selling the world-wide services of one company rather than the individual services of discrete offices would give us the competitive edge needed."

"We are exchanging people worldwide to acquaint each office with the strengths of others."

"We have developed a strategic plan that lets us market on a worldwide basis."

"We have devised a concept called World-Net that ties together our people on the four continents in terms of the kind of marketing they do for the firm and clients."

"Today, offices around the world still cater to local clients. But . . . they are alert to the needs of other Hill and Knowlton clients around the world who have business to be done in their area and they are encouraging local clients who may be investing in other countries . . . to use Hill and Knowlton offices there."

10. *Help them develop senior executive access*: Counselors can build a deep reservoir of good will with their advertising counterparts by opening up access to client senior executives.

"Public relations people deal with a higher corporate level than the agency that owns them," Burger said. "This is key because advertising people have millions and millions of dollars riding on their proposals being approved by top decision makers."[77]

11. *Keep them briefed*: The same principle that works within any organization of assuring lateral, as well as vertical communication, may be especially important in a merger situation into which a traditionally misunderstood discipline is introduced.

"A very real peril is that they may be so frightened that some public relations person is not as well informed on the marketing segment and may do some ill advised thing that will jeopardize tens of millions of advertising dollars," Burger said[78] in illustrating the point that counselors should brief advertising executives, as well as elicit reciprocal exchanges.

Be sensitive to keeping them briefed on corporate problems. They don't normally get such intelligence in their channels from clients' advertising and marketing directors. Suppose a client is considering going to the equity market for more funding: It might be important to tell the advertising people privately. If there's a possible acquisition of the company or a federal regulatory problem coming up, it might make a strategic difference in advertising.[79]

It is implicit that trust begets trust and that sharing confidences that help other parts of the client team will tend to prompt reciprocity. Information, then, is exchanged on a perceived need-to-know basis by advertising and public relations. If a person in one discipline thinks of another as helpful, it's axiomatic that the other will tend to cooperate. But if a person perceives people on the other side of the house as competitors, they won't cooperate.

12. *Understand the advertising business*: Counsel reviewed earlier about the importance of understanding the client's business could be extended to learning about the advertising side of a communications conglomerate.

If the client CEO expects a counselor to thoroughly understand his business, it stands to reason that senior management of a parent advertising firm would expect similar knowledge from public relations persons who wish to play important roles in the early phases of researching and planning.

In the case of positioning oneself to counsel a client CEO, Burger said that "it's easy to find out through data bases what's happening in the industry or company."[80] It would be even easier to find out what's happening in the parent advertising agency.

13. *Earn respect through accountability*: Campbell, chairman of Continental Public Relations, said that one of the fastest growth areas in his firm results from the provision of marketing public relations services "as inevitable companions to advertising." But it is because of its increasing accountability that the Canadian firm has earned "growing respectability." That respectability has allowed public relations to become "a disciplined marketing function, a research-based, problem solving communications activity and an integral part of the marketing mix."[81]

14. *Take initiative in educating*: Counselors frequently recommend to client public relations staffs that they take the initiative in educating others in their organizations. In the case of public relations firms, themselves, there's additional reason for counselors to take the initiative:

"Since public relations people probably understand advertising better, and since public relations is basically an education process, it's up to us to take the initiative," according to Drobis of Ketchum Public Relations. In remarks at a workshop of the Association of American Advertising Agencies, he recommended that this education come to grips with:[82]

> The most common misconception among advertising people, the idea that public relations is one specific entity: "They need to know what PR isn't." He listed a number of public relations activities, preceding each one with the words, "It's not." Then Drobis made the point, "It's not any one of these because it's all of these."

The misconception that public relations is an adjunct to advertising:

"PR is a special independent communications method that requires special skills. It's not another form of advertising or sales promotion. It may share objectives when the three are part of a particular assignment, but it's not similar to, subordinate to or a replacement for advertising or sales promotion."

The misconception that one is better or more effective than the other: "The two techniques are used differently. Each has its specific advantage."

The misconception that professional separateness rules out in-house togetherness: Drobis offered as a "rule for peaceful co-existence" education in the concept of " 'We are a team.' It's a natural tendency for people to root for their immediate sector . . . but ad and PR people shouldn't compete for business. They shouldn't be resentful if the lion's share of a budget goes to one or the other. The main thing is that the agency got the business, not how that business is divided up within the agency."

15. *Teach other advantages of counseling*: Gerald Voros, who presides over Ketchum Communications, added several points to the lesson plan. These include such differences as:[83]

"While PR people also work for the client, they must work through a third party—the media. . . . PR people have to convince outsiders that the message is worth printing or broadcasting in a way that will not distort the message. They must be less direct and more attuned to the needs and mentalities of a whole group of people outside the agency or corporation. . . . The PR person must be more of a 'negotiator' if the client's message is to be delivered."

"The PR person can't always say what he wants to say in the firm manner in which he would prefer to say it. If his material is not compatible with the media, it will not be used. As a result, the PR writer often is an in-depth writer . . . who must weave his message into material that seeks audience impact over a long period of time."

"PR also provides a continuing long-term program for reaching target audiences through various media. . . . Even where short-term impact is desirable, the delivery of messages to large audiences on a multimedia basis over a period of time not only expands the audience . . . but also keeps the message working effectively for the client's benefit far beyond the normal life of most ads."

Counselors can design a series of events that give a marketer "the opportunity to touch people in ways advertising never can." Print and broadcast coverage of corporate supported events can also significantly increase the depth and frequency of marketing messages.

16. *Integrate education in agency's training program*: Barbara W. Hunter, former PRSA president, as well as president of Dudley-Anderson-Yutzy as it was acquired by Ogilvy & Mather, suggested that one way to do an effective educational job on public relations is to "plug it directly into the parent firm's training program for account management groups."[84]

17. *Become agency educator*: Schoonover went a step further by becoming a lead educator in the Ogilvy & Mather system for advertising-side personnel and client product managers.[85]

She visits various O&M offices and explains to advertising people what public relations can do in situations ranging from crises to corporate philosophy presentations.

"We have to be client advocates as well as educators," Schoonover said. "It's a matter of making sure that concerns we might see—issues or other problems of that kind—are presented. And, sure, sometimes there will be an argument with advertising people about whether their strategy is on target or not."

Demands for education within an agency account team may arise in a given situation. For example: "We may see some of the product advertising at cross-purposes with what should be the corporate stance and position."

One of the more important lessons that may have to be taught to others in a communications conglomerate is that "product messages can benefit if a corporation enjoys a good reputation. Counseling on corporate actions, as well as product promotion and publicity, can help build that image."

For example, advertising people can learn that "we get the best results for a product by linking it with benefits for the public."

"We have to help people make sure that the totality of the client is realized. With all the messages that are produced, all of us have to think in longer range terms on what's it all going to do for the company."[86]

18. *Educate next management generation*: Just as clients of counselors are advised to educate future consumers, stockholders and regulators before attitudes are crystallized, public relations executives may benefit from educating the next generation of advertising agency management.

Although the president of Creamer Dickson Basford feels comfortable with the orientation of the current generation of communications industry management, he is concerned with the future. "Sometimes I wonder what will happen when the next generation of management comes along. There has to be a building of understanding for the roles of public relations counselors and the respect that goes with that in developing the next generations of management in both disciplines," according to Kozikowski.[87]

19. *Work into business school curricula*: Young shared Kozikowski's concern and saw

the need to get into business school curricula some work on communication theory so managers understand what we're doing. Conversely, we need to influence communications schools to require students to take financial, marketing and management courses so they will understand more about the thinking of executives. Normal fears of people who come from different disciplines can be resolved by their learning about each other and working together when they're young.[88]

20. *Getting together is key to understanding*: Familiarity, according to the cliché, breeds contempt. According to the chairman emeritus of Bozell & Jacobs, familiarity between the disciplines can breed understanding, if managed well.[89]

"We have taken a position that is difficult, a position that Burson-Marsteller took through the years, that public relations should be very closely linked to advertising wherever possible in planning and development of strategic communication programs. There should be a lot of conversation and working together, a lot of sharing."

With this familiarity should come an understanding of each other's techniques and respect for each other's knowledge. Jacobs, however, said he saw situations in which "the advertising commission was huge, and the public relations fees smaller, and the advertising people sought to lord it over the public relations people. That won't work. We have insecure advertising people from time to time. If they're uncomfortable with public relations, they should resign."

"Absolute confidence" of public relations management is necessary to deal with insecurity or lack of understanding on the part of advertising people, he said. "To build their confidence and security, you better be damned good."

"Each office around the country is an individual profit center, but if that is all the manager is concerned about, he's a failure. Each office manager has to participate in national accounts that require regional and local service. We feel we're a cohesive organization and each manager's got to know about business in other parts of our organization."

21. *Win over as client*: Increasingly, counseling firms are winning the business of advertising agencies—including their own parent corporations—as clients.

Jean L. Farinelli, for example, decided that "if you really are going to win over your advertising colleagues, one of the best ways to win them over is as a client."[90]

After she became president of Dallas-based Tracy-Locke/BBDO Public

Relations, she researched a year's issues of *Advertising Week* and *Advertising Age* and performed content analysis measurements on the coverage of her parent advertising agency and its competitors. She went beyond numbers of stories and column inches to the tone and substance of coverage of such topical areas as accounts, people and campaigns. At the same time, she analyzed industry trends.

Then she interviewed the heads of the agency's media, research and creative departments before holding a group session with three of the top advertising people. "That was my version of a focus group. I wanted to know how they thought the business was going, how they felt they were perceived and how they wanted to be perceived."

She also did an analysis of news releases about the advertising agency and explored opportunities for stories to mesh with the needs and objectives of its executives.

The next step was to follow through with interviews of account executives preparatory to developing her proposal for the president of the advertising agency. She won the account.

And she educated her advertising colleagues as she, herself, was educated. This helped her get invited into agency new-business strategy sessions and client presentations.

22. *Build for reciprocity*: The president of Geneva Marketing Services recommended a public relations campaign to build for reciprocity in business leads and other support. Hoods offered several suggestions:[91]

"One very easy and good way to get attention of advertising people is to come to them with new advertising business opportunities. You come to them with a good public relations client who is ready to select an advertising agency."

Another way to build good will leading to reciprocal help is "to walk in the door with a pragmatic, profitable new-business idea for advertising."

A third way is to propose joint presentations for prospects who need both public relations and advertising representation. "If public relations and advertising are in at the very beginning of a new-business conquest, then you would be thought of as part of the team that brought in the new business."

Hoods recommended increased visibility among advertising people, "including taking an active part in the social side of their business," such as offering to help with their internal special events.[92]

Other modes might include becoming involved in the same civic organizations or public causes that attract the agency's executives or attending professional advertising organization functions.

23. *Analyze interdisciplinary potential*: Counselors may find it advantageous to analyze interdisciplinary potentials, focusing on the pros and cons in different types of situations.

For example, the president of Diversified Communications Inc. of Findlay, Ohio, has questioned some of the attitudes toward interdisciplinary involvement of advertising and public relations:[93]

"This may border on heresy," Little said, "but to draw too narrow boxes around advertising, public relations and sales promotions processes at a medium-sized company can be dangerous. Each brings something special to the communication process, from listening through research to telling the client's story.

> *I think that people need to be aware of disciplines and how they work individually and in interaction. From the counselor's side, it's important that you don't try to sell public relations when they need advertising or vice versa. That takes a lot of self-discipline. We're not only counselors but also business people. You earn a position of trust with these people and have a big responsibility to them as their counselor.*[94]

That orientation to professional responsibility, however, did not appear heretical at all based on field research with more than 200 executives of counseling firms. It seemed to fit with the ethic of an emerging profession.

10

BUILDING PROFESSIONALISM

Perhaps the greatest factors in the market development, growth and alliances of firms relate directly to the struggle of counselors to move from a traditionally service-dominated discipline toward more creative, research-based, client-objectives-oriented counseling.

To that struggle, thousands of individual counselors and their firms have contributed varying measures of substance. The emergence of professional alliances such as the Counselors Academy has propelled that struggle to a new and higher level.

Public relations counselors are not professionals in the *classic* sense. Instead, they are members of what may be called an emerging profession. As such, they tend to concentrate more on looking to change than on reinforcing traditions.

This chapter looks at professionalism as a goal and at the role played by the Counselors Academy and other professional organizations. It acknowledges that those counselors whose vision includes growth and increased sophistication of the business must be professional in their development of the discipline's future.

PROFESSIONAL STATURE AS A GOAL

A fundamental, salient question is not whether public relations counseling is a profession in the classic sense, but whether counselors deliver service characteristic of professionals.

For example, Loet A. Velmans, chairman of Hill and Knowlton through 1986, cited the challenge to counselors in the marketplace from legal and management consulting firms and said "the future means a continued emphasis on the kinds of in-depth, quality service that marks 'a profession.' The key here is education and training."[1]

318

The Quest for Professionalism

Professional Legitimacy   Some say that a counselor can be a professional
without being a member of a profession because "profession" has a meaning of its own. Regardless of the semantics, regardless of the standards for
defining "professional" and "profession," public relations counselors are
engaged in the quest for professionalism.

That quest is essential in elevating perspectives of corporate and institutional executives on the services they can buy; attracting to counseling
careers well-qualified young persons in an increasingly competitive market; raising the caliber of public relations with the media, government
leaders and other important publics and strengthening the self-image so
important in the delivery of quality service and in the reaching of individuals to attain more.

Integral to the quest for professionalism is achievement—and
recognition—of professional legitimacy. Harold Burson, chairman and
CEO of Burson-Marsteller, supported this concept and said there has been
substantial progress:[2]

> Public relations has a legitimacy today that it has not had in the past.
> Along with the law and accounting, that professionalism reputation is
> likely to increase. As time goes on, more companies will have the same
> feelings of pride about their public relations firms as they do about the
> legal and accounting firms that represent them.
>
> Public relations is a tool of which a CEO can avail himself. Just as he
> gets up at an annual meeting and says, "I want the best legal or ac-
> counting source I can have," he will tend to look to public relations
> firms as resources to cite to his board.

Although he shared with Velmans a dedication to education and training
in building that professional quality of service, Burson seemed most concerned with the future ability of counseling "to attract good people with
high intelligence, emotional stability, motivation and initiative."

Those qualities are needed for "the advice part of the business," that the
Burson-Marsteller chairman said is "limited only by the ability of the
counseling firms and individuals. You start getting a blending of where
public relations stops and management begins. That's where public relations is heading."

Cynicism May Impair Professional Self-Image

While some counseling leaders hesitate before using the term *professional*
to mean something more than quality of service and individuals, others
seem to shrink from using the word in any relationship with public relations.

Perhaps part of their motivation is to avoid inflating the status of public relations. And, yet, there seems to have been a trendy cynicism at work among some individuals, a sarcastic perspective that may date back to journalistic roots, a defensive cynicism that belittles the tremendous strides taken by counselors lest they be disparaged by other practitioners.

Differing Views—From "Pompous Labels" to "Emerging Profession"
Counselors are not monolithic in their thinking on the topic. Even the co-authors of this book differ in their views of where counseling falls on the spectrum of professionalism. *Public Relations Quarterly* cited the following by Truitt as one of the viewpoints on the credentials of public relations:[3]

> It's about time that we shed the presumptions and abandon the inappropriate and pompous labels that so many in our craft have promoted for so long. The thought that a public relations practitioner should be called a professional . . . is simply the illusion of those who would build the business by affixing terms of endearment rather than training for quality and respect.
>
> Public relations practitioners are not professionals. We are not like doctors or lawyers or accountants. We are not supported by massive libraries or by a strong body of knowledge. . . . We look hard at the present and thoughtfully into the future, unlike those bona-fide professionals who must, by ethical obligation, look first to the past. . . . Public relations is a great business and a fascinating craft. It is not likely, however, that we ever could achieve recognition as professionals. . . .

Others, however, feel public relations is an emerging profession, and they base their thoughts upon several criteria for professional designation, as presented by Nager at a 1986 PRSA leadership meeting:[4]

1. *Significant body of knowledge:*

> If you take a purist attitude, we can't touch law's or medicine's centuries-old amassing of tomes. Instead, we have borrowed liberally from business and the social sciences. But doesn't that enrich us? We have a significant body of knowledge that encompasses the sciences of business administration, economics, psychology, sociology, organizational communication, mass communication, philosophy. . . .

2. *Breadth, depth and quality of research:*

> The researchers in counseling firms, corporations and institutions, and in academe have really just begun in the past few decades to do serious work worthy of the designation of professional research. But we have begun. And if we have to place a qualifier in front of the word "profession" such as primitive, young or emerging, so be it.

3. *Enforceable code of ethics*:

Unlike some in journalism and other would-be professions, by God, we actually have the machinery and the provisions for enforcement. We do need to get down to crystal-clear definitions that are open to no misinterpretation or waffling on exactly what we mean in the provisions. We do need to do a much better job in communicating to people outside their professional organizations what that code entails. Most important, we have not yet extended the reach of the code to enforce it on non-members.

4. *Formalized education system*:

We do have accreditation. We had the Bateman-Cutlip commission to develop curriculum guidelines for undergraduates. We've had the Alvarez-Hesse commission on graduate education. And we now have the Plank-Ehling commission, the first to represent the several major professional organizations and member educators in business, marketing, speech communications and mass communications. We still have weaknesses, but we're working on them.

5. *Public service and social responsibility*:

A roster of professional public relations association members documenting their voluntary involvement in civic, social, environmental, charitable, cultural and other causes and organizations would tend to show far greater commitment than could be found in many of the established professions.

6. *Control on designation as members*:

We do not do this. We have individual accreditation examinations and screenings in several of our professional associations. We even are exploring in some of our organizations second-tier accreditation, a requirement for continuing education credits after becoming accredited.

7. *Passion for improvement*:

A true profession is branded clearly by the passion its members evidence for upgrading their calling. The attention given professionalism by the national and local bodies within public relations is symptomatic of that passion. Let's take a positive perspective and concentrate on how this business might continue to advance to best serve the interests of its members and society without worrying about mimicking law or medicine, two other imperfect professions.

"Thank God we do not have the same degree of 'professionalization' as law or medicine," said Timothy V. Conner, executive vice president-worldwide creative director for Hill and Knowlton.[5]

"Let's stop apologizing for what we do for a living and for those who don't live up to our standards. The only way is to have a majority earn respect with their performance. Learn the business—not your own business, but your client's business—and earn your way on the board."

Building Identity and Professional Pride

A Time for Professional Identity   More than performance and learning may be needed to earn respect and position counselors with client executives and boards. In counseling their own clients, public relations persons have found value in designing campaigns to build identity and instill pride. What works for the client also may work for the counselor.

Consultant F. John Pessolano, for instance, made a plea for identity of the calling of counseling:[6]

> In our history, we have entertained nothing of the rational dialogue that must precede our transition from trade to skilled craft to whatever stature, recognition and authority we keep saying we want and may some day deserve. Perhaps we're too young to have done it all already; but there is nothing, except perhaps inertia, to keep us from making a start, and to keep at it until we know who we are, what we know and what we do, collectively as a profession.
>
> You see, we have no identity, even among ourselves. How can we hope to project a unified identity to the outside? We are beginning, but only beginning, to raise some of the questions to which we need consensus about identity; mission and purpose; methodology, talent, and skill; domain and structure.

Pessolano presented this challenge:

> Do we owe our primary loyalty to the organization, to a professional discipline, or the society at large? If we are mechanics, turning the valves that route whatever our employers want said and whatever conscience they have into the pipelines at the right times, then I don't suppose it makes any difference. But if we are managers of relationships, then it makes a great deal of difference and imposes heavy responsibilities on how we apply that knowledge, to what ends and with what effects on society.

Professional identity is important not only to counselors and the practice of public relations, but also to client executives. This is supported by the research of Judy van Slyke Turk, 1986–1987 head of the Public Relations Division of the Association for Education in Journalism and Mass Communications:[7]

"Public relations is faced with an inescapable ambiguity: defining or describing just what it is. Perhaps that crisis of identity can be overcome, or a least minimized, if we accept the possibility that it can become a mature and effective science."

She said:

> A would-be profession can be recognized as a profession only by common consent of both those within and outside the field. If public relations is to be defined as a profession, it must therefore have followed the path of other skills—law, medicine, accounting, which have been transformed into professions by convincing clients that those services are indispensable to survival and success.

Research indicated that clients and counselors remain uncertain "about the legitimacy of public relations' professional claims, and the field is only on the threshold of gaining professional status."

A Time to Instill Professional Pride   In established professions, such as law and medicine, one common characteristic is professional pride. The founder of Chicago's Daniel J. Edelman Inc. said professional pride serves as a key to success. "Let's eliminate the hangdog feeling about being in public relations. We're no longer second-class citizens, if we ever really were," he said.[8]

In a *Public Relations Review* article, the former Counselors Academy chairman wrote, "we're in a *real* profession. We do make a tangible contribution." He called upon his colleagues as professional counselors to take a leadership position in instilling that pride.

> The potential of our contributions to our clients' future—and hence to our own—is vast. We provide critical support in a wide variety of ways that significantly affect the success, growth and public understanding and acceptance of our clients' policies, their products and their actions. We are leaders in helping clients make decisions that will determine how they will fare in the public interest and the public mind.

Edelman also said: "And as we succeed in firming up our primary role, let's be sure we also get across the point that our services are worth fees commensurate with those paid to these other professional services."

Building Professional Responsibility

More Than Enunciating Lofty Principles   Identity and pride are built upon the bedrock of professional responsibility. That translates into social responsibility combined with a dedication to principles inherent in the long-established professions. And that requires well planned follow-through on principles enunciated in professional society bylaws, speeches and books but occasionally overlooked in practice.

Patrick Jackson, for example, agreed with Edelman that counseling is a

profession. But the senior counsel of Jackson, Jackson & Wagner of Exeter,
N.H., and past president of PRSA recognized a difference between accepting principles and following through on them:[9]

"Practitioners know the power—and the social responsibility—of our
profession. The barrier has been in applying these lofty principles to daily
practice in hospitals, schools, corporations, governments and associations."

Among his predictions for those who do follow through and "who can
influence the policies and actions of our organizations in the direction of
public relations philosophy," Jackson included:

1. *Raising our sights*: "Topical issues like whether public relations is a
profession or a vocation are insignificant beside one seminal query: 'Do I
truly believe this field has an underlying body of knowledge based in the
behavioral sciences and the humanities? More to the point, am I able to
apply it to my work?'"

2. *Learning without end*: "The body of knowledge grows so fast that
continuing education has become a necessity." Among topics to be studied
for new product development are organizational development, policy sciences, arbitration, visual literacy and graphic psychology, futures forecasting and strategic planning.

3. *Embracing research*: "We will master informal research techniques as
well as using the blind statistical sample."

4. *Becoming managers of change*: Jackson interpreted this as "no more
reactively apologizing, but proactively gaining approval of plans that anticipate issues and events."

5. *Presenting options*: "I think" will give way to "Here are the options."

6. *Building consensus*: "Building public relationships has no room for
victor and vanquished because losers rise again. We will seek consensus or
at least compromise."

7. *Listening vs. telling*: "Learning to trust the people means less telling
them what's best for them, more listening to what they really expect of
our organizations. Participation is basic to the public relations philosophy."

8. *Emphasizing policy, not publicity*: "We'll recognize the lack of power
of publicity in dealing with most public relations problems. Then we'll
stop expecting the media to do our job for us. We'll get out there and build
relationships, not one-way communications."

Necessity Demands Professional Actions Actually, despite myths to the
contrary, public relations practice has not been held in low regard compared to such institutions of society as the media. Both disciplines have
found that necessity dictates professional action to command high public
esteem.

As far back as the Watergate era, public opinion surveys concluded that public relations was regarded more favorably than advertising and in about the same measure of esteem as journalism.

James F. Fox, chairman of New York's Fox Public Relations and former national president of PRSA, traced criticism of the sources of communications to "frequently irrational" critics, problems of defining public relations, misunderstandings by outsiders or neophytes of the roles of public relations beyond publicity and incompetence of some in the field."[10]

He saw a combination of PRSA's Code of Professional Standards and the public's own "social code" as giving incentives and exerting pressures to induce higher levels of ethical behavior.

Michael Campbell, chairman and CEO of Toronto's Continental Public Relations, said that "by 1990, practitioners will—out of necessity—act in a more professional manner." He said this will require several actions:[11]

"Industry associations will have to police members far more aggressively. Standards will be more clearly defined. Guidelines for acceptable practice will be more widely recognized. Public relations as a discipline will be forced to disassociate itself from activities which degrade its status."

Similarly, another opinion leader in counseling stressed action over the trappings of professionalism. The public relations firm principal told an interviewer, "Behavior on the part of some of the so-called 'professional' people could use a good scrubbing."[12]

One of the more important parts of professionalism applies to ethics. He said it is not enough for PRSA to have an enforceable code of ethics: "Each section, including the Counselors Academy, should have its own code and be doing its own policing." He recommended "even stiffer" provisions and policing within specialized areas.

"Sometimes when a person or group is not looked upon as they would like to be, it suggests they have to act more professionally. Often you have to act more professionally than any other profession if you want a better chance of attaining that status," he said.

Donald K. Wright, the researcher who organized the 1986 and earlier PRSA National Conference professional development programs, said that results of international surveys suggest "we should measure factors such as responsibility and ethics in terms of individual practitioners rather than occupations or professions."[13]

He said that the emphasis on whether individuals are responsible holds as true for physicians, clergy, lawyers, journalists, teachers and accountants as it does for public relations practitioners. "What this all means to us essentially is that public relations will never be any more ethical or responsible than the level of basic morality and responsible behavior of the people who work in our occupation."

Research found "relative high levels of social responsibility thinking and moral value judgments exist among the people who practice in our field" compared to other occupations. "It appears we're as decent, moral and ethical as the rest of our society."

In research done in 1985 with 105 U.S. and 104 Canadian practitioners, Wright isolated factors that "clearly have significant impact upon moral values of public relations people." They include social responsibility and five types of morality: basic, socioeconomic, religious, puritanical and financial.[14]

Perhaps among the morality factors may lie an explanation of the traditional restrictions counselors seem to place on their practice. For instance, Davis Young, former Counselors Academy chairman and president of Cleveland's Young-Liggett-Stashower Public Relations, said some counselors are "highly prone to almost an inferiority complex" and are "very defensive."[15]

What makes public relations' ethical responsibility different from that of other callings is that "our responsibility is based on the fact that significant numbers of people make important decisions because of what we do and say," Young said.[16]

"The only real objective of a communications program is to enhance trust—trust in a product, trust in a service, trust in the integrity of a company, trust in its qualities and its service. Public relations is a business. It is not a profession. It can, however, be a business practiced with professional standards."

To achieve professional recognition while moving more into strategic thinking and management counseling, the practice may have to stretch and grow intellectually.

New North American Joint Initiatives

Public Relations Council Unites 30,000 to Advance Discipline That growth process together with the achievement of professional recognition and other professional goals must rely on more than the efforts of a single individual or firm. It takes a collective strength and sustained campaign—perhaps to the point of crusade.

That kind of strength and campaign was envisioned by the founders of a new North American alliance. In 1986, a Counselors Academy member who previously served as president of the Canadian Public Relations Society galvanized a dozen organizations representing more than 30,000 practitioners. Luc Beauregard, council president, led an alliance representing:

Public Relations Society of America

Canadian Public Relations Society

American Society of Hospital Marketing and Public Relations

Agricultural Relations Council

National School Public Relations Association

Religious Public Relations Council

Baptist Public Relations Association

Texas Public Relations Association

Florida Public Relations Association

Southern Public Relations Federation

Women in Communications Inc.

Council for the Advancement and Support of Education

International Association of Business Communicators

"We should take steps to have public relations become recognized as a profession in all jurisdictions," said Beauregard, president of Montreal's Beauregard, Hutchinson, McCoy, Capistran, Lamarre et Associés. By "all jurisdictions," he meant not only among the ranks of member organizations but, particularly, among other professional groups and in the executive suite.[17]

"Certainly, we want to increase the impact of the public relations discipline in management's decision-making process." The steps to gain recognition "would reinforce the importance of public relations among members of management teams" as well as with lawyers, financial specialists and other professional disciplines.

Those steps were initiated on three fronts:

1. *Definition of public relations*: He said the council would seek to gain consensus on a common definition of public relations.

A model that had strong support in 1986 was the statement endorsed a few years earlier by the PRSA National Assembly:[18]

Public relations helps our complex, pluralistic society to reach decisions and function more effectively by contributing to mutual understanding among groups and institutions. It serves to bring private and public policies into harmony.

Public relations serves a wide variety of institutions in society such as business, trade unions, government agencies, voluntary associations, foundations, hospitals and educational and religious institutions. To achieve their goals, these institutions must develop effective relationships with many different audiences or publics such as employees, members, customers, local communities, shareholders and other institutions, and with society at large.

The managements of institutions need to understand the attitudes and values of their publics in order to achieve institutional goals. The goals themselves are shaped by the external environment. The public relations practitioner acts as a counselor to management, and as a mediator, helping to translate private aims into reasonable, publicly acceptable policy and action.

As a management function, public relations encompasses the following:

> *Anticipating, analyzing and interpreting public opinion, attitudes and issues which impact, for good or ill, on the operations and plans of the organization.*

> *Counseling management at all levels in the organization with regard to policy decisions, courses of action and communication, taking into account their public ramifications and the organization's social or citizenship responsibilities.*

> *Researching, conducting and evaluating, on a continuing basis, programs of action and communication to achieve informed public understanding necessary to the success of an organization's aims. These may include marketing, financial, fund raising, employee, community or government relations and other programs.*

> *Planning and implementing the organization's efforts to influence or change public policy.*

> *Setting objectives, planning, budgeting, recruiting and training staff, developing facilities—in short, managing the resources needed to perform all of the above. . . .*

2. *Code of ethics*: Although most of the council's member organizations have codes of ethics, "what we're trying to achieve is a basic code upon which any organization could expand for its own needs," Beauregard said. Such a basic code would consist of a number of short, simply stated ethical prescriptions.[19]

3. *Accreditation*: Even before the council emerged, PRSA and CPRS had bilateral agreements that recognized each other's accreditation of members. The council's goal was to establish a joint program or some common requirements for individuals to be accredited.

"I have the feeling we have only a few years in which to make the decision on whether to go the professional route. If we hesitate, other factors will evolve and may take control." Among these factors, he mentioned pressures of the advertising discipline and national and local governmental bodies.

> *We have the elements now of what can be turned into a profession. We have 40 to 75 years' experience. We have a certain body of knowledge. We are involved in programs about which the public interest is at the focal point.*

> *Now is the time to move in that direction. It can't be done overnight. We're talking about a process that will probably take 10 to 15 years.*

Canadian Consultants Institute Teams with Counselors Academy   Before the
1986 North American alliance initiative, PRSA and CPRS and the Consultants Institute of Canada and the Counselors Academy already had
established close relations to encourage involvement in each other's professional development activities.

Beauregard, who presided over CPRS in 1984 and 1985, stressed that he
wanted to retain Canadian identity for both the Society and the Institute.[20]
"We have sought strong relationships with PRSA and the Counselors
Academy, and that has proven fruitful. We look forward to strengthening
the links."

In addition to recognizing each other's accreditation, the Americans and
Canadians exchange publications at reduced rates, attend each other's conferences and share professional development materials.

National identity does not deter practitioners from holding joint mem-
berships. "The strategy behind belonging to the Counselors Academy as
well as the Consultants Institute is to know what's going on in the other
nation's professional development" and to allow for "crossfertilization of
concepts and ideas," Beauregard said.

He brings a perspective from counseling relationships with such professional organizations as the Canadian Bar Association, Canadian Association of Management Consultants and Quebec Federation of General
Practitioners. As he sees it, the fundamental reason for the existence of
any professional association is: "They should be there to serve public
interest and protect the public."[21]

When Public and Private Interests Coincide

Public Relations, as Other Callings, Must Be Janus-Faced   The Roman god
Janus is characterized as having two faces, each looking in a different
direction. In a sense, a professional organization—public relations, medical, dental, legal, accounting, management, educational—is Janus-faced.
One face looks to the interests of the publics to which it is dedicated. The
other looks to the concerns of the organization and its members.

To serve the interests of their publics, members require more than
ideals; they require know-how and capabilities. Moreover, they need to
attract and retain strong practitioners, develop and update professional
skills, keep up with knowledge in business and technology and do such
fundamental things as meet payrolls, pay for office space and equipment
and cover the bills of vendors.

Survival is the ultimate objective of any organization, professional, trade
or blue-collar. Survival enables a higher order of life and service to others.
That is inherent in Abraham Maslow's hierarchy of needs. Maslow's theo-

ries said that humans move up a ladder from basic wants to more selfless motives.[22]

A professional organization such as PRSA, CPRS, IABC, Consultants Institute or Counselors Academy does not meet one level of needs at a time before proceeding to the next, but actually cuts across the various kinds of human motivations in its various programs.

The complexity within an individual member's physiological, business and psychological needs is such that an organization may have to fulfill many roles for the same person. Multiply that by the number and diversity of its members, and the Janus-faced analogy may be too simple to capture the essence of the professional organization.

PRSA and Other Organizations Meet Special Needs   Public relations organizations such as PRSA, parent organization of the Counselors Academy, meet special needs. Paul H. Alvarez, chairman of Ketchum Public Relations and past head of the Counselors Academy, said "the Academy leadership has been very much in support of PRSA and its objectives. PRSA has dramatically strengthened its programs and membership services. We carry some weight with PRSA and enjoy the respect of their leaders."[23]

Dwayne Summar, the counselor elected to lead the Society in 1988, said "PRSA has provided the vehicle for the Counselors Academy and other sections to exist." It has given them the strength, unity and backup resources to be "more than massive clubs." According to the senior counsel of Miami's Robinson & Weskel Communications, PRSA's "whole purpose is to meet needs of aspiring professionals."[24]

Among the largest areas of need he identified are professional development, networking, ethics and strengthening the reputation of PRSA and its members. In regard to reputation, Summar said "the best thing we can do as a society is to practice what we preach." Beyond that, he called for educating people outside the practice.

"Let client executives know the contributions public relations can make. Draw attention to the profession as it should be so they'll be better able to recognize the difference. We have got to let the publics know public relations is serving their interests."

Another mission is to help close the trust gap between media and organizations they cover.

Management has to be educated to shortfalls on the part of the media, and media have to be educated about the fear of organizations of being mistreated because of incompetence or lack of fairness in reporting. The public relations person can help bridge that gap by teaching corporate executives about the media and by educating the media about corporations.

THE ACADEMY'S CONTRIBUTION

Networking for Profits, Ideas, Camaraderie

One of the principal membership benefits of the Counselors Academy has been to find new perspectives that help organize and manage public relations firms more effectively and profitably. This results from informal networking as well as from highly organized programs.

Idea Makes Member Hundreds of Thousands of Dollars   It is by way of the Academy's informal networking that counselors have derived measurable business advantages.

"The Academy is the only game in town for exchange of ideas, problem solving, management assistance. It's probably been the one thing that's kept me linked into PRSA," a member told an interviewer. "The greatest value for my dues has been in allowing me to belong to the Academy; that's worth every nickel I've ever spent on PRSA. Anything else I got— the *Journal*, local meetings, national conferences and the like—was icing on the cake."[25]

"For less than $20 per month I get about $2,000 a month in information that's helpful to me." The member, a consultancy principal, cited one example of an idea that produced six-figure savings for his firm:

He was attending an Academy conference social function and sat next to Daniel Edelman. "I asked Dan how a technique worked. He told me. It made us hundreds of thousands of dollars." Although he called the technique "simple," he said "it paid for my dues in PRSA and the Academy thousands of times over." The technique had to do with cancellation clauses in letters of agreement.

"If I come away with one good idea from each session, it's worth 50 times the cost of admission. I never leave a Counselors Academy meeting without at least one good idea that helped in my business and in my professional life."

Networking Provides Place to Be Heard and to Gain Ideas   If networking is to serve the interests of an organization it must be of value to members, ranging from a place to be heard to pragmatic insights that can be used on the job. The Counselors Academy has done that well enough to expand its horizons overseas.

The 1987 chairman of the Counselors Academy, the founder of Miami's Bruce Rubin Associates, said "the networking aspect is one of many tangible benefits of Academy membership that, when added all together, make it truly hard for me to conceive of functioning as a professional without that kind of backing."[26]

Rubin said he sees the Academy becoming more of an international organization by the mid-1990s. "I see us interfacing with British counselors now; that will lead us into Europe. Counselors from around the world say we've got the best organization in the world by far. The Academy can take a worldwide leadership position in counseling."

He said that it should be regarded as "a basics group—whenever we get together, we talk the basics of doing business. There's a willingness to share. It's a refuge where senior counselors interface with each other without having to be 'on,' where you can be yourself.

"It's one of the few environments into which you can go and come back to your office the next day and implement ideas. We're not an esoteric association, but a pragmatic organization."

Michael V. Sullivan, chairman of Harris, Baio & Sullivan of Doylestown, Pa., called networking "extremely valuable, probably the biggest service the Academy has."[27]

The 1986–1987 member of the Academy's executive committee said: "The Academy is the best place for counselors to come together to benefit from the interaction in what is essentially a small group and to have some effect on where the profession is going. Somebody once said the future is inventable. If you want to have a voice in where the profession will be, this is a great place to be heard."

Business relationships and professional friendships form readily. "Associations built through Academy meetings make it possible to go back to the office and call up 10, 12, 15 people and ask each the same question—and they will answer the question," according to Sullivan.

There is an openness and willingness to share information, that is a mark of a profession. The openness is fed by a sense of professionalism, whether we are a profession or not. We certainly have the sense of it, the sense of doing something good for the practice, the profession. It's not an altruism exactly, but certainly a feeling that "if I open my feelings on this and bounce my ideas off other people, everybody will benefit."

He said "the return on our investment is outstanding. I always go to each conference with a set of questions, quite apart from whatever's on the program as part of the meeting theme."

For example, he remembered his first spring conference when he wanted insight into the best size of firm to build. "I talked to 15 people and came away with a real good understanding, a new business venture, a business relationship with another counselor and nice relationships with people I liked and respected."

At conferences, members place greatest value on mind stimulation. "I'd call it 60-40 in favor of stimulus of mind over information. It's stimulating in the sense of discussing common problems and getting divergent views from people who face the same kinds of questions I do and who are willing to share their information."

A special strength of networking lies in making possible interactions among a diversity of counselors. Another is in the cumulative impact on the practice of counseling. "Through the years, the Counselors Academy has provided an umbrella under which have stood sole practitioners and chief executive officers of giant, multinational firms," Young said.[28]

For a quarter of a century, we have been committed to the principle that a single public relations counselor in a small community and with a tiny client roster renders services every bit as important as any professional in a large firm in a major city. These men and women have shown through words and deeds that public relations counseling can be pursued with both ingenuity and integrity.

Special Resources for Firm Management

Source of Data on Fees, Taxes, Legal Interpretations   Whatever their motives, members of the Counselors Academy pool and share information in the interests of their own and each other's practices. This includes facts and experience concerning fees and compensation, state tax legislation alerts and legal interpretations.

In pursuit of effective firm management, counselors have shared:

1. *Fees and compensation intelligence*: Nearly 400 Academy members participated in a recent study of client fee structures and formulas for staff compensation.

2. *Directory of membership*: Annually the Academy distributes to members a directory designed for ready use in helping them get in touch with their colleagues.

3. *State tax legislation*: As legislators in some states have begun to look at counseling services as commodities for applying sales taxes or at public relations firms as possible sources of licensing fees, the Academy has served as an information repository and provided alerts through its newsletters and forums so members could mobilize efforts to table or kill such bills.

4. *Litigation risks*: As the nation's courts and government regulatory agencies have moved in new directions that pose additional legal risks for counselors, the Academy has brought in experts to share intelligence on how to reduce the dangers or respond to actions brought against public relations firms. For example, the Academy sponsored a session on "How To Protect Yourself and Your Client" at the 1985 National PRSA Conference and then reviewed the counsel of legal experts in a 1986 issue of *The Counselor*.[29]

5. *Job descriptions*: As part of his agenda for 1986, Academy Chairman Joe S. Epley launched a study aimed at producing "clear definition of job descriptions within public relations firms."[30]

He explained that "we should have a clear definition of what each of these jobs are, and what level of expertise is required for the job title. For example, in the 1985 fee and compensation report, some folks call themselves account executives, some account managers, some account supervisors. What's the distinction?"

Consensus on job descriptions would be useful to clients who want to know what level of service they're getting when promised services by different grades of professionals. It also would help those who are appointed to positions to better understand what their job entails and what qualifications they need in order to advance.

Monographs Help Counselors Improve Management The Counselors Academy has commissioned its members and outside specialists to write dozens of monographs.

In-depth, focused and well-documented monographs provide desk-top references and complement spring and fall national conferences, meetings of local PRSA counselor groups and monthly newsletters in providing members the intelligence and stimulation for improving the state of the art. Here are sample titles of Academy monographs:

The Management of a Public Relations Firm, Chester Burger

Computerizing the Counseling Organization, Bob Dorf

New Business Acquisition, Dana T. Hughes

Time Accounting for Public Relations Firms, Joe S. Epley

Creativity and Public Relations, Donald MacKinnon

Fees and Compensation (periodic survey results)

How to Make More from Your Money, Sidney Jarrow

Controlling Group Insurance Costs, David L. Glueck

Strategic Planning for Your Firm, Jacob L. Engle

Public Relations Practice and the Law, Theodore Baron

Issues Management: PR Comes of Age, Raymond P. Ewing

Other topics addressed by monographs include various aspects of financial relations, public affairs, international public relations, recruitment and retention of personnel, professional development, operating smaller and medium-sized businesses and productivity.

Survey of 1,500 Puts Management First A survey of 1,500 public relations professionals and educators has demonstrated a shift in emphasis on what future practitioners need to learn to manage effectively, it was reported by the Commission on Undergraduate Public Relations Education.[31]

The commission presented the following ranking:

1. Management
2. Research
3. Accountability
4. Technology

Although all planning topics rated high, the commission survey found that "setting goals, objectives, strategies and tactics" came in first by a wide margin.

PR Reporter editor Patrick Jackson commented that educational guidelines are useful for professional development and "all of us need to be retreaded continually."

Academy Presents Annual Professional Management School   One way of improving upon the state of the art involves going back to school. The Counselors Academy has developed its own school where members go for new knowledge rather than for refurbishment.

In October 1986, the Academy programmed its second annual "Professional Management School (PMS) for Senior Executives and Profit Center Managers in the Public Relations Industry," a week-long, intensive postgraduate course developed by a former professor of the Harvard Business School.

In inviting members to the first program, Alvarez noted that "this is hard-nosed professional training in state-of-the-art management. If you are part of a large firm, and you have profit center responsibility, the techniques and insights will enable you to manage your operations more efficiently, more effectively and more profitably."[32]

It also was designed to prepare individuals who are in line to "take over a profit center or firm to accept profit responsibility and perform with a sureness that comes from knowledge and training."

David Maister, researcher and consultant specializing in professional firm management, organized the first PMS at Princeton for 30 counselors who paid a tuition of $2,990 for the five-day program.

He brought in as additional faculty Harvard's Jeffrey Sonnenfeld, a specialist in human resources management and researcher in corporate public affairs management; McGill University's MBA Dean Roger Bennett, a specialist in marketing and executive training; and Christopher Lovelock, a former Harvard professor with specialization in the marketing of professional services.

Maister augmented the course with expert panels, including one consisting of client and counseling firm executives. In what may be an enduring model for the PMS, the curriculum dealt with issues affecting a firm's marketing strategy, economics, personnel and ownership structure and covered such topics as:

Market positioning—focusing on segmentation of the public relations marketplace and distinctions between selling a firm's expertness, experience and ability to execute programs

Client service—management practices to ensure client satisfaction with the quality of service

Branch-office management—including questions about when to open new branches, deciding between full-service or partial-service offices and determining how to account for branch profitability

Economics—forces that determine firm profitability and new ways of analyzing, tracking and managing performance

Balancing a firm—covering interaction among a firm's economic structure, market position, organizational structure and ability to attract talent to compete in critical markets for new clients

Motivating professionals to increase productivity

Building human capital to raise a firm's stock of skills, abilities and talents

Meaning of partnership—focusing on alternatives for rewarding senior professionals, such as allocation of profit shares

Financial aspects of ownership transition—how to value a firm and its equity and alternatives to buying and selling partnership and ownership positions

Leadership aspects of ownership transition—identification and development of leadership skills

Sullivan, who headed professional development for the Academy when the PMS started, said "it is necessary for us to professionalize the management function of our firms" to keep abreast of changing business environments and an increasing need to sell services.[33]

"If we're going to adapt to change, we're going to have to get real hot, first-class professional training. Today's client wants to deal with the firm that is better managed, more stable, and that better understands the environment in which the CEO lives."

Sullivan said client executives have been becoming more cognizant that professionalization of management leads to greater cost effectiveness and efficiency in delivery of the public relations counseling product.

"Management of growth of firms requires special skills that are hard to come by. A lot of firms founder there or become very inefficient." The PMS course, monographs, conferences and newsletters combine "to give us insights and expertise to manage and sustain growth of our companies properly."

In the case of the PMS course, the teaching follows the Harvard Case Study Method, which is adapted ideally to 25 to 30 participants and certainly no more than 50. The PMS program grew out of research of executive MBA programs at Harvard, Stanford, MIT, Yale and Princeton. "We borrowed a little here and a little there and adapted ideas to fit the Academy's needs," Sullivan said.

Skills Development May Be Left to PRSA, IABC, Universities

To help counselors succeed, the Academy has increased membership resources that emphasize firm management and help enhance the level of sophistication of public relations counseling.

"The Academy's role in the future must be toward firm management. Professional skills will be left to PRSA, IABC and university workshops and academic degree programs," Paul H. Alvarez said.[34]

"I think criticism of training in colleges and professional organizations is exaggerated. I think that if the Academy felt that an important problem were not being addressed we might step into it. What we have to do, because nobody else has an interest in it, is concentrate on management."

Professional development "works for Exxon, IBM, other companies that are big—they have lots of management training programs." But large public relations firms are fairly small businesses under the best of circumstances. So one of the things the Counselors Academy "can do well for members is institute in-depth training programs that would be unaffordable for most firms, even large ones," Alvarez said.

The Academy has had programs and presentations on measurement, evaluation and other subjects, but, "by and large, we've tried to help firm owners and top management upgrade their skills to make useful and intelligent business decisions."

Public relations can be studied in the context of other professional service businesses, Alvarez said.

We're now finding that public relations, legal, architectural, medical, dental and accounting firms have similar management problems.

We'll probably spend more time in the future teaching principals and potential successors how to manage the business. We've turned heavily into a project-oriented, execution business.

We've become a price-sensitive, but not rate-sensitive, business. We conceivably could charge $3,000 an hour for time; but what we get asked frequently is: "I've got $250,000 to budget this year; what can you do for that?" It's price-sensitive on what we can deliver as far as the client is concerned. He's not terribly concerned with our rates, but rather with the kind of results he can anticipate. That means both client and counseling firm have to focus on the bottom line, on what we can do on a cost effective basis.

Alvarez said it's in the Academy's and discipline's interest to encourage PRSA, other professional organizations, universities and member firms to increase and upgrade skills development programs.

At Ketchum, we're part of a much larger company that offers people tuition money that will help our agency in the long run. We pay thousands of dollars for people to go to special seminars where skills are improved, thousands more in dues for professional organizations in which meetings are devoted to improvement of specialized skills.

The business is loaded with some very aggressive people who are interested in putting their mark into their own areas. These are educated people, unlike the traditional employees of previous years who simply knew how to write for newspapers. They're into cable, into teleconferencing, into issues management.

You have to make sure you have the environment in which to do that. This type of encouragement or support goes on in 50 to 60 percent of the industry. If you don't do it, and they think they're not learning it, you'll lose them. Today's employees demand training, opportunity. Maybe you can ignore the bad ones and hope they will move on, but you have to keep the good ones well trained and interested.

He said skills training in the industry will continue to accelerate. "Good employees and the competition of the marketplace will put more pressure on the management of our firms. Professional development is a cost, but it's probably the best place where we can invest our money." But as he and other agency principals have agreed, skills training is not enough.

Professional Standing

Membership in the Counselors Academy Membership in the Counselors Academy itself confers a certain standing of professionalism on a practitioner which goes somewhat beyond that of the parent Public Relations Society of America.

As Epley put it: "Our membership is the leading edge of public relations excellence. The impact of our leadership is demonstrated in the manner in which we conduct our practice and personal development, in the examples we set for our employees, in the performance we give our clients, in the legacy we set for others to follow."[35]

The Academy's literature summarizes the organization's purposes and stipulates membership criteria:

The Counselors Academy was established a quarter of a century ago to meet the specialized needs of counselor members of PRSA. Its goals are to advance the profession of public relations counseling and to increase the knowledge and proficiency of public relations counselors through programs and activities of special interest to the field of counseling.

Academy officers and committee chairpersons come from both large and small firms. Volunteer committee members build research and knowledge in many diverse areas. The Academy publishes regular monographs and papers, sponsors conferences and helps its members to manage their firms for maximum profitability.[36]

Membership in the Counselors Academy is open to any member of the PRSA who is actively engaged in providing counseling service either as a full time principal, officer, partner or employee of a public relations firm or of a department or organization which is fully compensated on a fee basis in rendering such service to clients.

In addition, an applicant must meet two or more of the following criteria: be PRSA Accredited; be a PRSA member for at least two years; have been a professional counselor for at least two years, or if a resident of Canada, a member in good standing of the Canadian Consultants Section.[37]

In interviews with unaffiliated consultants and client executives as well as members of the Academy, in reviewing the literature and in observing national conferences, it becomes apparent that regardless of whether they regard themselves as professionals or members of a profession, those who belong tend to have a high professional esprit de corps and a reputation among their peers and customers for professionalism.

That was part of the vision of the founders who created the Counselors Academy in 1961. Actually, Burns Lee, a founding member of the board of the parent PRSA, remembered calling the first meeting of counselors to discuss common interests in Los Angeles in 1955 and chairing a meeting on new business and client relations in Milwaukee the following year.[38]

The president of Southern California's Bergen & Lee remembered joining with several colleagues in starting the first local counselors section in the country in 1960.

Lee said Academy founders sought to create an organization that would recognize the special problems and interests of counselors, help newcomers as well as veterans and generally upgrade the practice.

Heritage of Accreditation

By 1986, 66 percent of the Academy's members had passed PRSA accreditation examinations. By 1987, the Academy aimed for 80 percent of its more than 1,100 members to attain APR status. The Counselors Academy originated the idea for PRSA accreditation and then gave it the support to get it adopted, according to Lee. "We wanted it for clients."[39]

Hallmark of Professionalism, but Views Are Varied Most seniors in the business have considered accreditation one of the hallmarks of professionalism within public relations. There are compelling reasons for taking the accreditation exam in addition to the feeling of personal achievement in passing the test. Accreditation is one of several standards that measure an individual's professional ability, and thus is the symbol of the serious practitioner, Epley said.[40]

But even within the Counselors Academy, there are differing opinions on the value of accreditation. "APR is meaningless," said William Schechter, senior vice president of Ruder Finn & Rotman. He told *Public Relations Quarterly* that in his 25 years in the business, "I have never once heard accreditation mentioned by anyone as being pertinent or meaningful—not by PR personnel, clients in the field, management or recruiting firms."[41]

James B. Strenski, past chairman of the Counselors Academy and the head of Public Communications Inc., said that beyond his personal commitment to accreditation—because "it really means acceptance by my peers and within PRSA, and it represents me and what I do—APR means little or nothing, unfortunately."[42]

Yet "proper front-end credentialing, by whatever form, may help insure dependable, competent performance," Strenski said. "I'm supportive of whatever means will improve the level of performance. But performance is the key. In the final analysis, public relations will be judged by the practice of its members."

Although many counselors say the examination for APR was an enriching experience, some maintain, as Truitt was quoted in *Public Relations Quarterly*, that "the designation has not done much for me recently."[43]

Any shortcoming in what APR does for the reputation of accredited practitioners may come about because PRSA has not developed its potential adequately, he said. Few who favor APR do so because of what it does today—only because of what it could do tomorrow.[44]

The founder of Chicago's Philip Lesly Co. said his studies of accreditation programs of several associations indicated that they do provide "benefits in stature for individuals in their firms or in establishing credentials with potential clients."[45]

Lesly advocated more education of the publics important to the practitioners of public relations. "Constantly improved levels of performance, helped by education and professional development, are gradually having an enhancing effect."

The late Kerryn King, who was president of both PRSA and the Foundation for Public Relations Research and Education, said "one-shot, for-all-time accreditation" is inadequate.[46]

"Accreditation should be earned, not once, but year after year," according to the late senior consultant to Hill and Knowlton. "Continuing education credits, pragmatically offered and applied, could serve as incentive to continually upgrade the skills and abilities of the practitioner."

Judith S. Bogart, former president of PRSA and vice president of Diversified Communications, said she envisioned "a ladder of professionalism which starts with basic education, leads to a midpoint of accreditation and then provides an opportunity for accredited practitioners to become certified in the specific area of public relations they practice."[47]

Jacqueline K. Schaar, past member of the PRSA board of directors, told the South Pacific District Leadership Conference in 1986 that she advocated "second-tier" accreditation. She said such accreditation would be given for "proving oneself by taking a certain amount of credits per year to improve skills and keep up with new bodies of knowledge."[48]

Alvarez said that the instrumental role of the counselors in getting PRSA to adopt the accreditation program "was for the good of the profession. The rest of the industry picked it up, and that was fine." But he favored continuing education requirements to further enhance accreditation.[49]

"Our skills can go dormant, just as those of a physician or attorney. There will always be bad lawyers and doctors. Some people live in a time warp; they get ideas and hold on to them for a long time and don't build their practices." He said the forces of competition in the marketplace will tend to drive out those who don't invest in continuing education and professional development.

But the existing accreditation program still means something at Ketchum, he noted in an institutional advertisement.[50] "We're working with our people to get as many accredited as rapidly as we can. For new hires, the accredited applicant seems to get the nod over those who are not accredited. The reason is accreditation is a tangible demonstration of a long-term commitment to the profession."

Norman P. Teich, a past national officer of PRSA and vice president of Tracy-Locke Public Relations of Dallas, indicated that public relations persons have an opportunity to improve the reputation of their calling not only by their performance but also by helping publics understand what their accreditation symbolizes.[51]

By earning and using your APR certification, you tell the world that public relations is indeed a profession with a high purpose, high standards of practice, meaningful measures of quality performance and a desire for constant improvement. And when you look for APR among the credentials of people you are hiring, you tell the world that only the very best will do.

Accreditation does serve as a "badge of commitment" for counselors and is of value to potential clients and employers in recognizing an individual's dedication to his work, serious approach to business and desire to advance his self-worth, according to Dwayne Summar, who was elected PRSA president for 1988.[52]

But the Miami counselor shared the perspective of a growing number of his peers that until accreditation becomes a process that involves continuing education or re-examination to maintain APR status, it will continue to lack credibility.

"Accreditation right now is on the eve of making progress in that direction," Summar told an interviewer following a 1986 professionalism symposium for PRSA national, section and district leaders in Itasca, Ill.

The consensus "clearly directed the leadership" of PRSA to explore such questions as should accreditation be a requirement for membership; should there be a process in which an APR is reaccredited, reexamined, or renewed every few years; should a refined continuing education units program be tied into it and should accreditation be offered to non-members.[53]

Instilling Professionalism in the Young

Academy Representatives Work with Universities With projections for opening student-operated agencies running as high as 95 percent of all PRSSA-chapter campuses by 1989, the Counselors Academy designated Carolyn S. Burford, vice president of Neal Spelce Communications of Austin, and Carole Pettit of Carole Pettit Public Relations, Lexington, Ky., to a task force to "encourage high standards of professionalism in the operation of student agencies" and to provide other support.[54]

Counselors Academy members also have sponsored internships for university students, joined adjunct faculties at schools of communication and business to teach counseling seminars and other courses and given guest lectures on campuses as part of their investment in the next generation.

Alvarez co-chaired the Commission on Graduate Education in Public Relations, and other Academy members have taken active roles in educational commissions and task forces.

Challenge from Academe Counselors and PRSA members have been challenged to join additional programs to upgrade the quality of future practitioners. It is not unrealistic to envision:[55]

The time when veteran practitioners will take year-long sabbaticals to become visiting professors. They'd become an even more powerful catalyst for change in academe. They'd return to their jobs invigorated by the infectious spirit of inquiry.

The time when practitioners of public relations—as did lawyers and doctors before them—face the reality that it takes more than four or five years of formal university education to equip them with the depth and breadth of knowledge and analytical strengths that the complexity of their work demands.

The time when they reach out to attract the best and brightest in high schools, curbing the flow of business and journalism school dropouts who come to the practice because they "like people."

A call also has been made by the senior author of this book for accreditationlike examinations for university students:[56]

> *Would you consider a voluntary examination of students just before graduation, perhaps an extension of that examination to others who wish to switch over to our field and claim that their education and experience qualify them for that move?*
>
> *Would you consider an examination that tests entry-level qualifications, such as knowledge of public relations principles and pragmatics, business and communication theory, economics and psychology principles, command of the English language?*
>
> *If you would, you'd provide powerful incentives for our students and place some pressure on educators to see to it that our students had the caliber of education to pass such an examination.*

Toward the Future

Innovative Group on the Cutting Edge   Bruce Rubin, the counselor elected to lead the Academy in 1987, forecast increased growth, prestige and membership service.[57]

> *We are becoming recognized as spokespersons for the counseling industry to business editors and reporters in much the same way as the American Medical Association might be a source on medicine.*
>
> *Our professional development program has been breaking into new and exciting areas. We've crossed another boundary with our Management School.*
>
> *This is one group that's not afraid to say that "this has worked well in the past, but it's time to try something new." The Academy is innovative and on the cutting edge of the profession, a "we'll be the first to try it" group.*
>
> *Seldom does a professional organization rise to as high a level of service to its members as does the Academy. It provides both a forum for futurists and a vehicle for formal and informal information exchange.*
>
> *The Academy is atypical in another, important way—it provides members with a commonality of purpose, particularly crucial in a profession that many consider to be still emerging.*
>
> *Its achievements notwithstanding, the Counselors Academy is al-*

*ready becoming more and more important to its members and acceler-
ating in its value.*

*After all, an organization comprises individual members, and with
counselors only beginning to flex their creativity and establish new
disciplines, the Academy—and its members—can only be destined for
greater achievement that transcends professionalism.*

Individual Counselors Provide Leadership on the Job   Organizations such as
America's Counselors Academy and Canada's Counselors Institute, indeed,
have provided leadership in counseling. Their roles, and that of the many
counselors who have shaped them and the calling they serve, is ever
changing. Market forces, new technological systems, new cultures and
new values all bear heavily on the counselors' work. Their tools for keeping apace are manifest.

Within, and beyond, the professional organizations are individual counselors who are extending the leadership they give in helping client executives select actions and communicate for the good of business, institutions
and the public sphere today while girding for the changes of tomorrow.

The quest for professionalism continues.

NOTES

CHAPTER I

1. Bruce S. Rubin, interview, March 26, 1986.
2. Ideas stimulated by Paul H. Alvarez, interview, April 8, 1985.
3. Rubin, interview.
4. Joe S. Epley, interview, April 21, 1985.
5. Alvarez, interview.
6. Davis Young, interview, March 2, 1985.
7. James B. Strenski, "The Future of the Consultancy," *Public Relations Quarterly*, Spring 1983.
8. Findings of *Mercury Survey*, published by PRSA Communications Technology Task Force, Nov. 13, 1985. The survey was a joint venture of New World Decisions, Ketchum Public Relations and the PRSA Task Force's Research Subcommittee.
9. "21st Annual Survey of the Profession" and "1985's Most Important Issues/Problems by Industry," *PR Reporter*, Dec. 2, 1985, pp. 1–4.
10. "How Practitioners Spend Their Time," *PR Reporter*, Jan. 6, 1986, p. 1. The data was based on the publication's "21st Annual Survey of the Profession, 1985."
11. Davis Young, "The State of the Public Relations Consultancy in the United States," address to the Public Relations Consultants Association of Great Britain, London, June 1, 1985, pp. 6–10. The poll was conducted in Spring 1985.
12. Findings of 1985 *Mercury Survey*.
13. "More Than 200 New Firms Opened," *Jack O'Dwyer's Newsletter*, Dec. 18, 1985, p. 5.
14. "Top PR Stories of 1985," *Jack O'Dwyer's Newsletter*, Dec. 18, 1985, p. 5.
15. *1986 O'Dwyer's Directory of PR Firms*, cited in "Top 50 Firms Up Approximately 20% to $520 Million," *Jack O'Dwyer's Newsletter*, March 5, 1986, pp. 2, 6.
16. *1985 O'Dwyer's Directory of PR Firms* (New York: Jack O'Dwyer, 1985).
17. Jube Shiver Jr., "PR Boom Isn't Drum Beating: Public Relations Industry Expands Beyond Publicity," *Los Angeles Times*, March 24, 1985, Business Section, pp. 1, 2.
18. "Public Relations in the 80s: Trends and Challenges," *PR Casebook*, October 1983, pp. 4–5, 7.
19. David J. Speer, cited in "Public Relations in the 80s," pp. 5, 7.
20. Bill Cantor and the Cantor Concern, "4th Annual Review of and Forecast of Public Relations Trends," cited in *PR Reporter*, Jan. 27, 1986, p. 3.
21. Cantor, "Forecast '85: The Year in Public Relations," *Public Relations Journal*, February 1985, pp. 22–24.
22. Patrick Jackson, "A Modest Proposal: Dropping Use of the Word 'Agency' to Delineate Public Relations Firms Will Benefit Everyone in the Profession, as Well as Those We Serve," *PR Reporter*, Aug. 1, 1983, pp. 1, 2.
23. E. Bruce Harrison, "PR Counseling: Pat's Firm Stand," *The Counselor*, February 1984, p. 6.
24. Rubin, interview.

25. William H. Stryker, correspondence, April 20, 1984.
26. James F. Fox, "Re-thinking the Role of Public Relations Consulting," keynote address, Consultants Section, Canadian Public Relations Society, Vancouver, June 23, 1980.
27. Luc Beauregard, notes for an address at a joint conference organized by the Canadian Public Relations Society (British Columbia) and the PRSA (Northwest), March 22, 1985.
28. Harold Burson, interview, May 5, 1985.
29. Burson, interview, May 12, 1985.
30. Burson, interview, May 5, 1985.
31. Burson, interview, May 12, 1985.
32. Davis Young, "Toward 2005: the State of the PR Consultancy in the United States," in the *1985 Public Relations Yearbook* (London: Public Relations Consultants Association of Great Britain, 1985), pp. 13, 16.
33. Loet A. Velmans, cited in "A Boardroom Presence," *MBA Executive*, publication of the Association of MBA Executives Inc., March–April 1985.
34. Duncan T. Black Jr., interview, Feb. 1, 1985.
35. Daniel H. Baer, notes for speech to San Francisco Bay Chapter of PRSA, September 1984.
36. Michael Campbell, original manuscript of "PR through a Crystal Ball: Consulting in the Year 1990," written for *Stimulus* (a Canadian advertising journal), April 1985, p. 5.
37. Alfred Geduldig, "Opinion: Is Hay a Four Letter Word?" *Public Relations Journal*, March 1986, p. 12.
38. Burson, interview, May 5, 1985.
39. Young, "Toward 2005," pp. 13, 16.
40. Ibid.
41. Fox, "Re-thinking the Role of Public Relations Consulting."
42. Richard W. Darrow and Dan J. Forrestal, *The Dartnell Public Relations Handbook*, 2nd ed. rev. (Chicago: Dartnell Corp., 1979).
43. Burson, interview, May 5, 1985.
44. Robert L. Dilenschneider, interview, Feb. 22, 1986.
45. Fox, correspondence to Nager, March 2, 1985.
46. Rubin, interview, March 26, 1986.
47. Lee Thayer, "Thinking Leadership," 1985 Annual Lecture sponsored by the Foundation for Public Relations Research and Education, National Conference of the PRSA, Detroit, Nov. 10, 1985.

CHAPTER 2

1. See documentation and systems for applying MBO to creativity in Norman R. Nager and T. Harrell Allen, *Public Relations Management by Objectives* (White Plains, N.Y.: Longman, 1984).
2. Thomas E. Eidson, interview, Jan. 31, 1985.
3. Richard H. Truitt, "Creativity in Public Relations," speech to J.C. Penney Co., Public Relations Conference, New York, Dec. 6, 1984.
4. Davis Young article cited in *The Counselor*, May 1985.
5. Truitt, "Creativity in Public Relations."
6. Nager and Allen, *Public Relations Management by Objectives*, pp. 48–49, 80–86, 89–286.
7. Jean L. Farinelli, interview, Feb. 26, 1985.
8. Farinelli, interview, Feb. 22, 1986.
9. Identification of interviewee withheld to protect confidentiality.
10. S. Judith Rich, interviews, April 1985.

11. Truitt observations as one of the judges.
12. David S. Hill, " 'Goose-Bump' Corporate Advertising," *Public Relations Journal*, November 1984, pp. 17–19.
13. Identification of interviewee withheld to protect confidentiality.
14. Ibid.
15. Thomas J. Peters and Robert H. Waterman Jr., *In Search of Excellence: Lessons from America's Best-Run Companies*, (New York: Harper & Row, 1982), pp. 223–224.
16. James A. Little, interview, March 8, 1985.
17. Jack F. Agnew, interview, April 7, 1985.
18. Nager, 1986 lectures on persuasive communication, based on research for "Anatomy of the Aftermath of Cover-Ups" (doctoral dissertation), University of Southern California, January 1978.
19. Agnew, interview.
20. Little, interview.
21. Agnew, interview.
22. Ibid.
23. Nicholas E. Kilsby, interview, May 15, 1985.
24. Ibid.
25. Andy Cooper, interview, May 15, 1985.
26. Kilsby, interview.
27. Cooper, interview.
28. Loet A. Velmans, "Public Relations—What It Is and What It Does," in Bill Cantor, *Experts in Action: Inside Public Relations*, ed. Chester Burger, (White Plains, N.Y.: Longman, 1984), p. 4.
29. Eidson, interview.
30. Dennis L. Wilcox, Phillip H. Ault and Warren K. Agee, *Public Relations: Strategies and Tactics* (New York: Harper & Row, 1986); Scott M. Cutlip, Allen H. Center and Glen M. Broom, *Effective Public Relations*, 6th ed. (Englewood Cliffs, N.J.: Prentice-Hall, 1985); Norman R. Nager and T. Harrell Allen, *Public Relations Management by Objectives*, (White Plains, N.Y.: Longman, 1984), pp. 80–86, 232–234.
31. Eidson, interview.
32. Daniel J. Edelman, "Managing the Public Relations Firm in the 21st Century," *Public Relations Review*, vol. 9 (Fall 1983), pp. 3–10.
33. Nina Palmer, interview, July 23, 1986.
34. E. Bruce Harrison, "Planning Notes," written for internal distribution, Aug. 1, 1984.
35. Carol J. Gies, "Employees Make the Rules," *Public Relations Journal*, October 1984, pp. 19–21.
36. Cynthia Pharr, interview, Feb. 24, 1985.
37. Edelman, "Managing the Public Relations Firm."
38. Pharr, interview.
39. Alyse Lynn Booth, "Who Are We—Part Two," *Public Relations Journal*, July 1985, p. 18.
40. Ed Stanton, quoted by Alyse Lynn Booth, "Who Are We—Part One," *Public Relations Journal*, June 1985, pp. 17–18.
41. Booth, "Who Are We—Part One," pp. 14–18.
42. David Maister, "Firm Management," *Public Relations Journal*, August 1985, pp. 15–18.
43. Ibid.
44. Mitchell C. Kozikowski, interview, May 20, 1985.
45. Charles Lipton, interview, May 10, 1985.
46. Paul Alvarez, interview, April 24, 1985.
47. Sue Bohle, interview, Feb. 10, 1985; and David Finn, interview, May 9, 1985. Also see Walter W. Wurfel, "Well-Nurtured Interns Can Reap Benefits and Bring Rewards," *Public Relations Journal*, April 1985, p. 37.

48. Curtis Hartman, "Selling the Brooklyn Bridge," *Inc.*, November 1983, cover feature.

49. E. W. Brody, p. 27 of original manuscript for *Business of Public Relations* (New York: Praeger Publishers, 1987).

50. Lou Brum Burdick, interview, Feb. 26, 1985.

51. Alvarez, interview.

52. Ibid.

53. John Softness, "Not for Sale," *Public Relations Business*, Feb. 18, 1985, p. 7.

54. Norman Brown, "Harvesting Creativity," *FCB Person to Person*, July–August 1985, pp. 4-5.

55. Thomas E. Kuby, "Developing Creativity in Public Relations," *Counselors Academy Monograph Series*, August 1983.

56. Pharr, interview.

57. Paul Watzlawick, seminar on organizational communication, University of Southern California, Aug. 1, 1975. Also see Paul Watzlawick, John Weakland and Richard Fisch, *Change: Principles of Problem Formation and Problem Resolution* (New York: W.W. Norton, 1974).

58. Farinelli, interviews, Feb. 26, 1985, and March 1, 1985.

59. Ibid.

60. Identification of interviewees withheld to protect confidentiality. See Chapter 5, "Client Relations Strategies."

61. George Hammond and Edward DeBono, cited by Farinelli.

62. James Arnold, presentation at communications conference at Honeywell Inc., New York, September 1984.

63. Michael Wagman, "Read Kierkegaard, Wrinkle Your Brain and Throw Deep! Or, How To Be More Creative," *FCB Person to Person*, July–August 1985, pp. 17–18.

64. Ibid.

65. Thomas S. Kuhn, *The Structure of Scientific Revolutions*, 2nd ed. enlarged (Chicago: University of Chicago Press, 1970).

66. Alvarez, interview.

67. Rich, interviews.

68. Agnew, interview.

69. Rich, interviews.

70. Agnew, interview.

71. Ibid.

72. Rich, interviews.

73. Ibid.

74. Farinelli, interviews.

75. Rich, interviews.

76. Kay Berger, "Creativity," address to Public Relations Management Conference, Los Angeles PRSA Chapter, Palm Springs, Calif., March 2, 1985.

77. Rich, interviews.

78. Robert E. Keating, interview, April 19, 1985.

CHAPTER 3

1. Dennis L. Wilcox, Phillip H. Ault and Warren K. Agee, *Public Relations: Strategies and Tactics* (New York: Harper & Row, 1986).

2. Fraser P. Seitel, *The Practice of Public Relations*, 2nd ed. (Columbus, Ohio: Charles E. Merrill Publishing, 1984), pp. 57–58.

3. Scott M. Cutlip, Allen H. Center and Glen M. Broom, *Effective Public Relations*, 6th ed. (Englewood Cliffs, N.J.: Prentice-Hall, 1985), pp. 93–98.

4. Chester Burger, cited in *Effective Public Relations.*
5. David Ferguson, interview, Feb. 5, 1985.
6. David A. Meeker, interview, April 5, 1985.
7. Peter Finn and Mary-Kay Harrity, "Research," in Bill Cantor, *Experts in Action: Inside Public Relations,* ed. Chester Burger (White Plains, N.Y.: Longman, 1984), pp. 273–287.
8. "The Public Relations Audit: A Management Tool" (tape recording), produced by the National Professional Development Committee of the Public Relations Society of America for the PRSA Professional Library (PRSA Tape M-002).
9. John C. Pollack (representing Research & Forecasts), John M. Harding (Internorth) and Joseph C. Calitri (American Cyanamid Co.), in "The Public Relations Audit: A Management Tool," PRSA Tape M-002.
10. Ibid.
11. Ibid.
12. Finn and Harrity, "Research."
13. Pollack, "The Public Relations Audit."
14. Daniel H. Baer, "Selling Management on Public Relations Research," *Public Relations Quarterly,* Fall 1983, pp. 9–11.
15. Walter K. Lindenmann, "Dealing with the Major Obstacles to Implementing Public Relations Research," *Public Relations Quarterly,* Fall 1983, pp. 12–16.
16. Ibid.
17. Joe S. Epley, interview, April 20, 1985; Baer, "Selling Management"; Baer, interview, Jan. 18, 1985.
18. Baer, interview.
19. Burson-Marsteller, "The Marketing Audit" and "Marketing Audit Form," made available to Nager, March 5 and March 31, 1985, by Lloyd Kirban.
20. Lloyd Kirban, interviews, Feb. 21 and March 27, 1985.
21. Epley Associates, Inc., "Proposal for Communications Audit for ——— Company" (identity withheld for client confidentiality), and "Outline for Presentation about Conduct of a Public Relations Audit" (used for staff training). Outline used as background by authors for editing of proposal. "Client" or "organization" is substituted for company's name in text.
22. Winthrop C. Neilson III, in "The Investor Relations Audit," available from PRSA Investor Relations Section.
23. James B. Strenski, "The Communications Audit—Basic to Business Development," *News,* publication of the Society for Marketing Professional Services, 1984.
24. Ibid.
25. Kate Connelly, cited by Gladys Hearst in "Conducting Communications Audits," *PRO COMM,* February 1985.
26. David M. Dozier, "Planning and Evaluation in PR Practice," *Public Relations Review,* vol. 11 (Summer 1985), pp. 17–25.
27. David Finn, "The Elements of Sound Public Relations Planning," *The Forum* (published by Ruder Finn & Rotman), Summer 1984, pp. 1–2.
28. Cutlip, Center and Broom, *Effective Public Relations,* pp. 68–71.
29. Ibid.
30. James H. Dowling, "Creating a Common Language," speech presented at annual convention of the International Association of Business Communicators, Montreal, Canada, June 4, 1984.
31. William F. Noonan, "Finding and Growing Public Relations Talents—Some Realities of the 80s," speech presented at Counselors Academy Spring Conference, Las Vegas, April 30, 1984.
32. Joan Parker, interview, May 9, 1985.
33. *Epley Public Relations Manual,* revised edition, internally distributed document (Charleston, N.C.: Epley Associates, 1985).

34. Epley, interviews, April 7–14, 1985.
35. "Opportunity 85," *PR Reporter*, Jan. 7, 1985, pp. 1–4.
36. Dan Thomas, cited in "Developer of 'The Strategic Management Process' Questions Traditional Planning; Sees Limitations, Need for Line Manager Involvement," *Tips & Tactics*, supplement to *PR Reporter*, April 15, 1985, pp. 1–2.
37. Dale E. Zand, *Information, Organization, and Power: Effective Management in the Knowledge Society* (New York: McGraw-Hill, 1981), pp. x, 8.
38. Phillip J. Tichenor, "The Logic of Social and Behavioral Science," in *Research Methods in Mass Communication*, ed. Guido H. Stempel III and Bruce H. Westley (Englewood Cliffs, N.J.: Prentice-Hall, 1981), pp. 27–28.
39. Michael Rowan, cited in "An Interview with Michael Rowan," Strategic Information Research Corp. *Bulletin*, internally distributed Hill and Knowlton publication, sent to authors July 30, 1985, pp. 1–4.

CHAPTER 4

1. The reader is referred to another Longman book for a public relations research glossary and sections on scientific surveys, sampling procedures, probability sampling, non-probability sampling, tests to measure results, computer-assisted analysis, Q-sort, content analysis, participant observation, unobtrusive measures and futures research. See appendix "Glossary of Research Terms" and Chapter 6, "Research-Evaluation" in Norman R. Nager and T. Harrell Allen, *Public Relations Management by Objectives* (White Plains, N.Y.: Longman, 1984), pp. 167–230, 379–386. Also see pp. 10–18, 35–39, 41, 46–49, 66–68, 83–85, 115–116, 118–122, 139–140, 232–234, 250–251, 300–04, 315, 318–320, 350–353, 365–366.
2. Public Relations Society of America National Conference research workshops and regional professional development meetings, 1982 and 1983.
3. Lloyd Kirban, interview, Feb. 21, 1985.
4. Kirban, "What's the Impact?" adapted from Winter 1983 *Public Relations Quarterly* article and published as a monograph by Burson-Marsteller in 1984.
5. Kirban, interview, Feb. 21, 1985.
6. Ibid.
7. Michael Rowan, cited in "Rowan Named to H&K Research Unit," *Public Relations Business*, March 4, 1985.
8. Rowan, cited in "An Interview with Michael Rowan," Strategic Information Research Corp. *Bulletin*, internally distributed Hill and Knowlton publication, sent to authors July 30, 1985, pp. 1–4.
9. Rowan, *Public Relations Business*.
10. Richard H. Truitt, observations based on experience with case during tenure as executive vice president, Carl Byoir & Associates.
11. Jan Rogozinski, seminar for Honeywell executives, Minneapolis, Sept. 10, 1984.
12. "Vaughn Grid" graphic illustration from "Public Relations Research," presentation by Carl Byoir & Associates, New York, 1985.
13. Rogozinski, interview, March 17, 1985.
14. *The Byoir Planning Model*, internally distributed document (New York: Carl Byoir & Associates, 1985).
15. Lloyd N. Newman, "Developing Persuasive Programs for Results," presentation to 38th National Conference of PRSA, Detroit, Nov. 12, 1985.
16. Nager observations based on his doctoral studies of network analysis and subsequent review of reports in the literature and at conferences from such researchers as James A.

Danowski, Peter R. Monge, Richard V. Farace, Gerald R. Miller, Georg Lindsay, George A. Barnett, Matthew Friedland, Timothy Mabee and T. Harrell Allen.

17. Richard V. Farace, Peter R. Monge and Hamish M. Russell, *Communicating and Organizing* (Reading, Mass: Addison-Wesley, 1977), pp. 177–203, 245–247.
18. Ibid.
19. Peter R. Monge and Gerald R. Miller, "Communication Networks" in *Social Science Encyclopedia* (The Netherlands: Routledge and Kegan Paul, in press). Citation from Monge's galley proofs.
20. James A. Danowski, George A. Barnett and Matthew Friedland, "Interorganizational Networks via Shared Public Relations Firms: Centrality, Diversification, Media Coverage, and Publics' Images," paper submitted for presentation at annual conference of the International Communication Association, Chicago, May 23–25, 1986. Citations from Danowski's copy of original manuscript.
21. Ibid.
22. Farace, Monge and Russell, *Communicating and Organizing.*
23. Richard V. Farace and Timothy Mabee, "Communication Network Analysis Methods," in *Multivariate Techniques in Human Communication Research* (New York: Academic Press, 1980), pp. 387–388.
24. Adapted from definition in Nager and Allen, *Public Relations Management by Objectives,* p. 120.
25. Ed Zotti, "Thinking Psychographically," *Public Relations Journal,* May 1985, pp. 26–30.
26. Adapted from Truitt CASE speech, Jan. 28, 1985.
27. James Atlas, "Beyond Demographics," *The Atlantic Monthly,* October 1984, pp. 49–58.
28. Ibid.
29. Paul H. Alvarez, presentations at PRSA national and regional conferences, 1984.
30. "Values & Lifestyles Opinion Research—A Resource for Public Affairs Programs," client prospectus published by Ketchum Public Relations, 1985.
31. John L. Paluszek, interview, May 9, 1985.
32. Ibid.
33. Paluszek, cited by Zotti in "Thinking Psychographically."
34. Robert L. Dilenschneider, "Platform: A Call for Unity," speech presented at annual meeting of United Dairy Industry Association, Kansas City, Mo., March 2, 1985.
35. Ibid.
36. Zotti, "Thinking Psychographically."
37. Kirban, cited by Zotti in "Thinking Psychographically."
38. Atlas, "Beyond Demographics."
39. James B. Strenski, "New Concerns for Public Relations Measurement," *Public Relations Journal,* May 1981.
40. Nager and Allen, *Public Relations Management by Objectives,* pp. 216–218.
41. Alvarez, cited by Nager and Allen, p. 217.
42. Ruder Finn & Rotman, "Evaluating Public Relations Results," *Forum* (RF&R publication), Fall 1983, pp. 1–4.
43. Rogozinski, interview, May 5, 1985.
44. Kay S. Cushing, interview, May 7, 1985.
45. Kirban, interview, Feb. 21, 1985.
46. Albert J. Barr, "High-Technology Tracking on a Low-Tech Budget: Setting up Your Own System May Seem Tantamount to Climbing the Himalayas, But the View of What Can Be Done Will Be Worth All the Effort," *Public Relations Journal,* July 1984, pp. 28–30.
47. Dilenschneider, full text of Public Relations Foundation of Texas monograph, based on "Marketing and the Global Corporation," address presented to the Texas Public Relations Association, San Antonio, Feb. 22, 1986, pp. 24–26.
48. Rowan, remarks at the Food Commodities Promotion and Marketing Symposium, Washington, D.C., July 25, 1985, p. 3.

49. "Getting Results through Strategy and Action," capabilities brochure published by Hill and Knowlton, 1985, p. 22.
50. "Simmons," *Bulletin*, newsletter published by Strategic Information Research Corp. subsidiary of Hill and Knowlton, mailed to Nager March 14, 1986, p. 5.
51. Judith Reitman, "Taking Measure of the PeopleMeter," *Marketing and Media Decisions*, August 1985, pp. 62, 114–115, cited in "New Technology Used for TV Audience Measurement," *Purview*, Oct. 28, 1985, pp. 1–2.
52. Danowski, "Automated Word-Network Analysis: An Illustration with Electronic Mail," paper submitted for presentation at annual conference of the International Communication Association, Chicago, May 23, 1986. Citations from author's copy of original manuscript.
53. Truitt, based on participant observation as executive vice president, Carl Byoir & Associates, through August 1985.
54. Donald S. Knight, conversations as recalled by Truitt.
55. Timothy J. Doke, conversations as recalled by Truitt.
56. Ibid.
57. Correspondence to TRIP, cited by Truitt.
58. Doke, conversations.
59. Kirban, interview, March 27, 1985.
60. Kirban, interview, Feb. 21, 1985.
61. Ibid.
62. Rogozinski, "How To Make Public Opinion Work for You," speech for internal continuing education, Carl Byoir & Associates, January 1984.
63. Ford Rowan, "Predicting Public Attitudes," literature for potential clients published by Rowan & Blewitt Inc., Washington, D.C., 1985.
64. Robert S. Duboff and F. J. Baytos, *Use of the Focus Group Technique in Public Relations Research* (Lexington, Mass.: Counselors Academy and Decision Research Corp., July 1982). Jointly copyrighted material published as part of the Counselors Academy ongoing series of monographs. Such monographs are restricted to dues-paying members of the Academy.
65. Richard Weiner, interview, March 2, 1985.
66. *Jack O'Dwyer's Newsletter*, "Cabbage Patch Seminar: Research is Key," p. 4; and citation of the NYU/PRSA seminar Aug. 16, 1984.
67. Weiner, interview.
68. Ibid.
69. Burson-Marsteller, entry 6A-16, 1984 PRSA Silver Anvil Awards competition.
70. Ibid.
71. Don DelVecchio, "Cabbage Patch Fever: America Takes the Cherub-Faced Dolls to Heart, While an Enterprising PR Firm Reaps a Bountiful Harvest of Publicity," *Burrelle's Clipping Analyst*, July 1984, pp. 1–4.
72. "What a Doll!" *Newsweek*, Cover and Business feature and sidebars, "Oh, You Beautiful Dolls!" Dec. 12, 1983, pp. 78–82, 85.
73. Ravelle Brickman, interview and seminar at 37th annual National Conference of PRSA, Denver, Oct. 17, 1984.
74. Weiner, interview.
75. Truitt, recollection as judge of 1984 Silver Anvil competition.
76. Brickman, interview and seminar.
77. Weiner, interview.
78. Ibid.
79. Strenski, interview, March 31, 1985.
80. Rogozinski, extracted from 1984 and 1985 speeches.
81. Glen M. Broom and David M. Dozier, proposed Contents for *Using Research in Public Relations: Applications to Program Management*, tentatively scheduled for publication in 1988.

CHAPTER 5

1. Interviewees' identity withheld for confidentiality.
2. Ibid.
3. Ibid.
4. Ibid.
5. Otto Lerbinger, "Trends Affecting the Future of Public Relations," speech presented at California State University, Fullerton, May 1, 1985.
6. *PR Reporter* "Survey of the Profession," cited by Lerbinger.
7. Davis Young, cited in "Product of PR Counsel Is Counsel," *The Counselor*, December 1984, p. 1.
8. James F. Fox, "Who's That Knocking at Your Door? The Crisis of Spokesmanship," address before the National Association for Corporate Speaker Activities, Southeastern Region, Atlanta, March 8, 1985.
9. Fox, "Corporate Communications Strategies in a Topsy-Turvy World," speech presented at the Life Advertisers Assoc. Southern Round Table, Williamsburg, Va., May 9, 1983.
10. Fox, interview, March 13, 1985.
11. See, for example, William J. McGuire and Demetrios Papageorgis, "Effectiveness of Forewarning in Developing Resistance to Persuasion," *Public Opinion Quarterly*, Spring 1962, pp. 24–34; Papageorgis and McGuire, "The Generality of Immunity to Persuasion Produced by Pre-exposure to Weakened Counterarguments, *Journal of Abnormal and Social Psychology*, May 1961, pp. 475–481.
12. Fox, interview.
13. Ibid.
14. Interviewees' identities withheld for confidentiality.
15. Ibid.
16. Ibid.
17. Fox, interview.
18. Anthony J. Alessandra, cited in "Spring Conference Report: Counselors Share Secrets to Sales Success," *The Counselor*, May 1985, pp. 3–4.
19. E. Bruce Harrison, interview, March 9, 1985; and "Client Goals and Objectives for 1985" (internal-planning document of E. Bruce Harrison Co.).
20. Harrison, "How Love and Fear Affect Clients and the Counselor," column in *The Counselor*, December 1984, p. 8.
21. David Finn, "Public Invisibility of Corporate Leaders," *Harvard Business Review*, vol. 58, no. 6, 1980, pp. 102–110.
22. Michael V. Sullivan, interview, April 22, 1985.
23. Chester Burger, interview, March 15, 1985.
24. Ibid.
25. Ibid.
26. Ibid.
27. Harold Burson, interview, May 12, 1985.
28. Ibid.
29. Peter G. Osgood, interview, April 20, 1985.
30. Stanley C. Pace, cited by Robert L. Jackson in "New Dynamics Chief Pledges Ethical Regime," *Los Angeles Times*, Jan. 17, 1986, pp. 1, 5.
31. As reported by national print and electronic media.
32. Osgood, interview.
33. Osgood and Burson interviews.
34. Joe S. Epley, interviews, April 7 and 20, 1985, and Epley & Associates internal professional development and planning documents.
35. Ibid.
36. Ibid.

37. Terence A. McCarthy, interview, March 3, 1985.
38. Ibid.
39. David Davis, "The Client/Agency Relationship," *PR Casebook*, vol. 4 (October 1983), pp. 9, 20.
40. Ibid.
41. McCarthy, interview.
42. Byron G. Sabol, "Does Your Company Need a PR Agency?" *Business to Business*, November 1984, pp. 32–33. Sabol wrote the article while West Coast operations director for Hill, Holliday, Connors, Cosmopulos, Inc., Advertising.
43. Kenneth S. Drake, "Company Executives Need Information on When to Turn to a Counselor," *The Counselor*, December 1984, p. 4. Drake founded Kenneth Drake Associates.
44. Alan K. Leahigh, "PR on a Two-Way Street," *Public Relations Business*, Dec. 3, 1984, p. 7. Leahigh wrote the article as senior vice president of Public Communications Inc.
45. Rene L. White, "In the Market for a PR Agency? Consider This," *Computer & Electronics Marketing*, October 1984, p. 19. White is vice president and director of technology in the Los Angeles office of Fleishman-Hillard.
46. Jean L. Farinelli, "Auditing Your Counselor's Performance," *Public Relations Journal*, October 1983, pp. 20, 27–28. Farinelli wrote the article as president of Tracy-Locke/BBDO Public Relations.
47. James B. Strenski, "Ten Criteria for Selecting PR Counsel," *Office Guide to Tampa Bay*, reprint made available by Tampa, Fla., offices of Public Communications Inc.
48. Richard A. Barry, "What Every Client Should Know," *PR Casebook*, vol. 4 (October 1983), p. 8; Strenski, "Ten Criteria."
49. Bernard E. Ury, interview, March 18, 1985; "A Client's Guide to Better Public Relations Programs," published by Bernard E. Ury Associates, June 1984; and sample issues of Ury newsletter for clients, 1983–1985.
50. Ury, "Client Guide."
51. Ury, interview and sample issues of newsletter.
52. Robert L. Dilenschneider, "Platform: A Call for Unity," speech presented at annual meeting of United Dairy Industry Association, Kansas City, Mo., March 2, 1985.
53. Robert F. Smith and Kerry Tucker, "Looking Back: 'Backcasting' Moves into the Driver's Seat," *Public Relations Journal*, December 1984, pp. 29–30.
54. Nager, "The Judo Approach to Persuasion," seminar presentation, California State University, Fullerton, Feb. 5, 1986; and "Executive Education Strategies," computer data base developed 1980–1986.
55. Ibid.
56. Ibid.
57. Daniel J. Edelman, abstracted by authors from speech in collection made available during February–March 1985 interviews. Details that would identify the specific company withheld by authors.

CHAPTER 6

1. Members of the audience and David H. Maister in seminar "Achieving Excellence in Client Service," National Spring Conference, Counselors Academy, Carefree, Ariz., April 7, 1986. Nager developed data as participant-observer.
2. Maister, "Achieving Excellence in Client Service."
3. Thomas E. Nunan, interviews for Norman R. Nager and T. Harrell Allen, *Public Relations Management by Objectives* (White Plains, N.Y.: Longman, 1984); and conversations, 1980–1982.
4. Nunan, interviews and correspondence, November 1984–January 1985.

5. Ibid.
6. Peter J. Dowd, interview, March 17, 1985.
7. David Ferguson, interview, Feb. 5, 1985.
8. William Pruett, interview, April 3, 1985.
9. Joseph F. Awad, interviews, October 1984 and November 1985; correspondence, November 4, 1984.
10. Sunshine Janda Overkamp, interview, April 17, 1985.
11. Based on participant observation of Nager as communications consultant to the California State Legislature and as chairman of the Southern California Hospital Public Relations Directors.
12. Overkamp, interview.
13. David J. Metz, interviews, March 6 and 18, 1985.
14. Robert L. Lauer, interview, April 30, 1985, and speech to Counselors Academy, "What Corporations Look for in Reviewing Agencies," Orlando, Fla., April 16, 1985.
15. Lauer, interview.
16. Ibid.
17. Richard H. Truitt, conversation with co-author, Nov. 5, 1985.
18. Bruce S. Rubin, interview, Nov. 10, 1985.
19. Charles C. Dayton, "A Voice of Experience from the Corporate Side Discusses Choosing a PR Firm," *Public Relations Business*, Jan. 7, 1985, p. 7.
20. John F. Budd, cited in "Guidelines for Firms & Clients," *PR Reporter*, May 2, 1983, pp. 3–4.

CHAPTER 7

1. Regis McKenna, *The Regis Touch* (Reading, Mass.: Addison-Wesley, 1985), pp. 21–25.
2. Robert G. Wilder, "The Shoemaker's Children," *Public Relations Business*, Feb. 11, 1985, p. 7.
3. Ibid.
4. Jack F. Agnew, interview, March 23, 1985.
5. Ibid.
6. Gerald S. Schwartz, "Coping with Growing Pains," *Public Relations Business*, Sept. 17, 1984, p. 7.
7. Agnew, interview.
8. Ibid.
9. Ibid.
10. Ibid.
11. Ibid.
12. Ibid.
13. Ibid.
14. Ibid.
15. Ibid.
16. Jacqueline K. Schaar, interview and remarks in panel discussion, "Public Relations: Vocation or Profession?" South Pacific District PRSA Leadership Conference, California State Polytechnic University, Pomona, Calif., Feb. 7, 1986.
17. Ernest Wittenberg, 1985 interviews; 1986 promotional literature on forums.
18. E. Bruce Harrison, "What Do You Say When They Ask You to Explain Harrison Co.?" "Management Goal #1: Create Customers," and "How to Keep the Client–Counselor Relationship Strong," internal planning and professional development documents made available to authors March 1985.
19. David Maister, "Firm Management," *Public Relations Journal*, August 1985, pp. 15–18.

20. Harrison, internal planning and professional development documents.
21. Maister, "Firm Management."
22. Ibid.
23. John Naisbitt and Patricia Aburdene, *Re-inventing the Corporation* (New York: Warner Books, 1985), pp. 20, 107.
24. Lloyd Kirban, interviews, Feb. 21 and March 27, 1985.
25. Ibid.
26. James Reiner, cited by Stephen E. Nowlan, Diana R. Shayon et al., *Leveraging the Impact of Public Affairs* (Philadelphia: HRN, 1984), p. 26.
27. Naisbitt, "The Year Ahead: 1985," study released by Naisbitt Group, Washington, D.C., January 1985.
28. Naisbitt and Aburdene, *Re-inventing the Corporation.*
29. Alvin Toffler, *The Adaptive Corporation* (New York: McGraw-Hill, 1985), pp. 3–4.
30. "How to Make Your New Business Pitch," *Public Relations Journal*, November 1985, pp. 36–37.
31. Marshall McLuhan, "The Medium Is the Message," in *The Process and Effects of Mass Communication*, rev. ed., ed. Wilbur Schramm and Donald F. Roberts (Urbana, Ill.: University of Illinois Press, 1971), pp. 100–115.
32. Herbert W. Simons, *Persuasion: Understanding, Practice, and Analysis*, 2nd ed. (New York: Random House, 1986), pp. 108–115.
33. Norman R. Nager, observations of student-counselor interactions at California State University, Fullerton.
34. E. William Brody, introductory chapter to original manuscript, *The Business of Public Relations* (New York: Praeger Publishers, 1987).
35. Ibid.
36. Nager, extension of Brody model.
37. David Ferguson, interview, Feb. 7, 1986.
38. William Bennington, cited in "Colonial Penn PR Staff Becomes Agency," *Jack O'Dwyer's Newsletter*, March 13, 1985, p. 1.
39. Cherie Grigas, cited in "Is Public Relations Expense to Be Charged to General Overhead? Or Can It Be Profit Center?" *PR Reporter*, Sept. 10, 1984, pp. 1–2.
40. C. Thomas Wilck, interview, Feb. 12, 1986.
41. Jack O'Dwyer, "Ex-GE PR People Form Two Agencies," *Jack O'Dwyer's Newsletter*, Dec. 18, 1985, p. 2.
42. Joyce Hergenhan and Ralph Brush, cited in "Ex-GE PR People Form Two Agencies."
43. Truitt, cited in "Another Model Is Placing Firm Employees in Client Offices," *PR Reporter*, Sept. 10, 1984, p. 2.
44. S. Judith Rich, interviews, April 3 and Nov. 13, 1985.
45. Ibid.
46. Ibid.
47. Ibid.
48. Ibid.
49. Ibid.
50. Charles Lipton, interview, May 10, 1985.
51. Ibid.
52. Ibid.
53. Ibid.
54. Ibid.
55. Chester Burger, "The Management of a Public Relations Firm," monograph published by the Counselors Academy, June 1983, pp. 8–9.
56. Ibid.
57. Paul Alvarez, interview, April 24, 1985.
58. Michael Campbell, interviews and materials furnished April–May 1985.

59. Ibid.
60. Alvarez, interview.
61. Ibid.
62. Ibid.
63. Ibid.
64. Campbell, interviews.
65. Michael V. Sullivan, cited in Alvarez interview.
66. Alvarez, interview.
67. Lipton, interview.
68. Ibid.
69. Ibid.
70. Ibid.
71. Burger and Peter Brooks, "Time Management and Reporting in Public Relations," interactive seminar with members of the Public Relations Special Interest Group (PRSIG) over CompuServe telecomputer network, Sept. 20, 1984.
72. Harrison, interview, March 9, 1985; and Harrison, "Lessons Learned after 12 Years in Business," internal planning document, E. Bruce Harrison Co., March 13, 1985.
73. William F. Noonan, "Finding and Growing Public Relations Talent: Some Realities of the 80s," speech presented to PRSA Counselors Academy Spring Conference, Las Vegas, April 30, 1984.
74. Renee Miller, "How to Keep Clients: 11 Mistakes to Avoid," *Public Relations Journal*, June 1985, pp. 34, 36.
75. Janet Laib Gottlieb, "Tips and the 3 E's . . . List for New Business Agendas," *Public Relations Business*, Dec. 24, 1984, p. 7.
76. *The Random House Dictionary of the English Language*, unabridged ed. (New York: Random House, 1981).
77. "Code of Professional Standards for the Practice of Public Relations," *Public Relations Journal 1986–87 Register Issue*, June 1986, pp. 12–15.
78. Truitt, participant observation notes while executive vice president, Carl Byoir & Associates.
79. Observations based on interviews with Burson-Marsteller executives following new product roll-out campaigns and client crises.
80. Joe Epley, interview, April 7, 1985.
81. Davis Young, "Ethical Considerations in Public Relations," address presented to Greater Cleveland PRSA and Cleveland Advertising Club, Oct. 8, 1985; and "We Are in the Business of Enhancing Trust," *Public Relations Journal*, January 1986, pp. 7–8.
82. Richard Weiner, interview, March 2, 1985.
83. Ibid.
84. Ibid.
85. Ibid.
86. Ibid.
87. Ibid.
88. Ibid.
89. Frank Walsh, John P. Scanlon and Alan J. Berkeley, cited in "PR Counselors at Risk as Litigation Increases in Business Situations," *The Counselor*, January 1986, p. 1.
90. Weiner, interview.
91. "PR Counselors at Risk," *The Counselor*.
92. Berkeley, cited in "Seven Situations Involving Information, PR and Litigation," *The Counselor*, January 1986, p. 6.
93. Bernard E. Ury, "'Errors & Omissions' Can Spell Trouble for Growing PR Firms," *The Counselor*, February 1984, p. 2.
94. Weiner, interview.
95. Ibid.

CHAPTER 8

1. "The PRSA Communications Technology Task Force *Mercury Survey*," joint project of New World Decisions, Ketchum Public Relations and the Task Force Research Subcommittee, Nov. 13, 1985.
2. *1985 O'Dwyer's Directory of PR Firms* (New York: Jack O'Dwyer, 1985).
3. Peter G. Osgood, interview, April 20, 1985.
4. Ibid.
5. Dana T. Hughes, "New Business Acquisition," monograph published by the Counselors Academy, August 1983, p. 1.
6. Harold Burson, interview, May 5, 1985.
7. Theodore Levitt, "The Globalization of Markets," *Harvard Business Review*, May–June 1983, pp. 92–101.
8. Robert L. Dilenschneider, interview; and "Marketing and the Global Corporation," address presented to Texas Public Relations Association, San Antonio, Feb. 22, 1986.
9. Ibid.
10. Levitt, "The Globalization of Markets."
11. Philip Kotler, cited by Jube Shiver Jr. in " 'Micro-Marketing': Firms Get Personal in Sales Quest," *Los Angeles Times*, Feb. 27, 1986, pp. 1, 20–21.
12. Shiver, " 'Micro-Marketing,' " *Los Angeles Times*.
13. Alvin Toffler, *The Adaptive Corporation* (New York: McGraw-Hill, 1985), pp. 103–107.
14. "PR-MBO as a Management System," in Norman R. Nager and T. Harrell Allen, *Public Relations Management by Objectives* (White Plains, N.Y.: Longman, 1984), pp. 25–53.
15. Dilenschneider, interview.
16. Richard Phalon, *The Takeover Barons of Wall Street* (New York: G. P. Putnam's Sons, 1981), pp. 66, 241–242.
17. Osgood, interview.
18. Ibid.
19. Ibid.
20. Ibid.
21. Paul H. Alvarez, interview, April 24, 1985.
22. Daniel H. Baer, "Preparing Now for an Excellent Future," speech presented at Counselors Academy 1986 Spring Conference, Carefree, Ariz., April 9, 1986.
23. *Jack O'Dwyer's Newsletter*, "Ketchum PR Acquires the Bohle Co.," Nov. 27, 1985, p. 1.
24. Sue Bohle, interview, Feb. 10, 1985.
25. Alvarez, interview.
26. Ron Gossen, interview, Feb. 23, 1986.
27. Dilenschneider, interview.
28. Gossen, interview.
29. "Top PR Stories of 1985," *Jack O'Dwyer's Newsletter*, Dec. 18, 1985, p. 3.
30. Daniel J. Edelman, interview, Feb. 28, 1985.
31. Ibid.
32. Jay Rockey, interview, March 26, 1985.
33. Edelman, interview.
34. David Finn, interview, May 9, 1985.
35. Ibid.
36. Edelman, interview.
37. Finn, interview.
38. Edelman, interview.
39. Finn, interview.
40. Peter F. Drucker, *Innovation and Entrepreneurship: Practice and Principles* (New York: Harper & Row, 1985), pp. 76, 83–86.
41. Ibid.

42. "The PRSA Communications Technology Task Force *Mercury Survey*," joint project of New World Decisions, Ketchum Public Relations and the Task Force Research Subcommittee, Nov. 13, 1985.
43. "Media Leaders Panel Predicts Quantum Growth in High-Tech Uses," summary of article from *Video Monitor*, October 1985, abstracted by Communication Research Associates, College Park, Md.
44. Kari Bjorhus, "Strategies for Sleuthing," book review, *Public Relations Journal*, February 1985, pp. 32, 33; Leonard M. Fuld, *Competitor Intelligence: How To Get It; How To Use It* (New York: John Wiley & Sons, 1985).
45. Ibid.
46. Susan Willner, "Behind the Scenes at Disclosure," *Online Today*, February 1986, p. 23.
47. "SEC Filing Documents" chart, *Online Today*, February 1986, p. 22.
48. Mary Mitchell, "Disclosure II: Data on Companies," *Online Today*, August 1985, p. 22.
49. Kathy Baird, "Micro 10K Plus Assists Investors," *Online Today*, February 1986, p. 24.
50. Kathy Baird, "Standard & Poor's Offers Online Data," *Online Today*, January 1986, p. 25.
51. William J. Kostka Jr., interview, March 2, 1985.
52. Bohle, interview.
53. Ibid.
54. Michael V. Sullivan, interview, April 22, 1985.
55. Ibid.
56. Bohle, interview.
57. Joe Basso, interview, Oct. 13, 1983.
58. "Young-Liggett-Stashower/36," brochure, Young-Liggett-Stashower Public Relations, Cleveland, October 1984; and "Young-Liggett-Stashower/36 Computer Information System," prospectus, p. 3.
59. Ibid.
60. Bohle, interview.
61. Charles Lipton, interview, May 10, 1985.
62. David H. Simon, interview, Feb. 12, 1985.
63. Bohle, interview.
64. Simon, interview.
65. Darryl R. Lloyd, interview, Feb. 16, 1985.
66. Simon, interview.
67. Bohle, interview.
68. Simon, interview.
69. Mark Nigberg, cited by Christopher Policano in "The Road to High Tech," *Public Relations Journal*, January 1985, pp. 12–15.
70. Loet A. Velmans, cited in "A Boardroom Presence," *MBA Executive*, published by Association of MBA Executives, March–April 1985.
71. Bob Dorf, "Computerizing the Public Relations Counseling Organization," monograph published by the Counselors Academy, December 1983.
72. Merton Fiur, "Information Technology: Form or Substance for Public Relations?" in *New Technology and Public Relations*, ed. Kalman Druck, Merton Fiur and Don Bates (New York: Foundation for Public Relations Research and Education, 1986), p. xvi.
73. Ronald D. Solberg, interview, Dec. 3, 1986.
74. Joel A. Strasser, cited in "Technology Section," *Public Relations Journal*, December 1985, "PRSA News Briefs" insert.

CHAPTER 9

1. Lou Brum Burdick, interview, Feb. 26, 1985.
2. Sue Bohle, interview, Feb. 10, 1985.

3. Ibid.
4. Burdick, interview.
5. Darryl R. Lloyd, interview, Feb. 16, 1985.
6. Ibid.
7. Ibid.
8. Ibid.
9. Ibid.
10. Ibid.
11. Ibid.
12. Ibid.
13. Michael Campbell, interview, March 19, 1986.
14. Luc Beauregard, interview, March 30, 1985.
15. Robert J. McCoy, interview, March 11, 1986.
16. Davis Young, interviews, March 2, 1985, and July 18, 1986.
17. Young, interviews.
18. James B. Strenski, interview, March 5, 1986.
19. Young, interviews.
20. Interviews with Ohio counselors, 1985 and 1986.
21. Sally I. Evans, interview, March 16, 1985.
22. Ibid.
23. "How to Take a Fresh Approach to Public Relations (And Profit from the Experience)," prospectus of The Public Relations Council, made available to the authors by Kenneth A. Murphy.
24. E. William Brody, "The Advantages of Adopting an Association with Other Counselors," *Public Relations Quarterly*, Summer 1985, p. 31.
25. "PR Firms, Others Unite against Deadbeats," *Jack O'Dwyer's Newsletter*, Jan. 2, 1986.
26. James Little, interview, March 9, 1985.
27. Patrick Jackson, interview, March 24, 1985.
28. Jackson and Little, interviews.
29. Ibid.
30. Glen A. Dell, cited in "PR Newsfront," *Jack O'Dwyer's Newsletter*, Jan. 2, 1986, p. 4.
31. Kay Berger, "Public Relations: 2001 and Beyond," address at the PRSA South Pacific District Leadership Conference, Pomona, Calif., Feb. 7, 1986.
32. Daniel H. Baer, "Trends," address presented to San Francisco PRSA Chapter, September 1984, pp. 9–10.
33. Chester Burger, interview, March 3, 1985.
34. Edward Gottlieb, cited by Jack Bernstein in "PR Merger Maven Gives Rules of M&A [Mergers and Acquisitions] Game," *Advertising Age*, Jan. 17, 1985, p. 7.
35. Robert Pfundstein, cited in *Advertising Age*, May 13, 1985, p. 70.
36. Jack Bernstein, "Merge Advertising and PR?—Yes and No," *Advertising Age*, May 13, 1985, pp. 70, 72.
37. Jean W. Schoonover, interview, March 12, 1985.
38. Burger, interview.
39. Ibid.
40. Identity withheld for confidentiality.
41. John Suhler, cited in *Advertising Age*, May 13, 1985, pp. 70, 72.
42. Burger, interview.
43. Schoonover, interview.
44. Mitchell C. Kozikowski, interview, May 20, 1985.
45. Alan J. Jacobs, interview, May 11, 1985.
46. David R. Hoods, interview, Feb. 12, 1985.
47. Jacobs, interview.
48. Kozikowski, interview.

49. Gerald J. Voros, "Can This Marriage Be Saved?" *Madison Avenue*, September 1984, pp. 18, 20.
50. David R. Drobis, "Survival of the Advertising/PR Marriage; or, How to Live Harmoniously and Profitably," address presented at public relations workshop, Association of American Advertising Agencies, San Francisco, August 1984, pp. 5–6.
51. John Becker, cited in *Advertising Age*, May 13, 1985, p. 70.
52. Burger, cited by Jack Bernstein in "PR Merger Maven Gives Rules of M&A Game," *Advertising Age*, Jan. 17, 1985, p. 7.
53. Young, interviews.
54. Robert Marston, cited in *Advertising Age*, May 13, 1985, p. 70.
55. Robert Schwartz, cited in *Advertising Age*, May 13, 1985, p. 70.
56. Schoonover, interview.
57. Campbell, interview; and "Some Friendly Advice to Ad Agencies," *Stimulus*, November–December 1984, pp. 28–29.
58. Edelman, interview, Feb. 28, 1985.
59. Dana T. Hughes, "New Business Acquisition," monograph published by the Counselors Academy, August 1983, p. 2.
60. Schoonover, interview.
61. Burger, interview.
62. Schoonover, interview.
63. Burger, interview.
64. Hoods, interview.
65. Young, interview.
66. Jacobs, interview.
67. Hughes, "New Business Acquisition."
68. Harold Burson, interview, May 8, 1985.
69. Ibid.
70. Ibid.
71. Ibid.
72. Robert L. Dilenschneider, interview, Feb. 22, 1986.
73. Ibid.
74. Ibid.
75. Dilenschneider, full text of Public Relations Foundation of Texas monograph, based on "Marketing and the Global Corporation," address presented to Texas Public Relations Association, San Antonio, Feb. 22, 1986, pp. 8–10.
76. Ibid.
77. Burger, interview.
78. Ibid.
79. Ibid.
80. Ibid.
81. Campbell, "Public Relations Not a Substitute But a Supplement to Advertising," *Stimulus*, September 1984, pp. 19–20.
82. Drobis, "Survival of the Advertising/PR Marriage," address presented to Association of American Advertising Agencies, San Francisco, August 1984, pp. 1, 3–4, 6.
83. Voros, "Can This Marriage Be Saved?" *Madison Avenue*, September 1984, p. 20.
84. Barbara W. Hunter, interview, March 14, 1985.
85. Schoonover, interview.
86. Ibid.
87. Kozikowski, interview.
88. Young, interview.
89. Jacobs, interview.
90. Jean L. Farinelli, interviews, Feb. 26, 1985, and Feb. 22, 1986.
91. Hoods, interview.

92. Ibid.
93. Little, interview.
94. Ibid.

CHAPTER 10

1. Loet A. Velmans, "An Overview," *Experts in Action: Inside Public Relations*, ed. Bill Cantor and Chester Burger (White Plains, N.Y.: Longman, 1984), pp. 5–6.
2. Harold Burson, interviews, May 5 and May 12, 1985.
3. Richard H. Truitt, cited in "The Credentials of Public Relations: Licensing? Certification? Accreditation? A Symposium in Print," *Public Relations Quarterly*, Summer 1984, pp. 25–26.
4. Norman R. Nager, "Emerging Profession: Today's Realities and Visions for Tomorrow," opening address presented to panel, "Public Relations: Vocation or Profession," PRSA South Pacific District Leadership Conference, Pomona, Calif., Feb. 7, 1986.
5. Timothy V. Conner, panel remarks, PRSA South Pacific District Leadership Conference, Pomona, Calif., Feb. 7, 1986.
6. F. John Pessolano, cited in "Public Relations—Its Scrutable Future," *The Counselor*, special issue, Summer 1981, pp. 1–6.
7. Judy van Slyke Turk, interview, March 2, 1985; and "Defining Public Relations: Toward a Theory of Science," paper presented to Public Relations Division, Association for Education in Journalism and Mass Communication, Boston, August 1980.
8. Daniel J. Edelman, "Managing the Public Relations Firm in the 21st Century," *Public Relations Review*, Fall 1983, pp. 9–10.
9. Patrick Jackson, "The Future of Public Relations—and Maybe the World," *Perspectives*, vol. 7 (1983), pp. 4–5, 21.
10. James F. Fox, "Public Relations: Some Ethical Considerations," in *Ethics, Morality and the Media: Reflections on American Culture*, ed. Lee Thayer (New York: Hastings House, 1979), pp. 153–162.
11. Michael Campbell, copy of original manuscript for "PR Through a Crystal Ball: Consulting in the Year 1990," *Stimulus*, April 1985, pp. 5–6.
12. Interviewee identity withheld for confidentiality.
13. Donald K. Wright, "Moral Values and Ethics in Public Relations," address presented to plenary session, 10th Public Relations World Congress, Amsterdam, June 7, 1985.
14. Wright, "Measuring Moral Values in Public Relations," research paper presented at the National Convention of the Association for Education in Journalism and Mass Communications, Memphis, Tenn., Aug. 5, 1985.
15. Davis Young, interview, March 2, 1985.
16. Young, "We Are in the Business of Enhancing Trust," *Public Relations Journal*, January 1986, pp. 7–8.
17. Luc Beauregard, interview, March 18, 1986.
18. "Official Statement on Public Relations," *Public Relations Journal*, 1986–1987 PRSA Register Issue, June 1986, p. 6.
19. Beauregard, interview, March 18, 1986.
20. Beauregard, interview, March 30, 1985.
21. Beauregard, notes for address to joint conference of the Public Relations Society of British Columbia and PRSA (Northwest), March 22, 1985.
22. Abraham Maslow, "A Dynamic Theory of Personality," *Psychological Review*, 1943, 50: 370–396; *Motivation and Personality* (New York: Harper & Row, 1954); and *Toward a Psychology of Being* (New York: Van Nostrand–Reinhold, 1962).
23. Paul H. Alvarez, interview, March 8, 1985.

24. Dwayne Summar, interview, Oct. 6, 1986.
25. Interviewee identity withheld for confidentiality.
26. Bruce Rubin, interview, Feb. 24, 1985.
27. Michael V. Sullivan, interview, April 22, 1985.
28. Young, blending of statements from "Report to the Membership"; remarks to annual meeting of the Counselors Academy, Denver, Oct. 16, 1984; and "The State of the Public Relations Consultancy in the United States," address presented to the British Public Relations Consultants Association, London, June 1, 1985.
29. "Issue Analysis: PR Counselors at Risk as Litigation Increases in Business Situations," and "Seven Situations Involving Information, PR and Litigation," *The Counselor*, January 1986, pp. 1, 6.
30. Joe S. Epley, correspondence with Nager, March 29, 1985; and interview, April 21, 1985.
31. Commission on Undergraduate Public Relations Education, cited in "Practitioners & Educators Now Agree on What PR Students Need to Learn," *PR Reporter*, Feb. 3, 1986, pp. 1–2.
32. Alvarez, correspondence to Academy members, April 22, 1985.
33. Sullivan, interview.
34. Alvarez, interview, April 8, 1985.
35. Epley, "Chairman's Comments–1986: A Year for Excellence," *The Counselor*, January 1986, p. 2.
36. "The Counselors Academy," introduction to *1986 Directory of Public Relations Counselors* (New York: Counselors Academy, 1986), p. 1.
37. Membership application, Counselors Academy.
38. Burns Lee, interview, March 9, 1985.
39. Ibid.
40. Epley, "Chairman's Comments," *The Counselor*, January 1986, p. 1.
41. William Schechter, cited in "The Credentials of Public Relations: Licensing? Certification? Accreditation? A Symposium in Print," *Public Relations Quarterly*, Summer 1984, pp. 21–22.
42. James B. Strenski, cited in "Credentials of Public Relations," pp. 24–25.
43. Truitt, cited in "Credentials of Public Relations," pp. 25–26.
44. Ibid.
45. Philip Lesly, cited in "Credentials of Public Relations," pp. 18–19.
46. Kerryn King, cited in "Credentials of Public Relations," pp. 17–18.
47. Judith S. Bogart, cited in "Credentials of Public Relations," p. 12.
48. Jacqueline K. Schaar, remarks to panel discussion, "Public Relations: Vocation or Profession," PRSA South Pacific District Leadership Conference, Pomona, Calif., Feb. 7, 1986.
49. Alvarez, interview, April 8, 1985.
50. Alvarez, "Who Cares about PRSA Accreditation? Paul H. Alvarez Cares," advertisement in *Public Relations Journal*, January 1986, p. 36.
51. Norman P. Teich, "Who Cares about PRSA Accreditation? Norm Teich Cares," advertisement in *Public Relations Journal*, March 1986, p. 42.
52. Summar, interview, Oct. 10, 1986.
53. Ibid.
54. "Counselors to Aid Student Agencies," *The Counselor*, January 1986, p. 8.
55. Nager, remarks made at presentation ceremonies, 1985 Outstanding Educator Award for Distinguished Service in Teaching, PRSA National Conference, Detroit, Nov. 11, 1985.
56. Nager, "Emerging Profession: Today's Realities and Visions for Tomorrow," Pomona, Calif., Feb. 7, 1986.
57. Rubin, interviews, Feb. 24, 1985, and March 26, 1986.

INDEX